BATTLE FOR THE CHURCH

AMERICA'S LAST STAND!

BATTLE FOR THE CHURCH

AMERICA'S LAST STAND!

Tired of the everyday routine of a Lukewarm Church experience? Ever dream of a life of pleasing God with your WHOLE heart and NO excuses? Want to get away from it all? I offer you ESCAPE! Designed to free you from the four walls of today's dying and ineffective Church. ESCAPE into teaching that may make you HOT or COLD but NEVER LUKEWARM! [1]

JAMES W. KEHRLI

Copyright © 2020 James W. Kehrli
All rights Reserved.
ISN: 13: 978057873473-6

GUIDELINES FOR STUDYING THIS BOOK

The purpose of this book is to enlighten the reader regarding the importance of the Scriptures and the necessity to believe, study, and obey them so you can defeat the enemy. The title of the book represents TWO statements. FIRST there is the Battle for the Church going on right now in America, and for generations to come, it will have ETERNAL consequences. SECOND Battle for the Church is a Command from God to do battle for the church in America! He is calling upon us to enter the fray ON HIS TERMS, using His weapons!

We need to develop the habit of checking everything we hear, see, or read with the Scriptures to determine what is true or false. It is especially true that we need to evaluate ANY and ALL teachings on the basis of what the Bible says. Even the opinions of great men such as Martin Luther, John Wesley, George Whitfield, Matthew Henry, Charles Spurgeon, A W Tozer and Martin Lloyd-Jones must be evaluated on the basis of what the Bible says and not on the basis of any other source. Particularly, in the last 50 years, we have had an inundation of poor doctrine that has little to do with Scripture and much to do with the unscriptural psychological arts, culture driven science and the frighteningly strong voice of the media.

When you read this book, please do the same. If you find something that goes against or is not supported by the Word of God, please contact me. Please evaluate what is being taught here on the basis of Scripture ALONE! I would strongly recommend several Bible aids that I have found helpful.

I have little knowledge of the Greek language and less knowledge of the Hebrew language. I depend upon this website: Bible Hub @ Biblehub.com. to help me understand the meaning of words or phrases throughout the scriptures.

For looking at various translations of the Bible, I use Bible Gateway @ Biblegateway.com. The best dictionary for Christians is the Webster's 1828 American Dictionary of the English Language @
http://webstersdictionary1828.com.

My favorite Bible commentary is Matthew Henry @://www.studylight.org/commentaries/mhm.htm

If you go outside of the Scriptures, you may well be entering the enemy's camp and you have lost the protection of the Word of God. You can be taught by great teachers IF they interpret the Word of God BY THE WORD OF GOD. Remember, the defensive weapons that are mentioned in the warfare chapter 6 of Ephesians, all have to do with the Word of God. You are protected by the Word of God, but when you go outside the Word of God you may be wounded and blinded by the enemy so you can no longer see the Word of God clearly. The major cults have done this and have come to believe unspeakable lies. The Jews in Jerusalem during the time of Jeremiah went outside the Word of God, practiced idolatry, and eventually were judged unmercifully by God. The Lukewarm Church today as it goes outside the Word of God and accepts teachings from the secular realm that are not backed up by Scripture will likewise be judged, if they won't repent. We do not need to be a part of that judgment if we are happy and satisfied to let the Word, empowered by the Holy Spirit be our SOLE protector. Unfortunately, many in the Lukewarm Church look at the unvarnished Word of God as too restrictive, so, they soften the supposed harshness of the Scriptures with humanistic psychology and false science.

THE VOICE OF THE GOOD SHEPHERD IS THE SCRIPTURE OF GOD

John 10:14,26-28 (NASB) I am the good shepherd, I know My own and My own know me 26 but you do not believe because you are not of My sheep. 27 MY SHEEP HEAR MY VOICE, and I know them, and they follow Me; 28 and I give eternal life to them, and they will never perish.

Stick with the Word, the whole Word and nothing but the Word of God and you can't go wrong. Edit out the uncomfortable parts and add to the Scriptures cultural interpretations and you will not experience the fullness of God's power to either make you holy or to make you strong in the Lord.

2 Timothy 2:15-16 (NASB). Be DILIGENT to present yourself approved to God as a workman who does not need to be ashamed, ACCURATELY HANDLING THE WORD OF TRUTH, 16 but avoid worldly and empty chatter, for it will lead to further ungodliness.

I often use capital letters to highlight a portion of the Scripture or teaching that I feel needs to be emphasized. I'm not attempting to change the meaning of the Scripture or teaching, but I am trying to draw it to your greatest attention. In quoting from the Holy Scriptures, I often will use Italics when I'm writing or including a word that is not in the Scripture itself. For example, if the Scripture says "He" in referring to Jesus, the name Jesus may be written in italics.

BIBLE VERSIONS CITED:
AKJV Authorized (King James) Version
AMP Amplified Bible,
AMPC Amplified Bible, Classic Edition
GNV 1599 Geneva Bible
KJ21 21st Century King James Version
KJV King James Version
NABRE New American Bible (Revised Edition)
NASB New American Standard Bible
NIV New International Version
NKJV New King James Version
NLT New Living Translation
PHILLIPS J.B. Phillips New Testament

CONTENTS

GUIDELINES FOR THIS BOOK

SECTION 1: THE DUTIES AND POWER OF THE CHURCH	1
CHAPTER 1: POLITICS AND RELIGION	**3**
CHAPTER 2: HISTORY LESSONS	**17**
SECTION 2: CAN JUDGMENT OR SEVERE CHASTENING BE CLOSE?	33
CHAPTER 3: SHRINE PROSTITUTES IN THE TEMPLE OF GOD	**35**
CHAPTER 4: CORRUPTION IN AMERICA & THE CHURCH	**45**
CHAPTER 5: EVIDENCE THAT DEMANDS A VERDICT	**57**
CHAPTER 6: GODLY PUNISHMENTS	**69**
CHAPTER 7: JOSIAH REVIVAL	**83**
SECTION 3: PREPARING FOR DIFFICULT DAYS	93
CHAPTER 8: TEACHING GOD'S PERFECT WORD	**95**
CHAPTER 9: JUDGING MEN & DOCTRINE	**109**
CHAPTER 10: LAWLESSNESS IN THE TEMPLE OF GOD	**123**
CHAPTER 11: GRIEVE AND LAMENT FOR THE SINS OF THE CHURCH	**133**
SECTION 4: ENEMIES LIST	141
CHAPTER 12: KNOWING THE ENEMY	**143**
CHAPTER 13: HAPPY MEALS FROM HELL: COMFORT CLUB CHRISTIANS	159
CHAPTER 14: WE MUST FIGHT HARDER THAN HELL!	**169**
SECTION 5: HAS GOD RESCINDED THE SUPERNATURAL GIFTS?	183
CHAPTER 15: IS SUPERNATURAL MINISTRY FOR THE CHURCH?	**185**

CHAPTER 16: CONFLICTING VIEWS OF THE ROLE OF MIRACLES	**193**
CHAPTER 17: THE USE AND MISUSE OF THE MIRACULOUS GIFTS	**203**
SECTION 6: GAME CHANGER-- THE DESTRUCTION OF THE FAMILY	215
CHAPTER 18: FOUNDATION FOR WARFARE:LOVE & SUBMISSION	219
CHAPTER 19: MARRIAGE AND DIVORCE	**233**
CHAPTER 20: AN EPISTLE FROM HELL. DOES THE BIBLE SAY THE WIFE IS SUPERIOR TO THE HUSBAND?	247
CHAPTER 21: AN EPISTLE FROM HELL! DOES "SCIENCE" SAY **THE** WIFE IS SUPERIOR?	**257**
CHAPTER 22: TO BE OR NOT TO BE …. A DOORMAT!	**265**
CHAPTER 23: EXTREME SOLUTIONS	**273**
SECTION 7: LAST WORDS	285
CHAPTER 24: THE RULE OF LAWLESSNESS	**287**
CHAPTER 25: THE GREAT SHAKING, THE SECOND STORM, AND PEARL HARBOR - THE GREATEST AWAKENING!	**297**
ENDNOTES	309
BIBLIOGRAPHY	315
ABOUT THE AUTHOR	317

SECTION 1: THE DUTIES AND POWER OF THE CHURCH
CHAPTER 1: POLITICS AND RELIGION
CHAPTER 2: HISTORY LESSONS

When I began to write this book in 2018, my opening paragraph was the following:

"Over the last several years, we've seen some great strides in our nation. God has once again extended His grace to us. Donald Trump's policies both at home and abroad have strengthened our nation. His policies, for the time being, have stopped the Progressives from completely taking over our culture and our country. His recognition of Jerusalem as the capital of Israel is an extension of God's grace both to Israel and America. His immoral past is hopefully behind him. His stance regarding his lack of need to ask forgiveness for his sins has been softened somewhat. It has been a great pleasant surprise to see a Republican President that is not afraid to attack the enemies of the United States and the Church. Most importantly, in choosing Donald Trump to be President, the Lord has given us more time to repent of the Church's plummet into pornography, unscriptural divorce and people pleasing, positive preaching that excludes or diminishes the fear of the Lord and the consequences of our sin. He has given us time to avoid or prepare spiritually for the terrible judgment that many lukewarm countries have experienced."

As written at this date, March 18, 2020, I'm not as sure that we will get as much time as I had hoped for. The Coronavirus Pandemic has caused 8,951 deaths worldwide. As of May 1, 2020, the total reached 239,443 [2] and business has been virtually shut down. In the United States, this has created a reaction from both conservatives and Progressives alike. Even at the height of World War II, we didn't see commerce disrupted as we see today. We have NEVER seen our people directed by the government to QUIT WORK! Restaurants, sporting events, churches, and even gatherings of more than ten people are being shut down. Both the federal and state governments are implementing massive programs that cost trillions of dollars. Perhaps, from a scientific and health perspective these measures will be proven necessary and effective. In the meantime, you can be sure the Progressives and their partners in crime, the media, will do everything they can to make the Conservatives look bad. They will do their level worst to take back the Presidency and the Senate and turn America into a Progressive Paradise. Perhaps we in the Church will have much less time than I originally supposed to become the strong army of Christians that we MUST BECOME to defeat the enemy.

As of my re-write on July 18, 2020, in Portland, Oregon where our family lives, the Fascist organization Antifa still has had little resistance: 50 straight nights of "demonstrations". To thwart their attack on a government building, 20-25 arrests were made, but many believe they will be released soon. If the Marxist democrats take over the White House in the next election, this election may be America's Last Stand as a nation powerful enough to prevent the destruction of freedom both in America and around the world.

The following section will go into detail regarding the relationship of politics to religion. It will also discuss how the spiritual condition of the Church influences the state of the nation. This section will take a close look at the decline, the fall, and the RISE of God's people and the nations they have affected throughout history.

CHAPTER 1: POLITICS AND RELIGION

The Role and the Purpose of the Church
What is a Lukewarm Church?
Consequences of this Church's Attitude
The Cultural Crisis in America
Who Bears the Most Responsibility?
What Must the Church Do?
   We Must Wake Up!
   We Must Repent!
   We Must be Zealous!
   We Must Change Now!
Judgement May Come Soon
The Focus
The Stakes
Now is the Time
The Power of the Church of Jesus Christ
Conclusion

THE ROLE AND PURPOSE OF THE CHURCH

The Church of Jesus Christ in America is the only Army that battles the REAL enemies of our country and the only people that possess the power to protect our culture and way of life from destruction. We alone patrol the spiritual borders of the people of God and this nation. We set our watchmen on the walls to make sure that we can identify any attack coming that threatens our country or our church. We alone can prepare for any attack that may come, but the power behind the attack is always SPIRITUAL. We are the only rescue force that can save the people that are in danger of being weakened, deceived and damaged both in this life and the next. We alone can bring home the shellshocked and the battle-weary and help them to recover to fight again. We are the protectors of the innocent and will gladly give our lives to make sure that our young ones will not be picked off by the sniper fire of the enemy and destroyed by the subtlety of Satan.

We are the one and only people that have the antidote to death. We have the secret to eternal life and every one of our soldiers knows that secret. We are to be the gold standard of goodness and Biblical morality in our culture even if the culture refuses to recognize us. We are the firemen that put out the fires of lust that destroy the purity and the power of our people. We are the educators that train up our children and young people to do what is right and just before God and fight for and protect the next generation. We are the first responders in every attack on our freedom to worship Jesus Christ and follow Him into a lifetime of holiness. We are the ones that go to the front lines of every war. In history. You will find us saving England from the ravages of the People's Revolution which destroyed France. In England and America, you see us laying the groundwork for the Great Awakening that led to the formation of the two most powerful nations that the world has ever seen. Because of the spiritual revivals that we have experienced, our economies and our militaries have been powerful, and most importantly we have printed more Bibles, preached more Biblical sermons and spread the gospel to the ends of the earth as no other nations have ever done. BUT, since world war II, we have forgotten that our SPIRITUAL victories have been the foundation for both our economy and our military success and has allowed us to stay free in a world that is fast losing its freedom.

To continue to be effective and defeat our enemies, we must be legitimately born again from above; we must be filled with God's love and our Lord's Holy Spirit and what's more important is that we must be filled with the precious and powerful Word of God which guides, encourages, and empowers us. We must fight with a terrible resolve to see the Church made holy, powerful, and raised up to GLORIFY GOD GREATLY in this land.

For the last 50 or 60 years, the Christian soldiers of America have been asleep to the damage that Hell's warriors have done to the walls that protect our culture, our government, and our churches. The Church has become complacent. The Church has become LUKEWARM and there is a steep price that every lukewarm church must pay.

WHAT IS A LUKEWARM CHURCH?

Revelation 3:15 (NKJV) "I know your works, that you are NEITHER COLD NOR HOT. I wish that you were cold or hot.

First of all, the Lukewarm Church is not hot nor cold. This Church is a MODERATE Church. Certainly not a zealous church that would embarrass people in the congregation with loud praise or noisome gifts of the Spirit. Also, the pastor would seldom grieve any in the congregation because he preaches repentance from sin. This Church will mouth correct doctrine but does not demand that the hearers LIVE this doctrine. This Church is not cold towards the world and sin and not on fire for God and holiness. Lukewarm indicates that there is a mixture of hot and cold teachings because the Church is influenced by both the words of the world and the Word of God, but not really committed to either one. This Church is mildly holy and slightly concerned about sin. This Church is trying to please both God and man.

Revelation 3:17(NKJV) Because you say, 'I AM RICH, HAVE BECOME WEALTHY, AND HAVE NEED OF NOTHING' and do not know that you are WRETCHED, MISERABLE, POOR, BLIND, AND NAKED.

This Church has a high opinion of itself. This Church has the highest self-esteem of ANY CHURCH IN HISTORY. God does not share the Church's opinion, however. He says that this Church is wretched, miserable, poor (essentially SPIRITUALLY BANKRUPT), blind, and naked. This Church LITERALLY offers NOTHING GOOD TO JESUS CHRIST in its present condition.

CONSEQUENCES OF THIS CHURCH'S ATTITUDE

REVELATION 3:16-19 ((NASB) So because you are lukewarm, and neither hot nor cold, I will spit you out of My mouth. 17 Because you say, "I am rich, and have become wealthy, and have need of nothing," and you do not know that you are wretched and miserable and poor and blind and naked, 18 I advise you to buy from Me gold refined by fire so that you may become rich, and white garments so that you may clothe yourself, and that the shame of your nakedness will not be revealed; and eye salve to anoint your eyes so that you may see. 19 Those whom I love, I reprove and discipline; therefore, be zealous and repent.

This lukewarm spirit is extremely offensive to God. He wants NO PART of this Church. The Lukewarm Church can expect God to eventually vomit it out of His mouth. This is a serious response. For the sake of the delicacy of its hearers, the NASB translate the word that is rendered as "spit out." Young's Literal Translation and others use the word "vomit". Food in the stomach, if it is not digested and become part of the body, is vomited out. Spiritually speaking, it means that if a church or a church member does not allow God to break him down so that he will become part of His body, then that member or church will eventually be expelled.

God tells this Church that they must purchase from Him gold refined in the fire. Likely this fire is the fire of tribulation, judgment, or severe punishment. With this step of sacrifice and faith they will then be Spiritually rich. With this gold they will buy white garments and clothe themselves with the righteousness of Christ so that the shame of their nakedness will not be revealed when they stand before God and He judges their faith, love, and deeds. In order for them to see CLEARLY He commands them to purchase eye salve to anoint their eyes. This eye salve may well be the un unaltered WORD OF GOD. At first glance, this eye salve may be uncomfortable or even painful. But if they will endure this period of discomfort, they will be able to see CLEARLY with eyes that have been healed BY SCRIPTURE and the power of God.

THE CULTURAL CRISIS IN AMERICA

Our government's educational system from kindergarten through graduate school now teaches our young people how evil Christianity is and how it has corrupted America and influenced most of its adherents to become economic and social conservatives. The American educational system now focuses on multi-culturalism. Our children are forced to study the religions of a multiplicity of heathen countries. They are taught about the GREAT religions of the world, which include the Muslim religion, the Hindu religion, American Indian religions, Buddhism, Voodoo, Wicca, and many other African and eastern religions. When Christianity is discussed, it is usually in the context of how cruel and thoughtless the Christians have been through the ages. American school history focuses on how evil the founding fathers were (many of which were Christians) and how Christians have been and still are Haters that abuse women, people of color and anyone who is not a Christian. The Church is no longer concerned that this terrible educational system not only does not care for holiness and sexual purity, but they mock it! We have become so weak that we CONTINUE to send our children to government schools where they likely WILL BE BRAINWASHED into believing that other religions are just as good or better than Biblical Christianity.

Today, both the movies and the media promote fornication, adultery and even homosexuality as daring and courageous behavior. We have essentially erased the concept of sexual sin. Most believe that any sexual activity is okay if it is between consenting human beings. Truth is no longer valued. In some cases, the good liar is a hero, particularly in the realm of entertainment. Bill Clinton's obvious lies, because he promoted liberal causes such as abortion and a nonjudgmental attitude toward adultery and homosexuality, was deemed to be a good man by the Progressives. Respect for people in authority depends solely upon who is in authority. If left-wing or progressive people are in authority, for the most part, anything goes. It is understood that they are to be respected or even revered. If a Christian or a conservative is in authority it is equally clear that they are NEVER to be respected. Those who don't support the left-wing agenda are never to be respected. Most fathers and some mothers are not to be respected, especially if they demand that their children obey Biblical principles. A wife that submits to her husband is thought to be a weak woman in our culture and even in some of the churches. Husbands who dare to function as the head of the wife even as Christ is the head of the Church suffer both at the hands of the world and often from other Christians. Policemen ESPECIALLY are not to be respected. We are more likely to honor criminals than cops. Our culture is in a moral shambles and many are glad!

WHO BEARS THE MOST RESPONSIBILITY?

Most Christians believe that Hollywood, the liberal media, the ACLU, Planned Parenthood, the left-wing progressives, our corrupt educational system, and television are the ones responsible for the cesspool that our culture has become. They are especially concerned about groups that mock Christians. Most in the Church believe that the world hates us because we have a holier than thou attitude.

Most churchgoers believe that if we just work hard to elect conservatives and Christians to positions of power in the executive branch of our government and in Congress then we will have a great opportunity to change this nation for good. We can make America great again, if we could just take the Presidency, the Senate, and the House of Representatives. If we can get the politics right, then we can be a strong Church again! Unfortunately, historically speaking, this is not the case.

As we study the Bible, Church history and secular history we find that the only one who can make America great again is God, and He only does this through His people by the power of His Holy Spirit, the Words of His Holy Bible and men and women who are willing to exhibit sacrificial, holy love. We will discover that ONLY when the Church humbles herself, prays, seeks the face of God and TURNS FROM HER WICKED WAYS (1 Chronicles7:14), only then will God bless the Church and consequently bless the nation.

The Church MUST take the lion's share of the responsibility concerning the terrible moral decline in America and the great punishment or judgment that we will someday experience. We have not fought the war against Hell with the Word, the whole Word and nothing but the Word. We have grown blind to the enemy that has weakened us and caused us to be oblivious to our own spiritual failures, shortcomings and sin.

In America, in the 21st century, the Church has so deteriorated that it has virtually no power. We have willingly been compromised by the culture. We are no longer able to change the culture in our country. And we have not been able to change enough hearts of the people in our country because the gospel we present is cheap and the Jesus we present is more like a sympathetic psychologist than a Savior from sin. Because of this, there is a smaller percentage of truly born-again Christians in America today than ever before.

The MAIN issue in America is neither cultural nor political. The main issue in America today is the SPIRITUAL condition of the Church. We must recognize that the Church is in dire need of spiritual help. We must combat the Laodicean, lukewarm error that we have comfortably and willingly embraced. We are neither fervently hot for holiness nor dead cold to sin. We must pray that God would open our eyes so that we can see this and raise up men with prophetic insight concerning the Word of God and His will. We must pray that God would raise up men like Martin Luther, George Whitfield, John and Charles Wesley, John Calvin, Charles Spurgeon, and A. W. Tozer. But, most important, we must pray that WHATEVER IT TAKES, He will raise up a people that have hearts like David that are willing to do ALL that He desires.

The protection of our families, as the deception increases and when terrible punishment or judgment occurs, will likely depend on what we do now and how we trust and obey the Scriptures. We must stir ourselves to be fully awake and warn God's people about the further and increasingly more virulent attacks that will occur. We must teach our families the whole Word of God with no worldly trimmings. We must seek to understand what God expects our conduct to be. We must see clearly in His Word what our responsibility is to Him.

WHAT MUST THE CHURCH DO?

WE MUST WAKE UP!

If we don't wake up, and it seems almost inevitable that we will not, we will most certainly be viciously attacked, and the Church will suffer GREAT loss! Because the Church of Jesus Christ in America has become tolerant of evil, tolerant of evil doctrine and unable and unwilling to judge from Scripture what is of God and what is not of God, it is no wonder that God has not sent us a country changing revival. This revival for which we have prayed will likely never come until our hearts have been purified by judgment, persecution, and tribulation. This Church MUST WAKE UP to its lukewarm ways. It must once again become zealous for the Lord and His holiness and hunger and thirst after His righteousness so that we can once again have the spiritual strength to defeat our powerful enemy! If we want to win the *Battle for the Church*, we must know who our real enemy is and what is our real spiritual condition.

We MUST realize that we have been asleep to God's will, asleep to God's battle, and asleep to God's call to speak THE TRUTH, THE WHOLE TRUTH, AND NOTHING BUT THE TRUTH of HIS WORD. Many have embraced the very Church that God Himself separated us from in the 16th century – the Roman Catholic Church. We have systematically dismantled the Protestant Reformation of 1517. We no longer recognize the necessity of Sola Fide (Only through Faith), Sola Scriptura (Only the Scriptures reveal this truth perfectly), Sola Gratia (Only by the Grace of God), Solus Christos (Only Christ), Soli Deo Gloria (Only for the Glory of God).

Before World War II, all Americans knew that there was a war going on in Europe and the Far East, but America would not risk the lives of its soldiers. Our country sent ships and money to some of our friends overseas, but we felt that we were beyond the reach of Japan or Germany. We didn't wake up to our weakened military condition until we were attacked viciously and without warning at Pearl Harbor on December 7, 1941. After the slaughter of 3,000 of our finest men, we woke up and began to fight. We sent troops overseas to Europe, Africa, the Pacific region and the Far East and we sacrificed hundreds of thousands of men and billions of dollars; but in four years we won an overwhelming victory and saved America, Western Europe and much of the rest of the world from the Nazis and the Japanese Imperialists.

We must wake up to the reality of what is happening in our nation and in our churches! Over the last 60 years, we have never lost so many battles. In fact, we have virtually no victories in the courts, the colleges, and the culture. The enemy has beaten us at virtually every turn. We have not assessed Satan's true power and our true weakness. We have greatly diminished the power of the sword of the Spirit which is THE WORD OF GOD by adding to and subtracting from the Scriptures. We have dulled that mighty weapon by grinding off the parts that we don't like. We have corroded the Word of God and rusted the Sword of the Spirit with the water of the world. Until we cease these practices, we are not ready to fight and defeat the enemy. The SPIRITUAL STRENGTH OF THE CHURCH is the issue! We must be focused on making sure that we present the gospel OF THE SCRIPTURES that will cause people to become new creatures in Christ and have new hearts that will love Him, trust Him, and obey Him. We desperately need to wake up and prepare to fight like we never have before. We will likely need another devastating Pearl Harbor judgment to wake up the Church. We are still living the dream of lukewarm prosperity and do not want to wake up to the TRUE will and the TRUE purposes of God.

The establishment media hates any person or party that keeps the godless left wing from achieving its ends. These people have become increasingly sympathetic to the community organizers and their mobs that continue to vilify and attack both conservative policies and anyone who speaks out against progressive policies in our country. Even Muslims are being treated more sympathetically. Someday we may well see an open alliance between the Left and the Muslims, hell-bent to destroy all that is good in America.

WE MUST REPENT!

We will be judged by God because we have failed to acknowledge that WE, not the unsaved liberals in our country, nor the entertainment industry, nor the abortionists need to repent; WE are the ones that need to repent so that the Church can have the strength and be the leaven of righteousness that can change this country and the world for Jesus Christ.

THEN, many Christians will finally be able to identify and understand the lukewarm Laodicean Church mentality that brings judgment and tribulation. When this happens, we will no longer be blind. We will no longer say, "We are rich and in need of nothing!"

WE MUST BE ZEALOUS.

JB Phillips in his New Testament perfectly describes the Lukewarm Church when he interprets the Scripture, 'be zealous' to mean **"SHAKE OFF YOUR COMPLACENCY"**. No Church in history has ever been so confidently complacent of its standing before God then the lukewarm Establishment Church in America. We need to repent of our HALF-HEARTED holiness. We must see the terrible consequences that sin brings. We need to quit leaning on a cheap grace that is not scripturally consistent with God's expectation of who we are to be to Him. We must recognize that the grace of God is not merely so we can avoid the penalty of sin, rather that grace is the grace that ENABLES US TO CONQUER SIN AND LIVE A HOLY LIFE that pleases Him and is a joy to His heart.

WE MUST CHANGE NOW!

This book is about preparing people to fight against an unshackled enemy that has weakened and conquered many in the Church and still is waging war and preparing to launch his greatest attack in the greatest battle that the Church of Jesus Christ in America has ever faced. The Battle to destroy the Church in America has been raging for decades and we have been too simple-minded to notice. We have given up on depending exclusively upon the overwhelming power of the Word of God and His Mighty Holy Spirit. We've chosen the easy broad path in making Christians. Our words are less biting, our sermons no longer judge sin and our lives reflect the compromises we are taught from the pulpit.

In many churches, it is common to see Christian parents turn a blind eye to college-age children and their girlfriends or boyfriends that are sleeping with each other in their own home. For many, keeping our homes pure from sexual sin has become a losing battle. Demanding obedience to the Words of Scripture is becoming increasingly rare in 21st century churches. Even the terrible sin of pornography runs rampant and unconquered in the leadership of many evangelical and charismatic churches. Therefore, we have created a huge spiritual void. Unfortunately, that spiritual void has been filled by the cults, eastern religion, humanistic psychology, and secular philosophy. Under the rule of the far-left leaning Democrat Party, WE have allowed much damage to be done to the Church of Jesus Christ and the American culture through the social engineering of this antichrist political system. To avoid judgement and win The *Battle for the Church*, WE MUST CHANGE!

JUDGMENT MAY COME SOON

With the labor unions, the entertainment industry, the legal profession, academia, the print media and most of television on their side, they still have not been able to destroy and enslave America. Only God's grace has kept us from devastation. This painful punishment or judgment from God will most certainly happen if the Church in America does not wake up soon.

This punishment of the people of God will come IF WE DON'T REPENT of embracing doctrines of demons. We have become convinced of our need to balance the Scripture with the best of secular psychology. We have devious ways of raising money to build "the kingdom." We have added to the Word like no other supposedly Christian movement since the Roman Catholic Church of the Dark Ages. We have softened the commandments of Scripture and cheapened the grace of God. We have been more concerned about unity than we have been about truth.

God is warning us NOW to wake up! Most of God's people will not respond to this message. Great trials and even judgments generally serve the purpose of exposing a man's true heart and occasionally a man or woman, out of desperation, will repent, submit to and believe in the Lord Jesus Christ and His Scriptures. More often, judgment throws most religious people into great fear or great doubt. The Word to us today is to get our hearts ready by letting God purge us of idols and to seek Him diligently in the Scriptures and in the prayer closet. We must seek out people or congregations of like mind who can compassionately and passionately correct us, exhort us, admonish us, and encourage us in righteousness

Proverbs 14:34 (NLT). GODLINESS makes a nation great, BUT SIN IS A DISGRACE to any people.
Jeremiah 10:25 (NLT) POUR OUT YOUR WRATH ON THE NATIONS THAT REFUSE TO ACKNOWLEDGE YOU—on the peoples that do not call upon Your name.

The tragedy is that whenever a nation refuses to acknowledge God and does not call upon His Name, that nation will experience the judgment of God. When the Church falls away from the principles of Scripture and invites either a worldly philosophy or an unscriptural belief system into their midst, that Church will weaken the power of the nation and THAT NATION ALSO will be judged.

THE FOCUS

IT IS SO IMPORTANT that we NOT judge sinners in the world.. Paul says:

1 Corinthians 5:12 (AMP) For what business is it of mine to judge outsiders *that is* **non-believers? Do you not judge those who are within** *the church* **to protect the church as the situation requires?**

We do so because it is much easier to focus on sinners in the world than focus on why the Church is so powerless. We need repent of OUR OWN sins and the sins of the Church in America. We CHRISTIANS IN THE CHURCH are the ONLY ones that can fight and defeat Satan and his warriors. Most are blind to the very existence of this devious enemy. Our focus must now be on the spiritual Reformation and Revival of God's people in America. The revamping of the political landscape in America may eventually cause some temporary changes to occur, but the only satisfactory solution to America's problems is to have a significant percentage of the population become born again and have new hearts to do new things that will please God. This solution can only come because we have sought the Lord, trusted the Scriptures, and changed our ways

and become a strong enough Church to fight the REAL enemy in our land. There may be some that are called to be involved in the political process, but PRIMARILY we must realize that time is running out for the Church of Jesus Christ and we need to seek God and His power and His program with all our hearts, minds, soul, and strength.
THE STAKES

America is perhaps the last stronghold of Christianity on planet Earth. Eastern Europe, Southern Europe, Northern Europe, Canada, Mexico, the Middle East, the Islamic countries, China, Japan, Africa, and Israel are all countries that have rejected the real Jesus Christ and Christianity. South Korea remains with some elements of Biblical Christianity, but much of that Church leadership is on the fringes of Christianity. BUT, America, despite the takeover of churches by a lukewarm mindset, still has pockets of people who are committed to the Scriptures and love the Lord Jesus Christ. Over the last 60 years, however, we have given up much ground in the *Battle for the Church*. If American Christianity falls, the nation of America will also fall, and Satan will have little resistance to a final takeover of the earth. The next few years may well be THE LAST STAND for America. Preparation for the *Battle for the Church* must not be half-hearted. Likely, as judgment comes, a remnant of God's people will repent and eventually blossom into the most powerful Warriors of the Word and the Spirit that the Church has ever seen. But it may take the Lord another 1,000 years to bring His people to a place where they cry out for mercy and repent of their worldly ways and finally receive the full power to conquer the enemy for one last time. We may lose our country, BUT GOD WILL SURELY EVENTUALLY WIN THE BATTLE FOR PLANET EARTH.

NOW IS THE TIME

There are some who are waking up to the fact that there will eventually be a debilitating spiritual attack launched on the Church of Jesus Christ in America. Unfortunately, most believe the difficult times will come because the Church has taken a strong stand against gay marriage and abortion. Likely, most people in this complacent, overconfident, self-satisfied church will believe just that. We need to see our own weakness and responsibility in the decline of the culture in our country.

EVEN NOW we are being given time to prepare our families, our fellowships, and our churches. This preparedness will be a sacrifice that most will not want to make. However, as we see that things get worse and worse in our country regardless of what party is in charge and regardless of how much we pray and vote, more people will wake up and realize that WE IN HIS CHURCH need to seek the face of the Lord and repent of our wicked ways and THEN pray and ask God for deliverance and victory. Then we will finally be able to identify and understand that the lukewarm Laodicean Church mentality has brought judgment and tribulation to both our country and the Church. When this happens, we will no longer be blind. We will no longer say, "we are rich and in need of nothing!"

But we must make major changes in the way we think, the way we speak, the way we study, the way we teach, the way we preach, the way we evaluate the Scriptures, the way we allow the Holy Spirit to deal with us, the way we allow the culture to compromise us and even the way that we hold church services. Eventually, we will see that we have been vulnerable to attack because we have thrown away most of the protective armor and spiritual weapons which the Bible speaks about in Ephesians chapter 6. We have replaced the sword of the Spirit which is the Word of God with empty platitudes and psychological solutions. We need to stop seeing the Church as a business organization that needs to employ worldly philosophy and humanistic psychology to succeed, or worse yet, another Hollywood style production to entertain us. In the 19th century, Charles Spurgeon warned, "A TIME WILL COME WHEN instead of shepherds feeding the sheep, THE CHURCH WILL HAVE CLOWNS ENTERTAINING THE GOATS." Unfortunately, that time has come.

THE POWER OF THE CHURCH OF JESUS CHRIST

Neither Donald Trump, Hillary Clinton nor any other politician or political party will ever make America a great nation. The Church is not merely one aspect of the solution regarding the defeat of worldwide Communism, the Muslims and the antichrist legal system. the Church is the ONLY SOLUTION to these problems. ONLY GOD can make America great and the only way He will do it is through His Church. America will never be great until the Church is great and the Church will never be great until the Church accepts the responsibility for the fall of America into the hands of the Hollywood whores, the ACLU, the LGBTQ coalition, Planned Parenthood, the government education system, the Commu-crats, or Nazi-crats, if you prefer; both the Nazis and the Communists, like their latest incarnation, the Democrats, have murdered TENS OF MILLIONS OF INNOCENT PEOPLE. AND their inglorious leader – LUCIFER has given them power over the classroom, the courts, and the culture. All of this is because the Church has chosen to IGNORE the truth of the Scriptures that demand sacrifice.

Rich and powerful lukewarm televangelists and huge evangelical establishment mega-churches will NEVER defeat Satan! Small time churches and pastors who are willing to play the games that will increase their popularity, or the size of their congregations will NEVER defeat Satan. Phony apostles and prophets who are more interested in establishing a cult-like authority with their followers and receive lots of love and lots of money WILL NEVER defeat Satan! Until we cast aside these false leaders, spiritually ignorant ministers and quit catering to the Comfort Seekers, we will NEVER be able to build a Church that will cast down the gates of Hell and fill the earth with the Spirit of the LORD!

Satan and his soldiers can only be fought and defeated by holy people with holy hands, holy minds and holy hearts filled with the Holy Spirit, faith in God's Word and are desperately in love with Jesus Christ. He can only be fought and conquered by the Church of Jesus Christ which understands that the cost of victory over the enemy is TOTAL TRUST IN THE WORD, the WHOLE Word, and NOTHING BUT THE WORD of God and the power of His Holy Spirit!

CONCLUSION

It may be that the Church in America will not abandon preachers and places of worship that make us comfortable but don't care if we live holy lives; we may never see the Churches rise up in Reformation. We may never experience a Great Awakening as a nation.

BUT, all we need, AS FAMILIES, is to walk in the Word of God with a heart that is willing to sacrifice for our Lord and teach our children accordingly. THEN we can plant the seeds of Reformation and Great Awakening in THEM! Then, we can walk in the joy of the Lord as we watch our children and our grandchildren grow strong and joyful and plant even MORE seeds of Reformation and Revival in their families! What if ONLY one out of ten thousand Christian families did so? REVIVAL and God's Church would blossom like a rose and, as that sweet fragrance was breathed in, multitudes would be born again as NEW and POWERFUL soldiers in God's army.

CHAPTER 2: HISTORY LESSONS

Modern History: Secular and Church
Church History: Post Apostolic to the Present
The Establishment Churches
The New American Establishment Church
God's People Must Take Responsibility
We MUST Learn from HISTORY

MODERN HISTORY: SECULAR AND CHURCH

Over the last 50 years, we have seen a severe decline in American values and cultural standards. Even Biblical standards have been affected. Many in the Church have blamed television and other media outlets for the moral erosion. A good example of the moral erosion in our country is the following. In 1950, an American actress of Swedish descent (Ingrid Bergman) had an adulterous affair which produced a child with an Italian director (Roberto Rossellini). American producers and movie fans were upset with her behavior. She was reprimanded for this behavior on the Senate floor. Today, even in the Church, many would sympathize with Ingrid and Roberto. In the 1990s many in the Church poured out a great deal of sympathy for Princess Diana in England even though she was sexually involved with a man outside of marriage.

As we study both church history and secular history, we discover that the nations that embrace Scriptural Christianity were greatly blessed both economically and culturally and even become strong world leaders. However, when the Church strays from a strict adherence to the Word of God and the power of His Holy Spirit, both the church and the nation become weak and are easily conquered by Satanically inspired heathen forces. The following is a thumbnail sketch of Church history.

CHURCH HISTORY: POST-APOSTOLIC TO THE PRESENT

By the end of the 2nd century, bishops began congregating in regional synods to resolve doctrinal and policy issues. By the 3rd century, the bishop of Rome began to act as the leader of a court of appeals for problems that other bishops could not resolve. In 313 A.D., the struggles of the Early Church were lessened by the legalization of Christianity by the Emperor Constantine I. In 380 A.D., under Emperor Theodosius I, CATHOLICISM became the state religion of the Roman Empire.

Constantinople was the most prominent eastern city and Rome was the most prominent western city. The Bishop of Rome became the Pope and the most powerful man in the West and the Bishop of Constantinople was his counterpart in the East. The doctrine of the Catholic Church became more and more infected with unscriptural concepts. The Church developed seven sacraments which all members had to accept as absolute truth. From 325 A.D. to 787 A.D., there were seven ecumenical councils held in which Biblical doctrine was interpreted by the bishops. The doctrine that emerged from these meetings at times was suspect at best and heretical at worst. Mary, the mother of Jesus became the Theotokos or Mother of God. Priests and nuns were forbidden to marry. They also believed that the early church fathers (men who wrote and interpreted doctrine as far back as the second century A.D.) were as important a source of truth as the Scriptures. The Pope became the Vicar of Christ and the communion elements became the literal body of Christ.

In 1054 A.D., the Eastern faction of the Church in Constantinople declared the Western faction, the Roman Catholics to be in error and formed the Eastern Orthodox Church. The Eastern Orthodox Church retained most of the Roman Catholic doctrine but made some changes in practice. They did not demand that the clergy be celibate. They also did not recognize the Pope as the Vicar of Christ. They still believed that Mary was the mother of God but did not believe that she should be worshiped. The Eastern Orthodox Church believe that babies are born again at baptism, and after baptism, when they receive chrismation, they receive the Holy Spirit as did the disciples at Pentecost. Also, they believe, as the Roman Catholics do, that the seven books of the Apocrypha are equal in value to the rest of Scripture. They DO believe that faith in Jesus Christ is necessary and they stress that faith without works Is DEAD. Both of these churches used traditions, teachings, and sources outside of Scripture to determine church doctrine. Both these churches became increasingly weakened because they abandoned the Scripture as the only source of God's will for man. They selectively added to and subtracted from the Scriptures to suit their own needs.

The Roman Catholic Church and Eastern Orthodox churches resisted the Reformation which started in 1517. This new reform movement taught that men should not rely upon the traditions or practices of the Church that conflicted with Scripture but should ONLY rely upon the SCRIPTURES which are inspired by God and profitable for teaching, for reproof, for correction and for training in righteousness. Because both the Roman Catholic Church and the Eastern Orthodox Church resisted this foundational truth, and continued practices that were not sanctioned by Scripture, the countries in which they ruled became much weaker after the Reformation and lost their standing in the world as military and economic powers. Spain, Portugal, France, and Italy in the West were all at one time great powers in the world, but after they resisted the Reformation, they became minor powers in the world. The Eastern Bloc countries in Europe also were diminished to the point that eventually they were conquered by evil neighbors. Even Russia, which did become a world power was eventually taken over by godless leaders who were unspeakably cruel to the Russian people and murdered tens of millions of them.

In history, we see examples where the Church fell away from either believing in or practicing the Scriptures and the nation where they lived became weak and the culture became corrupt. We also see examples where God's people repented of their sin and embraced and practiced the Scriptures and the nation became strong. When the Church trusts God's word and depends upon nothing else, the Church becomes Reformed and Awakened to the power of the Holy Spirit and God's Word and the nation in which it dwells flourishes morally, economically and spiritually.

The Roman Catholic Church and the Eastern Orthodox Church ruled Christendom from the fourth century to the 16th century. Both churches had a few mighty men and women of God who loved Jesus Christ and the Scriptures and made some great contributions to God's people. In the third century, St. Athanasius wrote the Athanasian Creed which discussed the essence of the Godhead. He also wrote the biography of St. Anthony, a hermit monk who had a wonderful conversion and, according to Athanasius, a miraculous ministry of healing. St. Augustine of Hippo is another example of a man who wrote passionately and compellingly about his love for the Lord Jesus Christ, even though much of his doctrine was tainted by corrupt Roman Catholic beliefs. However, the Church practiced idolatry and perverted the doctrine of grace. The phrase, "The just shall live by faith alone" to this day means little to Catholics. Most believe that to be a good Christian you must trust in Jesus Christ, Mary, the Pope and the teachings and traditions of the Catholic Church. There is much more detail regarding the Roman Catholic Church in chapters 16 and 17 of this book.

"The Dark Ages... refers to the period of the time between the fall of the Roman Empire and the beginning of the Italian Renaissance and the age of discovery (476 A.D – 1500 A.D.). During this time... poor people had little opportunity to improve their condition in life. Religious superstition was also widespread. The Catholic Church was extremely institutionalized and often opposed the scientific and cultural advancements the Greeks and Romans had pioneered.

"The Dark Ages were a difficult time in which to live. Famine and disease were common. The Black Death (bubonic plague) devastated Europe in the late 1340s and early 1350s, killing an estimated 100 to 200 million people. Warfare was also a part of everyday life. The Europeans and the Muslims of the Arab world fought numerous conflicts. These conflicts, called the Crusades began in 1095 and ended in 1291. The Dark Ages have often been described as a backwards time in human history." [3]

During this long period of cultural and spiritual darkness there were virtually no evangelists because the Church did not teach the Gospel (good news or Evangelium.) The people were supposedly saved by faith in Christ AND trusting the Church, the traditions that were handed down through the ages, partaking of the Eucharist, the intercession of Mary, and good works. This historical period was most certainly a time of great spiritual darkness. There were countless plagues, invasions, and times of famine. The lifespan was short, and the quality of life was poor. In the initial stages of the Dark Ages, these churches should have divested themselves of their unscriptural and harmful doctrines and embraced the truths of the Scriptures. If they had done so, they likely would have conquered the Muslims and their false god.

In the 14th through the 16th centuries, there were some stirrings of resistance against the Roman Catholic Church, but only when Martin Luther called for a Reformation of the Church in 1517 did the Reformation of Christendom begin to greatly bless the nations. One year earlier, a Catholic priest by the name of Desiderius Erasmus published the Greek New Testament. His 1519 version was used by Martin Luther in his German translation of the Bible; and William Tyndale used Erasmus's Bible for his translation of the New Testament into English.

Martin Luther, along with Ulrich Zwingli, John Calvin, John Knox and others, encouraged people to leave the Roman Catholic Church and believe, live and proclaim the Gospel of Jesus Christ apart from the traditions and councils of the Roman Catholic Church. In Germany, Martin Luther proclaimed that salvation came Sola Fide (only through faith), Sola Scriptura (only the Scriptures) reveal these concepts perfectly), Sola Gratia (only by God's Grace), Solus Christos (only in Christ) and Soli Deo Gloria (Only for the Glory of God).

To establish correct Christian doctrine and Christian practice, one MUST NOT appeal to the sacraments, the ecumenical councils, the Words of the early church fathers, the words of great reformed or Arminian ministers of the past, scientific writings, cultural changes, or the words of ANY man. WE MUST ONLY INTERPRET THE BIBLE BY THE WORDS OF THE BIBLE ITSELF.

On October 31, 1517 after Martin Luther nailed 95 theses on the Wittenberg door, the people began to rise up in rebellion against the Roman Catholic Church. Many of these writings opposed the Catholic practice of selling indulgences. An indulgence was an official document from the Church granting an individual in Purgatory a reduced sentence. These indulgences could be quite expensive. Half of Germany was sympathetic to the Reformation and the Protestant movement was launched. In 1527 William Tyndale published the Greek New Testament into the language of the common English people and began to translate the entire Bible from the original Greek, Aramaic, and Hebrew languages into English. Because God, earlier, had provided for the European peoples a marvelous invention: the printing press with movable type, the Bible became available to tens of thousands of common people in Europe. In 1536, Tyndale was executed because he had translated and sold copies of the Bible to the English people without the permission of the Church. Right before he was strangled and burned at the stake, he prayed that God would open the eyes of the English King, Henry VIII, so that he would allow the publication of the Bible in the English language. God answered Tyndale's prayer and from 1536 to the end of the century, many Bibles were printed and purchased by the English people even though some were killed because it was illegal to publish or own a Bible in English during the reign of their Queen, Bloody Mary. More than any other country in the world at that time, the English embraced their English Bibles and the Reformation doctrines of grace. Protestant churches were established throughout the country. In the 1600s, the Establishment Church, the Church of England, began to fall away from Biblical principles. Some of the pastors were influenced by a new philosophy, called the Enlightenment. In the 1730s and 1740s, the British Isles began to experience the Great Awakening under the ministries of George Whitefield, Charles Wesley, and John Wesley. There was a powerful outpouring of the Holy Spirit and the British Isles were transformed. By the 19th century after this mighty outpouring, England surpassed all other nations in the world in its wealth, military power and most importantly, in the production of Bibles.

In America, the greatness of our nation began when a group of English Christians journeyed from England looking for a place where they could raise their children away from the increasing carnality of 17th century England. First, they went to the Netherlands but discovered that it was no better than England. In 1620, they sailed from England to Plymouth Rock in North America. This small group of people set out to establish a New Jerusalem on North American soil. Many of them were Puritans who had a strong belief in trusting God completely and obeying His Word scrupulously. God blessed them with some great spiritual leaders for the next 100 years, and finally in the 1720s with

Theodorus Frelinghuysen, William Tennent and Gilbert Tennent in New Jersey, there were men who prayed for a Great Awakening. In the 1730s in England the Great Awakening was fully ignited by George Whitefield who then journeyed to America, and met with Jonathan Edwards, a pastor in Massachusetts who had experienced the Great Awakening. This move of God swept through the colonies and produced a nation that became much stronger in their faith and love for God.

In 1776, the 13 colonies broke away from England and started their own nation: The United States of America. After the war was over, God brought another Great Awakening to America in the 1790s and early part of the 19th century. The birth of our nation was literally cradled between two mighty outpourings of God's truth and God's Holy Spirit.

The greatest contributing factors to the military and economic success of both England and America were the Reformation in 1517 and the Great Awakenings in the 1720s through 1740s. Initially, there are just a few men that realized the need for a spiritual awakening in their respective countries. Some had been forbidden to speak in the Establishment Churches and began preaching in open fields and even outside the doors of these churches that forbade them to preach.

These two countries more than any other in the world embraced the evangelical faith that God was offering. The power of the Word of God and the Holy Spirit emboldened God's people to preach the Gospel to every nation they could. Hundreds of thousands of lives were changed, and the reformed and revived Christians enabled thousands of evangelists, missionaries, teachers, and pastors to set up churches and missions all over the world. In the 17th and 18th centuries, England was the most powerful and prosperous nation in the world. In the 19th and 20th centuries, America became the most powerful and most prosperous nation in the history of mankind.

Before the Reformation, Spain, France, Portugal and Italy were the most powerful countries in Europe and each, at one time or another, had been world leaders. However, in the 16thcentury they completely rejected the Protestant Reformation and chose to remain under the control of the establishment Roman Catholic Church. When the Great Awakening swept through both England and America, these Catholic countries, by choice, remained untouched by that world changing revival. By the 18th century, they completely lost the worldwide influence and power that they once wielded.

Germany, on the other hand, was marked by division. Half of Germany clung to Catholicism while the other half practiced Protestantism. By the 19th century, the Protestant churches slowly slid into a corrupt doctrine called Higher Criticism. Even though this doctrine stripped Jesus Christ of His deity and discounted any miraculous power mentioned in the Bible, very few fought the errors that Higher Criticism had introduced to the German churches. Shortly after these doctrines infected the Protestant church, Germany became culturally corrupt and the politics of the country were in disarray. In the 1930s, the politics of Germany had been heavily influenced by the mob rule of a group called the Brownshirts. While Adolf Hitler was enflaming the mobs of Jew haters with his publication of Mein Kompf, anyone who would come against the National Socialist (NAZI) Party or Hitler would be attacked, beaten up or worse. Those who spoke out in public against the Nazis were likewise silenced. The people in the country embraced the Anti-Christ mob rule and hate-filled ideas of Adolf Hitler. The weakened, dead, and dying Church in Germany was unable to mount any kind of defense against Hitler and his storm troopers. It was during this decade that Hitler was democratically chosen to be the leader of the German people. He brought economic stability to the country that had not been seen for years. His mixture of big government socialism and crony capitalism was successful. His attempt to conquer the world was thwarted because there were still two nations that practiced a Christianity that was not yet terribly compromised by worldly morals and philosophies: England and especially America still clung to the Scriptures and believed in Jesus Christ.

Eastern Europe never embraced the Reformation and its principles of grace and faith. They had been blinded for centuries by the legalism, idolatry and the deadness of the Eastern Orthodox churches. They were easily taken over by first the Nazis in the 1930s, and then the Communists ruled them from the 1940s to 1980s.

THE ESTABLISHMENT CHURCHES

For 1,000 years in Western Europe the Roman Catholic Church was the ESTABLISHMENT CHURCH. In Eastern Europe for over 500 years, the Eastern Orthodox Church was the Establishment Church. In England in the 18th century, the Church of England became the Establishment Church. In Scotland, eventually the Presbyterian Church was the Establishment Church. In Southern Europe, the Roman Catholic Church still is the Establishment Church.

Over the last few years, the left-wing Progressives (Marxists) in the American political system have become more aggressive and much more successful. The Democrat Party has been taken over by men and women who are sympathetic and loyal to a Marxist ideology and a cultural cesspool that wants a society without Jesus Christ and His Biblical laws and principles. The goal of ANY Marxist organization is anarchy (lawlessness). But on the way to this Communist utopia, godless leaders impose inhumane and antichrist laws that discourage the Godly and enslave the useful idiots. All you need to do is look at China, Russia, North Korea, Venezuela, and Cuba and you see Marxism in action. They hate Biblical Christianity. Even in our country, they mock the Lord Jesus Christ, the Bible, the Ten Commandments, and God's people. They have become increasingly violent and cruel in their attacks on all that is good. The political left, if given the opportunity, would cripple or destroy the Church of Jesus Christ in America. In 1843, Karl Marx said, "Religion is the opium of the people." [4]

We have seen political events that are dangerously like political events that occurred in Nazi Germany in the 1920s and 1930s and in Russia in the early decades of the 20th century.

Barack Obama is no friend of America. Just like his birth father, his spiritual father the Reverend Jeremiah Wright, and his political mentor Bill Ayers, he hates capitalistic America. When I was a young Communist in the Bay Area in the 1960s, we met together as fellow combatants against Capitalism and America. We had weekly meetings where members of the Russian Communist Party, the American Communist Party, the Trotskyites, the Progressive Labor Party, and the Young Socialists gathered and discussed strategy for converting college students, poor people and counterculture people to Marxism. On more than one occasion, we were told how important it was to destroy our two greatest enemies so we could establish worldwide Communism; we had to destroy Capitalism and we had to destroy or take over America.

As young community organizers, we were taught to spread this message of hate and division. We were taught that we needed to stir up hatred for Capitalism, hatred for the rich, hatred for the police, and hatred for conservatives. We organized college students on campuses and poor people in minority neighborhoods. We all understood that the term Community Organizer was merely a euphemism for Communist Agitator. Barack Obama was a community organizer of poor minority neighborhoods in Chicago before he became the Community Organizer of America. He has been doing a tremendous job! Today, we have more hatred and more violence than the Progressives could have ever hoped for. If you understand that Barack Obama is sympathetic to Communist ideology, then much of his activity is explained. Many of the decisions that he made were harmful to Capitalism and were calculated to cripple America to the point where the America that we know would no longer exist. With America converted or destroyed, and the means of production and the military might of our country in the hands of the New World Order, Communism would finally be able to embrace it's supposedly inevitable destiny and conquer the world.

These leaders of the left will say or do anything to accomplish their goal of gaining more power in the American political system. In the 1960s, because we had the "correct" worldview concerning the evils of Capitalism and American Imperialism, we were taught that we had the right to do whatever was necessary to destroy any impediment that hampered the spread of our doctrine. We were taught because the proponents of Capitalism lie and mislead the people all the time, we Progressives could also lie and mislead the people. In his introduction to Rules for Radicals, Saul Alinsky acknowledges that Lucifer (The father of lies and liars) as "the very first radical, known to man, who rebelled against the establishment and did it so effectively that he at least won his own kingdom." [5] Hillary Clinton wrote her senior thesis at Wellesley College on Saul Alinsky. Saul Alinsky advised his readers to NEVER call themselves Communists. He said this term was offensive to the middle class that radicals needed to win over and that they would be offended by the term. He suggested to use terms such as Progressive or Democratic Socialist, BUT NEVER use the 'C' word.

The same horrible demonic force that controlled the Nazi Party in Germany and International Communism in the Soviet Union, North Korea, Red China and Cuba is NOW in charge of the Democrat Party in America. In the 1960s and 1970s, radicals like Tom Hayden and Andrew Young began to influence the Democrat Party. Our society underwent great changes and we saw our nation weakened to such an extent that a group of Muslim mullahs and their temporary allies, the Communists, could take down one of our strongest allies in the Middle East, Iran. This was done under the American leadership of Jimmy Carter, a man that morphed into one of the greatest useful idiots of the 20th century. President Carter also orchestrated a deal with North Korea that allowed them to have enough money to start a missile program and eventually have nuclear bombs. In 1980, the Reagan Revolution began and by the 1990s the Soviet Union fell, and Communism was dealt a terrible blow. Some believed that Communism was dead. However, after this time of political and cultural change, we entered the 1990s and on September 11, 1991, before a joint session of Congress, President George H. W. Bush echoing Woodrow Wilson, announced that he wanted the United States to be a part of "The New World Order". In 2008, we elected another left-leaning Democrat for president: Barack Hussein Obama. While Jimmy Carter was merely a useful idiot for the Communist movement, Barack Obama was a well-prepared and well-trained Marxist. He made deals with the devil that plunged America into a pit of military, cultural, moral, and spiritual decay like we had never experienced. Our old friend Israel was abandoned in favor of our new friend Iran to whom we delivered over $1.7 billion in cash and returned approximately $150 billion of previously frozen money. You may verify this at www.factcheck.org. For icing on the cake, Barack Obama through the United Nations, unsuccessfully instructed Israel to give up its home building program on the West Bank.

THE NEW AMERICAN ESTABLISHMENT CHURCH

In the 21st century America, another Establishment Church has emerged: THE COMFORT CLUB CHURCH. The model for this new Establishment Church is the Church that started in the 1960s and 1970s. In southern California particularly, many of the Churches began to meet the needs and desires of the counterculture generation. The song services were changed and many of the doctrinally charged hymns from past ages were exchanged for relatively simple songs that were somewhat repetitive in nature. These songs were easily learned and easily sung. No more long songs which often sounded more like musical sermons. The worship became more man centered. The songs talked more about what God would do for us than about His awesome magnificence.

No longer were people exposed to the strange and strident sounds of speaking in tongues and the offensively corrective prophetic utterances that one heard in the Pentecostal churches of the 40s and 50s. Charismatic Lite was the favorite drink of these churches. The music was comfortable. The message was comfortable and often entertaining. These churches emphasized a doctrine that assured its adherents that if they accepted Jesus Christ as their personal Savior, they had no need to worry about final judgment or tribulation. It didn't even matter if they were still bound by sin. Because they had accepted Jesus, they would surely be taken away by the rapture before the REALLY hard times started. These churches were the beginning of the COMFORT CLUB CHURCHES that were perfected in the early part of the 21st century. A little bit of spiritual gifts; many easy and friendly songs to sing, no offensive teaching from the pulpit or prophecies from the people. A full measure of grace that was ridiculously cheap and easy to appropriate and keep. All this with an upbeat message that was often humorous and pleasing to the people.

In the 1980s the community church movement began in earnest. This melding of the moderate churches with inoffensive charismatic doctrine and psychology proved to be an attractive and successful combination. The Church did everything they could to broaden their appeal. Many churches ignored their denominational affiliation on their signs and in some cases, even in their doctrinal statements. Others refused to even refer to their church as a denomination. To the average churchgoer, the term and concept of denomination became narrow, confining and consequently religiously incorrect. Often, in these churches, you heard people say, "We don't teach doctrine here: we just teach Jesus!"

The Establishment Church has been doing what every establishment organization has ever done. It does everything it can to control the people so that the movement itself will get larger and richer. It weeds out Biblical doctrines that give too much freedom to the assembly at large and expands the ministerial staff's ability to control people in a way that will both preserve and supposedly improve the finances and numbers of people in the assembly. Typically, it accomplishes this by never discussing offensive subjects such as divorce, except of course to remind the congregation that divorce is not the unforgivable sin and there are more reasons than just sexual sin to dissolve the Christian marriage. When they teach on pornography, they never refer to it as a sin; rather it is called an addiction.

The outsider churches such as the crazy apostles and prophet movement began in the latter part of the 20th century and proved to be rightfully scary to many people. Many Charismatics and Pentecostals correctly wanted no identification with these unhinged people. Their intrusion into Pentecostal and Charismatic churches is similar to a Ku Klux Klan member joining the Republican Party claiming to be a conservative. This movement, because of its radical and unscriptural nature, was criticized in the Establishment Churches. Unfortunately, they took the notion that if you honestly believed that all the ministries and gifts in the New Testament are available today, then you are probably as crazy as those in the prophets and apostles' movement.

The Establishment Churches in the 21st century are like the Republican Party. Donald Trump was vilified and castigated long before his perverted sexual activities were brought to public attention. Part of the reason the establishment did not like him was because his style conflicted with their style. Their style was to be very accepting and non-combative towards members of the other establishment party, the Democrats. For years, they allowed the Democrats to do what they wanted just so they could retain a measure of power in their own party and be respected by the Democrats. If they offended the Democrats too much, they knew that they would be charged as being racists or exploiters of the poor. Of course, they wanted to supplant the Democrats in all three branches of government, but only with their hand-picked establishment candidates. They felt the best way to do that would be to compromise with the Democrats.

So too, the Establishment Churches have felt that it is important to meet the needs of the people and fulfill their desires. In Charles Spurgeon's day, it was called Churchianity, then seeker-friendly churches. The Establishment Churches today are far beyond being seeker friendly. The Establishment

Church, like the Republican Party, is most interested in gaining and preserving its OWN POWER over the people so it can either grow or maintain its "success".

In America, in the 21st century, the Church has so deteriorated that it has virtually no power. We are no longer able to change the culture in our country and more importantly, we have not changed enough hearts of the people in our country to see any real change in our morals. There is a smaller percentage of born-again Christians in America today than ever before. It is true that for the first time in eight years, we no longer have a president that is more sympathetic to Communism then he is to Capitalism. But our political system is compromised. One party has been taken over by a Marxist/Progressive left-wing agenda and the Republican Party has no backbone and is willing to compromise with the Progressives. They seem almost terrified of being branded as radical conservatives, racists, or male chauvinists. They are more concerned about pleasing the people and maintaining control than they are about doing what is best for the country.

THERE IS A DEFINITE RELATIONSHIP BETWEEN THE SPIRITUAL CONDITION OF THE CHURCH AND THE MORALS AND POLITICS OF THE NATION! Strong spiritual churches produce improvement in the nation. The culture, educational system, and the economy ALL improve. When the Church is weak, and depends upon traditions and worldly philosophies, the Church has little influence over the nation or the culture. Inevitably, the nation and the culture become corrupt and the educational system fails and eventually, the military will fall into the hands of godless people. OFTEN, the state of the nation is the fruit of the Church!

The Establishment Churches and their leaders in America are most interested in keeping their large buildings, their high salaries, and congregations that love them. Where the Republican Party has not fought hard for the things that they claim to believe in, so Christians in the Establishment Churches do not fight hard against sin and especially don't discuss controversial issues such as divorce or fornication. Most churches understand that discussing divorce from the pulpit in scriptural terms would offend most people. They no longer REALLY believe that the husband is to be the head of the wife even as Christ is head of the Church. The scriptural view of a wife's submission to her husband is rarely taught, and if it is taught, there are many "explanations" mentioned to help soften the blow and more importantly hold back the husband from being the head of his wife. Sexual sin, particularly pornography, is not really a sin in these churches; it is merely an addiction and must be treated as a sickness. People who break God's law are no longer guilty of committing sins, they are merely people who make mistakes. The fear of God is slight at best and completely gone at worst. They no longer discuss the consequences of sin that the Bible talks about. Churches readily admit and are almost proud of the fact that half their leadership is addicted to pornography. We are in big trouble with God and we need to confront our own sin and lack of courage. We must believe that ALL the Scriptures are for our time and for all time.

GOD'S PEOPLE MUST TAKE RESPONSIBILITY

More prayer meetings, more Christian unity in spite of our differences, more Christian involvement with the current political system will NEVER defeat the real power behind Communism, the Democrat Party, the ACLU, Planned Parenthood, the corrupt educational system, and the corrupt media which has helped ruin our families and our culture.

Before any of these things can be destroyed, WE MUST TAKE RESPONSIBILITY for the national and cultural failures in the United States. We have UNDERVALUED SCRIPTURE and have not stood up BOLDLY and OBEYED and proclaimed ALL the Word of God in our churches, our schools, our places of employment and even in the political arena. How refreshing it would be, if we could hear a Christian politician say, "We can no longer fund Planned Parenthood because, not only does it slaughter innocent unborn children, but THE BIBLE SAYS THAT FORNICATION IS A SIN and enabling young people to fornicate by providing condoms to them is wrong before God." We have casually allowed Satan to suppress Christians from quoting the Bible or referring to the person of Jesus Christ in public places. Even our good brother Vice President Pence, when he quoted from 2 Chronicles 7:14 in his inaugural address, left out the part that says, "and TURN FROM THEIR WICKED WAYS." It is just not politically correct to discuss ANY people, as having "wicked ways."

The people of eastern Europe who would not leave the Eastern Orthodox Establishment Churches and the people of southern Europe who would not leave the Roman Catholic Church, suffered terrible judgment. We must learn from both secular history and the Scriptures that there is a price to pay for supporting a church that is lukewarm. God vomited the Lukewarm Church that remained lukewarm out of his mouth in Revelation chapter three. Ezekiel speaks about the judgment that came to Jerusalem where the only people who were spared were the ones who grieved and mourned over the terrible things that were done in the house of God (Ezekiel 9:4). We must take a careful look at the Church age that we live in. If we discover that there are things going on that offend God in the same way that the people of Ezekiel's time offended God, we should follow the example of those that grieved and mourned over the condition of God's people and their leaders. Perhaps we could be spared some of the terrible judgment that will most certainly occur if our churches are as guilty as those in Jerusalem were.

At one time, Puritans were held in high regard as the great spiritual founders of Christianity in our country. They were a people who valued the Word of God. They understood that it was the grace of God that enabled His children to obey the law of God. The Puritans were a wonderful, spiritual people that understood that when things were going badly in their community the fault may not be with the Indians that attacked them, or the bad weather that caused famine, but perhaps it came about because they had been disobedient to God. During especially difficult times they would call for days of prayer, fasting and mourning. They would spend much time searching their hearts to see if they had offended God. Often men heard from God and identified their sin. They were quick to repent. On at least one occasion, they found that the sin that brought the judgment of God was there overly exuberant appreciation for the material blessings and the comfort that God had given them. They realized that they were neglecting Him and were enjoying His blessings more than they were enjoying Him and His wonderful Word. When they repented of their sins, God restored the blessings of protection and provision that they had experienced earlier.

In the last century, the secular world has unmercifully mocked the Puritans who laid the spiritual foundation for our nation. Even many 21st century Christians consider the Puritans to have been stodgy, sour faced and legalistic (not to mention racists). The word puritanical has come to mean legalistic and inappropriately sacrificial. In the Church, this disrespectful and wrong-headed notion could have been easily dispelled by correct teaching of church history, but we seem to have become much too sophisticated to study and learn the ideas and practices of our spiritually successful ancestors. We would do well to emulate the practices of the Puritans.

WE MUST LEARN FROM HISTORY

Men and women who are willing to sacrifice in order to do what the Scriptures require give the nation the opportunity to become great and at the very least, the Church and the individuals who obey the clear message of Scripture will please God and experience His power to be holy and make disciples. We will discover that when CHRISTIANS in the Church humble themselves, pray, seek the face of God and turn from THEIR wicked ways (2 Chronicles 7:14), then God will bless the Church and consequently, He can bless the nation.

We must examine the Scriptures carefully and look at Israel when the people turned to idolatry and strayed from His Word. We must examine church history closely and see that when God's people ignored, added or subtracted from His Word, He had to chasten them or even JUDGE them by being conquered by THE ENEMY. It is IMPOSSIBLE that this nation changes except the Church repent and seek God with her whole heart. If men and women in the American churches today continue to live and to teach like they have for the last 60 years, we will not see America REALLY great again. Whenever a nation refuses to acknowledge God and does not call upon His name, that nation will experience the wrath of God.

However, IT IS EQUALLY TRUE that whenever a nation or a people or EVEN AN INDVIDUAL OR FAMILY unconditionally embraces the principles of Scripture and SHUNS every kind of worldly philosophy, teaching, or revelation that conflicts with Scripture, that nation, people, individual or family will be greatly blessed and be able to bless multitudes of other people. If we ALONE please God, we can see our families flourish during times of GREAT trouble.

SECTION 2: CAN JUDGMENT OR SEVERE CHASTENING BE CLOSE?

CHAPTER 3: SHRINE PROSTITUTES IN THE TEMPLE OF GOD
CHAPTER 4: CORRUPTION IN AMERICA AND THE CHURCH
CHAPTER 5: EVIDENCE THAT DEMANDS A VERDICT
CHAPTER 6: GODLY PUNISHMENTS no 2
CHAPTER 7: JOSIAH REVIVAL

This section looks at the state of America and the state of the Church. First we look at the sin of viewing pornography. Then corruption is defined. What does the country, the culture, the Church, and the Bible show us? If the country and the Church are corrupt, how does God deal with the country and the Church? Is there enough real scriptural evidence to justify God judging America or the Church? If a trial were held, what would the prosecution say about the Church and about America? What would be the defense of America and the defense of the Church? We know that God is the ultimate judge in these matters and where defense is warranted, He will defend America and the Church. But equally true, if God deems the conduct of America and the Church to be indefensible, then God certainly will judge America and the Church. We know that God is merciful, but for how long does His mercy extend to a church and a nation? The next five chapters will investigate all these issues and will come to a conclusion that seems fair and just according to Scripture.

CHAPTER 3: SHRINE PROSTITUTES IN THE TEMPLE OF GOD

Pornography Is the New Church Epidemic
"Christian" Therapy for the "Addicted"
It Has Been Said in the Lukewarm Church
   But the Lord Says:
The True Nature of the Sin of Pornography
Temple Prostitutes in the Old Testament
Pornography: Polluting the Temple of God
Cleansing the Temple of the Holy Spirit
      The Only Real Solution Comes from Scripture
      An Extreme Solution
      Develop a Scriptural Fear of the Lord
Forgiveness for the Worst of Sins!
It's Not the Sins that You Do
Blessings of Overcoming Pornography

PORNOGRAPHY IS THE NEW EPIDEMIC IN THE CHURCH

James Dobson of Focus on the Family calls pornography the new crack cocaine. 57% of pastors say that addiction to pornography is the most sexually damaging issue to their congregations. 51% of pastors say cyber porn is a possible temptation and 37% say it is a current struggle in their own lives. OVER half of EVANGELICAL PASTORS admit to viewing pornography last year. Of those who had visited porn sites, 53% had visited such sites a few times in the past year, and 18% visit sexually explicit sites between a couple of times a month and more than once a week. Largest consumer of Internet pornography: 12 to 17-year-old age group. In December 2000, the National Coalition to Protect Children and Families surveyed the Christian campuses to see how the next generation of believers was doing with sexual purity: 48% of males admitted to current use; 68% of males said they intentionally viewed the sexually explicit site at the school. [6]

In March 2002, Rick Warren's website, pastors.com conducted a survey on porn use among 1351 pastors: 54% of the pastors had viewed Internet pornography within the last year, and 30% of these had viewed Internet pornography within the last 30 days. [7]

Statistics on women with pornographic addiction: 34% of the readers of women's online newsletter admitted to intentionally accessing Internet porn in a recent poll and one out of every six women, including Christians, struggle with an addiction to pornography [8]

"CHRISTIAN" THERAPY FOR THE "ADDICTED"

The following is a typical example of how churches handle pornography problems: Safe Families recommends the following steps for ministry leaders when helping someone recover from an addiction to pornography.
1. Immediate Emergency Response
2. Church-Based Accountability Partner
3. Media Sobriety Covenant
4. Online Safety and Media Sobriety Manual.
5. Family Support.
6. Peer Support Groups.
7. Professional Counseling. [9]

Please Note: NONE of the Above-mentioned Church-Based Steps reference ANY SCRIPTURE. Most church programs today are little more than "Christianized" secular psychology programs. In a few churches, some Scriptures are thrown in, but the basic thrust of the program is a large dose of secular psychology methodology. Seldom will you hear the term sin: almost always you hear the term addiction. The words repentance, holiness and the concept of the fear of God are virtually never mentioned.

Pornography is NOT an addiction, an illness, a sickness or an epidemic. These are all medical terms and imply that pornography can be handled the same way you handle a breakout of typhoid fever, mumps, or a badly broken leg. Pornography is a SIN against our body, our families, our souls and most importantly, PORNOGRAPHY IS A SIN AGAINST JESUS CHRIST who paid a terrible price to deliver us from sin and its temporal and eternal consequences.

IT HAS BEEN SAID IN THE LUKEWARM CHURCH

"Do not be overly concerned about viewing pornography on the Internet. After all, no one is perfect. Many other men in your congregation including the leadership, in times past, have done the same thing. Even now there are those that are struggling with their addiction just like you. Remember, you are saved by grace and not by works."

BUT THE LORD SAYS:

1 Thessalonians 4:3-5 , 7-8 (NLT) God's will is for you to be holy, so STAY AWAY FROM ALL SEXUAL SIN. Then each of you will control his own body and live in holiness and honor- NOT IN LUSTFUL PASSION like the pagans who do not know God and His ways. God has called us to HOLY LIVES, NOT IMPURE LIVES. Therefore, anyone who refuses to live by these rules is NOT DISOBEYING HUMAN TEACHING BUT IS REJECTING GOD, who gives HIS HOLY SPIRIT to you.

Matthew 5:27-28 (NLT) You have heard the commandment that says, "you must not commit adultery." But I say to you, ANYONE WHO even LOOKS AT A WOMAN WITH LUST has already COMMITTED ADULTERY (pornea or sexual sin) with her in his heart.

Looking at pornographic material on the Internet or anyplace else and lusting after those pictures certainly constitutes committing adultery in one's heart. In men's church meetings OFTEN the subject of pornography comes up. The leader of the discussion usually makes it noticeably clear that the men who are struggling with "the addiction" to pornography were not alone. Typically, there are confessions of shame which were quickly countered by someone in leadership saying, "You don't need to walk in condemnation. Jesus loves you."

The leaders do their best to sweep away any feelings of guilt or shame. My experience has been that many in leadership themselves confess that they have watched Internet pornography on occasion and they too found the habit difficult to break. Sexual sin does not merely become a habit but often becomes SPIRITUAL BONDAGE. However, in several men's meetings that I have attended, many of the emergency responses listed previously from The Safe Family website were discussed and suggested. SADLY, as with these websites, no Scriptures were brought up. They did discuss several Scriptures which dealt with God's love for us and His patience. It is certainly true that God is patient and He loves us more than our hearts can ever imagine. In fact, He loves us so much He does not want us to experience punishment or miss out on eternal life with Him. He wants us to trust Him enough to battle against our selfish flesh, repent of this egregious sin, and yield to His Word. Often, they recite Romans 8:1(KJV): "There is therefore now no condemnation to them which are in Christ Jesus." But they always leave out the REST OF THE Scripture, which says, "who WALK NOT AFTER THE FLESH, BUT AFTER THE SPIRIT. And Romans

8:6 (KJV): 6 For TO BE CARNALLY MINDED IS DEATH; but to be SPIRITUALLY MINDED IS LIFE AND PEACE.

THE TRUE NATURE OF THE SIN OF PORNOGRAPHY

1 Corinthians 6:18 (NLT). Run from sexual sin! NO OTHER SIN SO CLEARLY AFFECTS THE BODY as this one does. For SEXUAL IMMORALITY IS A SIN AGAINST YOUR OWN BODY.

In preparing this chapter and researching the use of pornography among Christians, I was not shocked. It confirmed much that I had heard and seen. Pornography continues to be a terrible problem in the Church because of our willful neglect of the Scriptures. Please understand, I am fully aware of the multitudes of temptations that face both men and women every day regarding sexual purity, but that is NEVER AN EXCUSE for a Christian who has repented of their sins, trusts in the Lord Jesus Christ and His Scriptures, is born again, and is a NEW CREATURE IN CHRIST. We must remember that pornography is NOT AN ADDICTION; it is SPIRITUAL BONDAGE and it is a terrible sin against a wonderful God who gave His life so He could live in our bodies, HIS TEMPLE.

In men's meetings, I have heard repeatedly this phrase: "Don't worry about your sexual sin. When the Father looks at you, all He sees is His pure and perfect Son Jesus Christ." This is Christian psycho-babble at its WORST. We need more than psychological head-patting that essentially tells us that we are okay EVEN if we view pornography. We really need to repent and renew our minds by studying the Scriptures with a heart that is ashamed of that sin and seeks God for a strong sense of His forgiveness and an infusion of His Holy Spirit.

TEMPLE PROSTITUTES IN THE OLD TESTAMENT

HOSEA 4:14 (NASB) I will not punish your daughters when they play the harlot or your brides when they commit adultery, For THE MEN THEMSELVES go apart with harlots and OFFER SACRIFICES WITH TEMPLE PROSTITUTES, So THE PEOPLE without understanding ARE RUINED.
1 Kings 15:12 (NLT) He (King Josiah) banished the male and female SHRINE PROSTITUTES from the land and got rid of all the idols his ancestors had made.
2 KINGS 23:7 (NLT) He also tore down the living quarters of the male and female SHRINE PROSTITUTES that were INSIDE THE TEMPLE OF THE LORD.

Referring to the temple prostitutes one commentator said, "Thus, CORPORAL AND SPIRITUAL WHOREDOM'S WENT TOGETHER and THE VILE AFFECTIONS to which they were given up were THE PUNISHMENT of their vain imaginations." [10]

In other words, their physical whoredom was a manifestation of their spiritual whoredom or idol worship. When men or women succumb to the sin of watching pornography or engage in unscriptural sex, often that is a physical manifestation of their idolatry, which is spiritual adultery. In their case, the idol may be ANOTHER JESUS. Typically, our generation believes in a Jesus Christ who is never negative, never judges you, and tolerates unrepentant sin.

PORNOGRAPHY: POLLUTING THE TEMPLE OF GOD

1 Corinthians 6:19-20 (NLT) Don't you realize that your body is THE TEMPLE OF THE HOLY SPIRIT, who lives in you and was given to you by God? You do not belong to yourself, 20 for GOD BOUGHT YOU WITH A HIGH PRICE. So, YOU MUST HONOR GOD WITH YOUR BODY.

Pornography has terrible consequences. Our body is the temple of the Holy Spirit of God. We defile His temple in THE SAME WAY that the Old Testament Jews did when they had sex with temple prostitutes IN THE TEMPLE OF GOD. Many a so-called Christian has had sex with the Internet prostitutes and have allowed them to dwell in their imaginations and in their bodies. What they are doing is allowing them to dwell in THE HOLY TEMPLE OF GOD.

If we examine Scripture carefully, we will see the powerful and terrible effects if the leader of any family commits sexual sin. We see in David's life that one of his sons died in childbirth, Amnon was killed by Absalom because he raped Absalom's sister. Absalom was killed by Joab after shaming his father by publicly sleeping with his concubines when he tried to overthrow his father's kingdom. A fourth son, Adonijah, was executed after he attempted to usurp the throne from Solomon. Solomon, David's son who became king, married 300 wives and had 700 concubines. To please one of his wives, he built a shrine to the detestable god Moloch who accepted the sacrifice of children.

We may see this powerful spirit of lust grab hold of members of our family and our church. If we are not quick to repent and stay free of sexual sin, we are inviting the chastening hand of God to deal with our bodies, our minds, and our spirits. More tragically, we may have weakened the protection of God from our loved ones. What A TERRIBLE JUDGMENT it would be to watch OUR CHILDREN GROW UP AND BECOME ENSNARED BY SEXUAL SIN.

If any viewer of pornography is bound by that sin of polluting the temple of the Holy Spirit, they define themselves as practitioners of the sexual sin of pornography which is adultery and, if not abandoned, they may experience the horrors of Hell itself.

1 Corinthians 6:9-10 (NLT) Don't you realize that those... who indulge in sexual sin...WILL NOT INHERIT THE KINGDOM OF GOD.

CLEANSING THE TEMPLE OF THE HOLY SPIRIT

THE ONLY REAL SOLUTIOIN COMES FROM SCRIPTURE

Romans 10:17(NASB) 17 So faith comes from hearing and hearing by the Word of Christ.
1 John 5:4 (NASB) For whatever is BORN OF GOD OVERCOMES THE WORLD and this is the victory that has overcome the world – our faith.
2 Chronicles 7:14 (GNV) If my people, among whom my Name is called upon, do HUMBLE THEMSELVES, and pray and seek my presence, AND TURN FROM THEIR WICKED WAYS, then will I hear in heaven and be merciful to FORGIVE THEIR SIN, and will heal their land.

REAL spiritual success starts with HUMILITY and ends with TURNING FROM SIN or wickedness. To overcome the enemy, we need to have a faith that reflects the values and the dictates of Scripture. Many lukewarm Establishment Churches, even those that believe that fornication is prohibited by God's Word, are prone to not confront unscriptural sexual conduct.

1 Corinthians 7:3-5 (NLT) The husband should fulfill his wife's sexual needs, and the wife should fulfill her husband's needs. 4 The wife gives authority over her body to her husband, and the husband gives authority over his body to his wife. 5 DO NOT DEPRIVE EACH OTHER OF SEXUAL RELATIONS, unless you both agree to refrain from sexual intimacy for a limited time, so you can give yourselves more completely to prayer. Afterward, you should come together again SO THAT SATAN WON'T BE ABLE TO TEMPT YOU because of your lack of self-control.

This Scripture tends to put a sense of responsibility on the partner that is reluctant to engage in sexual activity. If the woman or the man deprives their spouse of sexual relations, this puts the other in great temptation. The Bible instructs both partners in the marriage relationship to yield to the desires of their partner. The wife has authority over the husband's body and the husband has authority over the wife's body. The transgression of this clear teaching of the Apostle Paul has done great damage to both the offender and the offended party in the arena of sexual relationships of a marriage. There is never an excuse for any kind of sexual sin, but it puts the responsibility of compliance on the reluctant party that creates dangerous consequences for both parties. If either party disobeys this Scripture, then Satan is able to tempt BOTH parties. Of course, this scripture does not command a spouse to engage in sexual activity that they believe is offensive to God.

AN EXTREME SOLUTION

Matthew 5:29 (NLT) If your eye even your good eye causes you to lust, gouge it out and throw it away. It is better for you to lose one part of your body than for your whole body to be thrown into hell.

The remedy for lust and viewing pornography is NOT to literally pluck out your good eye. The figurative meaning for this instruction is to arrange your life and your viewing habits so that you are not tempted to look at any unholy thing that enslaves you or offends God. You most certainly should never enter a strip club or watch a movie where you view nudity or anyone engaging in sexual activity. If you're constantly tempted by the Internet, be scrupulously attentive to avoid viewing anything that the Lord Jesus Christ would not want you to see. If you can't do that, stop going on the Internet! When viewing television, avert your eyes and ears during suggestive commercials or any scenes that the Lord does not want you to look at, or, better yet, JUST TURN IT OFF; or you could do as one famous evangelist did, he took his television set to a wooded area behind his home and shot his television set AND KILLED IT! Essentially you must blind your eyes to that which would ensnare your soul, compromise your walk and grieve the Holy Spirit.

.........DEVELOP A SCRIPTURAL FEAR OF THE LORD

Why are men in many churches, including pastors and board members, so addicted to pornography? It's because we have edited and interpreted the Scripture so that we no longer are taught to FEAR THE LORD. In some cases, in the New Testament the Greek word PHOBOS means respect or reverence. But in Matthew 10:28, it definitely means FEAR.

Matthew 10:28 (NASB) And do not fear those who kill the body but cannot kill the soul. But rather FEAR HIM WHO IS ABLE TO DESTROY BOTH SOUL AND BODY IN HELL.

Because we seldom hear about the consequences of an unholy or disobedient life, we are not really afraid that God would ever PAINFULLY punish us if we watch pornography. When people sin, MOST do so with absolutely no fear of the consequences, either temporal or eternal.

FORGIVENESS FOR THE WORST OF SINS!

1 John 1:9 (NLT) But if we confess our sins to Him, He is faithful and just TO FORGIVE US OUR SINS AND TO CLEANSE US FROM ALL WICKEDNESS.

Along with confessing our sins, we must trust with our mind and our heart that God GUARANTEES THAT IF WE CONFESS OUR SINS, He will most certainly forgive us and cleanse us totally. As we separate ourselves and steer clear of and avoid people and places of temptation, we can stay pure in our own hearts and pure in His eyes. If we fail and fall, we can still expect His forgiveness and cleansing if we are sincere in our confession and our repentance.

Likewise, we must never hold back from telling people who have chosen ANY SIN, even pornography, the simple, profound truth that God offers them unconditional grace if they would repent of their sins and trust in His Son Jesus Christ. God will forgive them strictly on the basis of what He has done for them at the cross and not on the basis of their good works or their own righteousness. If they believe in the Lord Jesus Christ, He will give them a new heart and a profound new power to overcome the besetting sins of their life. If we are Christians who have viewed pornography and are sick of our sin and have repented, then we know that He will forgive us and cleanse us of ALL wickedness.

IT'S NOT THE SIN THAT YOU DO

Repentance of sin is extremely important. In their first sermons mentioned in the Scriptures, John the Baptist, Jesus Christ and Peter, ALL OF THESE GREAT MEN called the people TO REPENT of their sins.

Matthew 3:1-2 (NLT) In those days JOHN THE BAPTIST came to the Judean wilderness and began preaching. His message was, 2 "REPENT of your SINS and turn to God, for the kingdom of heaven is near."

JESUS CHRIST in Mark 1:15 (NLT) The time promised by God has come at last! He announced. The Kingdom of God is near! REPENT OF YOUR SINS and BELIEVE THE GOOD NEWS!

Acts 2:38 (NLT) PETER replied, REPENT OF YOUR SINS and turn to God, and be baptized in the name of Jesus Christ for the forgiveness of your sins. Then you shall receive the gift of the Holy Spirit.

These Scriptures illustrate an important truth. "It is not the sin that you do that ultimately causes you problems; it is WHAT YOU DO WITH YOUR SIN." As with other sins, after God warns the people, He tells them to come to Him and confess their sins and repent, AND He will forgive their sin and He will cleanse them of all unrighteousness. They may be able to avoid some of the punishment or judgment that they otherwise would have experienced on this earth. If they are His but fail to continue a life of trust and repentance, then God's grace will create circumstances that will cause them much pain. This pain can be spiritual, physical, mental, or psychological. But they will experience the consequence of their sin: they will experience His chastening hand. If they are not His true children, and are merely Christians in name only, they may not experience much pain in this life but eventually they will be cast from His Presence and thrust into Hell itself.

BLESSINGS OF OVERCOMING PORNOGRAPHY

Psalm 103:17-18 (NKJV) But the MERCY of the Lord is from everlasting to everlasting ON THOSE WHO FEAR HIM, 18 and His righteousness to YOUR CHILDREN'S CHILDREN, to such as keep His covenant and to those who remember His commandments to do them.

If we fear God and remember His commandments and DO THEM, we can fully expect to live with Him forever in a glory that is beyond our imagination and be in a relationship that will produce a sense of His love and an ability to love Him in return. We can know the peace that passes understanding and the joy that is beyond our greatest expectations. We can know that we are His and He is ours FOR NOW AND FOREVER. And what is more, we can fully expect His righteousness to be passed on to our children and our grandchildren and with the Lord's help and mercy, they will have the best possible chance of avoiding the impurities that we have experienced. And remember THE LORD'S MERCY IS ON THOSE WHO FEAR HIM.

1 Timothy 1:19 (NLT) Cling to your faith in Christ and keep your **CONSCIENCE CLEAR. For some people have DELIBERATELY VIOLATED THEIR CONSCIENCES; as a result, their FAITH HAS BEEN SHIPWRECKED.**

Another great blessing that we experience is A CLEAR CONSCIENCE. When we stop viewing pornography, we will stop violating our consciences and we can expect that our faith will no longer be shipwrecked. We will be able to believe God for more than we ever have before. May God bless each of us to keep His temple clean with a pure heart, a clean conscience, and an increased faith to love Him more, trust Him more and serve Him more effectively.

CHAPTER 4: CORRUPTION IN AMERICA & THE CHURCH

We Must Use Correct Standards
Government Standards in America
Cultural Standards in America
The True Standard: The Biblical Standard
The Church and The Biblical Standards
Fake Scriptures
To Whom Much is Given, from Him Much Will be Required
If We Fail to Convert the Culture
Daniel's Law

WE MUST USE CORRECT STANDARDS

To evaluate both America and the Church, we must first establish a standard of corruption. The standards of corruption formulated by the Babylonians of antiquity, were different from those of the early Greeks, the early Hebrews and of course the early Christians. Even today, we have tribes and cultures that in the past were cannibals, and in their religious system that activity was not deemed to be wrong. However, most of those tribes and cultures no longer embrace cannibalism as being morally acceptable: they believe that cannibalism would corrupt their cultures. In many pre-Christian cultures, fornication and adultery were considered normal. Some of the earlier religions even had temple prostitutes who played a part in the worship of their gods and goddesses. Today, we have many in the secular world that believe that fornication and adultery are appropriate and in no way sinful.

Even among people that claim to be Christians, we have different standards. Some Christians believe that it is wrong to fight in a war. Others believe that it is wrong to eat any kind of food that is considered unclean by Old Testament standards. Some churchgoers believe it is wrong to have a blood transfusion. Others have believed or still believe that it was or is appropriate and even pleasing to God for men to have multiple wives.

So, standards must be established that people must obey. Obedience to the standards will either bless or curse a nation or a church. Some believe that the standards must shift and change as the culture shifts and changes. Others believe these standards should be ABSOLUTE. Those standards must coincide with what is pleasing to a higher power. We must also have standards that state what is offensive to this higher power and morally wrong. In our culture and in the world at large, we have people that passionately believe that the highest power we should recognize is Mother Earth. They believe that the earth, the plants, and animals that live on it should be protected and preserved, even if that preservation and protection deprives human beings of a better life. They believe that human beings are no more important than seals, bears, trees, and any other living things. In fact, they believe that human beings are the greatest threat to Mother Earth and all the plant life and animal life that abide in her presence.

GOVERNMENT STANDARDS IN AMERICA

The government, through its laws, political structure and educational system has standards that greatly affect the people in our country. Many embrace values that coincide with those who believe that we should value the earth and all other creatures more than we value human beings.

Many of these people believe all nations should form one great organization where the richer nations share with the poorer nations and all religions are viewed as being equally valuable. The God of the Muslims, the voodoo gods, the Rastafarian gods, the gods of the Orient, the gods of Africa, the God of Judaism, and the God of Christianity are all part of the Confederation of gods. We all should love and respect all the gods and all the groups and religions that worship these gods. We should teach our children the values of all religions. The Christian religion especially has no right to claim that their God is the only God. Our government through its laws and educational system has greatly limited the practice of Christianity.

Our educational system has changed dramatically in the last 60 years. From kindergarten through college and university education, we have seen government intrusion and indoctrination in the classes to convince people that Christianity is not the solution but the problem. The Bible has all but been outlawed in these schools. In 1962, Engel versus Vitale essentially outlawed school prayer. Prayer in the Name of Jesus Christ is considered morally repugnant and is forbidden. This decision made it virtually impossible for any Christian teacher or even student to pray on the school grounds in the Name of Jesus Christ. Thus, FREEDOM FOR RELIGION was cleverly changed to

FREEDOM FROM RELIGION. Discussion of the principles of the Christian religion and the person of our Lord Jesus Christ are essentially prohibited except when this is done in a way that makes the Christian religion look bad and Jesus Christ appear to be weak, foolish or a hater of mankind's freedom to enjoy and express himself. Not only are our public schools Anti-Christian, but many private institutions are also Anti-Christian.

Simply put, Christianity is basically viewed as a religion of white men that has been practiced to their great advantage over people of color, any other religion, and women. They believe that men have forced them to have children that they do not want and that women should have complete charge over their own bodies and whatever happens to be inside those bodies. Christianity claiming to be the one true religion is most offensive. More importantly, Christianity destroys the freedom of people to be what they want to be.

In 1973, Roe versus Wade was made the law of the land, and the right to life, liberty and the pursuit of happiness was altered to exclude unborn children. Abortion became legal and eventually acceptable to hundreds of millions of people in our country. This ruling legalized the murder of unborn or partially born children. The Nazis in the 1930s and 1940s murdered 6 million Jews. Since Roe versus Wade, Americans have murdered over 50-60 million unborn children.

Many other Supreme Court decisions have punished the Church of Jesus Christ in America and greatly harmed both believers and nonbelievers. Criminals have received rights and privileges that are not in agreement with the laws of God. Sinners have been given liberty to do just about whatever they want, when they want, and how they want.

CULTURAL STANDARDS IN AMERICA

The divorce rate in our country has increased more than TEN-FOLD in the last 150 years.[11] It is more common today than ever before for a child to live in a home where there is only one birth parent. These changes have increased depression, homelessness, and rampant dependence on drugs that cause even further confusion and pain. Among people born from 1949 to 1958, Americans ranked FIRST IN THE WORLD in the percentage who've earned high school degrees and THIRD IN THE WORLD in those who've earned college and graduate degrees. But Americans born from 1979 to 1988 only rank 10th in the world in high school diplomas, and they've dropped to 13th in attaining post-secondary degrees.[12] We have become lazy and selfish because of the change in our cultural morals. The work and study hard ethic has virtually disappeared.

There was a time in America when we were more concerned about the other person than ourselves. Today the doctrines of self-esteem and self-worth have helped us to be more concerned about our own needs and pleasures than we are about the other person's needs and pleasures. Even the Church has accepted and taught these doctrines of demons. We have excused the law breakers and sinners and rationalized that their crimes and sins were someone else's fault. Even Christians have bought in to these teachings. Dr. James Dobson said in one of his books that if Lee Harvey Oswald had been given more self-esteem by his parents, particularly his father, he never would've assassinated John F. Kennedy. "Lee Harvey Oswald, the rejected, unlovable failure, killed the man who, more than any man on earth, embodied all the success, beauty, wealth, and family affection which he lacked." [13]

Parents, society, capitalism, the rich, white people, the police, fathers, and ESPECIALLY Christianity are the culprits. They are the ones that cause the lawbreakers (who the culture says are the real victims) to commit the crimes that they do, whether it is a robbery, rape, or murder.

Is America really that corrupt? Absolutely! We have become corrupt beyond the imagination of anyone that lived in our country in the first part of the 20th century. Is America ripe for judgment? Without a doubt. No country, Christian or heathen, has so offended GOD with their unrighteousness and not been judged. Billy Graham's wife put it quite clearly, "If God doesn't punish America, He'll have to apologize to Sodom and Gomorrah!" [14]

Look at History! Has any previously Christian country ever gotten away with as much sin as we have and avoided the judgment of God? Look at the Jews during Jeremiah's time. Look at both Western and Eastern Europe. Look at Germany, the seat of the first Reformation. These countries under weak Judaism, a lukewarm Lutheranism, the Roman Catholic Church and the Eastern Orthodox movement all were judged terribly by God using both Nazis and Communists. LOOK AT AMERICA in the latter part of the 20th and the 21ST CENTURY!

Thus says America to God, "Really, we don't need you and your rules to be a wall to protect us from danger. We will raise up OUR OWN WALLS to protect ourselves from floods, plagues, wars, or invasion! We can take care of ourselves! And what's more if you expect us to trust You and obey Your Word to buy Your protection, WE DON'T WANT IT ANYMORE!"

THE TRUE STANDARD: THE BIBLICAL STANDARD

If Biblical standards are the standards that are pleasing to God, then we must evaluate both the nation and the Church by these standards. Because we are

His Church, we must do His will and He will show us what His will is through His Scriptures. Through the Scriptures we will understand what is holy and morally correct. In years gone by, when the Church was much more powerful and influential, the laws of our country and its states were based on the laws that God revealed in His Holy Scriptures: adultery was illegal in most of our states. Sodomy and homosexuality were also outlawed. These activities are forbidden in the Scriptures. In fact, any sexual activity that was identified by the Scriptures as sin, was outlawed, including pornography. Even literature was judged legal or illegal based on whether or not it met standards that were set by the courts and based on the Bible. Virtually all forms of media expression, such as books, plays or movies were evaluated and judged by these legal standards. In the past 100 years, we have seen a continual erosion of those Scriptural values. We are at the point now when the most egregious sins are not only considered allowable and appropriate, but the practitioners of these activities are hailed as heroes for their bravery in going against the old, outmoded cultural standards of Biblical morality.

All the Commandments, precepts, statutes, and ordinances in the Scriptures are words from God that are to be heeded. For future reference, in this book, when the word law is used, it is in the sense that would include any directive, principle or precept, in the Scriptures, that God tells us to do. The law of God is what God directs us to do or not to do.

Today, many Christians believe that the laws, precepts, directives and principles are to be obeyed for the most part, but we are under no obligation to obey directives from Scripture if they seem to be out of touch with our modern culture. The choice of obedience or disobedience is based upon the subjective sense of whether the command of God was for a former time or for all time. In particular, the relationship between men and women has been challenged by our culture and by many in the Church. False teachers teach that the wife needn't submit to a husband who does not love her like Christ loves the Church. However, if the wife does not submit to her husband, he is still obligated to love her as Christ loves the Church. Divorcing your spouse "for the children's sake" or because you no longer get along and do not really love your spouse anymore is no longer considered by our culture or our churches to be forbidden. The Lukewarm Church is clear that in many cases it is appropriate for a spouse to get a divorce for an unscriptural reason, particularly if your spouse is damaging your self-esteem or is verbally abusive.

THE CHURCH AND BIBLICAL STANDARDS

Are churchgoers in our churches REALLY born again? Have they repented of their sins? Do they REALLY trust Jesus? Do we teach them to be disciples? Can they embrace corrective teaching? Unfortunately, many churches have no desire to discuss these issues. Consequently, MANY IN OUR CHURCHES ARE NOT REALLY BORN AGAIN. They attend church. They laugh at the pastor's jokes. They enjoy times of fellowship and sharing. And they might even tithe. But they don't have the power of the Holy Spirit to live a holy life because they are not born again.

With the current lackadaisical attitude of leadership, churches today have little impact on their families and virtually no impact on the nation. Most are taught, because we are saved by grace through faith, it is not necessary for us to either love or obey God's law. The lukewarm Laodicean Churches are in GREAT TROUBLE.

FAKE SCRIPTURES

The lukewarm Establishment Church has incorporated into its doctrine many fake Scriptures. The Scriptures are either not in the Bible or have been twisted to mean something different. But they are presented as being ABSOLUTELY TRUE and many believe them to be scriptural. The following are a few of the more prominent ones:

1). "Divorce is not the unforgivable sin." I've heard this FAKE Scripture at Christian weddings where one or both parties have been unscripturally divorced in the past. OF COURSE, divorce, pedophilia, adultery and even murder are also forgivable sins. Singling out divorce is not the issue. Unscriptural marriage is sometimes the real issue. The implication is, that the Christian culture has been unfair in not recognizing that unscriptural divorces can be forgiven by God and should be forgiven by men. The problem is, this fake Scripture has encouraged people to become serial offenders. In my many years of walking with the Lord, I have seen pastors who were divorced two, and even three times. Often these pastors were guilty of adultery and felt completely free to enter a Christian marriage with their co-conspirator. New churches received them with open arms, did not judge them and allowed them to minister after a trial period usually lasting one year. However, Jesus says in His Word if you unscripturally divorce your wife and marry another you are committing adultery. It also says that If someone marries a woman who is unscripturally divorced, that person is committing adultery.

Matthew 5:32 (NASB) *Jesus says,* But I say to you that everyone who divorces his wife, except for the reason of unchastity (sexual sin), makes her commit adultery; and whoever marries a divorced woman commits adultery.

Matthew 19:9 (NASB) And I say to you, whoever divorces his wife, except for immorality, and marries another woman commits adultery.

2). **"When you sin, even if you commit sexual sin, when The Father looks at you, all He sees is His Son Jesus Christ."** In my naïveté, I had to look up this "Scripture" in the Bible, but it wasn't there. I had heard this so often, I thought perhaps it was Biblical. After searching the Bible, I found nothing to justify the truth of this Scripture or even of this concept. When David committed adultery, God had to remind him through the prophet Nathan that God saw him as a sinner. David had sinned terribly and when this was brought to his attention, he repented deeply and wrote Psalm 51. He cried out to God not to cast him from His presence and not take His Holy Spirit from him. He cried out to God to create in him a clean heart. He knew he had a dirty heart and he knew God could cleanse it, but through Nathan's ministry he had to see that his sin was grievous to God. Also, Nathan's ministry showed David THAT GOD SAW WHAT HE DID! This fake Scripture makes God more like the friendly, non-judgmental psychologist who views sin as merely a mistake.

3). **"Because you are washed by the blood of the Lord Jesus Christ and forgiven of all your sins both past and present and even future, you need NEVER feel any shame."** We should experience shame when we grieve the Holy Spirit of God. We should be ashamed when we offend God with our sin. Feeling shame for disobeying God helps us to understand His displeasure and helps lead us to repentance. It is only wicked people that can commit sin without feeling any shame. We call these people sociopaths.

Zephaniah 3:5 (NLT) ...THE WICKED KNOW NO SHAME.

4). **"In order to truly love other people, you must learn to love yourself first."** This New Age concept has been around for many years in the Church. It started in the liberal churches in the first half of the 20th century, but in the 1970s and 80s, when the Church began to be transformed by secular psychology, this FAKE SCRIPTURE became extremely popular. The Bible says something much different. The lukewarm churches tell us that our big problem is that we don't love ourselves and that many of God's children actually HATE themselves. But:

Ephesians 5:29 (NLT) ...29 NO MAN YET HATES HIS BODY.

There are proper ways to love yourself and there are selfish ways to love yourself. All of us understand the need to care for ourselves properly. To do so, we must feed our bodies healthy food and our minds and hearts the Scriptures. But we should not feed our minds and our bodies things that would damage them or grieve the Holy Spirit. In the realm of eating, treating yourself to a one pound box of See's candy for dessert is a bad way to love yourself.

5). **You are also encouraged to have HIGH SELF-ESTEEM**; you are encouraged in the lukewarm Establishment Churches to place great value on yourself. Scripture does not encourages us to have high esteem: rather it encourages us to esteem others BETTER THAN OURSELVES. Scriptures all through the Bible encourage also encourages us to have high CHRIST esteem.

Philippians 2:3 Let nothing be done through selfish ambition… but in lowliness of mind LET EACH ESTEEM OTHERS BETTER THAN HIMSELF.

In fact, Scripture warns us about inordinate self-love:

2 TIMOTHY 3:1-2 (NKJV) …in the last days perilous times will come: 2 For men will be… LOVERS OF THEMSELVES.

6). "Negative language produces negative experiences." LACK OF FAITH IN GOD AND HIS WORD produce negative experiences. Negative language was not merely spoken by Old Testament prophets, but also in the New Testament by Jesus Christ and others. Parents must negatively correct their disobedient children. Often, Jesus negatively corrected people: Scribes, Pharisee's, Sadducees, money changers, and those of little faith, just to mention a few. The New Testament contains MANY Scriptures of warning and correction and these must be taught as much as the positive promises of God.

PROVERBS 27:6 (NLT) Wounds from a sincere friend are better than many kisses from an enemy.

7).Do not touch my anointed ones has come to mean that a person must never speak ill of the pastor or leader in your church or denomination. This is more a FAKE INTERPRETATION than a fake Scripture. In the lukewarm Establishment Church of today, the implication of this Scripture is that we are never to criticize the spiritual oversight in the Church. That is not Scriptural. The real Scripture is:

,

I Chronicles 16:22 (NKJV) finishes with, "Do not touch My anointed ones, AND DO MY PROPHETS NO HARM."

PLEASE NOTE! This Scripture is not speaking of pastors or teachers, but of PROPHETS! Prophets at times criticized the leaders of God's people in both the Old Testament and the New Testament. In fact, often that was their main job. The real interpretation is an admonition to not harm those who have an uncomfortable message for God's people, especially for the leadership. It is not a warning to never criticize the pastor. However, if you do have a corrective word for the pastor you should speak to him in private. If he does not accept and heed that word, then you are to bring a brother with you. If he still does not accept that word, you are to bring it before the entire church.

8). "He is so heavenly minded that he is no earthly good!" The contemplation and expectation of dwelling with Jesus Christ and all of our brothers and sisters in the heavenly realm is a great motivator for holy living. Fruitful practical living often is the product of considering the glory of our heavenly existence. What better incentive is there for someone who loves Jesus Christ with their whole heart? Really this fake Scripture is employed by the "balance" people who want to balance the Word of God with modern secular philosophies and lifestyles. The implication is that to truly succeed in ministry, a person must throw off the shackles of excessive holiness. Of course, WE MUST NEVER go beyond the dictates of Scripture and make demands that add extra duties, OF SCRIPTURE in order to please God. HOWEVER, that certainly is not the problem with this generation of Christians. In order to build up congregations, ministers are more likely to relax the rules so people can enjoy earthly pleasures in excess of God's word. If the "no earthly good" person rejects that, and teaches or lives more like Jesus, Paul the Apostle and Jeremiah, he may well be censured by those in the lukewarm Establishment Church for doing so.

TO WHOM MUCH IS GIVEN: FROM HIM MUCH WILL BE REQUIRED

LUKE 12:48 (NKJV) ...For everyone TO WHOM MUCH IS GIVEN, from him MUCH WILL BE REQUIRED; and to whom much has been committed, of him they will ask the more.

Christians and congregations in America have advantages like no other Christians have EVER had. If we carry a cell phone, we have 50 or 60 translations of the Bible at our disposal. We have at our fingertips MANY concordances, Bible dictionaries, commentaries, biographies of great Christian men, and the writings of the great spiritual geniuses throughout the ages. We have Greek,

Aramaic and Hebrew Bible word studies. Because of this, God requires MUCH MORE from us!

The problem is, we ALSO have unbelievably carnal Bible teachers that desire to tickle our ears on CDs, television shows and radio shows. We have greedy shallow teachers selling their wares like snake oil salesman promising to fix your marriage if you buy their fluff filled teachings. We can use the very information on the Internet to either ruin our lives or bless our souls for eternity. We can communicate with people of like mind, and experience either a blessing or a curse. If we are born again with new hearts that love God and serve him faithfully, we can bless Him more easily than ever before.

When King Josiah was a young man, he and his people were blessed when they discovered the Book of the Law. They heard the Words of the Lord and many, including the king, cried out to God in repentance for their sins. Josiah even instituted changes that helped cleanse God's people of idolatry. Because of this, he was spared the terrible judgment of Jerusalem. Unfortunately, when he died, MOST of his people went right back into idolatry and were judged with the most horrific judgment the Jewish people had ever experienced.

NOW IS THE TIME to choose to expose false doctrine, false teaching and 21st century idolatry. We can choose to repent of our lukewarm ways, seek both the will and the Presence of the Lord in our lives, experience great blessings, perhaps even during the punishment or judgment of God's people. We can be properly responsive to the correction and chastening in our own lives. We can join the Battle AGAINST SATAN for the Church. In America, we can stand with other Christians against the most vicious assault we've ever experienced. WE HAVE BEEN GIVEN MUCH AND WE CAN USE THESE MAGNIFICENT GIFTS TO DRIVE THE ENEMY BACK TO THE GATES OF HELL!

IF WE FAIL TO CONVERT THE CULTURE

IF WE FAIL TO CONVERT THE CULTURE, THE CULTURE WILL CONTINUE TO CONVERT THE CHURCH! We will see a continuing erosion of both our culture and our churches. The Church will become more and more like the world and less and less like the New Testament Church or even the Church of the Reformation. Picking and choosing which scriptural laws we are to obey and judging our choices by the culture we live in will inevitably weaken the Church and strengthen the ability of Satan to alter our culture. Considering the depth and speed of the moral erosion and the growing weakness of the Church, in the not-too-distant future, if we fail to convert the Lukewarm Church, we will see the practice of unscriptural sexual sin and unscriptural marriage descend deeper and deeper into gross perversion.

We are the ONLY LEAVEN OF RIGHTEOUSNESS that America will ever experience, and we need to hold to a much higher standard than ever before. If we don't hold to the standards of Scripture, the nation and the culture will decline further and further into sin and lawlessness. It is not inconceivable that we will see a time when it will be appropriate for a boy of twelve and a man of fifty to be able to get married and have that marriage blessed by our culture and our government. This may be the way that it will happen.

DANIEL'S LAW

On an afternoon television program where the hostess interviews a variety of guests, a young boy of twelve years old is seated closely to a man in his early fifties. The man will have his arm around the boy and the boy will occasionally look up into the eyes of the older man with a slight smile on his face. The hostess of the show will introduce each by name and explain to the people that each has a very touching and important story to tell the TV audience. She will first question the boy, "Daniel, why are you here this afternoon?" Daniel will first say that he wants his parents to understand that he is incredibly happy and has experienced no harm whatsoever. He knows that they were worried about him because they had not seen or heard from him for over a year. Daniel wants them to know that he was very unhappy living under their roof because the conditions were oppressive. Even though he still loves them, he hates how they mistreated him. They forced him to go to an incredibly boring and weird church every Sunday. This act of cruelty also made him miss his favorite Sunday morning TV shows. He also was not allowed to watch any of the shows or movies that all his friends watched because his parents said they were not appropriate for him. They were either too violent, had what they considered to be bad language or had scenes that they felt he should not see. He was also extremely offended by the almost quarterly beatings that he received because of his supposed disobedience to their unfair rules. They were clever enough to never leave a mark on his body, but they were physically painful to him and what is worse, they were humiliating.

When George came along and invited him to go and visit him at his house, Daniel was a little afraid because his parents had warned him about going to the house of a man or a woman that he did not know. But he knew that this rule was mainly because they did not want Daniel to know what it was like to live in the real world that all his friends lived in. Their parents loved their children enough to give them the freedom to do pretty much whatever they wanted to do. Daniel felt that love from George and what's more, George gave him what he wanted and never spanked him or verbally abused him like his parents did. What's most important, George never forced Daniel to go to church with him; in fact, George felt the same way about church that Daniel did: he never enjoyed it. George let Daniel stay home on Sunday mornings and watch cartoons on television. George gave Daniel hot chocolate and fed him only foods that he liked. He was never forced to eat his vegetables and they always had dessert. He is especially pleased and thankful because this man introduced him to a life of freedom and joy that he never dreamt possible.

The man who picked him up will speak tearfully about how he could see how terribly this child was suffering and how he only wanted to bring him some peace and release from the cruel couple that was raising him and forcing their religion upon him. The boy will say that at first it was difficult, but as he experienced the love and concern of this older man, he grew to love him, and their emotional relationship developed into a physical relationship that brought them both great satisfaction and joy. I can see this couple being on the show and the hostess tearfully proclaiming, "How could anyone with a heart, deny this touching relationship to be ended! How could any court convict this man of any crime when all he wanted to do was to rescue and love this boy?" After this tear-filled plea, Daniel and his new friend announced the date of their upcoming marriage.

Never mind the distraught parents and the confused siblings that he left. The most important thing is that this man and boy were meant to love each other and express their love one to another in a physical sense. After all, all you need is love.

Of course, a movie of their unholy relationship will be made in Hollywood with major stars performing the parts of the man and the boy. The movie likely will win the Academy award for best picture of the year. The parents will be depicted as cold, hardhearted, cruel Christians. Not too many years after this film is made, the President and the Congress will pass laws that will allow this behavior and severely punish any unloving parents that interfered with such a relationship. This law will be called DANIEL'S LAW. LBGTQ will add a new letter, "P for pedophile".

IS AMERICA AND OUR CULTURE REALLY THAT CORRUPT?

WITHOUT A DOUBT!!!

CHAPTER 5: EVIDENCE THAT DEMANDS A VERDICT

Six Major Indictments Against the Church
    No Fear of the LORD
    Self Esteem and Self Love
    The Love of Money
    Adultery and Pornography
    Unscriptural Family Life
    Shepherds Lead the Sheep Astray
The Salt of the Earth
When the Church Was Salty
When the Church Ceases to be the Salt
Nothing Like this Has Ever Been Seen
Conclusion

SIX MAJOR INDICTMENTS AGAINST THE CHURCH

1) NO FEAR OF THE LORD!

The following is the definition of FEAR in Scripture in Noah Webster's 1828 dictionary.

"IN SCRIPTURE, FEAR is used to express a filial (AS A CHILD TO A FATHER) or a slavish passion. In good men, the FEAR OF GOD is a HOLY AWE OR REVERENCE OF GOD AND HIS LAWS, which springs from a just view and REAL LOVE OF THE DIVINE CHARACTER, leading the subjects of it to HATE and SHUN EVERYTHING THAT CAN OFFEND SUCH A HOLY BEING, inclining them to AIM AT PERFECT OBEDIENCE. This is FILIAL FEAR.

SLAVISH FEAR is the effect or CONSEQUENCE OF GUILT; it is the PAINFUL APPREHENSION of merited (DESERVED) punishment. "

Why is the divorce rate in evangelical and charismatic churches virtually equal to that of the secular realm? Why in many churches, is pornography so prevalent? One reason is because we have edited and interpreted the Scripture so that we no longer are taught the TRUE fear of the Lord. We have cheapened the term so that it merely means respect or reverence at best. In some cases,

PHOBOS does mean reverence. But in many others, like Matthew 10:28, which was mentioned in the last chapter, Phobos CERTAINLY means fear.

Matthew 10:28 (NKJV) And do not FEAR those who kill the body but cannot kill the soul. But rather FEAR HIM WHO IS ABLE TO DESTROY BOTH SOUL AND BODY IN HELL.

Proverbs 8:13 (NKJV) The FEAR OF THE LORD IS TO HATE EVIL

Most Christians are not really afraid that God will punish them for unscripturally divorcing a spouse or viewing pornography. We seldom hear what Scripture says about the consequences of an unholy or disobedient life. Consequences and punishments on this earth and the horrible reality of a soul being destroyed in Hell are seldom taught. We have preached a Gospel of CHEAP GRACE and CHEAP HOLINESS that is NOT scriptural.

With little or no concern for the outcome and certainly no fear of the Lord, we allow our children to play games on the Internet and watch movies that feature inappropriately dressed heroes and heroines. Dragons, witches, warlocks and other satanic manifestations are even depicted as heroic figures. We let them suck up Eastern doctrine and hidden demonic agendas in apparently innocuous cartoons, kids' movies, and TV shows. And then we wonder why when they leave home for college or a job, they fall away from the Lord and give up on Jesus Christ and live for the most part a completely secular life and are dabbling in fornication or various forms of the occult.

I John 4:18 (GNV) 18 There is no fear in love; but perfect love casteth out fear for fear hath painfulness: He that feareth is not made perfect in love.

Many in the Establishment Church when quoting the Scripture, "Perfect love casts out all fear." imply that the fear of the Lord will be cast out because we have the perfect love of Jesus Christ in our lives. This is a complete misrepresentation of the Word of God. Psalm 23 says, "I will FEAR NO EVIL for thou art with me." The fear that is cast out is the FEAR OF EVIL ATTACKS. THE FEAR OF THE LORD Is NOT cast out.

Proverbs 16:6 (KJV) by the fear of the LORD men depart from evil.

Many ministers preach a God that loves everybody all the time regardless of what they do. He loves you too much to give you the spanking that you deserve AND WOULD NEVER banish you from His presence because of your unbelief or disobedience. We have redefined and weakened the fear of the Lord to the point where it has all but disappeared.

IN ALL OF CHURCH HISTORY, WE HAVE NEVER SEEN SUCH AN UNSCRIPTURAL MISREPRESENTATION OF THE FEAR OF THE LORD AS WE NOW SEE!

2) SELF ESTEEM AND SELF LOVE

According to 2 Chronicles 7:14, the first thing the Church must do to experience the healing of their land and receive the forgiveness of their sin, is to HUMBLE THEMSELVES.

2 Chronicles 7:14. (KJ21) If my people, who are called by my name, shall HUMBLE THEMSELVES and pray, and seek my face and TURN FROM THEIR WICKED WAYS; THEN I will I hear from heaven, and will forgive their sin and will heal their land.

Thanks to the influence of secular psychology and "Christian" counseling, the Church has become excessively concerned about self-esteem. Look up the word SELF in the New Testament, you'll see that the Scriptures are most concerned about self-control, self-denial, and the abuse of self-love. the Church today is most concerned about a good self-image, high self-esteem and the cultivation of self-love. We ignore the warning in Scripture that says in the last days, "people will be LOVERS OF THEMSELVES" as a BAD thing (2 Timothy 3:2 NIV).

In the 1970s, Dr. James Dobson, a Christian who got his doctorate in psychology in 1967 (PhD in Child Development at the University of Southern California), urged people in the Church to cultivate a strong sense of high self-esteem for themselves and their children. The self-esteem movement, once owned entirely by the secular world, now became an integral part of most Establishment Churches. So-called Christian counseling ministries began to replace Biblical counseling in the Bible schools and seminaries.

Dr. James Dobson said "Feelings of self-worth and acceptance, which provide THE CORNERSTONE OF A HEALTHY PERSONALITY, can be obtained from ONLY ONE SOURCE. Self-esteem is only generated by WHAT WE SEE REFLECTED ABOUT OURSELVES IN THE EYES OF OTHER PEOPLE. It is only when others respect us that we respect ourselves. IT IS ONLY WHEN OTHERS LOVE US THAT WE LOVE OURSELVES. It is only when others find us pleasant and desirable and worthy that we come to terms with our own egos." [15]

No mention of how important it is to know that GOD LOVES US or that what God thinks of us is INFINITELY more important than what others think of us. On that basis, Jerimiah must have had pretty low self-esteem.

Philippians 2:3 (NKJV) Let nothing be done through selfish ambition or conceit, but in LOWLINESS OF MIND let each ESTEEM OTHERS BETTER than himself!

Luke 14:26 (NLT) If you want to be My disciple, you must, by comparison, hate everyone else - your father and mother, wife and children, brothers and sisters and - yes, EVEN YOUR OWN LIFE. Otherwise, you cannot be My disciple.

NEVER BEFORE IN THE HISTORY OF THE CHURCH, EVEN IN THE DARKEST DAYS OF THE ROMAN CATHOLIC CHURCH, HAVE WE SEEN SUCH RAMPANT CONCERN FOR SELF-LOVE AND HIGH SELF-ESTEEM!

3) THE LOVE OF MONEY

1 Timothy 6:10 (NLT) For the love of money is the ROOT OF ALL KINDS OF EVIL. And some people, craving money, have wandered from THE TRUE FAITH and pierced themselves with many sorrows.

Luke 19:45-46 (NLT) Jesus entered the Temple and began to drive out the people selling animals for sacrifices. 46 He said to them, "The Scriptures declare, 'My Temple will be a house of prayer,' but you have turned it into a DEN OF THIEVES."

John 2:14-16 (NLT) In the Temple area he saw MERCHANTS SELLING cattle, sheep, and doves for sacrifices; He also saw dealers at tables exchanging foreign money. 15 JESUS MADE A WHIP FROM SOME ROPES AND CHASED THEM ALL OUT OF THE TEMPLE. He drove out the sheep and cattle, scattered the money changers' coins over the floor, and turned over their tables. 16 Then, going over to the people who sold doves, he told them, "Get these things out of here. STOP TURNING MY FATHER'S HOUSE INTO A MARKETPLACE!"

In our generation, TV evangelists and pastors of mega-churches are among the most guilty. The possibility of yearly salaries and stipends exceeding one million dollars a year have tempted many to seek to become rich.

In all of the New Testament, we never see Jesus as angry as He was when he chased the moneylenders and the sacrifice sellers out of his Temple. He hated the idea of supposedly religious people using Biblical practices for their own profit. There are a number of practices that are in the Church today that expose a manipulative attitude that benefits money hungry ministers. The selling of Biblical literature and recorded sermons under the guise of the purchaser, "making a donation" of fifty dollars or more is transparently wrong before God. The generous salaries that pastors and evangelists either demand or negotiate is even worse. Even Christian ministers who are involved with charities can reap a healthy salary from the donations they inspire. In one case a prominent minister working for a charity and a Christian foundation, in one year, reaped a monetary reward of more than $600,000. Of course, if he plowed back much of that money into other Christian needs, I'm sure that would be pleasing to God.

Many Evangelists and pastors, both male and female, have homes and holdings worth tens of millions of dollars, several have well over ONE HUNDRED MILION DOLLARS of personal worth. This money came from donations and salaries they have received for ministering the gospel to the poor, needy, middle-class and rich.

Judas stole money that was given to the disciples for his own pleasure, but the fortune he amassed was minuscule compared to the money these people have received for the work they have done in the Kingdom today. Gone are the days, when most ministers sacrificed to minister to God's people. Today, SHEEP sacrifice to feed the SHEPHERDS or well-known speakers so they can live a luxurious lifestyle. When George Mueller received large donations for the charitable works that he supported, he would use virtually all of it to further the work of the Lord in missions and orphanages. Today, many ministers are asking the people to sacrifice so that God's work can be done. In most cases, they don't advertise what they are making from these donations. PLEASE UNDERSTAND! Even today, there are Godly shepherds that live sacrificially so they can minister the Gospel of Jesus Christ to their flocks.

Years ago, at a pastor's conference in California, Oral Roberts told 1400 pastors that it took a quarter of a million dollars a day to finance his ministry, the City of Faith Hospital. After this confession, he gave a rousing sermon on the value of money: a ludicrous misrepresentation of Scripture from Philippians 4. He even went as far as to lead the gathered clergyman in a chant of, "Sweet Smelling Money." Then with a "Louder! For the Lord!" They repeated it. Then with a "One more time!" the cries were deafening: "SWEET SMELLING MONEY!" The leader of the conference assured us that Oral's teaching on money from Philippians 4 was the most balanced teaching on money or prosperity that he had ever heard, and we were all encouraged to clap for Oral. This was followed by Oral's insistence that the pastors "Claim from God what they deserved." He said that many of us made only $18,000 a year ($1,500 a month) and we should rightly claim $80,000 a year ($6,667 a month). After this confession of faith, we would receive this great blessing and we could then live and minister in a manner befitting our efforts. As one body, the ministers stood to their feet crying out to God to get what they deserved. And, to God's great despair, many probably got just that.

JOHN WESLEY'S GODLY EXAMPLE "...In 1731 Wesley began to limit his expenses so that he would have more money to give to the poor. He records that his annual income was 30 pounds and his living expenses 28 pounds, so he had 2 pounds to give away. The next year his income doubled, but he still managed to live on 28 pounds, so he gave 32 pounds to the poor. In the third year, his income jumped to 90 pounds. Instead of letting his expenses rise with his income, he kept them to 28 pounds and gave away 62 pounds. In the fourth year, he received 120 pounds. As before, his expenses were 28 pounds, so his giving rose to 92 pounds.

Wesley felt that the Christian should not merely tithe but give away all extra income once the family and creditors were taken care of. He believed that with increasing income, what should rise is not the Christian's standard of living but the standard of giving." [16]

Both small churches and large denominations have played terrible games with money hoping to increase the coffers of their ministries but in some cases have given millions of dollars to scam artists because God did not protect them from liars because they were not concerned about truth. Many have made the Church a business. They have come to understand that in some cases it is "good business" to not teach on certain subjects or even certain Scriptures. They have come to understand the importance of the little white lie or worse yet, they ignore the truth that might offend some of their flock "for the sake of the people who may be injured and feel judged by talk regarding fornication or divorce". Many seem to believe that it is okay for us to merely IGNORE the subject, or to unscripturally justify it.

Often men are chosen for positions of leadership not because of their spirituality or their knowledge of the Bible, but because of their hefty tithes, business success or the assurance that they would always support the leadership and the views of the Church or denomination.

We have come to understand the concept that says at times we need to take small immoral advantages that will benefit our financial situation. We cheat on our income taxes. We preach enticing sermons to get people to give more money, so we could have a higher salary. We get upset with the Democrats because they give favors to certain Wall Street bankers and minority groups to gain their money, favor, and votes, but we edit the Scriptures to gain members that will stay in our churches and support our ministries. Pastors and evangelists make millions of dollars off of spiritually bankrupt churches.

NEVER IN THE HISTORY OF THE CHURCH, EVEN IN THE DARKEST DAYS OF THE ROMAN CATHOLIC CHURCH, HAVE WE SEEN SUCH RAMPET EXPLOITATION OF GOD'S PEOPLE.

4) ADULTERY AND PORNOGRAPH

Because the Church neither believes in nor teaches the FEAR of the Lord, both the sheep and shepherds are no longer concerned about committing adultery, fornication and in some cases engage in homosexual activities. Since the 1980s, we have seen many, many shepherds and sheep fall into adultery or homosexuality. Jimmy Baker and Jimmy Swaggart were just the tip of the iceberg. Many ministers were caught in sexual sin. In our denomination, our divisional superintendent was forced to resign because of his adulterous affair with a woman in his congregation and our district supervisor voluntarily resigned when it was discovered that he had had an adulterous affair with a female evangelist.

This behavior is no longer considered to be as serious as it once was. Repentant fornicators and even adulterers certainly should be forgiven, but immediate remarriage to your partner in crime and subsequent acceptance by a new church is unscriptural. Fornication is taken lightly, and adultery is often easily excused, especially if the adulterers have ministerial skills.

IN AMERICA WE HAVE NEVER SEEN SUCH AN EPIDEMIC OF MARITAL UNFAITHFULNESS AND ACCEPTABLE SEXUAL SIN IN THE CHURCH.

5) UNSCRIPTURAL FAMILY LIFE

Many men and women in the 21st century Church in America either rationalize or ignore the Bible's directives regarding both marriage and divorce. Many men are reluctant to assume or claim their God commanded role to be the head of the wife even as Christ is head of the Church and many have no desire to even attempt to love their wives as Christ loves the Church. Women in the Church, under the pressures of our culture have little desire to submit to their husbands as unto the Lord. Children are not expected to honor their parents. Because many single mothers are raising sons without fathers, there is an epidemic of disrespect for men in the family.

NEVER IN THE HISTORY OF THE CHURCH IN AMERICA HAVE WE SEEN SUCH A TERRIBLE PLAGUE OF DIVORCE AND DISRESPECT.

6) SHEPHERDS LEAD THE SHEEP ASTRAY

Jeremiah 50: 6-7 (NLT) 6 My people have been lost sheep. THEIR SHEPHERDS HAVE LED THEM ASTRAY and turned them loose in the mountains. They have lost their way and can't remember how to get back to the sheepfold. 7 All who found them devoured them. Their enemies said, "We did nothing wrong in attacking them, FOR THEY SINNED AGAINST THE LORD, their TRUE PLACE OF REST, and the hope of their ancestors."

When the pastor unscripturally divorces his spouse and marries another, his congregation may accept that this practice agrees with God's view of divorce. What is worse, the evangelical churches have excused adulterating pastors, youth leaders and worship leaders who have committed egregious sexual sins. One of the worst things we have done, is to advise the parents not to press legal charges against ministers who have molested their children. In many cases we have done exactly what the Roman Catholic Church has done. We just allow offending ministers to go to other churches. Our reason for doing so, is that God forgave David of murder and adultery; therefore, we should do no less. We have received into our churches unrepentant men and women who have committed gross sexual sin and given them positions of authority because of their grandiose oratory, business acumen, ministerial skills. or their bulging bank accounts.

God says that His people have been lost sheep! And the reason He gives is because, "Their shepherds have led them astray." As it was true in the day of Jeremiah, so it is true in the day of the 21st century church in America. We have leaders that are afraid to either live or teach the narrow path that leads to life but are content to preach the broad way that leads to destruction.

NOTHING LIKE THIS HAS EVER BEEN SEEN IN THE AMERICAN CHURCH!

THE SALT OF THE EARTH

Matthew 5:13 (NKJV) YOU ARE THE SALT of the earth.

From the context it is clear that the Bible says that a church that is the salt of the earth is a good church. Jesus characterizes the Church as the salt that flavors the earth. Peanuts, vegetables, even meat tastes much better when salt is added. When the Church is salty, wherever the Church is, the earth is a better place. The salty church brings flavor to MANY people that will savor LIFE in Christ is a wonderful, tasty experience.

WHEN THE CHURCH WAS SALTY

In the sixteenth century, England and other Northern European countries participated in the Reformation of the Church that started in Germany. England changed dramatically and in the 18th century experienced a mighty outpouring of God's Holy Spirit in the First Great Awakening. Some of the fruit of the Reformation in England was the emigration to America by the Pilgrims in 1620. For the next 120 years, the Gospel of Jesus Christ spread throughout the New England colonies and starting in 1740, America experienced TWO Great Awakenings. In both England and America, the salty leaven of the Church caused both countries to thrive. in the 18th century, England became the most powerful nation in the world. At one time it was correctly stated that the sun never set on the British empire. More importantly, they sent MANY missionaries throughout the world. They leavened their nation and the world with the righteousness of Christ.

In the twentieth century, as the gospel started to wane in Great Britain, America became the most powerful nation in history. In World War II, America saved the world from the Nazis and the Japanese imperialists and sent more missionaries and Bibles to other countries than any other country in history.

WHEN THE CHURCH CEASES TO BE THE SALT OF THE EARTH

Matthew 5:13 (NKJV) YOU are the SALT OF THE EARTH; BUT IF THE SALT LOSES ITS FLAVOR, how shall it be seasoned? IT IS THEN GOOD FOR NOTHING but to be THROWN OUT AND TRAMPLED UNDERFOOT BY MEN.

This is a dire warning to the people of God. When the salt has lost its flavor, it is good for nothing and must be thrown out and TRAMPLED UNDERFOOT BY MEN. Without the salt of the earth, life can become dull and lifeless and will then be awakened by the spicy dishes served up by Satan. Only the Church when it presents the TRUE GOSPEL of the Scriptures can life become filled with real joy and be a flavorful experience. When the Church becomes another psychological solution that sparks a little hope at first and then becomes a dying and eventually dead ember that neither sheds light nor gives comfort, IT IS GOOD FOR NOTHING. When the church becomes only exciting to the flesh and fills the void of existence with nothing better than a decent rock concert or symphony does, it has LOST ITS FLAVOR.

This New Testament Scripture is ominous. This is one of the promises of God that you will not find in a promise box. The word "You" in the phrase, "you are the salt of the earth", refers specifically to the Church of Jesus Christ in any century or in any country. This Scripture directly says that IF the salt (the Church) has lost its flavor, the salt will be cast out and TRAMPLED UNDERFOOT BY MEN. The Scriptures specifically says that if the Church has lost its flavor, it will be judged through men. The men that judge the Church could be a political system, a foreign conqueror or a culture that despises Jesus Christ enough to inflict pain and death upon the hapless body of churchgoers. The world is by its nature unsavory. The world without the compelling influence of the Church of Jesus Christ is meaningless, depressing, dangerous place, and needs jolts of excitement to survive.

In the last 60 years, Christians in America have been stomped on by the courts. Women in our country now have the right to kill their unborn children. The radical homosexual community has walked all over the Church and trampled on the rights of Christians in both the bakery and the bathroom. We now punish success that comes from hard work and we reward indolence. It seems as if we possess little power to influence the nation for good, and all that we hold dear has been trampled underfoot by men because the sweet scent of Christ and the powerful influence of the Holy Spirit is missing from our lives. Our words and our deeds have become useless. We have lost our flavor and lost our influence in the world. If we do not soon take on and manifest the flavor of our Lord Jesus Christ, we will be judged MUCH MORE PAINFULLY by our culture, our political system and possibly even foreign conquerors.

We may well receive a final terrible judgment like the Jews in the Old Testament experienced when they were judged by God as he used Nebuchadnezzar and the Babylonian army to destroy the city and kill and enslave many of its people. Because they had lost the flavor of the presence of God they were cast out and were trodden underfoot by men. According to Scripture this is the fate of the saltless Church.

NOTHING LIKE THIS HAS EVER BEEN SEEN

We have NEVER seen any conduct that is as ungodly as that of the evangelical and charismatic churches in this century. These churches are supposed to represent the best that God has to offer, yet we have never seen in the history of the Church in America so many divorces, so much sexual sin and so many of our children walk away from God and His Word. Sacrifice in order to obey God's Word has been replaced by making sure you love yourself and have high self-esteem. We have preached sermons and written bestselling books that denigrate husbands and wives that obey the Scriptures in the marriage relationship. Adultery in the pulpit is epidemic and a terrible disgrace to our churches. Even pedophilia has reared its ugly head in evangelical and charismatic churches. We dare to support some of the greediest, foulest and most disgraceful shepherds in the history of the Church. Pornography is an accepted "illness or addiction" of many men and even women. It is so rampant that we are afraid to call it sin, fearing that people might think that we were being judgmental. EVEN pastors and elders admit to this "illness". What is worse is that these supposedly anointed leaders reject the power of the Holy Spirit and the new birth to make Christians holy! Instead they seek out psychological solutions!

We must understand that when the Church in any given country no longer is able to influence the culture, it is because THEY ARE NO LONGER THE SALT OF THE EARTH! The Roman Catholic Churches of France, Italy and, and Spain and the Eastern Orthodox Churches of Russia and Eastern Europe are good examples. Because of their centuries long resistance to the Reformation, the Nazis and Communists rendered them virtually obsolete. The saltless church will ALWAYS be trodden under foot by men and cast aside by God. First, He must tear down the SALTLESS church that no longer has flavor, and then He can create a NEW church that IS the SALT OF THE EARTH.

We must understand the tenor of our times. If OUR 21st century church had the same high Scriptural standards of The Greatly Awakened Churches; if God's people today feared to grieve the Holy Spirit in the same way that the Church of the 18th and 19th centuries did; if the current Establishment Churches obeyed the Scriptures as those churches did; if OUR churches were not weakened and in some cases broken by unscriptural divorce and pornography; THEN, we could be salt to the culture and our country and be CONFIDENT that God would protect us. BUT WE ARE NOT EVEN CLOSE! Only if the 21st century church REPENTS DEEPLY and fights hard will America and the Church be spared being trodden under foot by men. The Church MUST take at least ONE LAST STAND for Jesus Christ and America.

CONCLUSION

When God's people are drawn away from God Himself to the world, the flesh or the devil, this withdrawal INHIBITS GOD'S GRACE FOR VICTORY over the powers of Satan and consequently that grace can only be manifested in His corrective punishment. Important examples from Scripture are: 1) The northern kingdom of Israel was judged terribly by God because it fell into idolatry and incorporated idolatrous worship into the worship of Jehovah. 2) Judah was even judged more severely because Judah had more light and was given a longer time to repent. 3) In the Book of Revelation, five of the seven churches were warned of judgment because they fell away from the purposes of God for His people. In history, we see the Jewish people judged extremely harshly after they rejected Jesus Christ as their Messiah. This judgment has lasted 2000 years. Devastation, Destruction and Death have characterized these judgments as He has done whatever it takes to bring His own people back to Himself. Backslidden Europe was judged by TWO World Wars, great loss of life and a loss of FREEDOM for many.

Such judgment may come upon America and the Church. NO CHURCH OR NATION HAS EVER BEEN GIVEN SO MUCH AND DONE SO LITTLE as have God's people in America in the early 21st century.

Even today God is preparing a people of the narrow gate and the narrow way that will embrace all the LAW, LOVE, GRACE, and HOLINESS of the Word OF GOD. HOLY will no longer be a neglected word by God's people but will be a way of life for God's people. The HOLY Spirit will once again be manifested in narrowness and purity that does not conflict with but instead reinforces and defines God's love. No longer will God's Church be defined as "We are a Church who just loves God and loves mankind." Instead, the Church will once again be thought of as a HOLY nation, SET APART for God's purposes! This love will be manifested not merely in terms of tolerance and good deeds to people, but in terms of corrective teaching that calls God's people back to holy living.

Those families who compassionately and accurately evaluate their children, their friends, their teachers, their doctrine, their churches and ESPECIALLY THEIR OWN LIVES may avoid the terrible consequences of God's judgment. They will be equipped to conquer the enemy and in the midst of battle enjoy The Presence of God and His pleasure!

CHAPTER 6: GODLY PUNISHMENTS

Introduction
Persecution for Righteousness Sake
Tribulation
The Chastening Hand of God
The Fruit of Chastening
Don't Condemn Everyone Who Suffers
Ongoing Punishment of God's People
Purpose of Scriptural Chastening
Judgment in Scripture
What Can We Do?

INTRODUCTION

We must understand the difference between PERSECUTION, TRIBULATION, CHASTENING (PUNISHMENT), AND JUDGMENT. So many in the Church believe that what is happening in America in the Churches of Jesus Christ is persecution because we have been outspoken about the sins of abortion and homosexuality. Some Christians definitely suffer because they speak and do righteous things for God. Randy Alcorn is a good example. He demonstrated at abortion clinics, was arrested, charged, and convicted of crimes, and suffered for righteousness sake. Still others suffer because God is chastening them because they have disobeyed Him. Others suffer because they are experiencing tribulation: either trials from God or temptations from Satan. We must be careful not to mistake punishment for being persecuted for righteousness sake.

PERSECUTION FOR RIGHTEOUSNESS SAKE

…..PERSECUTION for righteousness sake is a direct result of the world and the Satanic realm tormenting the people of God who have repented of their sin; obeyed Him and are walking in a way that pleases Him. Righteous living inevitably produces persecution AND GREAT BLESSING.

Matthew 5:10-11 (NASB) BLESSED ARE THOSE who have been PERSECUTED FOR THE SAKE OF RIGHTEOUSNESS, for theirs is the kingdom of heaven. 11 Blessed are you when people insult you and persecute you, and falsely say all kinds of evil against you BECAUSE OF ME. Rejoice and be glad for your reward in heaven is great; for in the same way they persecuted the prophets who were before you.

Being persecuted for the sake of righteousness occurs when you defend or proclaim Jesus Christ, His Father, the Holy Spirit, or the Holy Scriptures. This persecution can come either from the world or from the Church itself. Another form of persecution is when people in the world or in the Church spread LIES about you or accuse you FALSELY. Typically, this is to discredit your ministry, your doctrine, or your character so you or your word won't be trusted.

In the world, persecution can have both extreme, moderate, and mild forms. Extreme forms, such as murder or imprisonment usually occur when a God hating government is in control of a nation. Moderate forms of persecution include either being fired from a job or being prevented from holding a job because of your religious beliefs. In Communist countries one had to be silent concerning their religious beliefs if they expected to hold down ANY job. A more subtle form of persecution is one in which a Christian is able to work either for the government or a private industry but is forbidden to discuss or even mention their beliefs with anyone else in the organization. If an individual is led by God to speak to a colleague about Jesus Christ or His Word and is fired, then he is being persecuted for righteousness sake.

In the Old Testament, true prophets were persecuted in both Israel and Judah. In the New Testament times and later, since the beheading of John the Baptist many Christians have been persecuted. Previous to the Refomation, many non-Catholic Christians were killed by the Roman Catholic Church during the Spanish Inquisition. During the Protestant Reformation in Europe, the Catholic Church both under King Henry VIII and Bloody Mary, the Catholic queen of England, murdered Christians who either published or possessed Bibles in the English language. These men and women of God were being persecuted for righteousness sake.

Moderate forms of persecution include both imprisonment and excommunication by the ruling church body. One example of this is the imprisonment of John Bunyan who wrote Pilgrim's Progress. He was imprisoned by the Church of England for not conforming to their unscriptural doctrine.

In the twenty-first century, Christian churches use much more subtle forms of persecution. INFORMAL EXCOMMUNICATION is most common. This occurs when an individual speaks things that offend the delicate sensibilities of either the leadership or the people in the congregation. There is no formal letter of excommunication given to the offender, but the offender is essentially ignored or shunned by the leadership and the congregation. This typically occurs in churches that stress the positive and are extremely offended by anything negative.

Many public Christians, such as politicians, while not being worried about saying "God" in a public speech, would NEVER expose themselves to certain ridicule and MILD persecution by using the name of Jesus Christ in public. The Name above all names by which men may be saved, Jesus Christ is considered EXTREMELY offensive and can bring mild persecution.

ON THE OTHER HAND, there are Christians that say offensive things that won't necessarily help the church but will make them feel like they are functioning, "prophetically". Their badge of honor is to be run out of the church that they attend. BUT be careful, SOMETIMES EVEN A JACKASS CAN SPEAK FOR THE LORD. (NUMBERS 22:28)

TRIBULATION

For God's people tribulation is a series of trials and an outpouring of great difficulties that cause much pain. God is testing those in the Church and exposing their heart and their faith. If they pass the test, sometimes God will send them more tests. If they fail the test, they typically will experience ONLY the punishment aspect of tribulation, which is either great punishment or the FINAL HORROR of an existence without God in Hell.

When the people of the world experience tribulation, it is a time of testing, in which they usually fail and suffer great pain. Sometimes people in the world will be driven by tribulation, punishment, and judgment to repent. BUT, typically, there does come a time when the tribulation for people in the world is NOTHING LESS THAN AN OUTPOURING OF THE WRATH OF GOD. This outpouring of wrath is not a test; it is THEIR FINAL JUDGMENT ON THIS EARTH.

THE CHASTENING HAND OF GOD

This section is extremely important. Some in the Church today do not believe that God REALLY punishes His children. And if He does punish them, He virtually NEVER causes them pain. He may give them the spiritual equivalency of a timeout, but NEVER would beat them with a rod! He may severely reprimand them at times and if they don't respond obediently, He may withhold some pleasure from them, but God would never intentionally cause pain to any of His children. Others believe, the chastening MAY occur in other people, but they themselves typically suffer at the hands of the enemy because they have offended Satan, by fighting against abortion and gay rights. CHASTENING is when God punishes His children because of their sin. The Bible says, "Sin is breaking the law of God." (1 John 3:4 NLT). The law of God includes whatever God tells us to do or not do in His Holy Scriptures. These include His commandments, His Word, His ways, His statutes, His precepts, His judgments, and His testimonies. Please read the following Scriptures.

Hebrews 12:5-6 (NKJV) ...My son, do not despise the CHASTENING OF THE LORD, Nor be discouraged when you are rebuked by Him; 6 For whom the Lord loves He chastens, and scourges *(whips)* **every son whom He receives."**
Revelation 3:19 (KJ21) As many as I love, I REBUKE and CHASTEN. THEREFORE, BE ZEALOUS AND REPENT
Deuteronomy 8:5 (NKJV) You should know in your heart that AS A MAN CHASTENS HIS SON, SO THE LORD YOUR GOD CHASTENS YOU.
Job 33:19 (NKJV) Man is also chastened WITH PAIN ON HIS BED, AND WITH STRONG PAIN IN MANY OF HIS BONES,

These Scriptures clearly indicate that GOD INFLICTS PAIN UPON HIS PEOPLE when He disciplines them. This is NOT the PERMISSIVE will of God. This is God Himself His children. Sometimes God's people suffer from plagues or sickness; some even die of plagues. If a Christian continues in sin, he may experience great pain from disease or bodily harm that comes from the hand of God.

When you read the Old Testament, you see that God judged Judah and Jerusalem and inflicted them with every imaginable horror because they had resisted, rebelled and would not respond to lesser punishments with either repentance or sorrow for their sin. These lesser punishments were to prevent them from experiencing the horrific judgment of God for those that would not repent. PLEASE TAKE NOTE! God is NOT giving Satan permission to torment Judah and Jerusalem. GOD HIMSELF is punishing His wayward children! God takes FULL RESPONSIBILITY for causing His people pain.

The Lord CHASTENS WHOM HE LOVES! There are godly consequences to sin mentioned in both the New Testament and the Old Testament. Five out of the seven churches in chapters 2 and 3 of the Book of Revelation experienced the chastening hand of God. This was done so they would repent, trust and obey Him. Can we as Christians in the 21st century expect any less? God is not the friendly neighborhood psychologist who will teach you to love yourself and consequently have a great pain-free life. God manifests VERY TOUGH LOVE!

People can get sick because they disobey God. That does not mean that every sick person has been disobedient to God, but sometimes the physical and even mental pain that we experience is because God is trying to get our attention and turn our hearts back to Him.

In the second chapter of the Book of Revelation, the people of one church are cast upon a bed of sickness because of their sin. God did not send them that sickness to kill them and deliver them to Hell; God sent the sickness to have them cry out to Him in repentance and receive His forgiveness and glorify Him. Even if they died as forgiven sinners, they were able to be with Him in glory. Chastening or punishment is part of the package that EVERY CHRISTIAN is given as he walks through this life on his way to his final reward.

THE FRUIT OF CHASTENING

Hebrews 12:9-10 (NKJV) Furthermore, we have had human fathers who corrected us, and we pay them respect. Shall we not much more readily be in subjection to the Father of spirits and live? 10For they indeed for a few days chastened us as seemed best to them, but HE, FOR OUR PROFIT, that we may be PARTAKERS OF HIS HOLINESS.

Hebrews 12:11 (NKJV) Now NO CHASTENING SEEMS TO BE JOYFUL for the present, but PAINFUL; nevertheless, afterward, it yields the peaceable FRUIT OF RIGHTEOUSNESS to those who have been trained by it.

The grace of God does not merely deliver His people from the ultimate penalty of sin, which is damnation in hell. This GRACE also allows His people to experience shame and guilt when they sin. If we are not concerned when we grieve the Holy Spirit of God, we will be dealt with. But when we quickly and deeply repent of how we have offended Him; God's grace also delivers us from the BONDAGE OF SIN. This grace opens our eyes to the sin in our own lives through the Scriptures and the stirring of the Holy Spirit. The Word of God is quite clear regarding what is sin and what is not sin. Sin essentially is disobeying the law of God.

1 John 3:4 (NASB) ... Sin is THE TRANSGRESSION OF THE LAW.

The chastening hand of God PRODUCES THE PRECIOUS FRUIT OF HOLINESS in the life of those who can receive it and understand its power. Do you pray that God will make you more holy? He will. But he often uses His chastening rod to produce holiness and righteousness in your life.

Isaiah 26:16 (NKJV) LORD, in trouble they have visited You, THEY POURED OUT A PRAYER WHEN YOUR CHASTENING WAS UPON THEM.

Often when men are chastened, they are driven to prayer and seek God's help. This sincere humility is pleasing to God and often He will answer the sincerity of their prayer with the healing that will not only heal their bodies but strengthen their faith.

1 Corinthians 11:32 (KJ21) But when we are judged, we are chastened by the LORD, THAT WE MAY NOT BE CONDEMNED WITH THE WORLD.
Hebrews 12:8 (KJ21) But IF YOU ARE WITHOUT CHASTENING, of which ALL have become partakers, then YOU ARE ILLEGITIMATE AND NOT SONS.
2 Chronicles 7:13-14 (NIV) WHEN I SHUT UP THE HEAVENS so that there is no rain, or COMMAND LOCUSTS TO DEVOUR THE LAND or send a plague among my people, 14 if My people, who are called by My name, will humble themselves and pray and seek My face and TURN FROM THEIR WICKED WAYS, THEN I will hear from heaven, and I will forgive their sin and will heal their land.

The PURPOSE OF THIS CHASTENING is so that God's people would humble themselves and pray and seek His presence and TURN FROM THEIR WICKED WAYS." Please note verse 13. It says, "When I *God* shut up the heavens so that there is no rain, or command locusts to devour the land or send a plague among my people". This is not the devil that is attacking God's people. This is Jehovah God, the Holy Spirit, Jesus Christ CHASTENING His people. Our country and our churches have suffered plagues, economic disasters, and storms and floods that have almost destroyed our cities. If His people do what God tells them to do in verse 14, THEN AND ONLY THEN, will God forgive their sin and heal their land. The heavens will no longer be shut up, the rain of God's love and power will shower down upon them; the forces of evil that devour their land and the plague of perversion and lawlessness will be destroyed. Children will grow up to be strong oaks, unconquered by plague or adverse weather. Others will be vines bearing rich grapes that will produce fruit which will nourish and wine that will bring joy and the power of the Holy Spirit and the Spirit of Holiness to the people of God and salvation to the unsaved.

DON'T CONDEMN EVERYONE WHO SUFFERS

We must understand however, just because a believer is suffering a terrible disease or plague, has his business wiped out, or is violently attacked, that does not necessarily mean that he has been a terrible sinner.

John 9:1-3 (KJ21) And as Jesus passed by, He saw a man who was blind from his birth.2 And His disciples asked Him, saying, "Master, WHO SINNED, this man or his parents, that he was born blind?"3 Jesus answered, "NEITHER HATH THIS MAN SINNED NOR HIS PARENTS, but that THE WORKS OF GOD SHOULD BE MADE MANIFEST IN HIM."

Some sickness is to keep us from sin. Some sickness is to punish us in the flesh, so we won't need to be judged eternally. Sometimes it is for the glory of God. Some sickness is to encourage us to love God. Sometimes we have no idea why affliction comes. But, when affliction strikes us it is always a good idea to ask God IF there is any wicked or sinful way in us that must be forsaken. SEARCH MY HEART LORD AND SEE IF THERE IS ANY WICKED WAY IN ME is a good prayer.

Psalm 139:23-24 (AMPC) Search me thoroughly, O God, and know my heart! Try me and know my thoughts! 24 And see if there is ANY WICKED OR HURTFUL WAY IN Me and lead me in the way everlasting.

1 Peter 3:22-4:2 (NLT) Now Christ has gone to heaven. He is seated in the place of honor next to God, and all the angels and authorities and powers accept his authority. 4:1 So then, SINCE CHRIST SUFFERED PHYSICAL PAIN, you must arm yourselves with the SAME ATTITUDE he had, and be ready to suffer, too. For IF YOU HAVE SUFFERED PHYSICALLY FOR CHRIST, you have finished with sin. 2 You won't spend the rest of your lives chasing your own desires, but you will BE ANXIOUS TO DO THE WILL OF GOD.

It is obvious from the Scriptures that God is telling us that sometimes WE MUST SUFFER FOR CHRIST SAKE. And when we do suffer for His sake, we can be sure that we are not sinning. When we do suffer for His sake, we enter into a phase in our life when we are no longer seeking to please ourselves; rather we are seeking only to please Him.

There is yet another time when Christians will bless God in the midst of their suffering. Jonathan Edwards, a key figure in the Great Awakening in the 17th century wrote about Abigail Hutchinson, a woman of frail health who was touched mightily by the Holy Spirit of God and was given a spirit of humility and the miraculous ability to endure pain without complaining. There may be people like her today that experience a great illness that threatens their health and well-being and are able to quietly and sometimes passionately endure this painful sickness. These people never complain to God and never complain about what is going on in their lives and have an absolute trust that His will is for them to be in pain at that time. These people have the ability to melt hearts with their sweet surrender to the circumstances that God has put them in. These people manifest a trust in their Heavenly Father, His Son Jesus Christ and His Mighty Holy Spirit that transcends 21st century Christian behavior. ALL WHO SUFFER ARE NOT SUFFERING BECAUSE OF THEIR SIN! These cases ARE RARE, however.

ONGOING PUNISHMENT OF GOD'S PEOPLE

What more can God do to warn us of impending judgment? Our schools preach hatred for all that is good, including God, and make heroes of evil people. Our courts coddle criminals and are unfairly harsh to people who love our country or love God. Much of our entertainment mirrors Sodom and Gomorrah. Our churches are filled with leaders that love fame and fortune and curry the favor of men more than they want the approval of God.

Many Christians lose their sons and their daughters to the world and to the enemy as soon as they leave home. Unscriptural divorce has crippled children in the Church. The clergy may make more money than they ever have before, but many of their families have been ruined by adultery, pornography, and unscriptural divorce. The millionaire ministers are getting paid off by those they serve, but many of the spiritually bankrupt men and women of their churches are living disappointing lives with failing marriages and resentful children.

God has been dealing with His people severely over the last 50 years. We have watched the power of the Church overturned in the courts. The Supreme Court has decided that the willful murder of an in unborn child is a choice that every woman can legally make with the approval of the government and society. Consequently, tens of millions of babies have been murdered by selfish, evil women and their Godless doctors. Christians have had no power to stop the slaughter. The people of God are a laughingstock in the eyes of the world. The once somewhat sympathetic media is completely against the people of God and God's laws. Christians are depicted as jokes and men and women of purity are thought to be fools or worse.

Yet we still send our children to government schools and colleges from kindergarten through PhD programs and they are indoctrinated with the teachings of the antichrist. Our resistance to the government schools is essentially token in its nature. The divorce rate in the Church is higher than it has ever been, and the children of divorce are punished with the great pain of separation from those they love. They grow up with little or no respect for Christian marriage. Pornography is rampant in in our churches.

YET WE WILL NOT ACKNOWLEDGE His chastening hand; instead, we have rationalized our lukewarm conduct. We have not acknowledged our spiritual failures to change the culture and the legal system because we have compromised our beliefs.

We WILL NOT acknowledge that God's hand is CERTAINLY EVIDENT in the disasters that have struck us. GOD IS TRYING TO WAKE US UP so we can avoid more severe punishment or terrible judgment that will come to us if we don't repent. So, we continue to deny the fact that God has been punishing us for decades. We continue to deny that His hand is against us.

All the defeats that we have experienced in the courts, the classroom and the culture are supposedly because of the evil people in the world. The Lukewarm Church in America believes that they are the most balanced, the most reasonable, the richest and certainly the most attractive Church that God has ever raised up. The tragic changes in our culture are NOT unrelated to the condition of the Church. Because we have failed in our duty to live and preach HOLY love and embrace THE TOTALITY OF THE SCRIPTURES, the enemy has taken over realms that we once owned.

In the 18th century, Christians founded the leading universities in America. The great pastor and preacher Jonathan Edwards who helped launch the Great Awakening was chosen to be president of the College of New Jersey (Princeton). In the 19th century we led the fight against slavery, and we won both in the courts and on the battlefield. Over the years we sent more missionaries, more Bibles and built more churches than any nation in history.

In the past 50 years, we have seen our pulpits occupied by men with ungodly sexual practices in congregations filled with unrepentant men and women "addicted" to the sin of viewing pornography and many unscripturally divorced couples. The Church in America has never been filled with so much filth and poor doctrine. Is it any wonder that the nation is plagued with homosexuality, adultery and fornication when we in the Church have so polluted our assemblies? WE HAVE BEEN PUNISHED WITH THE PLAGUE OF DIVORCE and with the ultimate sadness of seeing our children fall away from the Lord. In spite of this, we CONTINUE to water down or completely forsake the notion that God is severely chastening the church. We no longer are concerned, and we certainly no longer fear the chastening hand of God. We have become blind to the cause of our failures and blind to the grief in God's heart.

We are similar to the people of Amos's time that experienced God's chastening hand MANY TIMES. We have become like the world and assumed the status of victimhood. It's not our fault! It's the fault of the media, the corrupt courts, and the entertainment industry.

PURPOSE OF SCRIPTURAL CHASTENING

Amos 4:6-12 (NLT) I ,*God*, brought hunger to every city and famine to every town.
BUT STILL YOU WOULD NOT RETURN TO ME," says the Lord.
7 I kept the rain from falling when your crops needed it the most. I sent rain on one town but withheld it from another. Rain fell on one field, while another field withered away. 8 People staggered from town to town looking for water, but there was never enough.
BUT STILL YOU WOULD NOT RETURN TO ME," says the Lord.
9 I struck your farms and vineyards with blight and mildew. Locusts devoured all your fig and olive trees.
BUT STILL YOU WOULD NOT RETURN TO ME," says the Lord.
10 I sent plagues on you like the plagues I sent on Egypt long ago. I killed your young men in war and led all your horses away. The stench of death filled the air!
BUT STILL YOU WOULD NOT RETURN TO ME," says the Lord.
11 I destroyed some of your cities, as I destroyed Sodom and Gomorrah. Those of you who survived were like charred sticks pulled from a fire.
BUT STILL YOU WOULD NOT RETURN TO ME," says the Lord.

God was punishing His people because he wanted them to wake up and return to Him! They were BEING PUNISHED because they would not repent. God wanted them to cry out in repentance and forsake their sin. He wanted them to cease the activities that brought on their punishment on at LEAST FIVE DIFFERENT OCCASIONS, God sent terrible punishment to the people of Israel. But they had no fear of the Lord and continued to do what they thought was right and most of their leaders never told them that these terrible things were punishments from the Lord Himself. He gave them MANY OPPORTUNITIES to avoid the ultimate judgment, but, THEY WOULD NOT RETURN TO THE Lord. Amos was just one of the many prophets that warned the people of God to return to the Lord, The Lord said: because Israel would not return to Him:

Amos 4:12 (NLT) Therefore, I WILL BRING UPON YOU ALL THE DISASTERS I have announced. PREPARE TO MEET YOUR GOD IN JUDGMENT, YOU PEOPLE OF ISRAEL.

God's people in the Book of Amos were punished with famine, crop failure, drought, plagues, war, death, and destruction of their cities and STILL WOULD NOT REPENT OF THEIR SINS AND RETURN TO GOD. The people of God in the Old Testament certainly experienced the judgment of God. God warned His people in both the Northern Kingdom of Israel and Judah in the South for at least 150 years that judgment was coming if they did not repent. They did not repent, therefore God Himself (not Satan) threw them into judgment and punished them grievously for their sins.

When God has repeatedly called for the people who are called by His Name to repent of their sin and they neither ceased from that sin nor even acknowledged that sin, then God, after years of dealing with His people by chastening or punishing them, needed to judge HIS PEOPLE with GREAT pain and suffering. This is called THE JUDGMENT OF GOD.

JUDGMENT IN SCRIPTURE

We have become far removed from the principles that changed a few struggling New England colonies into the most powerful country in the history of mankind. We ourselves have laid the foundation for the terrible punishments and judgment that will be brought against both the Church of Jesus Christ and the nation if we don't repent. Like the People of Israel, we have been punished for decades, but there is hardly any HINT that the Church in America will repent of its sins, let alone acknowledging them.

Not only do many reject ANY CRITICISM of the Church or any prospect of judgment coming to God's people, they most heartily accept an unscriptural CHEAP grace that allows them to avoid the consequences of their own sin or the sins of the Church. The Israelites of their time were punished and chastened by God VERY SEVERELY before their final judgment. We MUST understand that the punishments and chastening could get VERY SEVERE in America. Even at this date, May 16, 2020, our economy has ground to a halt because the world is threatened by a pandemic of the Chinese Coronavirus. Even more ominous is the weakening of our economy in hopes that regime change could occur. Many governors and mayors are demanding and receiving billions of dollars for their already bankrupt states and cities but will not allow people to work or attend church. The harsh and unfair actions of high-ranking bureaucrats in our country is a HARBINGER of what lies in the future. Prayer chains are forming all over the nation, but NO TALK of repentance by God's people for THEIR sins.

God did not judge the Amorites until their cup of iniquity was full (Genesis 15:16). We have reached the point where our cup is almost full! When that cup is full, God will pour out judgment or severe chastening upon the Church. Many who have lived in America long enough to see the country as it was years ago, understand that we are living in a New Age of corruption. There is filth, defilement, and unfaithfulness both in the culture and in the Church that has never been seen before. The easy-believism, unholy grace Gospel is just as defiling as the prosperity Gospel and the phony New Age Apostles and Prophets movement. In some ways, this Laodicean, cheap grace error is by far the most dangerous false teaching in the Church today. IT IS SO SUBTLE! THE FIG TREE IS NO LONGER BEARING FRUIT THAT IS SATISFYING TO JESUS CHRIST and He WILL put manure on it first and if that doesn't cause the fig to bear fruit then He will cut it down.

Luke 13:7-9 (AMPC) So he said to the vinedresser, See here! For these three years I have come looking for fruit on this fig tree AND I FIND NONE. Cut it down! Why should it continue also to use up the ground to deplete the soil, intercept the sun, and take up room? 8 But he replied to Him, Leave it alone, Sir, just this one more year, till I dig around it and PUT MANURE on the soil. 9 Then perhaps it will bear fruit after this; but if not, YOU CAN CUT IT DOWN.

WHAT CAN WE DO?

For the Christian Church to blame the world for the terrible defeats and punishments we have experienced since World War II is like Judah and Jerusalem blaming the heathen Babylonians for their judgment. Most tragically, American Christians have no understanding that an even greater and much more painful judgment both to the Church and the nation could come upon us. In the meantime, before the ultimate judgment comes, we will experience a number of unpleasant punishments just as the people of Israel did in the day of Amos. Perhaps these lesser punishments that God sends might awaken God's people to return to Him.

It is only the Church of Jesus Christ that can lead the nation out of chaos, immorality and lawlessness. Before America can even survive as a free nation, the Church needs to repent; the Church MUST turn from THEIR wicked ways.

UNTIL WE REPENT, we will continue to be punished by God, and these punishments will intensify. and then God will bring GREAT JUDGMENT upon us. HOWEVER, If the Church in America will not change, then INDIVIDUAL FAMILIES that seek His face and His presence and TURN FROM THEIR WICKED WAYS will survive and endure the chastening hand of the Lord. These families can expect to experience the power to endure the difficult and perilous times that will come upon America and the Church and THEY will thrive spiritually.

CHAPTER 7: JOSIAH REVIVAL

Introduction
Before, During and After Josiah's Reign
Proclamation of Judgment
Respite from Judgment
God's People: Today and Long Ago
Possible Respite from Judgment
NOW is the Time
Conclusion

INTRODUCTION

This chapter deals with the possible temporary extension of God's mercy before terrible punishments or judgment strike both the country and the Church in America. It is a didactic teaching based upon historical facts that are related in the Old Testament regarding God's people before the terrible Judgment of Judah and Jerusalem after the death of Josiah. My SUPPOSITION is that before and during the time of Josiah's reign, the people of Jerusalem and Judah were much like the churchgoing population in America in the early 21st century. There was rampant idolatry and disobedience to God's Word before and during Josiah's time. After discovering of the law of God in the Scriptures, Josiah expanded his restoration of the temple of God and make even more radical changes regarding the responsibilities of God's people. Because Josiah had mourned and wept over the sins that Judah and Jerusalem both committed before and during his reign, God told him through the prophetess Huldah that he would be spared having to see the slaughter of God's people. However, because the people would not repent, He would still bring terrible judgment upon both Judah and Jerusalem after Josiah was gone.

For decades, I have been praying for a Josiah Revival that would at least give Christians in America an opportunity to be more prepared for ANY severe punishment or judgment that may come upon the people of God and our nation. As the political and cultural deterioration became greater and greater, I all but gave up on that prayer ever being answered. I might have been wrong.

I was surprised that many evangelical Christians jumped on board to support Donald Trump early in the campaign. There were many rejected candidates that had more character and a deeper faith than Donald Trump, but the Republican party preferred him, his style, his strong convictions, and his fighting spirit. I was not pleased when he misrepresented the views of his opponents and was extremely insulting in his criticism of them: his systematic attacks on front runners was cruel and, in some cases, outright untrue. His characterization of Jeb Bush contained innuendos that were not true. The remarks he made about Dr. Ben Carson and his testimony about the way he had overcome a terrible anger problem in his youth was twisted into a supposed confession of his psychological inability to become President. His veiled insults of Megan Kelly, Ted Cruz's wife and Carly Fiorina that demeaned their womanhood, and, in some cases, their physical appearance were especially wrong. His accusation that President George Bush knew about the 911 attack ahead of time was particularly absurd. When candidate Trump questioned Ted Cruz's citizenship and insinuated that his father was part of the conspiracy to assassinate John F. Kennedy, he completely lost it and showed that he would use the lie to get what he wanted.

ON THE OTHER HAND, I had to admire his fighting spirit and when he was nominated I was confident that he would fight hard against Hillary Clinton, the values that she represented, and if he won, he would not hesitate to battle the left-wing media that had viciously attacked George Bush and other Republicans and conservatives for decades. So far, this has proven to be true. Donald Trump has fought hard for values that many Republicans did not feel were worth fighting for. When he decided to move the U.S. embassy in Israel from Tel Aviv to Jerusalem, I was jaw-droppingly surprised! The anti-Israel lobby in our country and especially in the democrat party has not honored Israel's desire to have Jerusalem recognized as their capital. They were against having the U S move their embassy to Jerusalem. This move undoubtedly, caused our Lord to smile. Even though Israel is still a secular nation that discourages Christian evangelism, it is a nation that God has promised to bring back to Himself.

I have hoped that our President would remain strong against the political, cultural, economic and military enemies of the United States. Specifically, I was concerned that he would not completely reject Planned Parenthood and be too generous in his praise for the LGBTQ community.

However, WHATEVER HAPPENS, we in the Church have had at least a little more time to change and become like King Josiah and the people who escaped the judgment of God because they grieved and lamented over the sins of His people. (Ezekiel 9:4). HOWEVER, the majority of the Jews during Josiah's administration did not change, and they experienced death and destruction. Jeremiah, Ezekiel and other prophets continued to exhort and warn God's people after the judgment, and likely some heard the Word, abandoned their idolatry, and were spared judgment in eternity. Donald Trump's POSSIBLE further tenure in office MAY give us a little longer respite from similar judgment.

BEFORE, DURING AND AFTER JOSIAH'S REIGN

2 Kings 21:1-15, 19, 20, 22 (NLT) Manasseh *(Josiah's grandfather)...* reigned in Jerusalem fifty-five years... 2 HE DID WHAT WAS EVIL IN THE LORD'S SIGHT, FOLLOWING THE DETESTABLE PRACTICES OF THE PAGAN NATIONS that the Lord had driven from the land ahead of the Israelites. 3 ...HE CONSTRUCTED ALTARS FOR BAAL and SET UP AN ASHERAH POLE... He also bowed before all the powers of the heavens and worshiped them. 4 He built pagan altars in the temple of the lord, the place where the Lord had said, "My name will remain in Jerusalem forever." 5 He built these altars for all the powers of the heavens in both courtyards of the Lord's Temple. 6 Manasseh also SACRIFICED HIS OWN SON IN THE FIRE. He practiced sorcery and divination, and he consulted with mediums and psychics. He did much that was EVIL IN THE LORD'S SIGHT, AROUSING HIS ANGER. 7 Manasseh even made a carved image of ASHERAH and set it up in the TEMPLE, the very place where the Lord had told David and his son Solomon: "My name will be honored FOREVER IN THIS TEMPLE and in Jerusalem—the city I have chosen from among all the tribes of Israel. 8 If the Israelites will be careful to obey my commands - all the laws my servant Moses gave them - I will not send them into exile from this land that I gave their ancestors." 9 But THE PEOPLE REFUSED TO LISTEN, and Manasseh led them to do even more evil than the pagan nations that the Lord had destroyed when the people of Israel entered the land.

PROCLAMATION OF JUDGMENT

10 Then the Lord said through His servants the prophets: 11 "King Manasseh... is even more wicked than the Amorites, who lived in this land before Israel. He has caused the people of Judah to sin with his idols. 12 so this is what the Lord, the God of Israel, says: I will bring such disaster on Jerusalem and Judah that the ears of those who hear about it will tingle with horror. 13...I will wipe away the people of Jerusalem as one wipes a dish and turns it upside down. 14 Then I will reject even the remnant of my own

people who are left, AND I WILL HAND THEM OVER AS PLUNDER FOR THEIR ENEMIES. 15 For they have done great evil in MY SIGHT AND HAVE ANGERED ME ever since their ancestors came out of Egypt." 19 AMON *(Josiah's father)* was twenty-two years old when he became king... 20 He did what was evil in the Lord's sight, just as his father, Manasseh, had done. 22 HE...REFUSED TO FOLLOW THE LORD'S WAYS.

RESPITE FROM JUDGMENT

2 KINGS 22:1-20 (NLT) JOSIAH was eight years old when he became king. 2 He did what was PLEASING IN THE LORD'S SIGHT and followed the example of his ancestor David. 3 ... He told Shaphan, 4 "Go to Hilkiah the high priest and have him count the money...5 to supervise the restoration of the lord's temple. 8 Hilkiah the high priest said to Shaphan the court secretary, "I have found THE BOOK OF THE LAW in the Lord's Temple!"

10... Shaphan read it to the king. 11 When the king heard what was written in the Book of the Law, HE TORE HIS CLOTHES IN DESPAIR. 12 Then he gave these orders to Hilkiah the priest and others... 13 "Go to the Temple and speak to the Lord for me and for the people and for all Judah. Inquire about the Words written in this scroll that has been found. For THE LORD'S GREAT ANGER IS BURNING AGAINST US BECAUSE OUR ANCESTORS HAVE NOT OBEYED THE WORDS in this scroll. We have not been doing everything it says we must do."

14 So, they... went to consult with the prophet Huldah...15 She said to them, "The Lord, the God of Israel has spoken! Go back and tell the man who sent you, 16 'This is what The Lord says: I AM GOING TO BRING DISASTER upon this city and ITS PEOPLE. ALL THE WORDS WRITTEN ON THE SCROLL that the king of Judah has read WILL COME TRUE. 17 for my people have abandoned me and offered sacrifices to pagan gods, and I am very angry with them for everything they have done.'

18 "But go to the king of Judah JOSIAH who sent you to seek the Lord and tell him: 'This is what the Lord, the God of Israel, says concerning the message you have just heard: 19 YOU WERE SORRY AND HUMBLED YOURSELF BEFORE THE LORD when you heard what I said against this city and its people ... You tore your clothing in despair and WEPT BEFORE ME IN REPENTANCE... 20 So I WILL NOT SEND THE PROMISED DISASTER UNTIL AFTER YOU HAVE DIED and been buried in peace."

GOD'S PEOPLE: TODAY AND LONG AGO

We need to carefully look at what Judah did during the reign of the three kings. We also need to look at what the Church in America has done over the last 50 years. In 2 Kings 21, under Manasseh, Judah followed the detestable practices of the heathen nations. Specifically, Judah rebuilt the pagan shrines, constructed altars for Baal and set up an Asherah pole. An Asherah pole was a female icon that was worshiped by the heathens living in the lands that God gave to the Jews after they left Egypt. Asherah was a strong female goddess that wielded great power and was extremely attractive to the Jews.

During and before the Protestant Reformation, Roman Catholicism was a popular religion in which Mary was virtually worshipped. Whereas the Asherah religion directly worshiped the goddess or the Asherah poles and artifacts, the Catholic Church chose to translate the feminine mystique of the goddess Asherah into the image of Mary, the so-called Mother of God and Queen of heaven. Jeremiah mentions that the queen of heaven was an object of worship and received offerings from the backslidden Jews (Jerimiah 7:18, KJ21). The Mary of the Roman Catholics shared many of the attributes of the pagan goddess Asherah. Besides being the Queen of Heaven and the Mother of God, she was referred to as the co-mediatrix between God and man along with Jesus. Mediatrix is the feminine equivalent of MEDIATOR.

Today in the Evangelical Church, we have no physical shrines to Mary or any other woman, but we do teach, sometimes openly and sometimes subtly that women in general are much better equipped to obey God than are men. In Christian feminist circles, some evangelical and charismatic teachers, both men and women, teach that women are physiologically and spiritually superior to men; they are more stable emotionally, more able to communicate, and after God created woman, Gary Thomas in *LOVING HIM WELL*, says,

"If you look at the line of creation, FEMALES ARE THE CULMINATION. Everything keeps getting more sophisticated, more intricate, until FINALLY a WOMAN appears – and ONLY THEN does God rest." [17]

All in all, as she is described by Gary and other churchgoing feminists, wives are considered to be vastly superior to their husband: physiologically, psychologically, and spiritually. Men are often depicted as verbally abusive, controlling, and more like little boys than men of God. (please see Chapter 20-22 of *Battle for the Church*. Gary's book is a typical example of Christian feminism. This, of course, is not direct worship, but it is an elevation of women that is not in the Scriptures. Gary's declaration that woman is the culmination of God's creation – and ONLY THEN DOES HE STOP, is a DANGEROUS embellishment of the Scriptures. Christian feminism essentially destroys the concept of the headship of the husband and the submission of the wife by supplying so called "scientific evidence" regarding the physiological inferiority of the male. This extremely high and unbiblical view of women approaches idolatry.

Manasseh sacrificed his own son to a heathen God and as was mentioned before, parents in the Church have sacrificed their children to the gods of pleasure and convenience when they blithely send them to government schools. Most do not pay close attention to what the government schools teach and therefore, their children grow up brainwashed by this antichrist system. These parents would rather satisfy their own material desires than spend the time or the money to prevent their children from being indoctrinated. By neglecting to consistently protect them from the schools and the entertainment media, they allow their children to be deceived. Today, like the people of Jerusalem who refused to listen to the Words of warning and correction, many pastors will not even teach the people to obey the Scriptures that demand correction or repentance either for themselves or their children, for fear of driving them away.

POSSIBLE RESPITE FROM JUDGMENT

We need to understand that tough love is not an invention of a male dominated culture. Jesus Christ, the Father, and the Holy Spirit ALL practice tough love. Tough love is not MEAN love, but it is FIRM love.

We MUST, as Huldah and Josiah did, REDISCOVER THE BOOK OF THE LAW OF GOD, which includes the precepts and directives of God. God's grace and God's love have been given to us so that we can function as new creatures. We have been given a new tender, responsive heart to obey His laws.

We must root out and tear down all the idolatrous doctrines and practices that have ruined MANY families in both the churches and the culture. Because of our negligence, we have allowed much of this nation to be transformed into an ally and willing and effective warrior of Satan.

Josiah desired to see the Lord's temple restored to its former glory. While the workers were doing so, his high priest, Hilkiah, found the Book of the Law. Shaphan then read the Words of the Book of the Law to Josiah. The king became aware that the Lord's great anger was burning against the people of God because both they and their ancestors had not obeyed the Words in the scroll. Huldah the prophetess sent a message to Josiah telling him that the Lord would bring disaster upon this place and upon its people. She prophesied that all the Words of the Book which were read to the people would come true because the Jews had turned away from God and judgment would not be stopped. Josiah humbled himself before the Lord when he heard what God said against this city and its people. He tore his clothing in despair and wept before God in repentance. So, God, through Huldah, said He would not send the promised disaster until after Josiah died and been buried in peace

NOW IS THE TIME

RIGHT NOW, we in the Church should be concerned about rebuilding the temple of the Lord. We need to tear down the idols in the Church. The first one to go must be the false Jesus that some follow. This phony Jesus, as was said earlier, has led more souls astray than Internet pornography. He NEVER Judges anyone in the Church and forgives both the repentant and unrepentant alike. NO ONE need fear this Jesus. We need to destroy this idol that frightens leaders and laity alike from uttering anything negative about the Church or God's people. We have filled His temple of worship with entertainment and allowed unrepentant people in the congregation who are bound by the sin of pornography to praise Him with lust in their hearts. Most importantly, we must rediscover the Scriptures that we have ignored for decades that deal with our responsibilities to be holy as He is holy and describe the terrible consequences the Lukewarm Church faces.

We may not have a great deal of time. The time between Josiah discovering the Book of the Law and the fall of Jerusalem was approximately 20 years. however, before that time, God did warn and severely chasten His people for well over 100 years. But most certainly the punishments that we will experience will increase in intensity. Whether God would give us more time or less time is not known to us. Much that is written in this book, *Battle for the Church*, is for the purpose of using that time to prepare ourselves and our families for whatever God brings us. We still have time to make sure that our children don't get brainwashed by the government school system, media entertainment or the Lukewarm Church. Most of the Church in America will experience punishment or judgment. But if we mourn because of the abominations committed in the Church in America, grieve over our sins and the sins of the Church; if we humble ourselves, seek His face, pray, and turn from OUR wicked ways, we and our families will receive God's best.

If the Church at large will not change and has no desire to rebuild the temple of God for His pleasure, then their churches, their cities, and eventually the culture and the country will someday be judged without mercy. BUT, the remnant of God's people who desire HIS PLEASURE more than their own comfort will EVENTUALLY thrive more than ever before.

TODAY WE SHOULD start the process of casting out all the idols which offend God. As we do so, we can expect to see our marriages bear the fruit of the Holy Spirit, our lives produce the power of the Holy Spirit and our families forever changed by God's grace and power. We can gather together with people of like mind and form home meetings to encourage one another, correct one another, and love one another. From these groups, we can launch out and warn others how important it is for them to clean up and rebuild their own temples.

In 10 or 20 years, we may look back on this time as a time that God gave us to prepare our families for extremely difficult times and thank Him. The key elements in using our time wisely has to do with our families. Husbands and wives must fully embrace and learn to love and obey the duties that God has given BOTH OF THEM in His Scriptures.

NOW is the time for soul-searching repentance of our own sins. Our prayer must be, WHATEVER IT TAKES, Lord show us our sin and our rebellion and by the power of Your Holy Spirit, forgive our sin and rebellion. Make us holy and pleasing to You in all our ways. Show us clearly the wonderful power that You have given us through the new birth to be new creatures with new habits and new loves. Help us to be Watchmen on the walls of Your Church and help us to warn both the Church and the country about the judgment that will fall if they don't repent. Make us bold and fill us with Your Holy Spirit, Lord God, and fill our minds and our hearts with Scripture. Help us to call out appropriately for Your sheep to come to Your fold. And give us the anointing to deliver this message in a way that would please You. If there is any self-righteous holier-than thou attitude in our hearts, deal with us as mercifully as You can, but WHATEVER IT TAKES GOD, get rid of it. Help us to be legitimately sorrowful for our own sins, for the sins of the Church in America and for the sins of America. Let us weep as we see the judgment and the destruction that is to come. AND let us have Your heart of mercy to be merciful and have the will and the power to function in your wisdom.

We are in greater danger than the people of both Israel and Jerusalem before the terrible judgment of God destroyed their cities, their temples of worship and killed their people. We have the COMPLETE Bible! We have been reintroduced to the doctrines of grace and the power of the Holy Spirit! We have resources on the Internet that allow us to research ALL of Scripture and find answers. But Christians MUST STOP merely using the Internet for recreation at best and pornography at worst. WE MUST search our hearts and turn back to our LORD and His PERFECT, unadulterated Word.

CONCLUSION

We can start raising our families according to the dictates of the Holy Scriptures and we can reap the great benefits of watching God work in our marriages and our children so that when they reach maturity, THEY WILL NOT DEPART FROM THE WAY! We can reap the benefits of even seeing our grandchildren transformed by the Word of God and His powerful Holy Spirit. These joys can be ours TODAY. BUT WE MUST SEEK HIM WITH OUR WHOLE HEART .

SECTION 3: PREPARING FOR DIFFICULT DAYS

CHAPTER 8: TEACHING GOD'S PERFECT
CHAPTER 9: JUDGING MEN AND DOCTRINE
CHAPTER 10: LAWLESSNESS IN THE TEMPLE OF GOD
CHAPTER 11: GRIEVE AND LAMENT FOR THE CHURCH

For the difficult times that are ahead, either in our family's life or the nation, the preparation has virtually nothing to do with stockpiling food or buying guns; rather it has to do with preparing yourself by KNOWING THE TRUTH that is contained in the Word of God and applying that truth, especially to your families. As some are sovereignly called into politics, some may be called to store food or buy guns, but ALL are called to learn the Scriptures, teach them to our families and OBEY the Word OF GOD!!

This section deals with the importance of studying, living, obeying, and teaching God's Word, especially to our families and the necessity to judge men and teachings correctly. What does the Bible say about lawlessness and can it affect the Church? Lastly, we will look closely at the state of the Church in America today. We will see compelling evidence of our need to grieve and lament over the state of the Church in America.

This section deals with critical teachings that we must understand and live in order to survive and thrive during the difficult days that lie ahead. We must prepare ourselves and our families rigorously regarding the dictates of Scripture. We must obey all of Scripture, but most importantly, we must believe, obey, and teach the Scriptures that deal with responsibilities of husbands, wives and children. These are critical concepts because they have been either ignored or perverted by the Establishment Churches of our times. Our wives and our children must be exposed to and taught these concepts so they in turn can practice and teach these concepts to their own children and possibly grandchildren. God may give us decades, scores of years or even generations before the end of days when the most difficult times will come, but even if they are not fulfilled in our lifetime, for us to change the world as we once did, we must eat, drink and breathe the Word to the extent that the Scriptures bring life to our dead and dying churches, the dead and dying people of America and in some cases to our dead and dying families.

CHAPTER 8: TEACHING GOD'S PERFECT WORD

Sufficiency of Scripture
No Compromising the Scriptures
Living Document Theory
We Must Love the Truth:
Horrible and Persuasive Deception.
Government Indoctrination
Lukewarm Christian Schools
Preserving the Truth that We Teach
Starting a Co-Op Church or Home School
    Curriculum Suggestions
    Great Urgency
    Most Important Mission Field

SUFFICIENCY OF SCRIPTURE

2 TIMOTHY 3:13-17 (NKJV) But evil men and impostors will grow worse and worse, DECEIVING AND BEING DECEIVED. 14 But YOU MUST CONTINUE IN the things which you have learned and been assured of, knowing from whom you have learned them, 15and that from childhood you have known the Holy Scriptures, which are able to make you wise for salvation through faith which is in Christ Jesus. 16 ALL SCRIPTURE is given by inspiration of God, and IS PROFITABLE FOR DOCTRINE, REPROOF, FOR CORRECTION, FOR INSTRUCTION IN RIGHTEOUSNESS, 17 that the man of God may be complete, THOROUGHLY EQUIPPED FOR EVERY GOOD WORK.

2 Timothy 3:13-17(AMPC) But wicked men and imposters will go on from bad to worse, deceiving and leading astray others and being deceived and led astray themselves. 14 But as for you, continue to hold to the things that you have learned and of which you are convinced, knowing from whom you learned them, 15 And how from your childhood you have had a knowledge of and been acquainted with the sacred Writings, which are able to instruct you and give you the understanding for salvation which comes through faith in Christ Jesus through the leaning of the entire human

personality on God in Christ Jesus in absolute trust and confidence in His power, wisdom, and goodness. 16 Every Scripture is God-breathed, given by His inspiration and profitable for instruction, for reproof and conviction of sin, for correction of error and discipline in obedience, and for training in righteousness, holy living, in conformity to God's will in thought, purpose, and action, 17 So that the man of God may be complete and proficient, well fitted and thoroughly equipped for every good work.

THE KEY to understanding the Scriptures is BELIEVING THAT ALL THE SCRIPTURES ARE TRUE AND SUFFICIENT! We must have faith in the Scriptures BEFORE we will understand them! In the book of John, Jesus is referred to as the Word of God. The Scriptures are the objective, perfect manifestation of the thoughts and beliefs of Jesus Christ. In the world, an individual must FIRST UNDERSTAND before he can believe. In God's realm, including the realm of the Holy Scriptures, you must FIRST BELIEVE, AND THEN AND ONLY THEN WILL YOU BE ABLE TO UNDERSTAND AND APPLY THE SCRIPTURES. THERE MAY BE TIMES WHEN YOU DON'T UNDERSTAND WHY THE LORD commands us through His Word to do something, but we must believe and obey that Word because the VOICE OF THE SCRIPTURE is THE VOICE OF OUR SHEPHERD and we do what He says, and we follow Him wherever He takes us. But WE MUST BELIEVE This is NOT BLIND FAITH because WE KNOW the Lord!

Studying the Bible along with the works of other men is important. There are great Bible scholars in history that help to explain difficult Scriptures. We have the creeds of the early Church that at times enlighten us regarding basic elements of Christianity. Great preachers and teachers such as Martin Luther, Mathew Henry, George Whitefield, Charles Spurgeon, A.W. Tozer, and Martyn Lloyd-Jones have contributed much to our understanding of the Word of God. But TRUE understanding only comes when they INTERPRET DOCTRINE FROM THE WORD OF GOD itself and not from traditions, creeds, observations of men or scientific discovery.

It is extremely important to interpret Scripture from other Scripture and make sure that one is not being led astray by the teachings of a man or a woman. We can validate the opinions of men by studying the Scriptures; we NEVER are to validate the truth of Scripture by the opinions or actions of men.

The reformers broke away from the Roman Catholic Church because that organization added to the Word of God. The Catholics said that we were NOT saved by faith alone. They said that it was necessary for believers to accept and practice the beliefs and the doctrines of the Roman Catholic Church along with the Bible. The Bible typically means exactly what it says. An exception is prophetic literature which often is symbolic in nature. However, people tend to read their own desires and cultural beliefs into the clear words of Scripture. We do so because we want to excuse our disobedience to God's Word.

Oftentimes the culture will determine what the Scriptures are supposed to mean. In the past, even though Scripture never declared that it is wrong for a person of one race to marry the person of another race, many people believed that interracial marriage was unscriptural. Today, our culture, for the most part, understands this is not so. It is vitally important that we only judge doctrine and practice based on what Scripture says and not rely upon the opinions of men, either in our culture or in the Church. There is a great danger when men go outside of Scripture to validate any so-called truth.

Even the great Martin Luther, who did more to bring back the doctrines of grace than any man of the Reformation, had some terrible and unscriptural views on the character of the Jewish people. He also had little confidence in one of the books of the Bible. He called the book of James "a right strawy epistle". He did so because he felt that James said that we are saved by works. This went against his belief that we are saved by faith alone. James did say in chapter two that "Faith without works is dead and I will show you my faith by my works." James is saying that when you have real faith in Christ, you will always have the fruit of good works that are pleasing to God. Our interpretation of the Bible should NEVER ADD TO OR SUBRACT FROMTHE BIBLE.

NO COMPROMISING THE SCRIPTURES

Jesus Christ NEVER compromised His principles. He was challenged by Satan, circumstances and even by His Father, but he never compromised. It is perfectly clear in the Bible what He wants us to do. The Holy Scriptures tell us that we are to study the Scriptures, trust Him and His Word, and obey Him. But Satan is not afraid to bend and twist the Scriptures themselves and compromise them a little bit at a time so that he can disarm us of their power. Every chance he gets, he will do what he can to corrupt and compromise pastors, teachers, and other leaders so they will weaken the Church. One of Satan's most effective strategies is to convince the Church that the Word was written only for the people of the time of New Testament. His argument is because of our advancements in psychology and sociology and even in some scientific and philosophical realms, we need to adjust the Word to fit our times.

The devil never compromises his principles. Barack Obama does not compromise his principles. The Puritans, for the most part, did not compromise their principles which were based on the Word of God. We need to be sure that WE NEVER compromise the Scripture. The *Battle for the Church* is being lost because we don't commit ourselves to the Lord Jesus Christ and we COMPROMISE His Scriptures that are written for EVERY GENERATION.

We must never negotiate the principles of Scripture. Jeremiah, Isaiah, Daniel and all the other prophets never held back the Word that God gave them concerning judgment for Israel or Judah, even though many did not live to see that judgment. Jesus Christ, John the Baptist. and Paul the Apostle never held back when God gave them a Word for the Scribes, Pharisees, Sadducees, the Roman hierarchy, and even people that they loved dearly such as Peter and the rest of the apostles. We must in these dangerous times seek AND DELIVER teachings from Scripture and even God-given prophetic words that might cause pain to some people and even drive away others.

LIVING DOCUMENT THEORY

"The Living Constitution... is the claim that the Constitution has a dynamic meaning or that it has the properties of an animate being in the sense that IT changes. The idea is associated with views that contemporary society should be taken into account when interpreting key constitutional phrases... The pragmatist view contends that interpreting the Constitution in accordance with its original meaning or intent is sometimes unacceptable as a policy matter, and thus that an EVOLVING INTERPRETATION IS NECESSARY.[18]

They believe that the Constitution is a LIVING DOCUMENT. For instance, the preamble to the Constitution says, "all men are created equal, that they are endowed by their Creator with certain unalienable Rights, that among these are Life, Liberty and the pursuit of Happiness." The living document theorists believe that the life mentioned in the preamble only pertains to life after birth. They believe that our science and our culture has evolved to the point where we understand that the baby inside the womb is not, as Scripture says, a child (the Bible says that Mary was WITH CHILD in Luke 2:5 NASB). Another example is Luke 1:41 (NASB) When Elizabeth heard Mary's greeting, THE BABY leaped in her womb and Elizabeth was filled with the Holy Spirit. The baby inside the womb is now referred to as a fetus and is merely a conglomeration of tissue and to many Americans it does not represent the Life mentioned in the preamble to the Constitution.

There are certain people in the Church of Jesus Christ in the 21st century that believe that the Bible is a living document and must be reinterpreted with every generation; as the culture evolves, they believe that so must the Word of God evolve. They ignore:

2 Timothy 3:16-17 (KJV). ALL SCRIPTURE is given by inspiration of God, and is profitable for doctrine, for reproof, for correction, for instruction in righteousness: 17 That the man of God may be perfect, THOROUGHLY FURNISHED UNTO ALL GOOD WORKS.

Our generation must return to an understanding that the Bible is NOT MERELY SUFFICIENT but is COMPLETELY trustworthy. For example, because of the fear of man (and woman), we have avoided, ignored, and disobeyed the Scriptures that deal with marriage and divorce. We have suffered greatly both in our culture and in the Church because of this disobedience. The introduction to this chapter refers to the fact that we can be doctrinally correct in any relationship or situation in our daily lives if we trust and obey the Scriptures. We will look at Scriptures that you have seen before. Even If you have been walking with God for many years, take a fresh look at them because many in the Church have been taught to avoid the simple straightforward truth that the Scriptures teach.

This chapter is especially important because the marriage relationship is a TYPE of the greatest relationship that any human being can have: the eternal relationship between Jesus Christ and His Church, the Bride of Christ. The Christian marriage is a living example of this relationship. Marriage is where the faithfulness and the fruitfulness of that relationship is physically (AND SPIRITUALLY) manifested for all to see. It is the ultimate tool of evangelism and discipleship. It is the special place where souls are born both into the world and eventually into the body of Christ. If the marriage is working in a scriptural way, the children will become believers and disciples of Jesus Christ. They will become selfless givers of their own lives to be used by the Lord. They will become apostles, prophets, evangelists, pastors, teachers, workers of miracles, healers, spiritual administrators in the Kingdom and helpers of all who have needs. They will become warriors that will defeat the armies of Satan and help win the *Battle for the Church*. They will become holy worshipers of our Lord and Savior Jesus Christ, the Holy Spirit, and the Father Himself. The world will see them give glory to God and glorify His name in what they do and what they say. And because they live for Him, they will cause His heart to rejoice! More importantly for us as parents, they will come to know God and ENJOY HIM FOREVER.

If we don't obey the Scriptures regarding this most important of relationships, we will bring little or no glory to God. In many cases, we will cause the Holy Spirit to be grieved. We will have wasted a tremendous opportunity to establish the Kingdom of God in at least one place: our family. And most tragically, in the Body of Christ today, we see the children of divorced or lukewarm parents reject their parents and eventually abandon the Lord Jesus Christ.

God will not bring any measure of revival to us as individuals or to the Church at large or to the nation in which we live until we, the Church, believe and obey the Scriptures regarding how we are to be husbands and wives and raise our children.

WE MUST LOVE THE TRUTH

In the dark history of mankind, truth has always been a rare commodity. We humans have learned to lie in ways that are exceedingly deceitful and are very persuasive and we are able to fool most people quite easily. Thinking human beings understand that many lawyers are good lawyers because they are good liars. They have a way of twisting the truth so that people are often fooled. I remember when in high school, a friend of mine and I would often go downtown to the courts to watch trials. I was always amazed how easily I could believe the first lawyer and be on his side and then watch the second lawyer and be on his side. In criminal trials, I often believed the prosecution. But when I heard the defense lawyer speak, I believed the defense lawyer. Lawyers, politicians, and salesmen understand the power of the lie, or twisting the truth. The entertainment industry well understands that good liars in movies make for good movies. The good liar has become a hero or heroine in Hollywood. Even in real life, good liars are at times good heroes. Bill Clinton is a hero to the Democrats because he's a charming liar! It's hard for them not to love this charming rogue.

In our own lives, we have become accustomed to speaking so-called white lies: these lies range from, "I'm too tired to talk now, honey. Just tell them I'm not here." to "Well, you've caught me. I did commit adultery. But I lied to you because I didn't want to hurt you." This last lie is a particularly effective weapon in disguising our sin. "I didn't tell you about that phone call, because I didn't want to hurt you." "I didn't want to tell you about that purchase because I didn't want to worry you." Another common Christian lie is, "We need to get together! No, I don't want to set the date now; I'll give you a ring when it's a good time!" Often, they do so because they want to make you feel good for the moment. They have no intention or even desire of getting together with you. The adulterous liar denied his or her adulterous affair, not because they didn't want to hurt you, but because they enjoyed illicit sex more than they enjoyed godly sex! Unfortunately for so-called Christians, this manipulative and unrepentant lie is one of Satan's biggest helpers in paving the way to hell for them. It is important to understand that some of the greatest excuses that we use to avoid responsibility or to maintain a false front do not come from our own minds, rather Satan's little helpers are planting these notions into our thoughts so he can weaken our walk or worse.

If we think there is a good reason to lie, we can do or say anything we want! After all, no spouse ever feels good about discovering that their mate is having an adulterous or romantic affair with another person. In the long run, the confession of guilt to adultery would give a strong indication to the offended party that at least their spouse had enough respect for them to tell them the truth. That marriage would have a much greater chance of succeeding because truth entered the picture. But unfortunately, even in Christian circles in the Laodicean Church, there is little chance that the guilty party would ever be honest. Success in small lies often gives the liar more confidence into telling much larger lies. Eventually, the liar is trapped. It becomes difficult to break loose. He has received a lying spirit, and only an honest confession, a repentant heart and the work of God will free him. Often. However, there is a great cost to the liar. He or she may experience a tragic punishment from the hand of God. THESE PEOPLE DO NOT LOVE THE TRUTH and they will suffer the consequences. In these last days, the truth is the greatest victim in the Church. If we don't DO the truth, SPEAK the truth and LOVE the truth, we will never agree with either the letter or the spirit of the Scriptures. We will learn to cleverly rationalize a meaning that we can accept. And either we will experience painful punishment from the hand of God, or the father of lies will have another soul for his wretched kingdom.

Psalm 15:1-2 (NLT) Who may worship in your sanctuary, Lord? Who may enter your presence on your holy hill? 2Those who lead blameless lives and do what is right, SPEAKING THE TRUTH FROM SINCERE HEARTS.

One of the conditions for spiritual worship and being in the presence of God is speaking the truth from sincere hearts.

2 Thessalonians 2:9 - 12. (AKJV) Even him, whose coming is after the working in Satan with all power and signs and LYING wonders, 10 And with all DECEIVABLENESS of unrighteousness in them that perish; because THEY RECEIVED NOT THE LOVE OF THE TRUTH, that they might be saved. 11 and for This cause, GOD SHALL SEND THEM STRONG DELUSION, that they should BELIEVE A LIE: 12 that they ALL MIGHT BE DAMNED WHO BELIEVED NOT THE TRUTH but had pleasure in unrighteousness.

Matthew 24:3 (KJ21) And as He sat upon the Mount of Olives, the disciples came unto Him privately, saying, "Tell us, when will these things be? And what shall be the sign of Thy coming and of the end of the world?" Among other things, *Jesus answered,*

Matthew 24:11,24 (KJ21) Many false prophets shall rise and DECEIVE MANY...24 For there shall arise false Christs, and false prophets, and shall show great signs and wonders; insomuch that, IF IT WERE POSSIBLE, THEY SHALL DECEIVE THE VERY ELECT.

Many Christians today cover up their sin because they believe that the grace of God will ultimately forgive them and because they have confessed Jesus Christ as their Lord and Savior, they will inherit eternal life. They are completely oblivious to the concept that there will be people that encounter Jesus in the spiritual realm when they die, and they will call him Lord, Lord. And He will respond to them, **"I NEVER KNEW YOU! DEPART FROM ME YOU WHO PRACTICE LAWLESSNESS!"** Usually contemporary Christians have never heard this Scripture or teaching before from the pulpit and if they have, it has been interpreted to mean something innocuous.

HORRIBLE AND PERSUASIVE DECEPTION

Rules for Radicals is a brilliant satanic presentation written by Saul Alinsky to further the Communist/Progressive cause in America. He discusses the importance of causing confusion and unrest even if it is necessary to spread lies. He justifies this because he says that Conservatives lie all the time. This is not a new concept in the world, however in America it is NOW the basic strategy for the Democrat Party.

GOVERNMENT INDOCTRINATION

Even when I was in school in the 1940s and 1950s, there was an element of liberal or progressive thought in the public-school system. However, if a teacher
was a Christian, there was no coercion that prevented him from discussing the Bible or Jesus Christ, particularly during Thanksgiving, Christmas or Easter. Even liberal teachers taught us about the Pilgrims and during every Christmas season we had manger scenes, Christmas trees and Christmas plays. And, the Christian teachers openly and fearlessly discussed the birth of Jesus Christ. Teachers even read the Bible to us during the holiday season. At times, we even prayed.

But in the 21st century, things have become intolerable. Teachers are not allowed to have Bibles placed on their desks. No one can pray in the name of Jesus at a football game. The Christmas break is now called the Winter break. We don't have an Easter break anymore; we have a Spring break. Children are exposed to four letter words as they watch contemporary movies in the auditorium, but the five-letter word Jesus or the six letter word Christ are never mentioned by any in authority, except to denigrate Him or His church. In my youth, creationism was taught alongside evolution and even defended by some teachers. Teachers never used foul language or told dirty jokes. Today, teachers feel comfortable doing both because then their students think that they are pretty cool when they do so. In elementary school (K – 6th) we were with our teachers for 6 to 7 hours every day and they definitely influenced our lives. Much of my worldview was shaped by three or four effective teachers that I had growing up. Today it's the same: students are with their teachers 6 to 7 hours every day and much of their worldview is being shaped by this experience. Because the government school system at heart is Anti-Christian and anti-conservative, our children are being indoctrinated to support progressive political causes and LBGTQ causes. Incidentally, they are even often taught to support progressive agendas and candidates. As Christian parents and grandparents, we need to strongly contend for the minds and hearts of our children and grandchildren. Our children are being turned into good little soldiers for the Progressives, which is merely one division of Satan's army.

LUKEWARM CHRISTIAN SCHOOLS

Christian schools are somewhat expensive, and many Christians cannot afford to send children to these schools. Some Christian schools are just as bad or even worse than public schools because they teach a lukewarm, religiously correct curriculum that is frighteningly inoffensive. In the Christian high school of one of our sons, the school proudly proclaimed that they used the curriculum of the state of Oregon. Unfortunately, my son was exposed to Arthur Miller's play The Crucible and Nathaniel Hawthorne's novel The Scarlet Letter. In the first book, the witches of Salem are depicted as heroines and Christians are depicted as mindless fools. The Salem witch trials certainly were Christianity's darkest hour in Puritan times, but there were women who did cast spells and they DID influence children to the Dark Side. The Scarlet Letter was a book that was quite daring for its time because it depicted a minister as an adulterous hypocrite. Both literary endeavors depicted Christianity in the worst possible way but the curriculum for the state of Oregon offered no examples where Biblical Christians were depicted in a positive light.

Many Christian schools are afraid of losing children if they teach the whole counsel of God. Like the churches that have founded them, they believe they must be positive and nonjudgmental. They talk about the love of God often, but seldom teach the fear of the Lord or the responsibility to trust and obey Jesus Christ and ALL of Scripture.

PRESERVING THE TRUTH THAT WE TEACH

We need to create an alternative to establishment Christian schools and Progressive government schools. But to do so will require a great sacrifice that most lukewarm Christians have no intention of making. It would require the sacrifice of TIME both to prepare and teach our children. The greatest sacrifice that it would require is obedience to the Scriptures and the casting away of cheap grace and half-hearted holiness. Our zeal and our sacrifice, to some, would feel as severe to us as leaving England and settling in Plymouth Rock Massachusetts was to the early Pilgrims.

ONCE WE GET OUR DOCTRINE CORRECT AND OUR PRACTICES BIBLICAL, the greatest responsibility and opportunity in the Church regarding making disciples is to start a cooperative Christian school within the Church among willing and able parents.

STARTING A CO-OP CHURCH OR HOME SCHOOL

1) Get together with other families, preferably, from the same church.
2) Require each family to provide one adult parent, grandparent, or college student to contribute 10 to 15 hours a week for teaching the children.
3) DILIGENTLY search the Internet for edifying teaching material.
4) Contact local doctrinally sound Bible colleges or seminaries to see if you could get volunteers or paid laborers for your school.
5).Scrupulously check the background, abilities, and doctrine of each potential teacher.
6) All teachers MUST love Jesus, children, the Scriptures, and teaching.
7) Develop communication lines with other Biblical home or church schools.
8) REMEMBER early grade education does not require great understanding of the subject but does require time spent, great patience and love for children.
9) BE SURE to have classes to teach the teachers how to prepare, what to expect and how to respond.

CURRICULUM SUGGESTIONS

1) Must be supportive of the Holy Scriptures and recognize the necessity of believing, obeying, and LOVING all of the Scriptures and not heeding any doctrine that conflicts with Scripture.
2) Must teach the children to be diligent, sacrificing and in love with Jesus.
3) Must teach the children how to think, how to reason, how to study and use the Bible to test the truth.
4) Reading, writing, mathematics, science, English literature, church history, secular history, rudimentary logic, rhetoric or argumentation should be offered.
5) Must teach the children how to evaluate or judge what is true and what is a lie using the Scriptures as the standard of truth.
6).Must teach them to be aware of the wiles of the devil, particularly in entertainment media and news media.
7) WE MUST TEACH THEM TO UNDERSTAND THAT IN ORDER TO KNOW THE TRUTH THEY MUST SPEAK THE TRUTH, LIVE THE TRUTH AND LOVE THE TRUTH!
8) We must understand that every class and every child is different and accommodate our teaching and our curriculum to each need and ability.
9) Christian principles from the Scriptures regarding home management skills and Biblical financial management must be taught.
10) We must let the children know that God is much more interested in their DILIGENCE than He is in their INTELLIGENCE. Success with the Lord Jesus Christ is not based upon IQ but on the spiritual fruit that we bear for Him.

If there is no real opportunity to start a school: Do home schooling or enroll your children in a Christian school that would be pleasing to God. If you would need to send your children to be taught in a system that is basically Anti-Christ, you must be completely aware of the dangers that the children will face. As parents and grandparents, we need to be scrupulously involved with their education. We need to closely monitor what they are being taught in class, what they read and what their homework assignments are.

You need to remember: CHRISTIANITY IS UNDER ATTACK IN AMERICA. We must be ready and willing to edit what our children are learning and, if we are able, be involved as parents in volunteer programs. It is not enough to simply fall back on that old cliché, "Well, I guess we're just going to have to trust the Lord." We must be willing to confront a teacher that has crossed the line into antichrist indoctrination. Above all, we must be willing to fight AND SACRIFICE for the truth and our children.

GREAT URGENCY

Never in the history of America has the educational system so dismally failed our children and our families. At one time, the government schools taught that sexual sin was against the law of God, but the government now teaches our kindergartners and elementary students all about transgenderism, gender choice and condom usage. They also teach our children many unscriptural and unscientific lies. BE PREPARED: anyone who is against their unscriptural and pseudo-scientific belief system is branded as a right-wing kook or an ignorant Hater.

From cradle to grave, our public teaching institutions and government are creating a New Master Race. This Master Race is not based on nationality, skin color, intellectual ability, education, or social standing in the community; rather it is based on the religion of political correctness and the laws and lies of Satan. This religion is destroying our freedom, corrupting our children and marginalizing Christianity. This well-educated army of the NEW Master Race has already slaughtered millions of unborn children and, like their predecessors, the Communists and the Nazis, they will imprison, torment and kill their enemies, both Christian and secular if they win the *Battle for the Church*.

Our government school system, and the private schools, are the most effective tools the Progressives have in alienating our children from Christianity. Vladimir Lenin, one of the geniuses behind the Russian Communist revolution OF 1917, is reputed to have said, "Give me four years to teach the children, and the seed I have sown will never be uprooted!" [19A]

MOST IMPORTANT MISSION FIELD

Churches or organized homeschools must incorporate solid, intellectually sound and SCRIPTURALLY ACCURATE online teaching to replace the secular propaganda of most schools in America. If any church wants to start such a school and felt they could not afford to make the financial investment in such a ministry, they should consider changing the focus of their outreach. While it is wonderful to minister to prisoners and their suffering families and it is equally important to support missions that only trust in the Word of God, it is MORE IMPORTANT for us to minister to our own children and meet their educational needs in the midst of a demonically inspired educational system. Mission trips can be little more than short vacations to another country, but even when they bear good fruit, there is no doubt the GREATEST NEED in the Christian community today is to make sure that OUR children are brought up to know the Bible and love Jesus Christ. Our children and grandchildren are THE MOST IMPORTANT MISSION FIELD in the world today!

On September 20, 1940, about a year after the start of World War II, Franklin Roosevelt said, "We cannot always build the future for our youth, but we can build our youth for the future." [19B] Our country and especially the Church of Jesus Christ, are facing a MUCH MORE dangerous time. How do we build our youth? We build them with the UNADULTERATED WORDS OF SCRIPTURE.

CHAPTER 9: JUDGING MEN & DOCTRINE

Judging is DEMANDED by Scripture!
Judging Others
Prayer and the Golden Rule
The Narrow Way and the Broad Way
It Hath Been Said in the Broad Way Church
A Tree and Its Fruit
The Two Foundations
Who and What to Judge
We Need to Judge Ourselves
RED HOT Consequences
Band-aid on a Bullet Wound
Division of Pure from Impure
Conclusion of the Matter

JUDGING IS DEMANDED BY SCRIPTURE!

In this New Age of Deception, Matthew 7:1 is one of the most misapplied Scriptures in the Bible. This Scripture is usually only partially quoted as, "judge not, lest you be judged", and even when it is quoted in its entirety, it is misunderstood both as to intent and context. The context of this verse is that it is the first verse of the third chapter of the Sermon on the Mount. It is preceded by chapters five and six which are in large part teachings that instruct us in righteousness. Matt. 7:1 "Do not judge, lest you be judged" is the first sentence of an entire chapter devoted to telling God's people How, What and Who to JUDGE. This whole chapter is an exhortation and teaching on judging or evaluating people as to whether they are of God and doctrine as to whether or not it is of God. The first section tells us HOW we are to judge and with what attitude are we to judge.

JUDGING OTHERS

Matthew 7:1-5 (NASB) Do not judge so that you will not be judged. 2 For IN THE WAY YOU JUDGE, YOU WILL BE JUDGED; and by your standard of

measure, it will be measured to you. 3 Why do you look at the speck that is in your brother's eye, but do not notice the log that is in your own eye? 4 Or how can you say to your brother, 'Let me take the speck out of your eye,' and behold, the log is in your own eye? 5 You hypocrite first take the log out of your own eye, and then you will see clearly to take the speck out of your brother's eye.

The Amplified Classic Version of this passage conveys the meaning most clearly.

Matthew 7:1-5 (AMPC) Do not judge and criticize and condemn others, so that you may not be judged and criticized and condemned yourselves. 2 For just as you judge and criticize and condemn others, you will be judged and criticized and condemned, and in accordance with the measure you use to deal out to others, it will be dealt out again to you.3 Why do you stare from without at the very small particle that is in your brother's eye but do not become aware of and consider the beam of timber that is in your own eye?4 Or how can you say to your brother, Let me get the tiny particle out of your eye, when there is the beam of timber in your own eye? 5 You hypocrite first get the beam of timber out of your own eye, and then you will see clearly to take the tiny particle out of your brother's eye.

We must never be merely critical in the pejorative sense so we can put someone down or make ourselves look better by comparison. The attitude that takes joy in exposing someone as a sinner is a terrible attitude. The "log" that is in the eye of the one who judges may well be the attitude that seeks to condemn people: it is a JUDGMENTAL, CONDEMNATORY, BITTER, HOLIER-THAN-THOU or SELF-CENTERED attitude. It is easy to see this attitude in other people, but it is hard to see it in ourselves. It is NOT the attitude that wants to see a fallen brother repent or a deceived brother return to the truth; it is only interested in "getting" the other guy.

The Lord warns us that if we treat others in that manner, then HE HIMSELF will see to it that we are dealt with in the same way. It is one of the promises of God. IN THE WAY YOU JUDGE, YOU WILL BE JUDGED This Scripture tells us that if we are overly concerned about other people's sins, and are quick to point out their faults, and speak without mercy we are in danger. We can expect to be dealt with in the same manner. The Lord promises that this will happen. Often, the person who condemns others without mercy, finds themselves to be victims of CONDEMNATION from others.

We must understand that if we are concerned about God's holiness and if we are concerned about a brother trapped in sin, we must function with as much mercy as the Lord would allow, and always judge with love for the victim and especially for the Lord Himself. If we correctly show mercy to others, then God will show us mercy. **(Blessed are the merciful, for they shall receive mercy (Matthew 5:7).**

The Scripture, "Do not judge so that you will not be judged" is better translated IN THIS CONTEXT as, "Do not CONDEMN so that you will NOT BE CONDEMNED." Also, if we judge them incorrectly or we lie about them, God Himself will see to it that we are judged incorrectly and are lied about also. A great example of that in our current culture is President Donald Trump. When he was running for office, he falsely accused some of his political opponents. He insulted them, belittled them and made fun of them. Specifically, he insinuated that Carly Fiorina was ugly. He judged by implication in an insulting way that Ted Cruz's wife also lacked good looks. When Ben Carson started to rise in the polls, he implied that on the basis of his testimony concerning an anger issue that Ben overcame as a teenager, he would never recover from that and was unfit for the Presidency. When Ted Cruz became a threat to Trump's presidential aspirations, he implied that Ted's father may have been part of the assassination of President Kennedy.

Much of what Donald Trump said at that point in his life was not the truth: it was FAKE NEWS. Today, in the first three years of his Presidency, God has been dealing severely with President Trump. No man in history has ever been the victim of so much FAKE NEWS. The treatment that he has received at the hands of the Progressive media has been even more cruel than the accusations that President Trump made against his opponents and their families in the primaries. Perhaps if President Trump would publicly repent of the way that he dealt with these individuals and their families while running for the office of President, God would cause less fake news to exist and Donald Trump would receive more honest reporting. It must be noted, however, that George W. Bush, even though he did not incorrectly judge people as Donald Trump has done, when he was President received a great deal of false accusations during his administration, but NOTHING compared to that which Donald Trump has received.

In the way that you judge, you will be judged and BY YOUR STANDARD of measure, it will be measured to you. If you judge with mercy, you will be judged mercifully. If you judge cruelly or dishonestly, you will be judged cruelly or dishonestly. Jesus tells us that we ARE TO JUDGE, but not according to appearances. He says we must JUDGE RIGHTEOUS JUDGMENT.

John 7:24 (KJ21) Judge not ACCORDING TO THE APPEARANCE but judge righteous judgment.

One reason many leaders in our churches do not want to deal with other people's sins is because they do not want their OWN sins to be dealt with. When we go about cleaning up the Body of Christ, we too will be cleaned up and exposed by God. This is NOT a grievous thing to a man who TRULY desires God's holiness in his own life and wants God's will more than his own will. This man KNOWS that God is fully aware of his sins and, if God chooses to expose his sins to others, he is not too concerned because he longs to be holy at any cost. But the admonition by the Lord in chapter 7 of Matthew is to judge as we would like to be judged: with wisdom, love and as much mercy as God would allow, but WHEN NECESSARY, with severity and even public exposure.

Matthew 7:6 (NASB) Do not give what is holy to dogs, and do not throw your pearls before swine, or they will trample them under their feet, and turn and tear you to pieces"

This section deals with TO WHOM we should NOT minister God's precious and holy truth. These are people that make it clear that they hate God and have no interest in hearing anything about Him. They especially hate Jesus Christ and usually despise Christians. This does not mean that they will never get saved. But while they are in this condition, as Saul of Tarsus was when he compelled Christians to blaspheme (Acts 26:11 NASB), they are, at that time, unable to hear and are more dangerous than rabid dogs and starving pigs. Until they are dealt with by God, they cannot hear the truth. In Saul of Tarsus' case, Jesus Christ manifested Himself to Saul at the PERFECT TIME and he was gloriously saved and transformed into the mighty Apostle Paul.

PRAYER AND THE GOLDEN RULE

MATTHEW 7: 7-12 (NASB) Ask, and it will be given to you; seek, and you will find; knock, and it will be opened to you. 8 For EVERYONE WHO ASKS, RECEIVES, and HE WHO SEEKS FINDS, and TO HIM WHO KNOCKS IT WILL BE OPENED. 9 Or what man is there among you who, when his son asks for a loaf, will give him a stone? 10 Or if he asks for a fish, he will not give him a snake, will he? 11 If you then, being evil, know how to give good gifts to your children, how much more will your Father who is in heaven give what is good to those who ask Him! 12 In everything, therefore, TREAT PEOPLE THE SAME WAY YOU WANT THEM TO TREAT YOU, for this is the Law and the Prophets.

This section seems to be an interlude in this great chapter concerning judging. Matthew 7:7-11 is a teaching on prayer and searching for and obtaining things that are of the greatest importance. One of the principles of this teaching is that if earthly sinners will give you what you ask for, how much more likely is it, IF YOU ASK HIM, that an all-righteous, all-holy, all-knowing, all-powerful and all-loving God would give you great gifts concerning the Kingdom of God?

Verse 12 is an exhortation to treat people in the same way that you want to be treated yourself. This is the Golden Rule. This also is a summation of all the law and the prophets. We should all want to be treated in a way that would be best for us and ultimately give us the greatest peace, joy and love that we could possibly have.

These Scriptures in the Sermon on the Mount sum this up with this statement: "IN EVERYTHING, therefore, treat people the same way you want them to treat you." If you want your best desires met and given to you by God, you must live your life to give the best desires of God to everyone that you encounter. It takes a miracle to live the Sermon on the Mount and that miracle can occur as we ask God, seek God and knock on the door of His Kingdom.

This interlude is included in this chapter because it is especially important for us to be able to judge righteous judgment and understand to whom we should listen, to whom we should minister, to whom we should not listen, to whom we should not minister. We need to learn how to evaluate and judge the issues of life and death that are discussed in this chapter IN THE RIGHT SPIRIT.

THE NARROW WAY AND THE BROAD WAY

Matthew 7:13-14 (NASB) Enter through the narrow gate; for the GATE IS WIDE AND THE WAY IS BROAD THAT LEADS TO DESTRUCTION, and there are MANY who enter through it. 14 For the GATE IS SMALL AND THE WAY IS NARROW THAT LEADS TO LIFE, and there are FEW who find it."

Jesus makes it clear that there is a way that seems right to a man but leads to utter and absolute destruction. That is the broad way and the wide gate. That is the way that most people go. FEW there are that find the narrow way and the small gate that leads to life. Most people love to travel on the broad way. It is much more pleasurable, much freer and much easier than the narrow way. The narrow road and narrow gate churches are too restricting for most people.

The narrow way churches may prohibit activities that you love; they will suffocate an individual that loves the broad way and the wide gate. They will stress a holy life, a life that is confined and dictated by the Word of God. A life that is run by an Absolute Ruler: Jesus Christ. The narrow way churches will eventually correct you if you allow fornication in your home and even correct you if you are a gossip! Broad way people consider the narrow way churches to be Intolerant and negative. The broad way churches are much more "realistic". They say that if any correction is necessary, Jesus Himself will tell the offender Himself. They will often say to the narrow road pastor: "Please remember pastor, you are not Jesus! Only Jesus can judge people."

The broad way pastor is always just a little looser in language and application in the broad way churches. He is much more understanding of how easy it is to fall into sin and stay there. His sermons are less critical and much more entertaining than those of the narrow way churches. He is an extremely positive pastor, and seldom torments his sheep with negative teaching. The broad way church and pastor are much more aware of modern psychological discoveries that indicate that you can catch more flies with honey than you can with vinegar. The broad way pastor believes that the best way to change people is to be positive and encourage them, rather than be negative and correct them.

IT HATH BEEN SAID IN THE BROAD WAY CHURCH:

"You must forgive yourself." Forgiving yourself is so much easier than forgiving others. This "forgive yourself" doctrine probably came about in the 20th century with the advent of "Christian" psychology. This teaching is not in Scripture. Only Jesus Christ can forgive your sins and only Jesus Christ can cleanse your heart from sin and bring you peace. Forgiving yourself may be helpful if you are NOT a Christian. If you ARE a Christian and are still plagued with guilt, you should read the Scriptures regarding the forgiveness of God, examine yourself and see if you have judged others too harshly and make sure that you have repented of the sin that costs you your peace. Human forgiveness of yourself is a useless drop of water compared to the vastness of the entire ocean of forgiveness offered by Jesus Christ. Forgiving one's self is a heathen substitute for the true forgiveness that only Jesus Christ can give you. Like other aspects of the broad way mentality, SELF-forgiveness is not mentioned in the Bible. The narrow way of the Lord says: There is no call in the Scriptures to forgive yourself! However, there is a call to forgive all who have sinned against you. If you do so, if you trust in Jesus, you will experience the forgiveness of the Father, which is infinitely more important and comforting than forgiving

yourself. If you do not forgive others their transgressions against you, you will not experience that comfort. Forgiving yourself is a cheap and shoddy SECULAR alternative to forgiving others. If you want to enjoy the joy and peace of the Fathers
forgiveness, you MUST from your heart, forgive those who have sinned against you. If you understand how terribly you have sinned against Jesus Christ, the Holy Spirit and our Heavenly Father, it will be most appropriate and relatively easy to forgive others. The debt we owe Him for causing His Son to suffer the loss of His fellowship with His Father is incalculable. Any affliction we have received from others is minuscule in comparison.

The problem is that the NARROW WAY churches are considered by broad way church goers to be intolerant. They are intolerant of sin and intolerant of Christian literature or ministers that do not take sin seriously. They are much more likely to talk about repentance and obedience to God's Word than the Broad Way Church. The BROAD WAY churches are likely to give a psychological or humanistic solution that focuses on yourself and how YOU FEEL.

Jesus Christ has been telling us what HIS WAY is. He says that the way into His Kingdom is the narrow way. Do we hear and trust the narrow way doctrine or is it broad way doctrine we crave? He says that the way that we live must be NARROW. He warns us that the Road to Destruction is BROAD and many walk this way. He tells us here that WE NEED TO JUDGE WHAT WE HEAR. He says that we must only receive doctrine that opens the narrow gate and leads us on the narrow way. Jesus tells us here to JUDGE AS IF OUR LIFE DEPENDS ON IT because it does! The WAY that we choose to walk upon will determine WHERE WE END UP!

A TREE AND ITS FRUIT

Matthew 7:15-20 (NASB) BEWARE of the false prophets, who come to you in sheep's clothing, but inwardly are ravenous wolves. 16 You will know them by their fruits. Grapes are not gathered from thorn bushes nor from thistles, are they? 17 So EVERY GOOD TREE BEARS GOOD FRUIT, but the bad tree bears bad fruit. 18 A good tree cannot produce bad fruit, nor can a bad tree produce good fruit. 19 Every tree that does not bear good fruit is cut down and thrown into the fire. 20 So then, you will know them by their fruits."

Beware means BE AWARE AND WATCH OUT for danger. It implies that we must be scrupulously careful. He tells us to BEWARE of false prophets. In this section, He tells us WHO to judge. He warns us against prophets and teachers that will lead us to or teach us the broad way which leads to destruction. We must BEWARE of those who supposedly speak for God but don't warn us about danger. We must BEWARE of prophets or teachers that almost ALWAYS have a positive nice word that tickles the flesh but does not minister to our spirit. If they do not teach or prophesy like Jesus, they may well be false ministers. A helpful spiritual exercise would be to get a red-letter edition of the Bible and JUST READ THE WORDS OF JESUS. In the midst of the Words of hope and love, you will see Words of warnings, punishment, and judgment.

We MUST judge these men regarding what they speak and how they act. Jesus warns us NOT to judge by outward appearance. These men are disguised to look like sheep or shepherds. When their heart is exposed, however, it is the heart of a wolf. He tells us to JUDGE the fruit of these men. Are they gentle, loving, selfless, holy, giving men of God who are concerned with the needs of the flock and the will of the Lord? Or are they merely smiling, selfish, impure TAKERS who cater to the desires of the unsuspecting sheep so they can be rich, loved or successful? Are they hungry for God or are they hungry for affection and love from the congregation? Have they married or divorced unscripturally? Are the children they fathered after they were saved walking with the Lord? PLEASE UNDERSTAND their MAY BE mitigating circumstances, but you still must examine them carefully. Jesus tells us we MUST judge or evaluate ministers of the gospel. Again, we judge because our spiritual lives depend on it! We must judge the fruit of their lips and the fruit of their lives. Do they stress the material and the psychological or do they stress the spiritual? Do they encourage people to love themselves and seek comfort or do they encourage people to love Jesus enough to obey Him and love their neighbors as themselves? Do they use the words "mistake" and "addiction" to describe sin? Are they most concerned about having happy, prosperous, comfortable people in their congregation rather than hearing OUR LORD say,

Matthew 25:21 (NASB) Well done, good and faithful slave. You were faithful with a few things; I will put you in charge of many things; ENTER INTO THE JOY OF YOUR MASTER.
Matthew 7:21-23 (NASB) Not everyone who says to Me, "Lord, Lord," will enter the kingdom of heaven, but he who DOES THE WILL OF MY FATHER who is in heaven will enter. 22 MANY will say to Me on that day, "Lord, Lord, did we not prophesy in Your Name, and in Your Name cast out demons, and in Your Name, perform many miracles?" 23 And then I will declare to them, "I NEVER KNEW YOU: depart from Me, YOU WHO PRACTICE LAWLESSNESS."

Jesus warns us not to trust a leader or minister, OR EVEN OURSELVES because of the use of religious terminology, such as, "Lord, Lord". Even if a person apparently or even actually prophesies, casts out demons or does miracles and does it all using the name of the Lord, it does not mean that these gifts are an indication that he has eternal life. We must remember that Balaam prophesied truth but also deceived the people of God. We see the phrase PRACTICE LAWLESSNESS to describe these apparent prophets, exorcists and miracle workers, but because they don't have a love for the law and they don't trust Jesus enough to obey Him, they are JUDGED by Jesus to be phonies and are told to DEPART from Him. We must judge people by the fruit of their obedience to our Lord and the uncompromising narrow way gospel that they walk or teach.

THE TWO FOUNDATIONS

Matthew 7:24-29 NASB. "Therefore, everyone who HEARS THESE WORDS OF MINE AND ACTS ON THEM, may be compared to a wise man who built his house on THE ROCK. 25 And the rain fell, and the floods came, and the winds blew and slammed against that house; and yet it did not fall, for it had been FOUNDED ON THE ROCK. 26 Everyone who hears these words of Mine and DOES NOT ACT ON THEM, WILL BE LIKE A FOOLISH MAN WHO BUILT HIS HOUSE ON THE SAND. 27 The rain fell, and the floods came, and the winds blew and slammed against that house; and it fell—and great was its fall." 28 When Jesus had finished these words, the crowds were amazed at His teaching; 29 for He was teaching them as one having authority, and not as their scribes.

Hearing the Words of Jesus is NOT enough! We must HEED them; we must DO them: WE MUST ACT ON THEM. In this section of Scripture, Jesus Christ is NOT THE ROCK! Clearly, the rock is obedience to or ACTING ON THE WORDS OF JESUS CHRIST. The foolish man, whose house fell, did not obey the Words of Jesus and did not act upon the Words of Jesus (he built his house on the sand). The sand in this illustration is DISOBEDIENCE TO GOD'S WORD: NOT acting on the Words that Jesus spoke. These Scriptures clearly exhort us to judge ourselves and make sure that we are obeying the Words of our Lord Jesus Christ, so that when the storm comes, we will not fall away and suffer destruction. This is not salvation by works; it is the works that James speaks of that are the fruit of real faith.

James 2:17 (NASB) Even so faith, if it has no works, is dead, being by itself. 18... I WILL SHOW YOU MY FAITH BY MY WORKS."

2 Corinthians 13:5 (NASB) Test yourselves to see if you are in the faith; examine yourselves!

The Lord tells us to judge ourselves by our response to His Word. These words at the end of Matthew chapter 7 definitely test us: if we don't act on the Words of Jesus, we face ruination. If we do act on the Words of Jesus and obey Him, when the storms come, our house will stand. Our families will stand; our relationship with Him will stand; we will remain strong even in the most vicious of storms. But we must act on (obey) His Words. Believers WILL believe Him ENOUGH TO OBEY HIM! Phonies DO NOT understand that real faith ultimately has the fruit of obedience to Him and these people will not obey His Words and will suffer the consequences. Jesus tells us to JUDGE ourselves and see if we are mere hearers of His Word that don't obey His Word or DOERS of His Word.

WHO AND WHAT TO JUDGE

1 Corinthians 5:9-11 (NIV) I wrote to you in my letter not to associate with sexually immoral people— 10 not at all meaning the people of this world who are immoral, or the greedy and swindlers, or idolaters. In that case you would have to leave this world. 11 But now I am writing to you that you must not associate with anyone who CLAIMS TO BE A BROTHER OR SISTER but is sexually immoral or greedy, an idolater or slanderer, a drunkard or swindler. Do not even eat with such people.
1 Corinthians 5:12 (NLT). 12 It isn't my responsibility to judge outsiders, but it certainly is YOUR RESPONSIBILITY TO JUDGE THOSE INSIDE THE CHURCH WHO ARE SINNING.

We love to judge people outside of the Church: the secular sinners. We love to judge the adulterers and homosexuals of Hollywood; we judge the progressive politicians who purposefully are weakening the morality and the military of our country; we judge the antichrist ACLU and those who promote LGBTQ propaganda, but God Himself will certainly judge those that don't repent and condemn them to Hell. IT IS NOT OUR RESPONSIBILITY TO JUDGE OUTSIDERS. We, however, are COMPELLED BY SCRIPTURE TO JUDGE THOSE THAT ARE INSIDE THE CHURCH. WE ARE COMPELLED TO JUDGE THOSE THAT CLAIM TO BE CHRISTIANS. If we look at the list of perpetrators with whom we are not to associate in First Corinthians chapter 5:9-12, we see those that we are not to fellowship with those who indulge in sexual sin, or are greedy, idolaters, slanderers, drunkards, or swindlers. We are FORBIDDEN to even eat with such people. We are not only compelled to judge them guilty, but we are compelled to not even eat with them. If they do not claim to be Christians, then we have no need to judge them. As Scripture says, God will judge those on the outside. We are to judge ONLY those on the inside who claim to be Christians. This includes our friends or relatives who claim to be Christians.

WE NEED TO JUDGE OURSELVES

We need to judge ourselves to see if we are hot (fervently alive and in love with Jesus Christ, hungry for holiness and the fullness of His Word and Holy Spirit; on fire for God), or cold (either dead to sin, or it could mean cold and dead to Christ), or LUKEWARM and ready to be vomited out of His mouth. If you know that you are cold and dead in trespasses and sin, it is better than being lukewarm. If you KNOW you are cold and dead in sin, you will be able to find the joy and peace that is in Christ. When you're caught somewhere in the middle and have a self-assurance but no real spiritual fruit in your life, no real hatred of sin, no great hunger for the law of God in your life and no passionate love and desire for the Lord Jesus Christ, then you are likely lukewarm and are in terrible danger. You have been inoculated with a small dose of Jesus: just enough to have you attend church, but not enough to have you repent of your sins and completely trust in His love, His grace, and His forgiveness.

RED HOT CONSEQUENCES

When washing dishes, if you come upon a dish that has been in the kitchen for a long time and has food on it that is stuck, you can't get it out with cold water. You can't even get it out with lukewarm water. You must use extremely hot water to remove the debris. Even if you are washing dishes that are dirty and you're able to get to them quickly, it is still best to use extremely hot water to remove the stains.

So, it is true with sin. You can't remove sin by appealing merely to the Scriptures that say that God loves you. You must use the UNCOMFORTABLE SCRIPTURES, the VERY HOT SCRIPTURES such as "Repent for the kingdom of heaven is at hand!" Sometimes you need to apply Scriptures that warn of punishment or judgment that will surely come if you don't repent quickly. These are HOT, UNCOMFORTABLE SCRIPTURES, but they must be used instead of the friendly Scriptures that speak merely of God's love.

The Lukewarm Church is like Goldilocks. This Church only wants to have the water of the Word that is not too cold nor too hot but is just right. Scriptures that are comfortable and make the person feel good are certainly appropriate and are important to use in their proper place. But these Scriptures are never to be used exclusively. Sometimes, the congregation needs to hear the HOT WORDS OF CORRECTION that cause pain to our flesh. In the Old Testament, teachers that would quote soothing Scriptures when the people needed to repent were classified as FALSE TEACHERS or FALSE SHEPHERDS.

BAND-AID ON A BULLET WOUND

Jeremiah 6:13-14 (NIV) From the least to the greatest, all are GREEDY FOR GAIN, PROPHETS AND PRIESTS ALIKE, all practice deceit. 14 THEY DRESS THE WOUND OF MY PEOPLE AS THOUGH IT WERE NOT SERIOUS. "Peace, peace," they say, WHEN THERE IS NO PEACE...

Jeremiah is speaking about the false teachers in the Old Testament that would look at a terrible wound in the Spirit that someone had suffered because of sin such as idolatry or adultery and the teacher would merely tell the sinner not to worry, after all, he was one of God's chosen people. Treating a serious wound like pornography or worshiping another Jesus as if it were virtually nothing to worry about is a terrible sin. This is putting A BAND-AID ON A BULLET WOUND. This treatment does nothing but give the offending person temporary peace, AND WORSE, FALSE HOPE. We must make doubly sure that we are not in a church that teaches COMFORTABLE SOLUTIONS to sin and ministers' lukewarm words of temporary comfort.

The prostitutes and the tax collectors KNEW they were dead in trespasses and sins; they knew that they needed a physician or a miracle worker to forgive them of their sin, heal the brokenness in their lives caused by unrepented sin and bring them real peace. They knew that JESUS CHRIST was the ONLY PHYSICIAN and miracle worker that could do that.

DIVISION OF THE PURE FROM THE IMPURE

There is great division happening in our country, and the great division also is beginning to happen in the churches. It is like a fountain gushing out of the earth and a stream that comes forth from that fountain. From a distance, the fountain looks relatively clear. When one gets closer to it, one could see debris in the fountain. The fountain contains clods of dirt, tin cans, waste, and garbage – but the debris does not make the water undrinkable, you just need to be careful. Suddenly, the fountain splits and there are two fountains. One of the fountains becomes clearer: with less and less debris and refuse as it continues streaming forth. The other fountain gets more and more filthy until eventually all that comes out of it is a horrible smelling, sludge-like material. Eventually the smelly, sludge-like material just stops, and that fountain runs dry. The stream that gets progressively clearer becomes perfectly clear and this stream floods over everything and even the fountain of filth is swept away. Then the pure stream became an ocean and covers the whole earth.

The single undivided fountain and the stream that came from it is the move of the Holy Spirit on the earth as it existed in the past. One stream has begun to split into two streams, because God is bringing division. There will then be two "apparent" moves in the churches upon the earth. One stream, the stream that becomes progressively purer, will be made up of people who HONESTLY look at the stream of the Holy Spirit in their own lives and in the life of the Church. Those who see the impurities (sins and unscriptural doctrines), and ACKNOWLEDGE, CONFESS AND REPENT OF THEIR OWN SINS will be a part of the move of His Spirit and will become progressively more pure and more like Jesus. The stream that gets dirtier, until it is completely filthy, is made up of people who will NOT acknowledge the impurities (sins and unscriptural doctrines) in their own lives or in the life of the Church. These people will stubbornly choose NOT to let God's Word and God's men JUDGE their hearts and doctrine. They will take the position that they do not need cleansing and that it is not necessary to JUDGE the Church with regards to matters of doctrine or the practices of the leaders and sheep. These people are SATISFIED to remain in their current condition and are confident that God will put this unacknowledged, unrepented sin and carnal ministry "under the Blood". They feel sure that His love will cover their multitude of sins and poor doctrine. These unrepentant, presumptuous people will become progressively more impure until they are totally defiled and the movement that they are involved with will also become totally defiled.

God will raise up men who will expose the filthiness in the Church, both doctrinally and personally. We must listen to these men, but we must make sure that these men are making their judgments from Scripture and not their own imaginations. Those who speak against and mock or IGNORE them are in danger of being part of the FILTHINESSS described above. But all who fall on their faces before God and repent of their terrible carnality and cry out against the abominations that are being committed in His Holy Temple will be spared the filth and the ultimate judgment that follows. In our day, it will be as prophesied by Ezekiel in chapter 9, "The Lord said to him, 'Go through the midst of the city, even through the midst of Jerusalem, and put a mark on the foreheads of the men who sigh and groan over all the abominations which are being committed in its midst.'" And ONLY THESE MEN were spared from the sword of judgment that fell so heavily on God's people.

CONCLUSION OF THE MATTER

Great Deception is both in the world and in the Church. During this time, the enemy has managed to slip into the Church a doctrine of demons which says that JUDGING doctrine, judging teachers and judging the lives of others WILL NOT BE TOLERATED. This is surely one of the greatest deceptions of our age. We NEED TO JUDGE AND BE JUDGED NOW more than ever before! If our lives are out of order with God and His purposes; if our doctrine is not the doctrine of Scripture, we who are members of His body and part of His Kingdom DESPERATELY need to know where we err. We must receive judgment, we must exercise judgment and we must, using the Scriptures, judge the conduct and doctrines of all men and women, especially those who are leaders in the Church. Above all, we must be careful to judge our own lives. If we fail to do so, we are in danger of condemning our children to terrible judgment.

Even if the Church at large in America chooses to continue to fail to judge itself, we can change the course of OUR families and OUR children for generations to come. If we will humble ourselves and have the courage to judge our own lives and the lives of the members of our OWN families and if we will teach our children to judge everything they hear and everything they speak and everything they do on the basis of Scripture, we can prepare them for a life filled with righteousness, peace, and joy in the Holy Spirit.

CHAPTER 10: LAWLESSNESS IN THE TEMPLE OF GOD

Could These Really Be the Last Days?
Why the Lord May Return Quickly
Nothing They Desire Will be Impossible
Knowledge Shall be Increased
The Man of Lawlessness
Relation of Faith and Works
The Terrible Fruit of Lawlessness
Obeying and Enjoying God's Laws
Conclusion

COULD THESE REALLY BE THE LAST DAYS?

Many evangelical and charismatic Christians today believe that these are the last days. Whether that means that there are 100 days left, 100 years left, 1000 years left, or 10,000 years left, no one really knows. The Last Days that were spoken of by Peter started on the day of Pentecost.

> **Acts 2:16-17 (KJ21). 1 This is that** *(that which occurred on the Day of Pentecost)* **which was spoken by the prophet Joel: 2 and it shall come to pass in THE LAST DAYS, saith God, I will pour out my Spirit upon all flesh..."**
> Hebrews 1:1-2 (KJ21) says, "God...hath in THESE LAST DAYS spoken unto us by His Son..."

In the context of these two verses, the last days started during the time the New Testament was written. We may have less than 200 years or more than 10.000 years until Jesus returns. Looking at the following facts about today, it could be closer to 200 years than 10,000 years.

WHY THE LORD MAY RETURN QUICKLY

The Jews are back in the land. This is one of the greatest miracles in history and it seems that the end of days cannot happen if the Jews are not back in their land. They speak the same language they did 2000 years ago. They are surrounded by enemies as they have been for most of their existence. These enemies seem hell-bent on destroying them, but they have survived wars and even a cataclysmic Holocaust. Through many quirks of fate and the power of God, Israel once again has a friend in the United States. America doesn't need to survive for Jesus to return, but Israel will exist when He comes back.

NOTHING THEY DESIRE WILL BE IMPOSSIBLE

In the book of Genesis, God confused the language of the people and scattered them throughout the earth.

Genesis 11:5-9 (NLT) But the Lord came down to look at the city and the tower the people were building. 6 "Look!" He said. 'The people are united, and they all speak the same language. After this, NOTHING THEY SET OUT TO DO WILL BE IMPOSSIBLE FOR THEM! 7 Come, LET'S GO DOWN and confuse the people with different languages. Then they won't be able to understand each other.' 8 In that way, the Lord scattered them all over the world, and they stopped building the city. 9 That is why the city was called Babel, because that is where the Lord confused the people with different languages. In this way he scattered them all over the world.'"

The people reached the point where they were on the verge of being capable of doing ANYTHING they imagined. God said that this must be stopped. This disturbed Him to such an extent that He decided to destroy their unity by confusing their languages and from the Tower of Babel the people were scattered throughout the whole world.

We are fast reaching the point where we will be able to do VIRTUALLY ANYTHING WE IMAGINE OR DESIRE. Because man is a fallen creature who is more controlled by Satan than by God, God may well need to step in once again. This time, He will likely purify, perfect and empower His church to thoroughly defeat Satan and his realm and then pour out His wrath on those that are not of His Kingdom .

Other indications that this could well be the last days is the phenomenal leap in knowledge that we have seen over the last 75 years.

KNOWLEDGE SHALL BE INCREASED

Daniel 12:4 (KJ21) "But thou oh Daniel, shut up the Words and seal the book, even to THE TIME OF THE END. Many shall run to and fro, and KNOWLEDGE SHALL BE INCREASED."

The TIME OF THE END is different than the Last Days. During the Renaissance, knowledge began to greatly increase, but with the advent of computers, the microchip, and the world wide web, knowledge has increased EXPONENTIALLY! The emergence of the Internet in the 20th century has been even more profound and world-shaking than was the emergence of the movable type printing press in Europe in the 15th century. The Renaissance was strengthened by this printing press and eventually became a world-changing movement that enabled men of like minds to get together and accomplish great things in their respective pursuits. The movable type printing press was the platform for the Reformation that started in 1517. It allowed the Scriptures to flourish and spread as never before. In many countries, the Bible was translated from the Greek and Hebrew languages into the language of the people. The Roman Catholic Church only printed Bibles in Latin. Few people, even in the Catholic Church we're able to read Latin. But, with the new technology, Bibles were printed in the language of the Protestant nations.

Unfortunately, WISDOM has decreased! Today, we have available even more powerful tools than the printing press. We have EVERYTHING that we will need to know about ANYTHING WE WANT TO STUDY, including the SCRIPTURES. We have the POTENTIAL PLATFORM to reconstruct the Church into an even more powerful and pure fighting machine than ever before. When Jesus does come back, He will come back to a Church that is ready for Him. Conversely, the enemy can use that same platform to pervert, weaken, or destroy the people of God that are WEAK in the Scriptures.

Ephesians 2:8 (NASB) For BY GRACE you have been saved THROUGH FAITH; and that NOT OF YOURSELVES, it is the gift of God.

For about 1,200 years, the world did not hear the Gospel of grace. The Roman Catholic Church added many requirements to the grace of God through faith. They believed it was most important to live according to the traditions and teachings of The Roman Catholic Church. They also believed that one had to abide by the ex-cathedra words of the pope. The Reformation led by Martin Luther in 1517, exposed these additions as being unscriptural and untrue. The Roman Catholic Church essentially believed and still believes in a GRACELESS GOSPEL.

THE MAN OF LAWLESSNESS
2 Thessalonians 2:3-4 (NASB) Let no one in any way deceive you, FOR IT

***(THE COMING OF OUR LORD JESUS)* WILL NOT COME UNLESS THE APOSTASY COMES FIRST, and the MAN OF LAWLESSNESS is revealed, the son of destruction, 4 who opposes and exalts himself above every so-called god or object of worship, so that he takes his seat in the temple of God, DISPLAYING HIMSELF AS BEING GOD.**

Across the face of planet earth, we see the apostasy taking place. In the last year, even in America, we have seen people renounce Jesus Christ and Christianity and join with Satan. Also, many Christians are painfully aware of a horrible being that will inhabit the last days. The Bible describes him in the NASB and NIV as the MAN OF LAWLESSNESS in 2 Thessalonians 2:3. In the same verse in the KJV, he is described as THE MAN OF SIN. It really makes no difference because the Bible equates sin with lawlessness:

1 John 3:4 (NASB) Whoever commits sin also commits lawlessness, and SIN IS LAWLESSNESS.

Our real enemy in the last days is THE MAN OF LAWLESSNESS and THE SPIRIT OF LAWLESSNESS that presently haunts evangelical and charismatic churches. And consequently, our country! Today, our real enemy is the one who peddles CHEAP GRACE, CHEAP HOLINESS and a LAWLESS GOSPEL. The enemy of our salvation is perfectly satisfied to have us "confess Jesus Christ as our personal Savior" but not desire to be holy or obedient to God's law. The enemy wants us to think if we DESIRE TO BE OBEDIENT to God, that is enough. But we never need to actually BE OBEDIENT. The enemy wants us to believe that we DON'T NEED to obey the law of God if we believe in Jesus and accept Him as our personal Savior. He wants us to believe that obedience to the law is LEGALISM.

When the grace of God is given to a believer by God's grace through faith, it is never merely a verbal confession that does not come from the heart. The seeker NEVER casually accepts Jesus Christ as his personal Savior. It is God's grace that enables him to cry out in repentance and plea for His forgiveness! It is God's grace that causes him to be born again and become a new creature who loves Him and His Word more than he loves himself. It is God's grace that gives him a love for His Scriptures. It is God's grace that invites him to humble himself, seek His presence, pray and turn from his wicked ways. And it most certainly is God's grace to see the land of His people healed and empowered to TURN THE WORLD UPSIDE DOWN.

Real faith is an attitude of hopelessness in any salvation outside of Jesus Christ. Real faith ESPECIALLY does not rely upon the merits of the seeker of salvation. Real faith always brings repentance to the heart of the seeker and a genuine sorrow for their sin. Real faith trusts God to accept and forgive them EXCLUSIVELY based on His love and the sacrifice of Jesus Christ on the cross. What's equally important is, that real faith produces hatred for sin and a deep dissatisfaction of remaining in sin. Real faith will always generate a cry from the heart that will always be heard and answered by God. Real faith causes us to now have THE POWER to trust, love, and OBEY GOD AND HIS LAW.

RELATION OF FATH AND WORKS

Simply put, taking the New Testament in its totality, we are NEVER justified by works of the law , AND, REAL FAITH always has the fruit of GOOD WORKS.

Galatians 2:16 (NASB) Nevertheless knowing that A MAN IS NOT JUSTIFIED BY THE WORKS OF THE LAW but through faith in Christ Jesus, even we have believed in Christ Jesus, so that we may be justified by faith in Christ and not by the works of the Law; SINCE BY THE WORKS OF THE LAW NO FLESH WILL BE JUSTIFIED.

James 2:17-18,24,26 (NASB) Even so FAITH, IF IT HAS NO WORKS, IS DEAD, being by itself. 18 But someone may well say, "You have faith and I have works; show me your faith without the works, and I will show you my FAITH BY MY WORKS." 24 You see that a man is JUSTIFIED BY WORKS AND NOT BY FAITH ALONE. 26 For just as the body without the spirit is dead, so also FAITH WITHOUT WORKS IS DEAD.

REAL FAITH WILL ALWAYS PRODUCE REAL WORKS of the law. Real faith loves his neighbor like himself. Real faith loves God. Real faith repents of sin because real faith hates sin. REAL faith will be manifested in all of God's REAL children by REAL works of the law. Without REAL works, faith is REALLY DEAD. FAKE faith cannot possibly produce ANYTHING good. But FAKE FAITH can smile beautifully, tell GREAT jokes and a good story. FAKE FAITH cab be ENTERTAINING! FAKE FAITH also can be stern and SERIOUS and sound holy and even know the Scriptures: but fake faith will NEVER weep over the sins of the church and will fail to walk a truly Holy life.

The lawless spirit will always encourage preachers to preach that real faith doesn't need to have any good works. Real faith will ALWAYS have the FRUIT of obeying God and doing GOOD WORKS. Remember, the man of lawlessness and those who follow him HAVE NO REAL FAITH because they are not born again.

Hebrews 11:8 (NASB) says, …by FAITH Abraham when he was called, OBEYED by going out to a place which he was to receive for an inheritance; and he went out, not knowing where he was going.

Because Abraham had REAL faith, he walked in real SACRIFICIAL obedience to the Word of God.

Matthew 23:28 (NASB) So you, too, Scribes and Pharisees outwardly APPEAR RIGHTEOUS to men, but inwardly you are FULL OF HIPPOCRACY and LAWLESSNESS.

Often, religious people can appear to be most holy and most righteous and even teach and preach some truths that reflect the Holy Scriptures. But often, since the 20th century, we have discovered that many of these religious teachers and preachers were guilty of everything from adultery and homosexuality to great greed and many are much more interested in enjoying the pleasures of this world than laying up treasures in heaven. They look righteous, they often sound righteous, but they have been filled with HYPOCRISY AND LAWLESSNESS.

THE TERRIBLE FRUIT OF LAWLESSNESS

Matthew 24:12 (NASB) 12 Because LAWLESSNESS IS INCREASED, most people's love will grow cold.

When lawlessness increases in the Church of Jesus Christ, we begin to lose our love for other people and for God. We focus on ourselves and what we can gain. We become materialistic and greatly increase our love for money. Instead of merely helping the poor, we help them only if we make a huge income from that ministry or we can appear righteous before men. We shower our excess on ourselves and build up for ourselves treasures on the earth. Instead of sacrificing for our children and their growth in Jesus Christ, we often sacrifice our children for the growth of our own wealth and pleasure. We don't invest our time in teaching them the Word of God and keeping them from being indoctrinated by the world. We love the world and what it offers us more than we love God and we invest our time and blessing on ourselves and our children with the treasures of the world and not the treasures of the Kingdom.

If we become practitioners of lawlessness and lawlessness becomes part of our life and we blithely depend upon the grace of God to save us in spite of our lawless lives, we are likely to share the fate of those who are Christians In Name Only (CHRINOS):

Matthew 13:41 (NASB) The Son of Man will send forth His angels, and they will gather OUT OF HIS KINGDOM ALL STUMBLING BLOCKS, and those who COMMIT LAWLESSNESS.

All who embrace lawlessness will be summarily purged from the Kingdom of God and will never be able to partake of the glories and joy that He has prepared for those that love righteousness and hate lawlessness. We must seriously consider how dangerous are all the platitudinous statements that tempt us to dismiss our shame and cast aside our concern about our sin. If you don't love the law of God and sacrifice to keep it, it is not true that God loves you just the way you are.

OBEYING AND ENJOYING GOD'S LAWS

Psalm 119 is the longest chapter in the Bible. God chose this marvelous chapter to teach us about the Word of God and the law of God. No other teaching in the Bible praises the law of God, the Word of God, the Words of God, the statutes of God, the commandments of God, the precepts of God, the ordinances of God and the testimonies of God more than this Psalm does. Time and again, it emphasizes the fact that those who obey God and follow His instructions will be mightily blessed by God and those who either ignore or disobey them will be punished by God. We must be quick to defend and incorporate into our own lives these words from Psalm 119 (NASB).

In this Psalm, His law is mentioned 25 times, His Word 36 times, His Words 6 times, His precepts 21 times, His statutes 22 times, His ordinances 16 times, His testimonies 22 times, His testimony 1 time, His commandments 21 times and His commandment 1 time. The following are some examples from this chapter. ALL but verse 70 come from the NASB.,

Psalm 119:18 OPEN MY EYES, that I may behold wonderful things from YOUR LAW. Psalm 119:34 GIVE ME UNDERSTANDING, THAT I MAY OBSERVE YOUR LAW and keep it with all my heart.

These two Scriptures are examples of the psalmist praying that God would enlighten him so that he would be able to clearly see and obey God's law from his heart. So many of our prayers are to obtain either relief from pain or receive material blessing or secular success. The best prayers are the prayers that will increase our ability to communicate with, obey, and love the Lord and His law more fervently.

Psalm 119:61 The cords of the wicked have encircled me, but I HAVE NOT FORGOTTEN YOUR LAW.
Psalm 119:85 The arrogant have dug pits for me, MEN WHO ARE NOT IN ACCORD WITH YOUR LAW.
Psalm 119:51 The arrogant utterly deride me, yet I DO NOT TURN ASIDE FROM YOUR LAW.

These Scriptures are great examples for us to understand that even though we will be threatened and experience great pain from the world, WE NEVER NEED TO TURN FROM GOD'S LAW.

Psalm 119:53 BURNING INDIGNATION HAS SEIZED ME BECAUSE OF THE WICKED, WHO FORSAKE YOUR LAW.

Rather than be tolerant of wicked people, we should be like the psalmist and be disgusted with the wicked, particularly when they flaunt their hatred and disobedience towards the law of God. Even Jesus Christ expressed indignation with the moneychangers and the Pharisees.

Psalm 119:70 (NIV) Their heart is callous and unfeeling, but I DELIGHT IN YOUR LAW.
Psalm 119:1 How blessed are those whose way is blameless, who WALK IN THE LAW OF THE LORD.

CONCLUSION

Even though other people, even churchgoing people, can be uncaring, unfeeling and callous about the law of God, we can still be like the psalmist. He was blessed and DELIGHTED IN THE LAW OF THE LORD. If we are born again from above, if we are new creatures in Christ, if we are believers who are expecting eternity with Jesus Christ, it seems impossible that we would do anything else but LOVE THE LAW OF GOD! THE LORD GAVE US HIS LAW FOR HIS GLORY AND OUR GOOD!

Even if the Church in America clings to a cheap grace and does not feel they need the fruit of obedience to God's law, you can make sure that YOUR FAMILY is taught the Scriptures regarding the relationship between the grace of God and the works of the law. You can make sure that YOU PREPARE YOUR CHILD-

REN for the incredible benefits that await those who obey God's law from their heart and for His glory. In the midst of a heathen culture, God chose Abraham because he would teach his family and his household to obey the laws of God (Genesis 18:19). The blessings that were there for Abraham and his family are still there for us and our families!

CHAPTER 11: GRIEVE AND LAMENT FOR THE SINS OF THE CHURCH

Introduction
God's Law and How Terrible is Sin
Old Testament Reveals Lessons for Today
Grieve and Lament for Sins of God's People
 READ Ezekiel 9:1-10 VERY CAREFULLY
Could these Scriptures Apply to Us?

INTRODUCTION

We have become a Church that excuses and ignores sin. We redefine sin as, "missing the mark," and refer to pornography as an "addiction." We minimize sin and even go so far as to rename sin in either medical or psychological terms, so we don't need to feel guilty about our sin. If one is addicted to something, he has a psychological problem. God, however, says that our problems before Him are not psychological. They are spiritual problems and can only be eradicated by the blood of Jesus Christ through our acknowledgment that they are sins and REPENTANCE. Breaking the law of God is exceedingly grievous to Him.

One clever way to minimize sin is to use the original languages in a way that helps us justify a much weaker meaning. The handling of the word hamartano is a good example. Gary Shogren in OPEN OUR EYES, LORD, says the following:

"Have you ever been told that the word for sin literally means 'missing the mark' in the original Greek? In fact, it does not. The verb "hamartano" was sometimes used in pre-Classical and Classical Greek to refer to missing a target... More generally it meant, 'to do wrong, err or sin' (see Liddell, Scott and Jones, abbrev. LSJ). By the time they were writing the New Testament, the average reader would not have heard the word as 'miss the mark', unless he or she was thinking about Homer's Iliad, written 800 years earlier. To import the use of the word from spear throwing to theology...to say that sin is literally 'to miss the mark' is about as useful as saying 'a hair comb is literally the top of a rooster's head'. It gives no help and is misleading." [20]

This is a great example of men using their Hebrew hammer or their Greek wrench to pound and twist the meaning of a word or phrase in such a way that conveys a much softer meaning that would please our culture than would the real meaning of a word. We love God's grace, but we do not like the law of God. We refer to strict enforcement of the law of God as LEGALISM. Also, we no longer teach about the painful consequences of breaking God's law. In the Church today we are working hard to make sin disappear from our vocabulary, our theology, and from our minds and hearts.

We are most scrupulous to avoid using the word S-I-N. To say that people sin is offensive, rather, we refer to the "mistakes" that people make and are quick to note that "nobody is perfect."

We must never call sin a disease, a mistake, or an addiction. GOD CAN NEVER FORGIVE A DISEASE, A MISTAKE, OR EVEN A PSYCHOLOGICAL ADDICTION. HE ONLY FORGIVES SIN. Sin may develop into spiritual bondage; sin may arise because of demonic attack or demonization. But we must never imply that the sinner is merely sick or in need of psychological counseling, psychiatric intervention or help from one of Oprah Winfrey's friends. Jesus never used half measures or worldly philosophy in dealing with the sins of the Scribes and Pharisees or even His own disciples. We must never minimize our own sin by pointing out that we have low self-esteem because of the way that we were raised. Even though people may have treated us badly, we can never blame them for our sin. We must concentrate and own the sin that we commit. Then we can acknowledge that sin, repent of that sin, be forgiven for that sin and be delivered from that sin. We can never argue that the reason we don't love Him is because our fathers or mothers never loved us. All our modern psychological defenses must come down. For Christians who need help, psychology and psychiatry are not healing arts: they are, as was mentioned before, only putting a BAND-AID ON A BULLET WOUND. They cover the DANGEROUS INFECTION, but the infection remains. MOST of our behavioral problems are spiritual. Scientific and psychological solutions, for the most part, are ideas that the enemy uses to destroy the concept of sin, our need to confess and repent of our sin, and our ability to receive His forgiveness and cleansing. Can we possibly avoid judgment when we MAKE SIN RARE AND VIRTUALLY HARMLESS?

We no longer are taught to be ashamed of our sin; we no longer are taught that sin brings painful consequences to our lives and the lives of those we touch; we no longer allow negative, offensive, or even corrective teaching into our assemblies. We talk about positional righteousness and explain that God NEVER judges us on the basis of what we do. Many believe that our sin and even the penalty for our sin was judged and satisfied on the cross and we need not worry about judgment or punishment. If we read the Scriptures carefully, we can see that God definitely chastens or punishes His people whom He loves and also, if they don't repent, HE WILL JUDGE THE HELL OUT OF THEM.

We seldom pray about the sins of the Church and if we do criticize the Church, we are careful to only criticize the crazy Pentecostals and the greedy televangelists that beg for money. We NEVER judge the moderate establishment evangelical church. Typically, we concentrate on the sins of our enemies in the world. We are rightfully concerned about the explosion of homosexuality, lesbianism and other perverse sexual sins in America, but we marginalize pornography's violation of our bodies, which are the temples of the Holy Spirit. We pollute the temple of the Holy Spirit with thoughts and experiences that are abominable to God and slough off our bondage to sin as a psychological problem or addiction. We no longer view our bondage to sin as offensive to God. We no longer believe that WE could possibly GRIEVE THE HOLY SPIRIT OF GOD! How can we possibly avoid judgment when we don't even grieve and lament over the abominable sin of unscriptural divorces in our churches, which God says typically leads to adultery? This abominable spirit of unscriptural divorce injures parents and children alike.

GOD'S LAW AND HOW TERRIBLE IS SIN

Romans 7:12-13 (AMPC) The Law therefore is holy, and EACH COMMANDMENT IS HOLY AND JUST AND GOOD.13 Did that which is good then prove fatal, bringing death to me? Certainly not! It was sin, working death in me by using this good thing as a weapon, in order that through the Commandment sin might be shown up clearly to be sin, that THE EXTREME MALIGNITY AND IMMEASURABLE SINFULNESS OF SIN might plainly appear.

1 John 3:4 (NASB) Sin is the TRANSGRESSION OF THE LAW.

As was mentioned earlier, some pastors and many modern commentaries define sin to be merely "missing the mark." The Bible says in the New Testament that sin is THE TRANSGRESSION OF THE LAW. The law of God in Scripture is not there to just make us feel guilty; rather it is there so we can see how WRETCHED AND TERRIBLE OUR SINS ARE IN GOD'S EYES and show us how important it is to repent quickly and avoid being punished by God. The law is there to allow us to be closer to Him in fellowship when we turn from sin.

OLD TESTAMENT REVEALS LESSONS FOR TODAY

1 Corinthians 10:1-11 (NLT) DON'T WANT YOU TO FORGET about our ancestors in the wilderness long ago. All of them were guided by a cloud that moved ahead of them, and all of them walked through the sea on dry ground.

2 In the cloud and in the sea, all of them were baptized as followers of Moses. 3 All of them ate the same spiritual food, 4 and all of them drank the same spiritual water. For they drank from the spiritual rock that traveled with them, and that rock was Christ. 5 yet God was not pleased with most of them, and THEIR BODIES WERE SCATTERED IN THE WILDERNESS. 6 These things happened as a WARNING TO US, so we would not crave evil things as they did, 7 or worship idols as some of them did. As the Scriptures say, "The people celebrated with feasting and drinking, and they indulged in pagan revelry." 8 And we must not engage in sexual immorality as some of them did, causing 23,000 of them to die in one day. Nor should we put Christ to the test, as some of them did and then died from snake bites. 10 And DON'T GRUMBLE as some of them did, and then were destroyed by the angel of death. 11 These things happened to them as examples for us. THEY WERE WRITTEN DOWN TO WARN US WHO LIVE AT THE END OF THE AGE.

This section of Scripture, containing quotes from the Old Testament Scriptures, was written by the Apostle Paul, to remind us how important it is to learn from the LESSONS OF THE PAST. It is important for us in America in the 21st century to accept this warning and carefully judge ourselves and the Church in America to see if the warning could apply to us. If we fail to do so, and are guilty of sexual immorality, grumbling against God, worshiping another Jesus or putting Christ to the test, then we are in danger of terrible judgment by God. We must even magnify the judgment of the Israelites on the basis that the light that God has given us. Our light is much greater than the light that the Jews of Israel and Jerusalem had. We have access to the Holy Scriptures and many scriptural aids to help us understand the Holy Scriptures. And if we are truly His, we have experienced the mightiest miracle of all: THE NEW BIRTH!

Today, most of the evangelists, pastors, and teachers in the Church of Jesus Christ in America are likely to dismiss negative messages. They particularly abhor messages that proclaim, prophesy, or predict judgment for God's people because of their displeasing, lukewarm lives. If this army of positive pastors, teachers and evangelists is right, then we have nothing to worry about. If this multitude of ministers is wrong and the minority of meddlesome men is right, then, we in the Church need to REPENT DEEPLY AND QUICKLY so that we don't experience a fate similar to the disastrous fate of those who perished in the wilderness. We must also remember that all but two (Joshua and Caleb) of the people that were 20 years of age or older did not survive to enter into the promised land. Joshua and Caleb, who were both over 20, continued to trust God.

It is also clear that these two men didn't grumble, they didn't worship idols, they didn't celebrate with feasting and drinking and indulge in sexual immorality and pagan revelry. They didn't put Christ to the test. and they DIDN'T GET JUDGED and they were able to enter the promised land!

Joshua and Caleb understood how important it was not to sin against God. They understood how important it was not to complain about the difficulty and blame others for their troubles, but to trust God and do what He said. They knew that God viewed sin to be exceedingly sinful and how important it was for His people to avoid sin.

GRIEVE AND LAMENT FOR SINS OF GOD'S PEOPLE

We must also take special note of the Scriptures in Ezekiel chapter 9. For scores of years prophets had warned the city of Jerusalem and the tribe of Judah that judgment was coming if they didn't repent. Most of the people denied that there was a real need for repentance because they were doing just fine. They were satisfied with what was going on in their places of worship. Many felt secure in the fact that they were the children of Abraham. Many of their priests and prophets proclaimed that because they were God's people, He would protect them, and they needn't worry about punishment from Him or even a disastrous attack from the enemies of God. Only a few meddlesome men disturbed their peace with warnings of God's impending judgment.

Ezekiel chapter 9 was likely written right before the time that the Jews of Jerusalem were severely judged. There's a principle here that shows us that we can avoid the terrible judgment that most of the people suffer when the righteous judgment of God strikes the people of God.US

READ EZEKIEL 9:1-10 (NABRE) VERY CAREFULLY!

EZEKIEL 9:1-10 (NABRE) Then He, the Lord, cried aloud for me to hear: Come, you scourges (executioners NASB) of the city! 2 And there were six men coming from the direction of the upper gate which faces north, each with a weapon of destruction in his hand. In their midst was a man dressed in linen, with a scribe's case at his waist. They entered and stood beside the bronze altar. 3 Then the glory of the God of Israel moved off the cherub and went up to the threshold of the temple. He called to the man dressed in linen with the scribe's case at his waist, 4 And the lord said to him: Pass through the city, through the midst of Jerusalem, and MARK AN X *(literally the Hebrew letter TAW)* on the foreheads of THOSE WHO GRIEVE AND LAMENT OVER ALL THE ABOMINATIONS PRACTICED WITHIN IT. 5 To the others he said in my

hearing: Pass through the city after him and strike! Do not let your eyes spare; **DO NOT TAKE PITY. 6 OLD AND YOUNG, MALE AND FEMALE, WOMEN AND CHILDREN—WIPE THEM OUT! But DO NOT TOUCH ANYONE MARKED WITH THE X** *(TAW)*. **Begin at my sanctuary.** So, they began with the elders who were in front of the temple. **7 Defile the temple, he said to them, fill its courts with the slain. Then go out and strike in the city. 8 As they were striking, I was left alone. I fell on my face, crying out, "Alas, Lord GOD! Will you destroy all that is left of Israel when you pour out your fury on Jerusalem?" 9 He answered me: the guilt of the house of Israel and the house of Judah is too great to measure; the land is filled with bloodshed, the city with LAWLESSNESS. They think that the Lord has abandoned the land and that He does not see them do their evil. 10 My eye, however, will NOT SPARE, NOR SHALL I TAKE PITY, but I WILL BRING THEIR CONDUCT DOWN UPON THEIR HEADS.**

Even though Jerusalem had already been dealt with severely by God many times in the past, there came a time when they were going to experience unmerciful judgment from God. Death and destruction were going to rain on these people. The standard that God used for who was to be destroyed and who was to be spared was very simple: the ones that generally did not notice anything wrong with God's people and the leadership of God's people WERE NOT SPARED. But there was a REMNANT that was spared! The only ONES THAT WERE SPARED TERRIBLE JUDGMENT were the ones that GRIEVED AND LAMENTED OVER THE ABOMINATIONS THAT WERE COMMITTED IN THE TEMPLE OF GOD AND IN THE CITY OF JERUSALEM. God told the man clothed in linen to put a mark on the foreheads and spare ONLY those who grieved and lamented over the sins that were committed in the dwelling place of God (Jerusalem and the Temple of God).

COULD THESE SCRIPTURES APPLY TO US?

It is of utmost importance for us to carefully assess what is going on in the Church of Jesus Christ in America today. We as individuals and as a Corporate Body are the dwelling place of God. Are there ANY or MANY detestable things done in the temples and households of God? Do we desire and demand holiness from the pulpit or do we demand entertainment and a gospel of comfort and compromise?

Why don't we hear grieving and lamenting from pulpits all over the country? Countless millions of Christian men and women are DEFILING their own bodies, which are the temples of God with pornography. The divorce rate in the Church is almost equal to the divorce rate in the secular community. We have sacrificed portions of the Word of God, so we wouldn't offend sinners in the Church or even people seeking salvation by mentioning that repentance of sin is necessary. Some have sacrificed their children by unscriptural divorce that breaks their hearts AND the heart of God Himself. Some have sacrificed true worship and a strong Word from the pulpit and replaced it with inoffensive entertaining worship and entertaining sermons that would be funny if they weren't sacrificing holiness and true faith. Whereas in Judah and Israel most believed that because God had forsaken them, He no longer could see the sins they committed, many in the Church think and teach that because viewers of pornography are Christians, when the Lord looks at them, HE DOES NOT SEE THEIR SIN, but only sees His son Jesus Christ.

We are the most entertained congregations in history! Once again, remember the words of Charles Spurgeon in the 19th century, **"A TIME WILL COME WHEN INSTEAD OF SHEPHERDS FEEDING THE SHEEP, THE CHURCH WILL HAVE CLOWNS ENTERTAINING THE GOATS."**

Do we worship the REAL Jesus who manifested both gentle love and tough love, or do we worship ANOTHER JESUS who is merely a soft-spoken, easy-going, inoffensive teacher of "love" with a good sense of humor? We have diluted the fear of the Lord with the words of men. We MUST cultivate a fear of the Lord that the unmarked Jews of Ezekiel's time lacked AND We must be careful about the attitudes of our hearts towards sin.

If we don't do so, judgment WILL come to God's people and ONLY those who weep and moan FROM THEIR HEARTS will be spared His judgment. We must vigorously warn the Church about the terrible events that will destroy those that are not marked by God. Revelation 9:4 (AMP) says that the locusts that God sent to judge the earth were told not to harm the grass of the earth or any plant or tree but, to hurt only those people WHO DID NOT HAVE THE SEAL (OR MARK) OF GOD on their foreheads.

Was the time when Ezekiel wrote this warning the only time in history that God dealt SO SEVERELY with a Jewish or Christian city, country or denomination? NO! In the last 100 years, we see many examples of a church or a denomination in countries that received similar terrible judgments from the Lord. In previous chapters, it was noted that the churches and the nations that did not accept Reformation theology, namely the Roman Catholics and Eastern Orthodox countries, were judged by God using the Nazis and the Communists.

As in the temple of Jerusalem during the time of Ezekiel, the first ones punished in these churches were the elders: pastors and other leaders. Then, many of the church members of these Eastern Orthodox Churches were killed by their new Communist leaders. In Cuba, many Roman Catholic priests and parishioners alike that worshiped Mary, the saints, and essentially worshiped ANOTHER JESUS were likewise dealt with by death and imprisonment.

Is it possible that God could do the same thing to ANY church or any people in a church that did not grieve and lament over the abominable sins that were being done in that church? EVEN the Church in America? In the New Testament, God judges the lukewarm Laodicean Church, so that the members of the Church could see clearly how corrupt they were. God said they had to buy eye salve with gold REFINED IN THE FIRE. This Church believed that they were rich and needed nothing, but He judged them to be wretched, miserable, poor, BLIND and naked. They were completely blind to their sinful attitudes and sinful deeds. They were incapable of grieving and lamenting for their sin because they simply could not see it. The Church of Jesus Christ in America in the 21st century IS NOT immune to such a terrible judgment of God. We have more Bibles and study resources in our homes, libraries and on the Internet than any people in history; yet we STILL have chosen to reject the clear intent of Scripture. We edit the Bible to satisfy our carnal natures and our current culture. God is CERTAINLY justified in judging us AS SEVERELY as He judged Jerusalem during the time of Ezekiel BECAUSE WE HAVE MORE LIGHT available to us.

During Ezekiel's time, there were men and women who mourned and grieved over the abominations that were committed in the temple and in the city. WE CAN BE THAT PEOPLE IN THE 21ST CENTURY AMERICAN CHURCH. Probably we would be few and most certainly we would be branded as legalistic, Puritanical, and lacking in the grace of God. Possibly we would be ostracized and even suffer physical death. But if we sincerely mourn and lament because of the terribly sinful condition of the Church in America today we would please God. Perhaps, like Josiah we would be spared the most horrific aspects of the judgment. We and our families certainly would not experience the ultimate spiritual results that condemn so many to hell. Those that do not see any need to grieve and mourn over the condition of the Church are in many cases willfully blind. The remnant may suffer physical death and even great pain, but if we suffer because we have been counted worthy to suffer for His Name (Acts 5:41), we will fill His heart with joy and love. Is there ANY greater reward in all the universe?

SECTION 4: ENEMIES LIST

CH 12: KNOWING THE ENEMY
CH 13: HAPPY MEALS FROM HELL FOR COMFORT CLUB CHRISTIANS
CH 14: WE MUST FIGHT HARDER THAN HELL

When fighting a war, one must understand who your real friends are and who are your real enemies. You must know how your enemies fight. During the Reformation in Western Europe, it was hard for people to see the Roman Catholic Church as the enemy. Most had been baptized by the local parish priest. Many had a great fondness for Mary, the mother of our Lord, and many had a sincere respect for the Saints and prayed to them for help. They believed in and loved the traditions of the Church and accepted them as gospel truth. They revered the pope as the earthly manifestation of Jesus Christ. It took great courage and deep insight to see that much they were taught was not Scripture and, in fact, contradicted Scripture. When the reformers came and pointed them to the Word, most could not accept the truth that the Catholic Church went beyond or ignored the Word and twisted the Word to fit their doctrine.

Some of the same practices and doctrines that infected the Roman Catholic Church also affected cults that sprung up later. The Mormon Church replaced the pope with a false prophet that led the Church and was able to speak for God and update doctrine periodically. These "Latter Day Saints" even had a supposedly brand-new book from God, The Book of Mormon. They believed that men could have 40 or 50 wives and Jesus Christ was the brother of Satan.

Today, these most dangerous cults have even subtly affected our modern lukewarm churches. The entertainment industry, the news media, the culture, the educational system, the courts, and the government have effectively influenced the doctrine of the Establishment Churches today. By compromising their doctrine, these churches have lost much of their savor and are in great danger of being trampled underfoot by men.

We must search the Scriptures diligently to make sure that we and our families are getting truth that will lead us deeper into the heart of God and be successful in converting our culture and our country. This section takes a close look at the doctrines of the government, the culture, , and the Establishment Church in America. Please judge what you read EXCLUSIVELY by the Bible.

142

CHAPTER 12: KNOWING THE ENEMY

Not-So-Subtle Enemies
Subtle Enemies: The Entertainment Industry
Social Engineering: Two Glaring Examples
   Glory Road
   Aeronauts.
Why is Hollywood So Anti-Scripture ?
What Do We Do with Hollywood?
Why Do We Support this Enemy?
Definition of Political Correctness
The 10 Commandments of Political Correctness
Useful Idiots in the Church
Definition of Religious Correctness
Their 10 Sacred Commandments

NOT-SO-SUBTLE ENEMIES

PLANNED PARENTHOOD.

The enmity of Planned Parenthood is obvious. They encourage women to kill their unborn children. They encourage teenagers to commit fornication and adultery by providing free condoms with no questions asked and then promise that their parents will never be contacted. Charismatic and Evangelical Christians DO NOT support this organization.

THE ACLU

Another obvious enemy. This group was founded by Communists and they continue to support their views. The American Civil Liberties Union typically defends atheists, Muslims, Communists, enemies of Christianity and enemies of Capitalism. They are ESPECIALLY quick to defend ANYONE who seeks to destroy the law of God and faith in Jesus Christ. They could just as easily be called the Anti-Christian Law Union. In their world, Christianity is the main culprit that keeps women in slavery, promotes racism, encourages white privilege, and has enabled men to be male chauvinists and the police to brutalize people of color.

EDUCATION: KINDERGARTEN THROUGH PHD

Many Christians correctly understand that the educational system in America, especially the government public schools, despises Christianity and alters the curriculum to reflect that viewpoint. PRIVATE SCHOOLS are also severely compromised. Most elite colleges and universities in America completely embrace an antichrist value system which will not even allow Christians or conservatives to speak their opinions in their hellish halls of learning. From kindergarten through graduate school, they pound their unholy hate into minds that have become malleable mush. These educators despise the name of Jesus Christ and do their best to keep His name out of every conversation except those which denigrate His Deity, His Holiness or His people. Most evangelical and charismatic Christians, even though they are aware of the corruption of public and some private American education, still support them by sending their children to these mind-numbing institutions.

THE MAINSTREAM MEDIA

Many Christians over the last several decades have become aware that the mainstream media edits and shapes the news to fit its own cultural and political bias. In the last decade, a new term has gained prominence: FAKE NEWS. For years, the news has been fake in many instances, but was always subtle in its presentation. Today, the news from the mainstream media is no longer subtle: it is in-your-face dishonest to anyone with even the slightest sensibility as to what is right and wrong or true and false. They can get away with this for two reasons. First, because the educational system and the entertainment industry have dumbed down and paralyzed the mentality of people in our country to the extent that most people have no clue as to what is true and what is false. The Big Lie is broadcast over and over, and of millions of people accept these lies as truth. The other reason they can get away with this practice is because tens of millions of people in America WANT TO BELIEVE THEIR LIES.

No longer does the mainstream media care anything about truth. They believe that there is no real moral code in the world, so they can do what they think is best for us. Those in the media, like most Progressives, believe that they are much smarter than most people in this country and are the ones who are best suited to convince the unconverted. Furthermore, many believe that the victory of Progressivism or Communism and the destruction of Christianity and Capitalism is historically inevitable.

THE DEMOCRAT PARTY

Hillary Clinton and Barack Obama, both have served their party well and both claim to be Christians. In the pantheon of Progressive gods, goddesses, and saints, these two have reached the pinnacle of adoration. In Hillary's case, even her unspeakable hypocrisy is not only excused but lauded and emulated by millions of men and women in America. Barack Obama, because of his strict adherence to the rules and purposes of Marxism, is no hypocrite. He is doing exactly what his teachers have taught him and is a True Believer. While Hillary apparently does what she does for power and the love of herself, Barack Obama knows what it takes to destroy America and Capitalism, and as an obedient follower of Saul Alinsky and Bill Ayers, he has become the most successful Marxist politician in American history.

Planned Parenthood, The ACLU, the educational system, the mainstream media, and the Democrat Party all have one thing in common: they are sworn enemies of Christianity, the Holy Scriptures, and Jesus Christ Himself. They understand that Christians can be tempted, polluted, and compromised. They know if this happens, Christianity will BE DEFEATED. If we are to win the *Battle for the Church*, we must STAND FIRM ON The Word of God and against the lies of these enemies. Since the 20th century, Planned Parenthood, The ACLU, the educational system, the mainstream media, and The Progressive Political Movement have been corrupting our nation and fundamentally changing our culture. The sexual morals of our country and the hatred of Christianity and Conservatism could never have been accomplished without their help.

But please take note. Hillary Clinton, Barack Obama, and all the leaders of the Democrat Party, and the useful idiots in Hollywood, the colleges, and universities, and even the entertainment dulled minds of hundreds of millions of TV watchers CAN be turned from serving Satan to serving the Lord Jesus Christ. If God could change Paul the Apostle, who prior to his conversion caused Christians to blaspheme, He can change ANYONE. But to change people He needs a Church that will stand against these enemies without compromising or diluting the Scriptures.

SUBTLE ENEMY: THE ENTERTAINMENT INDUSTRY

Over the last 90 years, Hollywood has depicted rich people as evil and poor people as good. They have taught us that virtually all Americans, except Christians and white men, are victims: people of color, women, Muslims, and the poor are all victims of white male privilege, rich people and Christians, whom they typically depict as hypocrites or fools.

Often, we in the Church treat sinners as victims in the same way that liberal politicians treat criminals in our society as victims. In some cases, we do it with the same bleeding-heart sympathy that liberals manifest when they look at the perpetrators of crimes as being the victims of society. Some prison ministries have a curriculum that is based on the premise that most of the prisoners were victims of an unloving father that had abused them either physically or psychologically and had damaged their self-esteem to such an extent that they became criminals. Because of this, it has been difficult to bring some prisoners to true, Biblical repentance. This victim mentality is still taught in many lukewarm churches. As was mentioned earlier, the women who pose for pornographic pictures on the Internet are not really the guilty ones; they are the victims of lustful men.

Hollywood taught us the need to get rid of our nuclear power, and the oil and pharmaceutical companies because they have been run by greedy capitalists that endanger mankind. Television continually shows us that our planet is burning up because of man-made climate change. Al Gore, in his 2006 movie documentary, An Inconvenient Truth, "tells the audience that, due to global warming, melting ice could release enough water to cause a 20-foot rise in sea level 'in the near future.' In 2007, the International Panel on Climate Change, an organization composed of scientists and policy makers around the world who monitor human caused climate change, estimated that sea levels would rise 0.18 to 0.6 meters (0.59 to 2.0 feet) over the next 100 years." [21]

Why do the Progressives insist that these disasters are imminent? The answer is simple: they would collect many trillions of dollars in carbon taxes and penalties for THE GOVERNMENT to redistribute wealth from Capitalist coffers to Progressive pocketbooks and causes. More importantly, they would scare some people into voting for Progressives.

SOCIAL ENGINEERING: TWO GLARING EXAMPLES

Watch the TV commercials and programs and you'll see that if there is a doctor, a judge, or a competent authority figure, this generally will feature a woman or a person of color as the authority figure. Especially in the commercials, women are the teachers while slow-witted white men are the learners. Most men are depicted as either oafish or acting like little boys; women are typically depicted as polite and mature in the best sense of the word. This is all very successful social engineering.

GLORY ROAD, Please read this review of the movie GLORY ROAD by movie critic William Arnold:

"It's a growing irony of today's Hollywood that, the more its filmmakers have come to rely on fact-based stories for their source material, the more inventive they've tended to become with the facts. These days, when we see that fateful kicker, 'Based on a true story,' experience tells us it's wise to be more than a little suspicious.

"In the middle of the film, Glory Road, there's a devastating sequence of events that begins when one of the traveling Texas Western Miners (a predominately black basketball team) is brutally assaulted in the restroom of a Southern restaurant by 'crackers' (white people), beaten bloody and then shoved head-first into a toilet in which we have just seen a man urinating.

"Frightened by the incident, their confidence shaken, the Miners shortly thereafter find, in an even more shocking scene, their motel rooms trashed, their personal belongings violated and the slogans 'Niggers Die' and 'Coons Go Home' scrawled all over the walls in what looks like either red paint or blood.

"From here, the battered team takes a long, solemn bus ride to Seattle for its next game. When they arrive, the mood is so grim that Haskins' assistant wants to give up. But Haskins can't, because it's become a moral crusade for him. 'Just think of how these boys have been degraded and humiliated just because they're black.'

"Cut to the Seattle University game, where the fans are booing just like all the rest of the rednecks we have seen. And as a consequence of this abuse the restaurant, the motel, the Seattle U fans -- the Miners lose the game: the only loss of their magical season. It's the low point from which they will rise to a thrilling climax.

"Now, there are several things wrong with this scenario. First, neither the restaurant nor the motel scenes actually happened to the Texas Miners. This was divulged to me by the film's producer, Jerry Bruckheimer, when I interviewed him a month before the film was released. Those incidents were made up, he said, 'for dramatic purposes.' Second, the racist reaction of the Seattle U fans is a fantasy. When I questioned the scene in my review of the film, a number of readers wrote to confirm my suspicion. 'I was at the game,' one writes. 'I was 12 years old at the time. ... It was a great game but there was no racial booing toward Texas that I remember.' WHEN THE MOVIE UNTRUTH SLAPS YOU IN THE FACE, IT'S NOT ARTISTIC LICENSE: IT'S A LIE. Hollywood takes liberties with true stories but 'Glory Road' is a flagrant foul!" By William Arnold, P-I movie critic. Published 10:00 pm PST, Thursday, February 9, 2006. [22]

This alteration of the truth is but one example of the ways Hollywood depicts white people as being mean and cruel and black people as being victims of white oppression. VERY CLEVER SOCIAL ENGINEERING.

THE AERONAUTS. Movie review by Johnny Oleksinsky: "On the surface, "The Aeronauts"- a movie inspired by a real, mid-19th century balloon adventure, would seem to be the inspiring story of a British man, James Glaisher, and a British woman, Amelia Wren, who soared higher into the sky than any persons before them. Riding their gas balloon in 1862, the scientist and pilot surpass the previous flight record of 23,000 feet, set by the French, and triumphantly defy the odds.

But after a quick Google search to check some facts...Amelia Wren, it turns out, NEVER EXISTED. The actually real Glaisher was joined by a guy named Henry Tracey Coxwell, who writer Jack Thorne has unceremoniously scrubbed from history to satisfy a politically correct agenda. Coxwell has been he-rased and sex-cised. It's as if I wrote a film called "The Story of the Airplane," and made the main characters Orville and Suzanne.

As the two...fly higher and begin to freeze, Glaisher passes out and Wren is forced to rescue the vehicle in an action-packed sequence. The audience cheers at her extraordinary perseverance. A woman, mocked and kept down for her gender during a highly sexist era, saves the day. Hurrah! Sorry, folks, SHE NEVER LIVED...you can't help but feel swindled by Hollywood's hot air." [23]

The movies and television have become one of the most persuasive Antichrist voices of Satan that we have ever seen on this planet. Particularly offensive to them is this Scripture, which depicts women as the weaker sex:

1 Peter 3:7 (NASB) You husbands in the same way, live with your wives in an understanding way, as with SOMEONE WEAKER.

Hollywood goes out of its way to depict women as STRONGER than men. If the Bible said that men were weaker than women, Lucifer and Hollywood would advertise THE STRENGTH OF MEN and make women look weak!

ABC, CBS, NBC and most of the cable channels that broadcast entertainment have been taken over by progressive elements and culture warriors that aim to turn America into a Progressive Paradise and has broadened the borders of sexual freedom to include and encourage virtually ANY and EVERY kind of sexual expression that is forbidden by the Holy Scriptures. New York is the Big Brother and Hollywood is the Big Mother of the sin-laden, perverse manufacturers of the Kool-Aid that is drunk by tens of millions of Americans day and night. They want their MTV, soft porn movies, hard-core Internet pornography, and "new culture" family sitcoms.

Our morals have been softened and all but destroyed with sympathetic depictions of fornication, adultery, divorce, and homosexuality. Liberals, Communists and Progressives are depicted as heroes while Conservatives and Christians typically are depicted as fools and basically evil. Occasionally, Roman Catholic or liberal ministers will be depicted as good religious leaders. Without this massive propaganda machine, there likely would never have been a radically Progressive Democrat party, Roe versus Wade, or a biased corrupt court system which has supported laws that oppose the laws of God.

WHY IS HOLLYWOOD,SO ANTI-SCRIPTURE?

Most people who choose show business as a career do so because they either want to be stars or they want to be those who serve the stars. In Scripture, the term star can identify an angelic or heavenly being. Revelation 12:4 And his (Satan's) tail drew the third part of the stars of heaven (fallen angels), and cast them to the earth: and the dragon stood before the woman..." These stars were angelic beings of great beauty and great power that came down to earth with Satan. These beings were apparently created before man and looked upon themselves as gods. They left the realm of heaven with Satan because they hated the law of God. Hollywood stars certainly are not fallen creatures who used to be angelic beings. However oftentimes, they are men and women who desire to be worshiped and loved like gods. Please note that most of the stars in Hollywood and New York hate the law of God. Many of them indulge in sexual practices that are forbidden by Scripture and they see no reason to cease their activities because the Bible says it is wrong. They are offended that the Bible does not agree with their lifestyle. They support political parties and organizations that hate the law of God, such as the ACLU and the LGBTQ. These people are COMMITTED to disobey the law of God.

Many of these people do not even believe in sin, except, of course, being Politically Incorrect. They feel particularly strong about the Bible's view of sexual sin, divorce, and lying. Hollywood typically glorifies those that go against the law of God: homosexuals, transvestites, and adulterers are lifted up as examples of sacrificial rebels who go against the grain of society and have the courage to do what they want, when they want, and with whom they want. These people are depicted as HEROES. Bonnie and Clyde, two vicious killers were glorified by Hollywood as star-crossed lovers who just happened to be caught up in the depression. Hollywood loves Bill Clinton because Bill was a charming adulterous rogue. Many people in Hollywood believe that fornication, adultery, and homosexuality are completely acceptable to the gods or god that they worship. They are absolutely correct, but they don't worship the God of the Holy Scriptures.

It is no surprise that they typically choose to support political candidates and organizations that war against Jesus Christ and the Holy Scriptures. Occasionally, a movie is made that will glorify God and lift up Christians, but that is rare. There are few Christians in Hollywood. The vast majority are haters of God and despise His Holy Scriptures.

WHAT DO WE DO WITH HOLLYWOOD?

We should be scrupulously careful about what we allow to enter our minds and hearts. We should be especially careful to guard the minds of our children. We must recognize that Hollywood and the entertainment industry are our deadly enemies. Their unspoken goals are to destroy the laws of God, weaken the faith of Christians and prevent the churches from being obedient to the Scriptures. They hate The One we love. They desire to do great damage to the Church of Jesus Christ in America. If they could destroy the Church of Jesus Christ in America, they would do so in a heartbeat. They pass their collection plate with every foul movie they make. We make an offering to Satan with every movie we watch that glorifies sin or mocks and vilifies true Christians or Jesus Christ Himself. It seems that we have lost our ability to know what is pleasing to God and what is not pleasing to God. We contribute greatly and often to this evil monster that preys on our personal purity, our children, our marriages, and our churches. This dark lord has weakened us to the point where we are on the brink of experiencing terrible judgment from God that can only be averted by deep repentance of our tepid attitude towards sin. A major reason that the *Battle for the Church* is being lost is because we are willing to be entertained by an unholy and evil being that continuously weakens and chips away at our faith in the Scriptures which warn us about the company that we keep. By allowing them into our living rooms night after night, we are fellowshipping with people and ideas that we would never otherwise allow into our homes.

Ephesians 5:11 warns us And **have NO FELLOWSHIP WITH THE UNFRUITFUL WORKS OF DARKNESS, BUT RATHER EXPOSE THEM.**
1 Corinthians 15:33 (NIV) says, Do not be misled: "Bad company **CORRUPTS** good character."

We must carefully preview and monitor what movies and television shows our children watch. We must be careful and quick to turn the television set off when we see that the program we are watching is damaging to our hearts, minds, and spirits. Even sentimental religious movies that depict people encountering God, hardly ever equate God to be Jesus Christ. It's always some nebulous being that all the people of the world worship in one way or another. The only name under heaven, JESUS CHRIST, by which men may be saved is SELDOM mentioned.

We must teach our children what is dangerous and what is safe. Even the enemy knows what is dangerous and what is safe for his people and his kingdom. Many college campuses have safe zones where people do not need to hear Christian or conservative truths that may damage their antichrist viewpoints. The safe zones that we need are minds that easily and quickly identify what is of God and what is not. SOLUTIONS: read, study, believe and obey the Scriptures. Trust Him and His Word and DOUBT anything and everything that does not agree with the Word of God. If you are not sure, search the Word of God for the answers. If you don't understand what you are reading in the Word, look up the Scriptures in an older commentary, such as Matthew Henry.

WHY DO WE SUPPORT THIS ENEMY?

Boycotting has become a dirty word. Most conservative commentators and some Christian pastors have been victims of boycott because they taught in their assemblies that homosexuality was a sin that grieves God's heart. Most Christian leaders, besides boycotting houses of prostitution, Planned Parenthood, and the local liquor store, would not have Christians boycott businesses that support abortion, adultery, and homosexuality. In the 1930s and 40s, many churches believed that it was important not to support the movie industry, because of its stance on divorce and adultery. Today, the mainstream Establishment Churches, both charismatic and evangelical, know of no such policy. However, how can we ever attend a movie that condones or glorifies homosexuality, adultery, fornication or insults the integrity of Jesus Christ? How can we attend a movie or watch a television show which insults, makes fun of or besmirches Biblical Christianity?

Chariots of Fire, BEN HUR and even Kenneth Branagh's Henry V are all great entertainment that glorify sacrifice or faith. HOWEVER, most movies depict a variety of sins that not only display but glorify sin. Virtually all of television situation comedies fall into the same categories. Should we support the advertisers of such entertainment who either directly or indirectly pay their bills? In some cases, ABSOLUTELY NOT.

CALL IT WHAT YOU WILL! We need to stop supporting our enemies. WHY DO WE CONTINUE TO SUPPORT THIS MONSTER FROM HELL? Because he entertains us! We love to be entertained! And we are not afraid to spend a small pittance of our integrity to do so! After all, we are told that we are not perfect, and many believe that God's grace will cover these slight indiscretions of INTEGRITY FAILURE.

HE WHO CONTROLS INFORMATION CONTROLS THE WORLD

This is a quote from an old TV series called *Babylon 5*. There is MUCH truth in this statement For over a thousand years the common Catholic was not able to read the Scriptures because they only used the 4Th century Latin Vulgate by Jerome in the Church. The laity did not know Latin This prevented them from receiving the unedited Word of God. The Roman Catholics CONTROLLED the doctrine delivered to the people through the teaching of the priests. John Wycliffe and his followers produced an English version of the Bible in the 14th century. For fear of losing control of the Scriptures, the Roman Catholic Church tried to kill him. The penalty for producing a Bible that the Catholics did not approve of was death. In 1534, they executed William Tyndale for doing so. After his death, The Church of England who had broken away from Catholic oversight, approved an English Bible.[23A]

For hundreds of years the Catholic Church had kept the people blind to the Scriptures. With the Protestant Reformation, and the northern European counties breaking away from Catholicism, they no longer could keep people ignorant concerning the truth of Scripture. They lost control of the most important information in the world – the Holy Scriptures. After1000 years of looking at the Bible through the shrouded eyes of ill-taught men, the people FINALLY were able to experience the freedom of Scriptural Salvation unhampered by Catholic control. The Reformation blossomed into TWO Great Awakenings and the Gospel spread throughout the World.

The Catholic Church today has much less power over people than it once did, but huge companies such as Google, Facebook, Apple, and Amazon decide what you should read, hear, and watch. These companies by and large are culturally and politically progressive Globalists and are run by men who gravitate towards an anti-Christian viewpoint. They at times forbid truth that does not support their views (they call this hate-speech) and allow lies and false stories about those who oppose their views. They are able to shape public opinion so that unwary and untaught individuals from both the world AND THE CHURCH are deceived. They are most dangerous enemies. We in the Church of Jesus Christ MUST create an alternative to the anti-Christ and anti-truth companies that twist truth.

In the 18th through 20th centuries, the Gospel Message actually produced salvation in many men who were wealthy, and these men allowed or supported Christianity. Even some who were not Christians felt a desire to support proponents of the Bible. Our current gospel message produces churchgoers and tithers, but FEW Biblical converts. In the meantime WE MUST BE CAREFUL and not allow the internet to pollute. Influence, or CONTROL our minds with

THEIR ideas of truth and fair play. We must ONLY rely upon the Scriptures to determine how we think, and what we should say and do.

DEFINITION OF POLITICAL CORRECTNESS

Political Correctness is an ideology of both written and unwritten ideas, definitions of words and redefinitions of words that are used to establish a code of conduct and a way of thinking that all people in the culture must adhere to or suffer painful penalties. However, if one does adhere to Political Correctness, the culture is quick to grant liberal rewards and great opportunity for advancement either politically or practically. Political Correctness encourages us to use appropriate terminology and discourage us from using inappropriate outdated and offensive language. For example: African American replaced Black which replaced Spade (typically only used by African Americans) which replaced Negro in describing African Americans.

USEFUL IDIOTS IN THE CHURCH

Many years ago, when I was involved in Communist politics in the Bay Area, we used the term "useful idiot" to describe people that fought for us but had no clue as to what we really believed. Our conservative enemies would use that phrase to describe virtually any college student who was involved and supported the left-wing agenda. The following are some examples of the useful idiots that we looked down on. 1) limousine liberals. We had little or no respect for the limousine liberals. They were the fat cats that provided us with the necessary funds to do what we felt was important. 2) churches that let us use their buildings for sanctuary when the cops were chasing us. 3) militant groups like the Black Panthers. We considered them to be useful as a threat against conservatives, but we were quite aware they were not real Communists. They had little understanding of Marxism or Communism. Looking back, it is quite evident that like many of my friends, I WAS MOST CERTAINLY A USEFUL IDIOT!

Today we see the entertainment industry used by the Progressives to spew their message of hatred and rebellion. Movie actors, musicians, singers, TV personalities, sports figures, movie producers, and sports team owners and players have become powerful and effective useful idiots. These people all have this in common: they are rabidly Politically Correct and have virtually no understanding of the REAL history and effect of Communism on countries where Communism took over. Most importantly, THEY DO NOT VALUE TRUTH.

THE 10 COMMANDMENTS OF POLITICAL CORRECTNESS

The entertainment industry, the media, the culture warriors, and Progressives have their own Ten Commandments that are much more sacred to them than the 10 Commandments of Scripture.

1) Thou shalt recognize The One World Government that is being created for all nations and all people to serve, enjoy and revere. No nation is better than any other and the richest nation MUST care for and feed the less fortunate nations.

2) Thou shalt not criticize nor judge any Communist, Progressive, Socialist, Democrat, or anyone in the LGBTQ. Because they believe correctly, they are above reproach.

3) Because Biblical Christians and Conservatives are inherently judgmental, they are not allowed to exercise ANY speech on ANY College campus, or educational institution. Especially speech that is critical of progressive people who are by their very nature, above reproach.

4) Man-made climate change MUST NOT BE CHALLENGED in any educational institution or in any political debate. It is after all, a universally accepted truth among right-thinking scientists and educators all over the world.

5) All men should acknowledge the scientific fact that women are inherently superior neurologically, morally, intellectually, logically and spiritually.

6) No man, except a Muslim, can claim or exercise headship over his wives or their families.

7) All religions are created equal and Christianity has no right to EVER CLAIM to be the only way to reach God. Especially, the Muslim religion must be recognized as a religion of peace and their customs must be accepted.

8) The public practice of Christianity in the secular realm must be outlawed to ensure the separation of church and state.

9) Because of white male privilege, NO heterosexual white male may EVER utter ANY critical comment regarding women or members of another race.

10) Because of white male privilege, only heterosexual white males can be convicted of any sex crime or receive the death penalty. It is time to balance the books.

DAMAGE TO THE CHURCH: USEFUL IDIOTS IN THE CHURCH

The greatest damage, however, has not been done in the secular realm. The greatest damage has been the weakening of the Church. Christians have actually felt guilty about being too judgmental regarding the sins of adultery, fornication, homosexuality and pornography. Parents have even felt guilty about inflicting corporal punishment because television and movies have depicted the use of the rod as being child abuse. Because of the subtle onslaught and manipulation of the news media and the entertainment industry by Satan, the Church itself has become even more compromised. The Word preached, the lifestyles lived and the hunger for more wealth and power by its pastors, traveling speakers, and even by its charity fundraisers has become epidemic. Divorce has been infinitely easier in this new age of tolerant Christianity. Adultery, fornication, and viewing pornography has been easily forgiven and fallen ministers and board members have been able to keep their jobs and their positions. Sometimes they need to move to another church, but they can even keep their new unscriptural spouses.

In the Church, Satan uses many useful idiots to preach his doctrine of compromise, moderation and rejection or rationalization of Scripture. These men and women are interested in being politically correct AND RELIGIOUSLY CORRECT. They willingly and gladly mix secular psychology and worldly philosophy with Scriptural truth to please the people. They are commonly acknowledged as balanced teachers because they willingly balance the teachings of secularism with the truth of Scripture.

DEFINITION OF RELIGIOUS CORRECTNESS

Religious Correctness is an outgrowth of the Political Correctness of the Left but is practiced by people who would identify themselves as Evangelicals or Charismatics. This Religious Correctness, however, is not Scriptural. In the religious culture of Evangelicals and Charismatics, Religious Correctness is ultimately a more damaging influence than Political Correctness. As Political Correctness has a political and cultural agenda in mind, so Religious Correctness has a spiritual or religious agenda in mind. Inadvertently many in the Establishment Church today have fallen into the same blind obedience that has affected the adherents of Political Correctness.

Religious Correctness is often a group of written or unwritten ideas, words, or thoughts that are used to establish a code of conduct that all Christians must adhere to or suffer painful penalties. However, if one DOES adhere to Religious Correctness, the Church is quick to grant liberal rewards and great opportunity for advancement. As in Political Correctness there is an attempt to change conduct and ways of thinking in the Body of Christ by, among other things, redefining, renaming and using terms or words in ways never used before. Religious correctness always caters to making the people happy and the Church strong and successful. Religious correctness is always balanced with the secular culture, is non-judgmental and very positive. Negative attitudes, actions, and words are forbidden, except when discussing critical or radical Christians.

THE SEVEN SACRED COMMANDMENTS OF RELIGIOUS CORRECTNESS

1) Doctrine is not important. We must ONLY TEACH JESUS.
2) Remember, only JESUS judges. You are NEVER to judge the doctrine or actions of ANY Christian, EXCEPT those Christians who negatively judge leadership or doctrine.
3) In counseling, especially when encountering those addicted to pornography, never use the word sin, sinner or other offensive or negative words. Remember you are dealing with hurting people who feel bad enough as it is.
4) Evangelicals must unite with Mormons and Catholics to defeat Satan. Unity is more important than truth and who are we to judge what is truth?
5) Husbands, all of which are really just BIGGER little boys, must NEVER make any decision apart from their wives. Without unity and reliance upon her innately superior wisdom, God is not pleased.
6) For purposes of spiritual growth, we must balance the Bible with teachings that promote high self-esteem.
7) NEVER allow negative teaching in the assembly. Jesus was always positive.

Religious Correctness is a much more dangerous enemy that political correctness. Political correctness basically addresses the secular realm. Religious Correctness addresses the Church of Jesus Christ and the spiritual realm. Religious Correction LITERALLY strengthens Satan's kingdom. The Church must maintain a SCRIPTURAL CORRECTNESS apart from the Religious Correctness that the Establishment Church now practices. The 7 sacred commandments of religious correctness are just the tip of the iceberg. The problem for the Establishment Churches, is that if you are not religiously correct, then you will have no ability to progress in influencing this lukewarm group of people.

The not-so-subtle enemies are easy to fight against. It's the subtle enemies, like the entertainment industry and the religious correctness of the Establishment Church that are difficult to combat and defeat. As in every previous church age, the religiously correct church movement must be soundly defeated by a Scripturally Correct movement. This is never an easy task. It takes great fortitude and great faith in the Scriptures to make the sacrifices that are necessary to defeat this most challenging and most dangerous enemy.

The enemies list concludes in the next chapter with the most subtle enemy of them all: The Comfort Club Church.

CONCLUSION

The Army that Satan has arrayed against the Body of Christ in America seems to be unconquerable. With virtually the entire culture, educational system and even the bulk of the churches in America virtually committed to compromising with the devil, it seems as if we have no hope.

DON'T BELIEVE IT! Just make sure that you and your family are on God's side. His side is clearly defined by the Scriptures, particularly the New Testament. Raise your children according to His Word. Don't make the mistake that David made and was severely judged; you MUST hold your children accountable to the Word of God and you must correct them and chasten them when necessary. Make sure that you and yours are on God's side, and you will have nothing to worry about and can only expect great blessing for your marriage, your children and even your children's children. This is the promise of God that you can trust completely. Remember, our hope is not built on any church or organization. Our hope is built on nothing less than Jesus' blood and righteousness. We dare not trust the sweetest secular philosophy but only lean on Jesus' magnificent Word: the Holy Scriptures. Trust and obey, for there's no other way to beat the devil and be happy in Jesus! You and your family when standing with Jesus Christ and His Scriptures are UNCONQUERABLE!

CHAPTER 13: HAPPY MEALS FROM HELL FOR COMFORT CLUB CHRISTIANS

Happy Meals from Hell's Kitchen
Friendly Enemies: The COMFORT CLUB Church
The Life and Death of the Lukewarm Church
Five Dangerous Errors of the Country Club Church
    1) Another Nicer Jesus Christ
    2) Special Writings
    3) Special Unscriptural Ministries
    4) Ignore-ance and Subtraction
    5) Phony Prophecy or False Teaching
Discerning Good from Evil
Conclusion

HAPPY MEALS FROM HELL'S KITCHEN

McDonald's serves Happy Meals to children. These meals have made McDonald's the most popular kids' restaurant in the United States. They even include a small gift with each meal. To accommodate parents who are concerned about their children's intake of fats and carbs they now offer 405 calorie meals that are low in sugar, salt, and fat, but children may choose other meals with higher calorie content. The meal also comes with a small toy. This is a dream from advertiser's heaven that satisfies both McDonald's and its clientele. McDonald's is the children's favorite fast food restaurant in America and, because of the small toy included, the nation's leader in the sale of toys. The Happy Meals that we buy for OUR OWN grandchildren from McDonald's are their FAVORITE meal at their favorite fast food restaurant. The title for this chapter, Happy Meals from Hell's Kitchen does NOT suggest that Happy Meals from McDonald's are unsuitable for children. When I go to a restaurant, I'm looking for food that is pleasing to my palate. I am looking for a meal that makes me and my grandchildren happy. The title is an indication that many churches have chosen to give their congregations spiritual food that makes them happy and comfortable but is not suited to make them holy or strong in the Lord and His Word.

Whereas the job of McDonald's is to please the customer and make his experience pleasurable, the Job of Hell's Kitchen is to please the flesh and damage the spirit of their enemy, the Church of Jesus Christ. The real chef that is producing these tasty morsels in the Country Club Church, is the head chef from Hell's Kitchen, Lucifer himself. Consequently, the lukewarm inoffensive word that the Country Club Churches serve up is more dangerous than the message of the crazy cults with their screwball ideas, phony prophets, apostles, and popes. But if you eat this Happy Meal, you will eventually figure out that it did not come from the Scriptures. It came STRAIGHT FROM HELL'S KITCHEN and was prepared to slowly but joyfully KILL YOU! If you stop now and start feasting on the milk, the meat, and vegetables of THE WORD OF GOD, you WILL get healthy and be strong enough to resist the steady diet of tempting, tasty but terribly UNHEALTHY food prepared by Hell's kitchen. The meals that the Comfort Club Churches serve up are high in sugar and fat but low in protein. Most importantly, they DO serve meals that no longer contain a salty taste. The problem is that according to Matthew 5:13, when this salt has lost its savor, that church will eventually be trodden underfoot by men.

FFRIENDLY ENEMIES THE COMFORT CLUB CHURCH

There are churches in America whose goal is to make their congregations large and profitable. To do so, it is important for them to draw as many people as they possibly can. The easiest way to do that is to make the people comfortable. These are the COMFORT CLUB CHURCHES. This Church provides a comfortable atmosphere and serves only tasty dishes that are pleasant to the palate. They know that you can catch more people with ice cream and candy than you can with broccoli or a slightly tough steak. They know that people are looking for entertainment in the form of humorous messages that make them chuckle rather than convicting sermons that make them squirm. They know that if they don't please the people, the people will go to another church that will give them what they want. The Comfort Club Churches give their customers a shame-free, guilt-free, repentance-free positive message that makes them feel good but neglects to make them good Christians.

The Country Club Church typically is interested in building a happy, growing church that does not challenge the members to eat their spiritual meat and vegetables. To the average churchgoer, the Comfort Club Church has the best of both worlds and the pastor and the people are really nice. The Jesus Christ that is preached is REALLY NICE TOO! These churches will always provide a comfortable experience. The leaders will never insult you or offend you with messages that are negative or chastise you for your sin. Negative, culturally inappropriate passages are replaced with teachings that emphasize HOW GREAT YOU ARE and define people as victims rather than sinners or lawbreakers.

Many in this crowd are quick to point out the faults or sins of the Democrats, Hollywood, Planned Parenthood, and the educational system. BUT they NEVER want to discuss the declining condition of God's people. They know how much you love fellowship and good food and they know how to play. This friendly enemy wants to make you COMFORTABLE. They want to like you AND THEY WANT TO BE LIKED BY YOU. They understand that the Country Club Christian is non-judgmental regarding the Church and does not get excited about either holiness or sin. He is extremely moderate. They will never burn you with the heat of critical conversation or preaching and will not cool down your desire to enjoy life, even if it is somewhat offensive to God. Scripture classifies them as lukewarm.

These churches will love you and tolerate much of your unscriptural behavior. They will not object to your third unscriptural divorce or even your next unscriptural marriage. They will not always condone your activity, but they will NEVER preach to you about it. They understand that every now and then, men fall into sin and they will be quick to remind you of the truth that Jesus Christ forgives sin. They will never bother you by warning you of the consequences of your sins. They will assure you that even if you make mistakes (they refer to sin as making mistakes) even if they are quite serious, because you trust in Jesus, you don't need to worry about Hell or even the chastening hand of God.

To the Lord however, they are an enemy of the Gospel. If any chastening does come to a member of the Comfort Club Church, they will say that it is AN ATTACK FROM THE DEVIL, probably because of their strong stand against abortion and gay rights. They seldom if ever mention that God REALLY punishes His wayward children. Because they really don't know the truth, their comfortable message will lead you into errors and either the pain of EXTREME chastening by God or the finality of His wrath.

This church is especially dangerous because it is not blatantly unorthodox like the cults, the liberal churches and is not joyless like the old-line dead churches. In fact, the Comfort Club Church dominates and defines the typical popular evangelical and charismatic churches in America in the 21st century. The Comfort Club Church however is dangerous because of its likability. It does everything to make churchgoers HAPPY and virtually nothing to make them HOLY.

THE LIFE AND DEATH OF THE LUKEWARM CHURCH

Revelation 3:15 (NKJV) 15 "I know your works, that YOU ARE NEITHER COLD NOR HOT. I wish you were cold or hot.

The Country Club Church is a Lukewarm Church where the icy waters of the world have cooled down the fervent zeal for holiness and the fiery power of the Holy Spirit of God. A Comfort Club Church is defined as an apparently orthodox church that is most concerned about pleasing the people. Humor will replace , and everyone will be the happier for it. Many will learn to laugh off the conviction of sin. The Bible classifies the Comfort Club Church as lukewarm.

Revelation 3:16 (NKJV) So then, because you are LUKEWARM, and neither cold nor hot, I will VOMIT YOU OUT OF MY MOUTH.

The fate of the lukewarm Comfort Club Church, as was spoken of in Chapter 1 in this book, is encapsulated in the phrase, "I will VOMIT you out of My mouth." Jesus Christ will expel the lukewarm church from His Body. Being expelled from the Body of Christ indicates that the one expelled would not allow God to absorb them into Himself and bring nourishment to His Body. Instead He defines the individual person or church as dead matter that will only bring unnecessary pain to His Body, so they must be EXPELLED.

Revelation 3:17 (NKJV) Because you say, 'I am rich, have become wealthy, and have need of nothing'—and do not know that you are WRETCHED, MISERABLE, POOR, BLIND, AND NAKED.

No church in history has ever been so confidently complacent of its standing before God than the lukewarm Country Club Church in America today. Because our financial situation is stronger than any church age in history, we boast many of the richest and largest mega-churches ever assembled. We are quite proud and feel that we are rich and in need of nothing. We feel comfortable in our extreme moderation: we are not over-emotional like the Pentecostals and we are not dead like the old-line churches. We shun the zeal of the Lord because we equate zeal with fanaticism.

This Church is rich in His grace, and if God loves the world, how much more does He love His Country Club Church in America? This church is not concerned about repentance. After all, they were taught that when they accepted Jesus Christ as their personal savior it was a done deal and His grace is sufficient. They were told that He will save them because of that confession of faith. **God will use drastic means to awaken this self-satisfied church.**

Revelation 3:18-19 (NKJV) "I counsel thee to buy from Me GOLD TRIED IN THE FIRE, that thou mayest be rich, and white raiment, that thou mayest be clothed and that the shame of thy nakedness may not appear, and anoint thine eyes with eye salve, that thou 19 As many as I love, I REBUKE AND CHASTEN. Therefore, BE ZEALOUS AND REPENT."

God goes on to explain that IF you are His own, He promises that He WILL rebuke and CHASTEN you. This is one of the promises of God that you will never see in a promise box. **JB Phillips** in his New Testament describes the Lukewarm Church PERFECTLY when he interprets the phrase BE ZEALOUS to mean **"SHAKE OFF YOUR COMPLACENCY"**.

FIVE DANGEROUS ERRORS OF THE COUNTRY CLUB CHURCH

1) ANOTHER NICER JESUS CHRIST

Any church that represents Jesus Christ as stressing your happiness more than He stresses your Holiness is just another lukewarm Country Club Church that is preaching ANOTHER JESUS. Paul warns us NOT to trust in Another Jesus.

2 Corinthians 11:3-4 (NASB): But I am afraid that, AS THE SERPENT DECEIVED EVE by His craftiness, your minds will be LED ASTRAY FROM the simplicity and purity of DEVOTION TO CHRIST. 4 For if one comes and preaches ANOTHER JESUS whom we have not preached... you bear this beautifully.

The Jesus Christ that many contemporary churchgoers believe in and trust is a God that is not to be feared; respected yes, but not to be feared. This god is tolerant of sinners, even unrepentant sinners. This god is not a god of judgment, but a god of ONLY mercy and love. The Comfort Club Christ is relatively tame. He would never wield a whip to drive out the money changers in ANY church. He would never lift His voice in anger at the hypocrites in these assem-blies. He would not challenge their faith with words that suggested there are those in the assembly who feel secure but were NOT REALLY HIS.

Because the Comfort Club Jesus is pure love, this Jesus would seldom speak of a fiery Hell that awaits insincere churchgoers and never discusses the judgment of the Lukewarm Church. This Jesus Christ is incredibly positive and His outlook on life is bright and cheery. When depicted in Christian movies, often He is playful; He laughs a lot and is always friendly to His disciples. His messages typically focus on what He has to offer and not on the disciples' responsibilities. He would never berate a church or denomination by calling them whited sepulchers, broods of snakes or hypocrites. What is more important: HE would NEVER allow his ministers to even hint that any in the assembly were anything but loving and kind brothers and sisters who were doing their absolute best. Any prophetic utterance that suggested God's people need to repent and change their wicked ways would NOT be allowed. However, a prophecy such as, "I, the Lord, love you and am PLEASED with you just the way you are" is always acceptable.

This Jesus Christ desires that His people have a high sense of self-esteem and self-love; in fact, without these qualities many Comfort Club Christians believe that it is impossible to love other people. It is true that this Jesus will pour out His wrath and severely punish unrepentant sinners in the world who have abortions, are homosexuals and don't vote Republican, but those inside their church are safe from His anger. This contemporary Jesus ignores or rationalizes the Scriptures to fit our culture. This Jesus understands that, all we need is love and a ridiculously cheap, non-consequential grace. This Jesus wants us to feel good.

Can you imagine the real Jesus saying to His disciples, "You guys are really great! You are wonderful. You are some of the finest men I have ever met in my entire life." That would certainly heighten their self-esteem, but we never see that in Scripture. In one case he complemented Peter because God had revealed to him a great truth. A little later, he was saying 'Satan get thee behind me' to him. He was more concerned about making Peter BE good then making him FEEL good.

If we ONLY KNOW the positive aspects of Jesus Christ, such as His love, His mercy, His grace, and His forgiveness, then WE MAY BE SERVING ANOTHER JESUS. If our Jesus is a god only of punishment, judgment, and fear, we ALSO may be serving ANOTHER JESUS. If we are trusting another Jesus, we are practicing a subtle form of idolatry. We must preach, teach, and trust the COMPLETE Jesus of Scripture. It is so easy for a teacher or a pastor to avoid the parts of Jesus Christ that make difficult demands. Unfortunately, we likely will only be preaching to goats and not to the sheep! Only the sheep of Jesus Christ will hear the Words of the REAL Jesus and exclusively trust the Holy Scriptures which are the voice of God!

Many lukewarm churches worship a Jesus that is half Savior and half Santa Claus. Their Jesus is much more like the indulgent mother that allows her children to disobey her and never punishes them adequately because she fears she will lose their love.

2) SPECIAL WRITINGS

Any church that supplements the Scripture with the traditions of men that are not supported by Scripture is in great error and is leading the congregation on the broad road that leads to destruction. The Roman Catholic Church, in its attempt to placate people in heathen cultures and make them more comfortable, incorporated unscriptural ideas and practices into their doctrines. Churches today often incorporate principles from our heathen culture. They embellish, ignore or edit the Scripture to fit in with more modern beliefs, thus making church members and seekers alike more at home.

The mission statement of a Comfort Club Church will NEVER reflect any unorthodox doctrine. But the message of the Church will always reflect a belief in many secular principles which are not in the Scriptures. These churches are particularly enamored with so-called psychological truths that are not Biblical.

The Comfort Club Churches choose to interpret the Scriptures concerning marriage and divorce to include both physical and verbal abuse as reasonable grounds for divorce. Some even teach that a wife need not submit to a husband if he does not love her like Christ loves the Church. This church has absorbed these ideas from pop culture, pop psychology, television and visiting speakers. At the Bible college I attended, we were taught in our psychology class by a licensed Christian psychiatrist. He said that if Paul the Apostle knew as much about psychology as we did, his ministry would've been much more successful.

3) SPECIAL UNSCRIPTURAL MINISTRIES

The most common and the most dangerous aspect of the Comfort Club Church is the inclusion of special counseling ministries that require learning secular skills and principles that are not identified by Scripture. The ministry of psychological counselor is not mentioned anyplace in the New Testament and is strictly a product of Hell's Kitchen. The word of the secular psychological counselor is often tainted with poisonous lies. Typically, however, they are positive and will often help you to understand that you are a victim of an abusive father or mother who made you feel worthless. Believe it or not, MANY are looking for that COMFORTING counsel that tells them that their unhappiness is NOT THEIR FAULT.

4 IGNORE-ANCE AND SUBTRACTION

The Comfort Club Church did not invent this stratagem, but they have mastered it. A successful and unobtrusive way to edit the Scriptures is to **ignore** or scoff at Scriptures that don't fit your theology. It is much better to ignore a doctrine than discuss it. Argumentation and debate can ruffle the delicate feathers of the average churchgoer. Typically, they do not ignore the entire Scripture, merely the parts they don't like. Another tactic is to adapt a new meaning to the Words of Scripture to fit in with our culture or the religiously correct position that is in vogue.

Comfort Club Churches often believe that shame and sorrow for sin are unscriptural. They tell the offending brother, "Don't worry brother, it is true that you sinned greatly before God, but YOU NEVER NEED TO FEEL SHAME for that sin because when the Father looks at you, all He sees is His Son Jesus Christ". Their desire to make the offender comfortable can harm him greatly! It is unscriptural to not feel shame for our sin. We should be ashamed when we sin against God. Our sin grieves His Holy Spirit. If we are saved, we can be confident that, if we repent, we will be forgiven and ultimately perfected in glory. However, we must realize that God exhorts us to be holy even as He is holy and expects us to live progressively holy lives even now. If we continue in sin, God WILL convict us of that sin and punish us.

Philippians 2:12-13 (NASB) … Work out your salvation with fear and trembling. 13 For it is God who is at work in you both to will and to work for His good pleasure."

In the Comfort Club Churches, Jesus does everything. We merely need to passively trust Him. The people are not exhorted to work out their own salvation. More importantly, they are not exhorted that they should work out their own salvation WITH FEAR AND TREMBLING. The phrase, fear and trembling, does not engender comfort in the hearts of the listeners or readers; but it is a command that should inspire us to be careful how we work out our salvation. We see from the Scripture, that as we fearfully work out our own salvation, it is equally clear that IT IS GOD who is working in us both to will and to work for His good pleasure. It gives Him great pleasure to see the external evidence of the inner work that He is doing.

5) PHONY PROPHECIES OR FALSE TEACHING

The major cults do not have a corner on fake prophecy and false teachings. The Comfort Club Church does the same thing. For years, many pastors have been teaching that we don't need to prepare for Great Tribulation because the Lord was coming back before then. They calculated the year of the rapture to be in 1981. Of course, the Lord did not come back in 1981 and God's people probably won't be bailed-out of Great Tribulation in the future. This teaching that Christians will avoid Great Tribulation comforts many but doesn't really comfort Christians in Muslim countries.

The Lord rebukes false teachers with the same gusto that He rebukes false prophets. Date setting seems to be an affliction of both the dangerous cults and some of the friendly Comfort Club Churches.

DISCERNING GOOD FROM EVIL

Hebrews 5:14 (NIV) But solid food *(KJV says strong meat)* is for the mature, who by CONSTANT USE have trained themselves to distinguish GOOD FROM EVIL.
1 Peter 2:2 (NLT) Like newborn babies, you must CRAVE PURE SPIRITUAL MILK so that you will grow into a FULL EXPERIENCE OF SALVATION. Cry out for this nourishment,

A steady diet of spiritual milkshakes, hot fudge sundaes, French fries and cheeseburgers is not food to make you a healthy child of the Lord or a STRONG MATURE Christian! God's healthy children crave THE PURE UNADUTERATED MILK OF THE WORD! And when you achieve maturity, you will not be attracted to a fast-food diet. You will hunger for solid food and strong meat that will prepare you to hunt down and defeat the enemy. We must CAREFULLY and CONSTANTLY chose a diet that does not cause sin and disease that cripples us spiritually. Hell's Kitchen constantly broadens a menu that include teaching that makes Christianity more pleasant and much tastier to our flesh. The Country Club Churches eat this stuff up.

These Scriptures tell us that we must train ourselves to distinguish good from evil by CONSTANT use. if we don't CONSTANTLY PRACTICE discerning truth and error and judging what is good and what is evil, we're not ready for more complex or difficult doctrines or situations. We just aren't MATURE enough. The lackadaisical approach to judging either conduct or doctrine leads to an inability to discern what is good from what is evil. In Country Club churches, we are told exactly the opposite. Whenever the subject of whether someone is teaching the true Word or not, many teachers and leaders make it clear that only Jesus Christ has the right to judge the conduct or the doctrine of His ministers and even the conduct of fellow churchgoers. These pastors do not constantly practice discerning TRUTH from ERROR and therefore are much more subject to further deception.

Besides lukewarm Comfort Club Churches, some of the most well-prepared Happy Meals from Hell can be found right in your own living room from the unfiltered god of this world himself. Television serves up MANY Happy Meals from Hell's Kitchen. Every evening, every morning, and every hour, we must constantly evaluate what we listen to and watch and REJECT what is unclean and what is offensive to God. When adultery is glorified or accepted as normal conduct, we must reject it. We must only partake of that which God approves. OF COURSE, we must be especially careful to evaluate any preaching, teaching, Christian movies or Christian music that don't represent either the Word or the Spirit of our Lord Jesus Christ. We must evaluate what we hear BY SEARCHING THE SCRIPTURES and make sure that what we partake of is confirmed by the Scriptures as pleasing to God. If we teach the Scriptures or deliver a prophetic Word, we must be careful and search the Scriptures for its accuracy and pray diligently that it is the right message for the right people at the right time.

This church can only survive if it sees that in God's eyes a spiritually successful church CAN NEVER cater to merely making the people feel comfortable. The Church that serves up the pure unadulterated milk of the Word, strong meat, and vegetables will produce the PRECIOUS FRUIT OF THE SPIRIT for all to enjoy! This church will empower the people to defeat the enemy, destroy the works of the devil, see our nation and our culture transformed, and cause the heart of God to rejoice. The job of the leadership in any Scriptural Christian church is not to make their congregations comfortable or even happy, but to feed them the complete, perfect and powerful Word of God that brings them joy as they drive the enemy back to hell itself.

CONCLUSION

The sad news is, the Church in America may never, in our lifetime, abandon the comfort of the Lukewarm Church. The good news is, even if the Church at large doesn't change, WE CAN CHANGE our lives and the lives of our families by not consuming Happy Meals from Hell's Kitchen. We can make sure that we only eat the meat and vegetables of the unedited Word of God and partake of the fruit of the Spirit in our own families. THEN, we can expect our children to NEVER abandon the Lord Jesus Christ and see them grow in grace and the knowledge of God.

CHAPTER 14: WE MUST FIGHT HARDER THAN HELL!

Fight the Good Fight for the TRUE Faith
The Battle Rages in America
Spiritual Warfare and Spiritual Weapons!
Gird Your Loins with Truth
We Must Fight Against the Flesh
Satan Against America and the Church
The Father of Lies is the Father of Liars
Satan's Soldiers Sacrifice
Satan's Morality
Lukewarm Politicians and Preachers
Only the Church
We Must Fight Harder than HELL!!!
Conclusion

FIGHT THE GOOD FIGHT FOR THE TRUE FAITH

1 Timothy 6:12 (NLT) 12 Fight the good fight for the TRUE faith.

The NLT translation is unique. All the other translations of First Timothy 6:12 omit the word TRUE before the word FAITH. The Scripture is generally translated "fight the good fight for the faith." The NLT inserted the word TRUE before the word faith. Considering the context of First Timothy 6:12, this is an accurate rendering of the Scripture. The fight that we are to wage is for the TRUE FAITH that is found perfectly in the Scriptures. This is the faith we fight for. This rendering implies that there is a FALSE faith. We are not to fight for just ANY faith or ANY creed, mission statement or doctrine. We are ONLY to fight for the TRUE faith written in the Holy Scriptures.

Jude:3-4 (NLT) Dear friends, I had been eagerly planning to write to you about the salvation we all share. But now I find that I must write about something else, urging you to DEFEND THE FAITH THAT GOD HAS ENTRUSTED ONCE FOR ALL TIME TO HIS HOLY PEOPLE. 4 I say this because some ungodly

people have WORMED THEIR WAY INTO YOUR CHURCHES, saying that GOD'S MARVELOUS GRACE ALLOWS US TO LIVE IMMORAL LIVES. The condemnation of such people was recorded long ago, FOR THEY HAVE DENIED OUR ONLY MASTER AND LORD, JESUS CHRIST.

The real battlefield in our war against Satan is the Battlefield of Scripture. There are men who creep in unawares and divert your attention FROM the Scriptures to science, psychology, and tradition. Satan is the father of lies and does everything he possibly can to corrupt the Scriptures. The example from Jude 3-4 is a perfect example. Even today we have Bible teachers who pervert the scriptural grace of God into an excuse for sin. They contend that for Christians who are saved by grace through faith, obedience is not necessary. Dietrich Bonhoeffer described this grace as CHEAP GRACE and dismissed it as being of no value. The Scriptures also dismiss this cheap grace and faith as having no value. James 2:18 (NASB) says: I will show you my faith BY MY WORKS. This point is discussed in greater detail in chapter 10, page 131-132 of this book. To encapsulate that teaching, James says that REAL FAITH always produces REAL WORKS of obedience to God's Word.

1 Timothy 6:10-12 (NASB) For the love of money is a root of all sorts of evil, and some by longing for it have WANDERED AWAY FROM THE FAITH and pierced themselves with many griefs. 11 But flee from these things, man of God, and pursue righteousness, perseverance, and gentleness. 12 FIGHT THE GOOD FIGHT OF FAITH; take hold of eternal life to which you were called, and you made the good confession in the presence of many witnesses.

Establishing the Kingdom of God in new territory, is difficult, but taking it back after it has been lost is even more difficult. To FIGHT THE GOOD FIGHT for the TRUE FAITH, we must lay down some important principles. First, ONLY MEN OF GOD, not men of the world, can fight THE GOOD FIGHT FOR THE TRUE FAITH. We must run from the love of money and the evil that springs from that love. We must pursue righteousness, godliness, TRUE FAITH. which ONLY comes from the Scriptures, and love with perseverance and gentleness.

Also, we must hold tightly to the fact that WE ARE NOT MERE MORTAL CREATURES. We have become eternal beings that are BORN AGAIN AS NEW CREATURES in Christ. We MUST be ready to risk our lives and our reputations. We are not fighting for an earthly reward or an earthly kingdom. We are fighting for an eternal kingdom that will be populated by born again new creatures in Christ that will look upon their earthly existence as an incredibly important but an extremely short battle with unimaginable eternal consequences. When we understand and live these things, then we will certainly fight THE GOOD FIGHT.

THE BATTLE RAGES IN AMERICA

There is a war going on going on in the world today. It is a World War in which Lucifer is doing battle to take over every country on the planet. He has been successful in most parts of the world. Many Far Eastern nations, Middle Eastern nations, Western and Eastern European nations already have quit fighting. Our country RIGHT NOW is reeling on the ropes under the heavy barrage of Satan's punches but is still feebly resisting. The only protector that America has, the Church of Jesus Christ, has been worn down by body blows that hit below the belt. This church has been gouged in the eyes and knocked down. Lately, the Church is so tired that it seems like it is sleepwalking. It has let down its guard and seems unwilling and unable to protect itself. The enemy has noticed this and is launching blow after blow. The Trainer keeps yelling instructions at the Church, but the Church won't listen. After the last fight, the Church hired a new modern trainer and has been using his tactics. It looks like the Church is heading for a fall. With virtually no defense and a feeble offense, the Church as it is in America, can't last long. the Church must wake up and follow the instructions of its First Trainer. If not, it's all over.

Make no mistake, the *Battle for the Church* is being waged. Satan understands that if he can weaken the Church, if he can knock the Church down, if he can knock the Church out of the ring, then HE CAN OWN THE CULTURE, THE COURTS, AND THE COUNTRY AND EVEN THE MILITARY. We have watched the left wing of the American political machine use every conceivable dirty trick and lie to conquer our culture and replace it with idolatrous beliefs and join the other nations in their worship of false gods.

To win elections, they stuff the ballot box with the votes of dead people. They enlist workers to disrupt the meetings of their opponents. Their CHIEF enemy is the body of Christ. Their goal is to destroy the incredible power of the United States of America and they can only do that if they destroy the Church. Our culture, our colleges, our political system, our families, and our morality have all been attacked and we have lost much. The media is completely complicit with every attempt to cast out the holy, the good and the pure in these United States. They are sold out to every progressive cause and do everything they can to denigrate Christianity. The filth-filled entertainment industry uses every possible weapon to corrupt the morals and the spiritual quality of life for families, parents, and especially the children in our country AND OUR CHURCHES. They have successfully removed Jesus Christ from our schools, our courts and our culture. Now they are attempting to replace the real Jesus Christ in the Church with Another Jesus Christ. They are totally in agreement with Lucifer. His rules are simple: lie, cheat, steal, bribe, and even murder when you can get away with it. You can even use truth, if you are very careful to only use it to attack the shortcomings and the failures of your MAIN enemy - Christianity. Satan's strategy is simple: ALL'S FAIR WHEN YOU FIGHT GOD AND HIS PEOPLE!

Incrementalism has been one of his most successful strategies. Destroy the walls that protect your enemies ONE BRICK AT A TIME. In the sexual morality wall, first you remove the brick of fornication. After all, the seventh commandment is "Thou shalt not commit ADULTERY". It doesn't mention fornication. Then you remove the brick of unscriptural divorce: after all, times have changed. Then you remove the brick of pornography: obviously, it is a victimless crime. Censorship, the legal act that prevents the publication of tantalizing but corrupt depictions of sin, must be done away with. The censorship brick is HUGE! With its removal, the country, the culture, and even the Church has been much more likely to commit sin in private. Eventually, if things progress naturally, the bricks of sodomy, child molestation, and LBGTQ lifestyles can be COMPLETELY removed. At that point, the enemy has free reign to convert the culture in the country. Typically, the enemy will use the media and the entertainment industry to describe people who engage in these activities as heroic champions of freedom that are to be emulated. Eventually, the culture will come to understand that ANY sexual activity is acceptable. The tactic of incrementalism can be used with any sin and in time and if it is tolerated, it will destroy a culture, a country, and the Church.

Regarding the Church, Satan subtly suggests that the Establishment Church must compromise its principles if it expects to maintain its power and grow in numbers. If they preach puritanical principles from Scripture, they will soon disappear. The only way you can keep large congregations is to avoid criticizing the new changes in the culture and you must modify your own doctrine to remain strong.

The problem is, WE WILL NEVER WIN THE *BATTLE FOR THE CHURCH* BY COMPROMISING THE HOLY SCRIPTURES just because certain sins have become acceptable in our culture.

SPIRITUAL WARFARE AND SPIRITUAL WEAPONS!

Ephesians 6:12 (NLT) For we are not fighting against FLESH-AND-BLOOD ENEMIES, but against EVIL RULERS AND AUTHORITIES OF THE UNSEEN

WORLD, against mighty powers in this dark world, and against evil spirits in the heavenly places.

We are not fighting merely against the ACLU, the government schools, the corrupt courts, planned parenthood and the entertainment industry. We're fighting against Satan, the evil rulers in his hellish hierarchy of hate and all the soldiers that he has enlisted in the heavens and on this earth.

We must strive to be MORE SENSITIVE to sin and become people who quickly and deeply repent. We know that we are saved by God's grace through faith and not of works. But, if we are born again, it is equally important to understand that God has given us the ability to believe, preach and live A LIFE OF HOLINESS. We must love Him and His Word and hate sin and ESPECIALLY we can't TOLERATE THE LIES of our enemy, whether inside or outside the Church.

Ephesians 6:13 (NASB) Therefore, take up THE FULL ARMOR OF GOD, so that you will be able to resist in THE EVIL DAY, and having done everything, to STAND FIRM.

THE EVIL DAY IS HERE! We have never seen such sin in our nation and in the Church. Many in the Church love a comfortable middle-class existence more than they do righteous education for their children. Many in the Church pollute their bodies and the temple of the Holy Spirit with pornography, unscriptural divorce and fornication. We must take up the full armor of God in order to resist the Enemy and his plan to take over the world. If he can conquer America , He may be able to take over the world. THIs is the time for the Church to STAND FIRM or we may witness AMERICA'S LAST STAND!

GIRD YOUR LOINS WITH TRUTH

We must stand firm and gird our minds and our hearts with THE TRUTH OF SCRIPTURE. We must exclusively depend upon the sword of the Spirit which is the Word of God and not allow ourselves to be tempted to depend upon secular psychology, culturally charged science, or the traditions of men. The TRUTH OF THE WORD OF GOD IS ALL WE NEED and all we should use in our battle against the dark world and the evil spirits in heavenly places. But we must not neglect ANY PORTION of the Word of god, either.

EPHESIANS 6:14-17 (NASB) Stand firm therefore, having GIRDED YOUR LOINS WITH TRUTH 15 and having put on the breastplate of righteousness,

and having shod your feet with the preparation of the gospel of peace; 16 in addition to all, taking up the SHIELD OF FAITH with which you will be able to extinguish all the flaming arrows of the evil one. 17 And take THE HELMET OF SALVATION and THE SWORD OF THE SPIRIT WHICH IS THE WORD OF GOD.**

The SWORD OF THE SPIRIT, which is the Word of God is to be our offensive weapon. We use the Word of God to attack the false doctrines of the enemy and the subtle temptations that he casts before the people of the lord.

But THE WORD OF GOD is also the weapon we use to defend ourselves. THE TRUTH of Scripture protects us as we spread the Gospel to unbelievers. The RIGHTEOUSNESS OF CHRIST settles our hearts, so we are not troubled. The GOSPEL OF PEACE keeps us safe in our daily walk. As the enemy hurls his fiery arrows of fear, compromise, doubt and temptation, we lift up our FAITH IN HIS WORD and we are shielded from their impact. OUR MINDS are protected, as we understand the full implications of our salvation as we study and contemplate the wonderful Word of God.

Satan's methods are, first and foremost, convincing lies and rationalizing away the truth of God's Scripture. He is the Father of Lies and will challenge the clear meaning of Scripture every chance he gets. He is a culture warrior and will appeal to the carnal nature of both Christians and unsaved people alike. He wields these weapons with great wisdom and power. We wield the sword of the truth which is the Word of God. WE must NEVER lie or obscure the true meaning of the Scriptures by appealing to the carnal nature of men. While Satan trusts the corrupt carnal nature of man and exploits that nature, we must ONLY TRUST GOD AND HIS WORD. We must use the full arsenal of THE TRUTH of the Word of God to protect ourselves and destroy the works of the enemy.

WE MUST FIGHT AGAINST THE FLESH

Galatians 5:17 (AMP) For the SINFUL NATURE HAS ITS DESIRE WHICH IS OPPOSED TO THE SPIRIT, and the desire of the Spirit opposes the sinful nature; for these two, the sinful nature and the Spirit are in DIRECT OPPOSITION to each other continually in conflict, so that you as believers do not always do whatever good things you want to do. 18 BUT IF YOU ARE GUIDED AND LED BY THE SPIRIT, you are not subject to the Law.

We must understand that as we fight Satan and His Kingdom , we need to fight against our sinful flesh. The two forces of our nature, sinful flesh and the indwelling Holy Spirit are constantly at war. People in the kingdom of Satan don't have this problem. Their flesh is on the side of sin and Satan. They have little or no inner conflict that may hold them back and compromise their sinful and evil intentions. If the Church is strong, or they were raised in church, they may have some moral conflicts, but today's cultural atmosphere generally exploits their fallen nature, and neutralizes any Godly thoughts. Born again Christians, on the other hand, even though our King is infinitely stronger than their king, still have this warfare going on in our minds and hearts. BUT if we fight HARDER THAN HELL, using our battle gear (listed in Ephesians 6:13-17) to full advantage and submit to the Holy Spirit we will most assuredly defeat the our sinful flesh.

SATAN AGAINST AMERICA AND THE CHURCH

In America, one of the two major political parties in America, fights like Hell to get what they want. These people essentially are motivated, advised and strengthened by Lucifer, a being that fought like Hell to become the ruler of his own kingdom: and became the god of this world. He has consistently chosen countries, political systems and kindred organizations to achieve his own lofty goals. He used the Nazi party in Germany. They were empowered by him to destroy both the Lutheran Church and the Jewish people whom he has always hated.

In Russia, China, many Eastern European countries, Cuba, and parts of Africa, he has used the Communist Party to destroy or weaken Christianity and any other religion that does not support his ultimate goals. In the Middle East, he has used Iran and the Muslim religion to establish caliphates to rule the people and train them to destroy Israel, America, and Christianity. In America, he is grooming the Democrat Party to join with the Communists, the Nazis, and the Muslims as champions in the destruction of innocent human lives and freedom.

THE FATHER OF LIES IS THE FATHER OF LIARS

Satan, the ruler of hell, PROUDLY bears the title of THE FATHER OF LIES.

> **John 8:44 (NASB) You are of YOUR FATHER THE DEVIL, and you want to do the desires of your father. He was a murderer from the beginning and does not stand in the truth because there is no truth in him. Whenever he speaks a lie, he, the devil, speaks from his own nature, for HE IS A LIAR AND THE FATHER OF LIES.**

He is also the father of LIARS. He has used liars and lies to achieve his goals throughout history all over the world. He also is the father of half-lies, half-truths, innuendos, sleight-of-hand, and outright deception. He even uses the truth to deceive people. He has no rulebook. He believes that playing fair is for suckers. He is far more brilliant than any human being. He cannot read our minds, but he can read our tone of voice, our facial expressions and body language, and can make a reasoned calculation concerning what he needs to do to bring us down. He plays on our weaknesses; he uses our pride, our selfishness, and the rest of our fallen nature to destroy us. He hates God: he views himself AS A VICTIM that God carelessly tossed out of heaven because Jesus Christ was jealous of him. He hates everything that God loves. He especially hates the redeemed people of God. He hates the truth! He especially hates the truth of God's Holy Scriptures. He will do everything he can to fill science, literature, philosophy, the courts, the culture, and the political system with LIES. He is constantly in search of willing suckers who will pervert the Word of God and will cause the people to look for another source of truth. He finds this false truth for them in libraries, courtrooms, political parties and the internet; he especially loves to use the Church. He is CONSTANTLY looking for and enabling authors and teachers to spew his twisted message that neutralizes the Holy Scripture. Satan is looking for liars and people who understand THE VALUE OF A GOOD LIE and people who understand that THE ENDS DEFINATELY JUSTIFY THE MEANS.

Satan has drafted an army of super liars in the moral realm; he has drafted LAWYERS to craft laws that are directly against the laws of God, he has filled them with a terrible resolve to get what they want at any cost and by any means. He has taught them to crush people and to disable them to get what they want because the ends CERTAINLY justify his means. The means are never the issue: a person who is in his Army can use any means that brings success to achieve the ends for their king. These super liars, the lawyers, don't care about the guilt or innocence of any individual: in fact, they feel much more comfortable defending the most terrible criminals who have committed the most heinous crimes no matter what it cost them in personal integrity or even money!

Many in his realm are willing to work for free in order to tear down the Holy Commandments of God and tear down God's morality that they believe is so confining to so many people. These men and women certainly are self-sacrificing fighters in the war against those who desire holiness and want to exclusively worship the God of the Scriptures. Even in the legislative branch of our government, these lying lawyers are LEGISLATORS FOR LUCIFER!

SATAN'S SOLDIERS SACRIFICE

America, which has the greatest and most powerful military force that has ever existed, faces an implacable and powerful enemy in the radical Islamic terrorists. These terrorists that are all over the middle eastern world and have migrated into Africa, Europe, and America are hell-bent to destroy any nation or individual that will not bow the knee to Allah, one of Satan's most powerful generals. They particularly hate Israel and the partially Christian nation of America. While they hate all those who do not embrace the Muslim faith, they particularly hate these two countries and what they stand for.

They are willing to make GREAT SACRIFICES to win the battle against the unbelievers. Their demon gods have convinced them that if they kill unbelievers for Allah and die in the process, they will be greatly blessed in the afterlife. It is common for a radical Islamic terrorist TO GIVE HIS LIFE FOR HIS FAITH. They know there is a war going on and they will wage it with the weapons that their demon god has given them to use. They have no obligation to be honest or loving to anyone. They have no mercy for those who will not bow the knee to Allah and in many instances, they have cut off the heads of these who refused to be converted to Islam.

In the political realm, throughout the world for the last hundred years, we have seen Communist armies fighting for International Communism using the tools of torture, murder, and brute military force. In the Russian Revolution in 1917, the takeover of China in the 1940s, and the annexation of most of Eastern Europe after World War II, they slaughtered millions who would not submit to their rule. But it must be noted that Communist billionaires have financed many uprisings throughout the world. Also, Marxist lawyers have donated their services to defend poor radical. Often, the name Che Guevarra has been brought up. Students are taught to emulate the great sacrifice that Che made for the cause of Communism: he gave up a promising and lucrative medical career and ultimately gave his life to establish Communism.

Satan's main goal is to rob mankind of the freedom that has allowed God's people to serve and worship Jesus Christ. He and his soldiers fight with everything they've got. They have made sacrifice after sacrifice. This revolution has also invaded grade schools and high schools. They know there is a war to be won and that it will require EVERYTHING THAT THEY HAVE, and they ARE WILLING TO SACRIFICE whatever it takes to win. Tragically, many of them have been quite willing to sacrifice their eternal souls to gain the victory for their god and king Lucifer in order to win the war against Jesus Christ and His church.

In America, in response to the sacrifice of the Muslim soldiers, our ESTABLISHMENT POLITICIANS under the leadership of Barak Obama, sacrificed many billions of dollars to Iran, a Muslim dominated nation. If things don't change radically in America, this money might be used to attack Israel or the United States.

SATAN'S MORALITY

Satan's morality is simple: destroy everything that God considers good. Absolute victory over our Heavenly Father, Jesus Christ, and the Holy Spirit is THEIR ULTIMATE GOOD. He is forever looking for people who are DISCONTENTED with the strict and confining doctrines of Scripture. God loves holiness: Satan is looking for haters of holiness. God loves purity and faithfulness in sexual relationships as defined by the Bible: Satan is looking for people who hate those limitations of personal freedom and consequently hate the Bible. Jesus Christ uses people that are disciplined, particularly in their understanding of the Scriptures. Satan uses people that WANT TO BE FREE from the shackles of the Old and New Testament so they can indulge in everything they desire. Satan is looking for people that will interpret the Scriptures to support his ideas of personal freedom, human rights, especially the rights of women and the LGBTQ. He HATES the strict authoritarianism that he lived under until he rebelled and was forced to leave the kingdom that was created by Christ Jesus. He wants people to see that the Bible basically ENSLAVES people to do the unreasonable bidding of this corrupt King of Kings who wants ALL the glory.

Hell, led by Satan, is a relentless opponent. Hell attacks and uses every aspect of our nation, our culture and the Establishment Church in America in its onslaught against the truth. Satan is looking for realists who understand that there are good lies and bad lies: good lies help tear down the CONFINING principles of God. Good lies can achieve great riches for anyone who has the courage to use them. Satan is basically looking for anyone who has the courage to go up against what the God of the Holy Scriptures teaches and the unnatural rules that He has set up for His people to obey.

The Democrat Party has learned well from this powerful ruler. They have learned that you need to fight the war with lies, half-truths, innuendos, insults, massive disrespect for your enemy, and by making alliances with whomever will join your army to defeat God and His narrow-minded people. Satan was able to convince one third of the heavenly army to become DISCONTENTED WITH THEIR KING and join him in his rebellion. Even in the Church he is using this same strategy of sowing discontent by raising up false teachers to reinvent the family and overthrow the authority of the husband as God's choice to be head. He has discovered that entertainment is one of the best ways to achieve these goals and win the war against God's love and God's law. He has enlisted men and women of questionable morality to be on his frontlines. These are men and women who love to be loved and are willing to pay any price to be adulated, loved and respected by as many people as possible. He has enlisted haters of holiness: people that are completely open to disobeying and encouraging others to disobey the laws of God in the Bible regarding moral purity.

Satan, the master political, military and cultural strategist is waging the war in America so that America will be defeated, and Christianity will be further weakened.

LUKEWARM POLITICIANS AND PREACHERS

Besides taking over the Democrat party and even many governmental agencies, he also has his people in the Churches. These are the lukewarm establishment pastors and teachers that have handcuffed the Christian soldiers by taking their weapons away. They want them to tone down their assault on the new cultural beliefs in our country, especially rights for women and homosexuals which conflict with Scripture.

Unfortunately, in the Church of Jesus Christ we have preachers who are more like politicians than prophets. Many spiritual leaders in the Establishment Churches seem to have no idea how serious the war is and how hard we must fight to win. These leaders seem to be afraid of demanding too much of their people. They are afraid of warning them of the consequences of losing the war in their marriages, their families, or in the country in which they live. They don't seem to understand that if we do not fight HARDER THAN HELL against our unyielding enemy, we will lose the spiritual war in America and we will experience terrible judgment from God. Like their political counterparts, the RINO Republicans, some of these preachers are Christians In Name Only (CHRINOS) pronounced CRY-NOSE. They are much more interested in pleasing people than pleasing God. They will be quick to attack the sins of the secular world, and even the sins of Christians outside of their lukewarm congregations. Poor churches will point out the sins of the rich. Rich, lukewarm churches will be sure to discuss the sins of the crazy Pentacostals. Each church must be careful to avoid the sins of their own congregations.

ONLY THE CHURCH

Because the battle for America is fundamentally a spiritual battle the ONLY soldiers that can successfully defeat Satan are Christians. All the weapons we need to fight our enemy are listed in the Holy Scriptures. Those Scriptures and His powerful Holy Spirit are all we need. We have tried to fight the enemy with politics, education, psychology, science and even human love. All you need to do is take an honest look at our culture and our country and even our churches and you will see that WE HAVE FAILED MISERABLY. Satan knows that ONLY THE CHURCH by cleansing itself of false doctrine and false teachers can cleanse the culture and the country. The only way our country can be changed is if THE CHURCH EXCLUSIVELY AND COMPLELY TRUSTS IN, TEACHES AND OBEYS THE SCRIPTURES. In Bible times this has always been the case. When God's people obeyed His Word, Israel was strong, and no nation could conquer her. When she fell into idolatry and would not repent, SHE WAS CONQUERED and judged horrifically. If we don't repent, God will vomit us out of His mouth! We must, like Jesus, chase the phonies out of the temple who sell us a religious bill of goods that lines their pockets with our money and their hearts with our love. BUT, MOST IMPORTANTLY, to defeat this terrible enemy,

WE MUST FIGHT HARDER THAN HELL!

Remember, we are fighting an enemy that has convinced 50-60 MILLION AMERICAN WOMEN to kill their unborn children and countless millions of men and women to divorce their spouses and greatly damage their children. We are fighting an enemy that has convinced the Democrat party to support and legalize the slaughter of the unborn. This terrible foe also has given freedom to the purveyors of perversion to continue their abuse of God's laws. This political party wields MORE POWER TO KILL than the Nazi party of the 1930s and 40s. You are fighting an enemy that hates God and ALL of God's law. You are fighting an enemy that has convinced many evangelical women that they need not submit to their own husbands and many evangelical men to give up leadership of their family to their wives. AND this enemy has convinced most evangelical leaders in the country to twist the Scriptures to make it convenient for spouses to unscriptural divorce their spouses and remarry. God, on the other hand, is looking for PURISTS who would never add to, subtract from, or twist the Scriptures for ANY victory.

Hell, certainly fights hard and uses every foul and wicked advantage that it can to defeat, compromise and ultimately destroy the people of God and, were it possible, frustrate the Lord Jesus Christ. They can get away with these tactics because they reject the Biblical standard of right and wrong. They easily and often lie without shame while Christians must sacrifice their pride, money, and sometimes their jobs or even their lives to please our wonderful Lord. We must not rationalize any abridgment of His Word because we know that we will be giving AID AND COMFORT TO THE ENEMY. We must be truthful, obedient, and deeply loving children of the living God and trust Him and His Word completely! THEN we will have fought Satan and His Kingdom HARDER THAN HELL!

We must return to lives of ABSOLUTE TRUST in God and His Word. We must exercise scrupulous obedience to what God tells us to do in His Word. We must settle for nothing less than a heart filled with love for God and His Word and a mind renewed by constant use of the Scriptures, fervent prayer and when FACED WITH OUR OWN SIN, quick and deep repentance. This is the only way that we can understand and use the power of the Holy Spirit to be strong and holy! We must make sure that our children grow up believing in, studying and obeying the Holy Scriptures. We must make sure they are filled with the Holy Spirit and His Holy Word, so they can have true faith, peace, joy and true love for God and all His people.

We must SACRIFICE our high self-esteem and start esteeming Jesus Christ and His Word to be PRICELESS. The real church that desires to do ALL OF GOD'S WILL like David must understand that SACRIFICE is an integral part of the Christian experience and is necessary in our war against Satan. One aspect of that sacrifice is that we will lose the respect of many of our churchgoing friends, but we must understand that WAR IS NEVER EASY. It is always hard and produces pain. BUT when victory does come for our families, our churches and perhaps our nation, it will be most pleasing to God and worth everything that we have sacrificed. We must sacrifice our guilty pleasures; we must sacrifice much of our precious entertainment; we must MOST CERTAINLY sacrifice our selfish, self-seeking modification of Scripture.

CONCLUSION

Even though, all of our enemies fight HARD in the flesh and make great sacrifices for their God and spend billions of dollars and millions of hours discrediting Scripture and the Churches that embrace the Scripture WE MUST SACRIFICE MORE! We must sacrifice our practices and desires that are not acceptable to God.

ACLU lawyers will work FOR FREE to limit the activities of God's people. Even the fake media will sacrifice advertising dollars and ratings points to go after any organization, political or cultural, that promotes Scriptural values. Many RINO Republicans and Lukewarm Church members fear the loss of their constituency, money, or the love of their friends or congregations if they fight too hard for the Scriptures. Even men who proclaim Jesus Christ as their Lord and Savior are fearful of mentioning His name in public speeches because they don't want to offend. Today, THE SOLDIERS OF SATAN SACRIFICE MUCH MORE THAN ESTABLISHMENT CHRISTIANS DO. THEY FIGHT HARDER THAN WE DO!

If the Church in America will not fight HARDER THAN HELL to drive Satan out of her midst, then WE can drive him out of our families and our marriages by fighting HARDER THAN HELL. We can teach our wives and our children how to recognize satanic activity in the TV shows and movies that they watch and the video games that they play. We can teach them to turn these games and programs off! We can teach them to edit out all that is offensive to God. We can teach them what to question as they listen to their secular teachers or even their Christian teachers. We can monitor their homework and pay close attention to what they're hearing in church and teach them how to discriminate between good and evil and what is false and what agrees with Scripture. We can be more scrupulous about what both we and our children say and hear, even in church. We can explain to them that we are at war with Satan and WE MUST NOT let him to influence or invade our family, our marriage, or even the Christian teaching that we hear. We must become bolder and be quick to identify false doctrine, even in our conversations. HELL FIGHTS HARD to destroy our family and WE MUST FIGHT HARDER THAN HELL TO KEEP OUR FAMILY SAFE. But if we care and IF WE DARE to be bold, WE CAN DO IT!

SETION 5: HAS GOD RESCINDED THE SUPERNATURAL GIFTS?

CH 15: IS SUPERNATURAL MINISTRY FOR THE CHURCH
CH 16: CONFLICTING VIEWS OF THE ROLE OF MIRACLES
CH 17: USE AND MISUSE OF THE MIRACULOUS GIFTS

SOLA SCRIPTURA: THE BATTLE CRY of the early reformers was an appeal to men to cast aside the legends, traditions, philosophy, and theological teachings of the Roman Catholic Church and ONLY TRUST THE SCRIPTURES. Sola Scriptura was a foundational truth of the Reformation. Sola Scriptura means ONLY THE SCRIPTURES. Over the centuries, leading up to the Reformation, the Roman Catholic Church added much new doctrine to the Bible. Monks and priests were not allowed to marry. The leader of the Church in Rome was called the Pope and the chief apostle. He was called the Vicar of Christ: the physical manifestation of the Son of God Himself. Much oral tradition was considered equal with the Bible. Cardinals, who were overseers of churches in other cities were called apostles.

There were many other doctrines and practices that were added to the Scriptures. Most of the reformers rejected these additions to Scripture. SOLA SCRIPTURA was the original intent of Martin Luther and the rest of the reformers. However, the reformed church did retain some traditions of the Roman Catholic Church that were not in Scripture. Infant baptism was one exception to Sola Scriptura.

OMNIS SCRIPTURA: Believing and practicing ALL the Scriptures. Omnis Scriptura was not practiced during Reformation times. They believed that the time of miraculous spiritual gifts, such as tongues, prophecy and healing ended with the death of the last apostle or the completion of the New Testament canon. The only miracles they had seen or heard in the Roman Catholic Church were not scripturally sound. Visions of Mary, which constituted many of the miracles, typically placed her in a superior position to her Son Jesus Christ.

Their observations of unscriptural miracles along with the opinions of some early church fathers that the miracle ministries ended with the death of the last apostle, convinced them that the age of supernatural miracles was over. These reformers nullified the need and usage of Scriptures that gave instruction regarding the practice of the supernatural miraculous gifts and ministries.

The premise of this section is that the Protestant Reformers, while they objected to adding to the Scriptures, should have seen that it was WRONG to INVALIDATE some Scriptures, even if they had been abused. Many evangelical Christians in America agree with the reformed view.

CHAPTER 15: IS SUPERNATURAL MINISTRY FOR THE CHURCH?

Presumptuous Faith and Little Faith
When God Changes Our Duties in Scripture
No Directive to Change ANY Gifts
What to do with Foolish Practitioners
Supernatural Miraculous Gifts

PRESUMPTUOUS FAITH AND LITTLE FAITH

This chapter is being written with the hope and the prayer that at least some of my Cessationist Reformed brothers would listen to some DIFFERENT arguments that defend the continuation of the gifts and ministries of the Holy Spirit (Continuationism).

If you were to arrange the Body of Christ in the same way that we arrange political parties, you would see that on the LEFT WING of the Body of Christ are the IRRATIONAL and PRESUMPTUOUS Continuationists (the Hyper-Faith Movement). These individuals twist the meaning of faith to be no more than a well-intentioned verbal utterance that will move the hand of God to do the bidding of the speaker. They ignore the scriptural dictates regarding the use of the gifts of the Spirit in the general assembly, particularly tongues and prophecy. They typically define positive emotional responses as being an evidence of the presence of the Holy Spirit. Some dismiss rational Scriptural study as being unnecessary or of little importance. They refer to seminaries as "cemeteries" (some are).

On the RIGHT WING of the Body of Christ are the Cessationists of Little Faith (Hypo-Faith) Movement. Tom Pennington, in his address to the STRANGE FIRE CONFERENCE, puts the position of the Cessationist very simply and very clearly. To quote him directly, "HE (speaking of God) NO LONGER GIVES BELIEVERS TODAY THE MIRACULOUS SPIRITUAL GIFTS, GIFTS LIKE SPEAKING IN TONGUES, PROPHECY, AND HEALING." [24]The Cessationists who believe that the gifts have ceased, rely in part, on the opinions of early church fathers, such as Augustine of Hippo and John Chrysostom. Many in the Little Faith Movement quote these men and others from church history who have also denied the continuation of the miraculous spiritual gifts and ministries after the time of the first century.

The often quoted Cessationists from the 16th century to the present time include such illustrious names as Martin Luther, John Calvin, Charles Spurgeon, and Benjamin Warfield. While the great reformers quoted Augustine of Hippo and John Chrysostom in support of their Cessationist views, they heartily condemned these early church fathers regarding their views on the Virgin Mary, the authority of the Pope, and the legitimacy of the (so-called) Divinely Ordained Holy Roman Catholic Church. They were certainly correct in their condemnation of the Roman Catholic Church and its UNSCRIPTURAL doctrines, but UNLIKE THE HOLY BIBLE, they were MERE MEN AND, LIKE THE REST OF US, WERE FALLIBLE. Only Scripture speaks UNALTERABLE TRUTH.

WHEN GOD CHANGES OUR DUTIES IN SCRIPTURE

When some of the Old Testament directives such as worshiping on the Sabbath, not eating certain food, and offering animal sacrifices changed God explained that they CHANGED and WHY THEY WERE CHANGED in the New Testament:

Hebrews 4:9-11 (NASB) So there remains A SABBATH REST for the people of God. 10 For the one who has ENTERED HIS REST has himself also RESTED from his works, as God did from His. 11 Therefore, let us be diligent to enter THAT REST, so that no one will fall...

Acts 10:13-15 (NASB) A voice came to him, "Get up, Peter, kill and eat!" 14 But Peter said, "By no means, Lord, for I have never eaten anything unholy and unclean." 15 Again, a voice came to him a second time, "WHAT GOD HAS CLEANSED, no longer consider unholy."

Colossians 2:16-17(NLT). So, don't let anyone condemn you for what you eat or drink, or for not celebrating certain holy days or new moon ceremonies or SABBATHS. 17 For these rules are ONLY SHADOWS of the reality yet to come and CHRIST HIMSELF IS THAT REALITY.

HEBREWS 10: 8-10 (NASB) After saying above, "Sacrifices and offerings and whole burnt offerings and sacrifices for sin You have not desired, nor have You taken pleasure in them" (which are offered according to the Law), 9 then He said, "Behold, I have come to do Your will." HE TAKES AWAY THE FIRST IN ORDER TO ESTABLISH THE SECOND. 10 By this will we have been sanctified through the offering of the body of Jesus Christ ONCE FOR ALL.

He says that the Sabbath rest NOW is Our Lord Jesus Christ. We rest in Him. We now have the freedom to center our worship on the Lord Jesus Christ on ANY DAY that we believe is appropriate. Regarding eating unclean food, He tells

Peter, "What I have made clean is now clean." So now, with the Scriptures as our guide, we are free to eat crab, pork, and other creatures that in the Old Testament God considered unclean and not to be eaten by His people. Both changes in behavior were explained by God. Regarding animal sacrifices, He tells us that He takes away the first in order to establish the second. 10 By Christ's sacrifice we have been sanctified through the offering of His body once for all. All of those changes were announced and explained in the Scriptures! The Sabbath rest, the cleansing of men's hearts, and the sacrifices for sin were ALL fulfilled in Christ!

NO DIRECTIVE TO CHANGE ANY GIFTS

In the Scriptures there is NO SUCH DIRECTIVE OR EXPLANATION regarding the cessation of the miraculous spiritual gifts and ministries for the people who are reading or hearing the newly compiled New Testament (before or around 90 AD). How absurd to believe that this BRAND-NEW BOOK, straight from the heart of God, the New Testament, WAS NO LONGER RELEVANT. For the sake of argument, let us suppose that the last member of the 12 apostles died OR the last elements of the New Testament were finished on November 1, the year 90 AD. According to the Cessationist teaching, that would indicate that on November 2, the year 90 A.D., the supernatural gifts of the spirit and supernatural ministries that are referred to in the book of Mark, First Corinthians, and Ephesians were no longer given to God's people for ministry. this is Completely Illogical. We must believe that our God is perfectly logical and reasonable. As with the rest of Scripture, His Word and His Words are not for one generation only. His Word and His Words are for ALL GENERATIONS, except where He tells us that they are not to be continued, such as sacrificing animals and exalting the Sabbath above all other days of the week.

The Cessationists insist that we need to alter the Scriptures; we need to ADD THE ADDITIONAL TRUTH that the practice of the miraculous gifts and ministries were cancelled by God upon the death of the last apostle. We must accept this as His truth! These men claim that they are speaking for the Lord, as they casually but clearly, ADD ANOTHER DIRECTIVE TO THE CANON OF SCRIPTURE!

2 Peter 1:18-21 (NLT) We ourselves heard that voice from heaven when we were with Him on the holy mountain. 19 Because of that experience, we have EVEN GREATER CONFIDENCE IN THE MESSAGE PROCLAIMED BY THE PROPHETS. YOU MUST PAY CLOSE ATTENTION to what THEY *(All the prophets: New Testament and Old Testament)* **WROTE, for their words are like a lamp shining in a dark place - UNTIL THE DAY DAWNS, AND CHRIST THE**

MORNING STAR SHINES IN YOUR HEARTS. 20 Above all, you must realize that no prophecy in Scripture ever came from the prophet's own understanding, 21 or from human initiative. No, those prophets were moved by the Holy Spirit, and THEY SPOKE FROM GOD.

2 Timothy 3:16 (NLT) ALL SCRIPTURE *(OMNIS SCRIPTURA in the Latin Vulgate)* **is inspired by God and is useful to teach us what is true and to make us realize what is wrong in our lives. It corrects us when we are wrong and TEACHES US TO DO WHAT IS RIGHT.**

2 Timothy 3:16-17 (NKJV) ALL SCRIPTURE is given by inspiration of God, and is profitable for doctrine, for reproof, for correction, for instruction in righteousness: 17 That the man of God may be perfect *(mature or complete)***, THOROUGHLY FURNISHED UNTO ALL GOOD WORKS.**

The New Testament is all solid PROPHETIC literature! How can we doubt what Paul and Mark wrote in the New Testament regarding the supernaturally miraculous gifts and ministries? How can we doubt that all the Scriptures are for EVERY generation? We must pay close attention to what these prophets who were moved by the Holy Spirit and spoke from God wrote in the New Testament! Equally important, we must never forget that ALL Scripture is useful to teach us, direct us, and correct us when we are wrong. No Scripture is cancelled out or invalidated unless God tells us in His Word! It is EXTREMELY DANGEROUS to remove the responsibility of obedience to ANY Scripture for ANY Christian of ANY time in history.

WHAT TO DO WITH FOOLISH PRACTITONERS

Many have never seen REAL FAITH in action but only the frauds and fools on television. They deny the Scriptures regarding the miraculous ministries on the basis of the actions of greedy or foolish men rather than the clear message of Scripture. This is basically the same argument that people in the world use: "The Bible can't be real because all I ever see in the Church are HYPOCRITES!" It is certainly true that there are hypocrites in the Church. There always have been and there always will be. Yet ALL THE SCRIPTURES are true, for EVERY generation Many Christians and heathens are led more by the actions of men than they are by the infallible Scriptures of Jesus Christ. Because of their unbelief, they adamantly reject the ministry of apostle, prophet and MIRACLE WORKERS, in part, because they have only seen the activity of the FALSE prophets, FALSE apostles, and FALSE miracle workers.

These men that teach that believers CANNOT function in the miraculous power of the New Testament Church have assisted in depriving many of God's people FAITH IN THE SCRIPTURES regarding the supernaturally miraculous gifts and ministries. We desperately need in these last days EVERY WEAPON that the Bible offers to defeat Satan. However, their righteous and CORRECT criticism regarding the misuse and even dishonest application of the gifts and ministries by some, is also important to note.

Satan uses his supernatural power to cripple and weaken the people of God and alter the culture. He ALSO uses shallow or phony Christians to bring the miraculous gifts and ministries into disrepute. Most certainly that is exactly what he did in both the New and Old Testaments: he used false prophets and teachers to discourage people from heeding the words of the true ministers of God's Word. This happened in both the Northern Kingdom and in Judah before and during the times of terrible judgment that virtually destroyed them. To dismiss the miraculous ministries because of SPIRITUAL malpractice is as absurd as saying that brain surgery is not a valid endeavor because many brain surgeons commit MEDICAL malpractice.

The road that the early reformers walked was much narrower than previously under the Roman Catholic Church, but it did not embrace the totality of Scripture. They practiced much of SOLA SCRIPTURA (Only Scripture could be completely trusted), but they did not embrace OMNIS SCRIPTURA (ALL of Scripture MUST be completely trusted). The way became narrower, but it must become even more narrow. The practice of rationalizing Scripture regarding the miraculous spiritual gifts, gifts like speaking in tongues, prophecy, and healing is not much different than telling wives that they no longer need to submit to their husbands because things are different now than they were when those Scriptures were written.

In order to defeat Satan, along with depending exclusively upon the Bible, we must embrace ALL the Bible and use EVERY weapon given so we can be supernaturally holy AND supernaturally powerful.

In 19th century Germany, many Higher Criticism pastors and theologians taught that the miracles of Jesus Christ were not real. They stripped Him of His supernatural power. They sincerely believed that He was a good teacher, but the miracles were just legendary. This terrible error was just one of many that rendered the Church in Germany too weak to prevent the Nazi takeover of their country in the 20th Century.

LOOKING AT SCRIPTURE, we must realize that it was the religious right (the scribes and the Pharisees) of Jesus time that turned out to be His greatest enemies. They COULD NOT BELIEVE that He could cast demons out by the power of the Holy Spirit and if He did, they attributed it to Beelzebub. They could not believe that this common carpenter, who was not even a member of the priestly tribe, could deliver anybody. These smug intellectuals of their time were too smart to be fooled by this phony "miracle worker". Gamaliel understood how important it was to be careful. He warned the people not to be too hasty in judging and punishing the disciples who had done miracles and were STILL not afraid to preach the gospel. Heed the words of Gamaliel:

Acts 5:34-36,38-39 (NASB) But a Pharisee named Gamaliel, a teacher of the Law, respected by all the people, stood up in the Council and gave orders to put the men outside for a short time. 35 And he said to them, "Men of Israel, TAKE CARE what you propose to do with these men. 38 I say to you, stay away from these men and LET THEM ALONE, for if this plan or action is of men, it will be overthrown; 39 but if it is of God, you will not be able to overthrow them; ... you may even be found FIGHTING against GOD."

Expose the frauds! Expose their misuse of the Scriptures! Expose their corrupt lives! Expose their manipulation and greed! BUT DON'T TEACH that Christians no longer have the responsibility and privilege of experiencing ALL the miraculous gifts and ministries of the Holy Spirit!

SUPERNATURAL MIRACULOUS GIFTS

Mark 16:17-18 (KJ21) And these signs shall follow THEM THAT BELIEVE: in My Name shall they cast out devils; they shall SPEAK WITH NEW TONGUES; 18 ... AND LAY HANDS ON THE SICK AND THEY SHALL RECOVER.
1 Corinthians 14:1 (NASB) Pursue love, yet DESIRE EARNESTLY SPIRITUAL GIFTS, BUT ESPECIALLY THAT YOU MAY PROPHESY."

These are SUPERNATURAL miracles, performed by men with SUPERNATURAL giftedness! Just as some have been given the gift of teaching (and if it's not a miraculous gift, it is absolutely no good), there are certain men that God has given supernatural and miraculous gifts of deliverance, healing and even other kinds of miracles. The miraculous God that we serve CLEARLY STATES IN HIS PERFECT WORD that He desires His people to earnestly desire spiritual gifts, but especially THAT THEY MAY PROPHESY. The word that is to be delivered is to be given is so we can BLESS OR WARN those whom He chooses.

Does 1 Corinthians 14:1 no longer tell our generation that we should desire earnestly that we may PROPHESY? Does ANY CESSATIONIST really believe that part of the Scriptures are out of date for God's people today?

We serve A SUPERNATURAL GOD who specifically speaks to a man and enables him to speak VERY specific words to another man or a group about a task they must do, a change they must make, or a blessing or an attack they must prepare for! We're talking about men being able to HEAR THE CLEAR VOICE OF GOD AND SPEAK A CLEAR WORD OF WARNING OR BLESSING. Prophets were used to prepare God's people in the Old Testament AND the New Testament for terrible or wonderful things that were going to happen. There are certain men that have been equipped by God to be more sensitive to His voice than other men. As was written earlier, many Cessationists BELIEVE that GOD NO LONGER GIVES BELIEVERS TODAY THE MIRACULOUS SPIRITUAL GIFTS, GIFTS LIKE SPEAKING IN TONGUES, PROPHECY AND HEALING.

The PURPOSE of the miraculous gifts of prophecy IS ALWAYS to glorify God and to confirm His Words and HIS truth in Scripture. Typically, prophetic words encourage people to shun idolatry and worship the one true God. Prophetic words often WARN people, so they can AVOID JUDGMENT OR PUNISHMENT and point people to the small gate and narrow way that leads to life.

We must remember that according to Scripture, we have been born again, are new creatures in Christ and, AS WE ABIDE IN HIM AND HIS WORD ABIDES IN US, we now have the supernatural power to LIVE A HOLY LIFE. If we believe that, how can we not believe the Scriptures that CLEARLY SAY that God will CONFIRM HIS WONDERFUL Word WITH SIGNS FOLLOWING? We lay hold of both BY trusting ALL of His unaltered word and make sure His word abides in us.

CHAPTER 16: CONFLICTING VIEWS OF THE ROLE OF MIRACLES

Scriptural Purposes of Miracles
    Confirm that the Father Sent Jesus
    Confirm Jesus as Messiah
    Confirm His Supernatural Compassion
    Confirm Jesus' Oneness w/the Father
    Confirm that Jesus is the Son of God
    Bring Glory and Praise to God
    Testify to the Word of God's Grace
    Confirm the Word of Believers
Why Miraculous Gifts Died Out
    Unbelief Hampers Faith
    Failure to Abide in Christ & His Words
Cessation of the Doctrines of Grace
Cessationists Say, No More Prophecy!

INTRODUCTION

As was spoken earlier in chapter 15, Cessationists believe He (God) has miraculous spiritual gifts, GIFTS LIKE SPEAKING IN TONGUES, PROPHECY AND HEALING. B.B. Warfield says **"Scripture leads us to expect the end of the miraculous gifts because of the unique role that miracles have ALWAYS played, as THE VALIDATION OF SOMEONE WHO SPOKE GOD'S OWN WORDS."** [25]

This is the Cessationist View of the role of miracles. This is NOWHERE substantiated in the Bible either directly or by implication B.B. Warfield is merely going by the teachings and traditions of some early Catholic Church fathers and early reformers. He does not EXCLUSIVELY depend upon the Words of Scripture or recognize that ALL the Scriptures are for EVERY believer of EVERY GENERATION, including those words that direct us to prophesy and teach us how to properly use the supernatural gifts. He does not believe that ALL the Scriptures are for ANY Christian after the last apostle died. He believes that MOST Scriptures, but NOT ALL SCRIPTURES are profitable for doctrine, reproof, correction, instruction in righteousness so that we may be THOROUGHLY equipped. But the Bible says ALL SCRIPTURE is profitable for doctrine, reproof, for instruction in righteousness. Scriptural purposes are much more complex. Please note the following. Please read the following:

2 Timothy 3:16-17 (KJ21) ALL SCRIPTURE is ... Profitable for doctrine, for reproof, for correction, for instruction in righteousness, 17 that the man of God may be perfect, THOROUGHLY EQUIPPED FOR ALL GOOD WORKS.

SCRIPTURAL PURPOSES OF MIRACLES

CONFIRM THAT THE FATHER SENT JESUS

Acts 2:22 (NLT) People of Israel, listen! GOD PUBLICLY ENDORSED JESUS the Nazarene by doing POWERFUL MIRACLES, WONDERS, AND SIGNS THROUGH HIM, as you well know.
John 5:36 (NASB) ...The works which the Father has given me to accomplish, the very WORKS THAT I DO, TESTIFY ABOUT ME THAT THE FATHER HAS SENT ME.

CONFIRM JESUS AS MESSIAH

John 7:31 But many of the crowd BELIEVED IN HIM and they were saying, "WHEN THE CHRIST COMES, He will not perform more signs than those which this man has, will He?"
John 10:2426 (NASB) The Jews then gathered around Him and were saying to Him, "How long will You keep us in suspense? If you're THE CHRIST, tell us plainly." 25 Jesus answered them, "I told you and you do not believe, THE WORKS THAT I DO in My Father's name, THESE TESTIFY OF ME, 26 But you do not believe because you are not My sheep."

CONFIRM HIS SUPERNATURAL COMPASSION

Matthew 14:14 (KJ21) And Jesus went forth and saw a great multitude, and was moved with COMPASSION toward them, and HE HEALED THEIR SICK.
Matthew 20:34 (KJ21) So JESUS HAD COMPASSION ON THEM and touched their eyes, and immediately THEIR EYES RECEIVED SIGHT, and they followed Him.

Mark 1:40-41 (KJ21) And there came a leper to Him, beseeching Him and kneeling down to Him and saying unto Him, "If You are willing, You can make me clean." 41 And JESUS, MOVED WITH COMPASSION, put forth His hand and touched him, and said unto him, "I will; be thou clean."

Mark 5:15,19 (KJ21) And they came to Jesus and saw him that had been possessed by the devil and had the legion, sitting and clothed and in his right mind... 19 Jesus ... said unto him *(the man previously possessed with a devil)*, "Go home to thy friends and tell them what great things the Lord hath done for thee, and how HE HATH HAD COMPASSION ON THEE."

Mark 8:2,6-7,9 (KJ21) "I HAVE COMPASSION on the multitude, because they have nothing to eat. 6 And He commanded the people to sit down on the ground. And He took the seven loaves and gave thanks and broke and gave to His disciples to set before them; and they set them before the people. 7 And they had a few small fishes, and He blessed them and commanded to set them also before them. 9 And those who had eaten were about 4,000.

Mark 9:22,23,25-27 (KJ21) *The father of a demon possessed boy says to Jesus* "And oftentimes the spirit hath cast him into the fire and into the waters to destroy him; but if thou canst do anything, HAVE COMPASSION ON US and help us." 23 Jesus said unto him, "If thou canst believe, all things are possible to him that believeth." 25 "Thou dumb and deaf spirit, I charge thee, come out of him and enter no more into him." 26 And the spirit cried...27 But Jesus took him, the boy, by the hand and lifted him up, and he arose.

Luke 7:13-15 (KJ21) And when the Lord saw her, HE HAD COMPASSION on her and said unto her, "Weep not." 14 And He came and touched the bier... And He said, "Young man, I say unto thee, arise." 15 And he that was dead sat up and began to speak. And he delivered him to his mother.

CONFIRM JESUS' ONENESS WITH THE FATHER

John 14:11 (NASB) "Believe Me that I am in the Father and the Father is in Me; otherwise BELIEVE BECAUSE OF THE WORKS themselves.

CONFIRM THAT JESUS IS THE SON OF GOD

John 10:36-38 (NASB) Do you say of Him, whom the Father sanctified and sent into the world, 'You are blaspheming,' because I said, 'I AM THE SON OF GOD'? 37 If I do not do the WORKS OF MY FATHER, do not believe Me; 38 but if I do them, though you do not believe Me, BELIEVE THE WORKS, so that you may know and understand that the Father is in Me, And I in the Father."

Clearly, when Jesus says, BELIEVE THE WORKS, so that you may know and understand that THE FATHER IS IN ME, AND I IN THE FATHER, these works of the father are MIRACLES. These are some of the works that are included in the passage in **2 Timothy 3:17 (KJ21)."THAT the man of God may be... thoroughly equipped for ALL good works. "**

CONFIRM THAT MIRACLES BRING GLORY AND PRAISE TO GOD

Luke 18:43 (NASB). Immediately he regained his sight and began following Him , GLORIFYING GOD; and when all the people saw it, THEY GAVE PRAISE TO GOD.

THIS IS SO IMPORTANT! Miracles cause people to praise and glorify God!

TESTIFY TO THE WORD OF GOD'S GRACE

Acts 14:3 (NASB) THEY *(Paul and Barnabas)* **spent a long time there speaking boldly with reliance upon the Lord, who was TESTIFYING TO THE WORD OF HIS GRACE, granting that signs and wonders be done by their hands.**

CONFIRM THE WORD OF BELIEVERS

Mark 16:17-20 (KJ21) And these signs shall follow THEM THAT BELIEVE: In My name shall they cast out devils; they shall speak with new tongues; 18 they shall take up serpents, and if they drink any deadly thing, it shall not hurt them. They shall lay hands on the sick, and they shall recover." 19 So then after the Lord had spoken unto them, He was received up into Heaven, and sat at the right hand of God.20 And they went forth and PREACHED...the Lord working with them and CONFIRMING THE WORD WITH SIGNS following.

The Miracles CONFIRMED THE GOSPEL MESSAGE preached by believers by THE SIGNS AND WONDERS THAT FOLLOWED them..

The PRIMARY REASON for miracles was not to validate "someone who spoke God's own words" but TO VALIDATE WHO JESUS CHRIST IS! The miracles testified of HIS GREAT COMPASSION; the miracles testified that THE FATHER HAD SENT HIM and HE IS IN THE FATHER AND THE FATHER IS IN HIM! The miracles testified that He indeed was THE CHRIST. The MIRACLES VALIDATED THE MINISTRY, THE MESSAGE and THE PERSON OF JESUS! MOST

IMPORTANTLY, the Miraculous signs and wonders confirmed the Gospel message concerning Jesus that is PREACHED BY "THEM THAT BELIEVE." And the miracles caused people to praise and glorify God!

WHY MIRACULOUS GIFTS DIE OUT

The Cessationists say that the gifts died out sometime after the 1st Century. They say that this a huge problem for the Continuationists. Sinclair Ferguson, a Cessationist says, "Continuationism provides NO CONVINCING THEOLOGICAL EXPLANATION FOR THE DISAPPEARANCE OF CERTAIN GIFTS during most of church history." **He says, "THERE'S NO WAY TO EXPLAIN IT."** [26A]

OF COURSE, THERE IS A WAY TO EXPLAIN IT. First of all, as has been stated earlier, Scripture NOWHERE tells us that the miraculous spiritual gifts would cease as a normative Christian experience with the death of the last apostle. There are a variety of reasons why the miraculous spiritual gifts and ministries died out sometime after the first century. The following Scriptures illustrate some of the reasons.

UNBELIEF HAMPERS FAITH

Mark 6:5-6 (KJV) And HE Jesus COULD THERE DO NO MIGHTY WORK, save that He laid His hands upon a few sick folk, and healed them. 6 And He marveled BECAUSE OF THEIR UNBELIEF.
Matthew 13:58 (NASB) And HE DID NOT DO MANY MIRACLES THERE BECAUSE OF THEIR UNBELIEF.
Hebrews 11:6 (NIV) WITHOUT FAITH IT IS IMPOSSIBLE TO PLEASE GOD, because anyone who comes to Him must believe that He exists and that HE REWARDS THOSE WHO EARNESTLY SEEK HIM.
Mark 5:35-36,42, While He was still speaking, they came from the house of the synagogue official, saying, "Your daughter has died; why trouble the Teacher anymore?" 36 But Jesus, overhearing what was being spoken, said to the synagogue official Jairus, "Do not be afraid any longer, ONLY BELIEVE. 42 Immediately the girl got up and began to walk, for she was twelve years old. And immediately they were completely astounded.
Romans 10:17 (NASB): So faith comes from hearing, and hearing by the Word of Christ.

Even the ministry of Jesus Christ was affected negatively by the people with whom he had grown up. Because of their unbelief, EVEN THE LORD HIMSELF, could do no mighty work except heal a few sick folk. It must be equally true that even His apostles could do no mighty work amidst unbelieving people.

After the apostles died, as the Church grew further apart from the Scriptures and began to embrace traditions and heathen practices, the Catholic Church began to lose faith in the Scriptures. By the third or fourth century, they were virtually without faith in the Scriptures. Their faith turned to the creeds and doctrines of the Roman Catholic Church. Also, they shaped the Scriptures in such a way that would please their heathen converts.

FAILURE TO ABIDE IN CHRIST AND HIS WORDS ABIDE IN YOU

For faith to be activated, YOU MUST ABIDE IN CHRIST AND HIS WORDS MUST ABIDE IN YOU. THEN and only then you shall ask what you will in His name, it shall be done to you. If you diligently seek miraculous spiritual gifts YOU ALSO MUST ABIDE IN CHRIST AND HIS WORDS MUST ABIDE IN YOU. If you don't abide IN CHRIST AND HIS WORDS DO NOT ABIDE IN YOU, what you ask for WILL NOT BE GIVEN TO YOU.

John 15:7,10-11 (NASB) If YOU abide in Me, and My Words abide in YOU, ASK WHATEVER YOU WISH, and it will be done FOR YOU. 10 If YOU KEEP MY COMMANDMENTS, YOU will abide in My love; just as I have kept My Father's commandments and abide in His love. 11 These things I have spoken to YOU so that MY JOY MAY BE IN YOU, AND THAT YOUR JOY MAY BE MADE FULL.

The Roman Catholic Church DID NOT abide in Christ and the Words of God did not abide in them. Consequently, the miraculous gifts and ministries of the Holy Spirit ended. You can only do the miraculous works of Christ IF YOU ABIDE IN CHRIST AND HIS WORDS ABIDE IN YOU.

This is the biggest reason why the Church lost the power to do miracles. They mixed local religious beliefs and the traditions of men with the Scriptures. They began to look to Mary the mother of Jesus as being more compassionate and, in some cases, more powerful than her son. They thought of Jesus as being too strict and if they went to Mary, they were more likely to get a sympathetic response. In Catholic theology, Mary eventually became the Co-Redeemer of mankind along with her Son; her title was The Mother of God. Even the Father in heaven was not exalted as much as Mary. When Roman Catholics prayed the rosary, Mary became the object of their prayers NINE times more than the Heavenly Father. For every ONE "Our Father" that was spoken while counting the rosary beads, there were NINE "Hail Marys' that were to be recited. The rosary recites a totality of 6 "Our Father" and 53 "Hail Mary" prayers plus the "HAIL HOLY QUEEN" as the closing prayer. [26B]

Abiding in Christ is abiding in HIS love and KEEPING HIS COMMANDMENTS and loving one another just as He has loved us. When we abide in Christ, we will never ask for anything selfish or foolish. We will never use "magic" words or phrases that are supposed to trigger God's favor. We will only ask what the Father desires. Even the honest, passionate desires of a carnal heart will not move Him. Abiding in Christ requires a relationship with Jesus that is an ongoing miracle of His love. The Scriptures that say. "He did not do many miracles there because of their unbelief," shows us the fruit of unbelief. And "If ye abide in Me, and My Words abide in you, ye shall ASK WHAT YE WILL, and it shall be done unto you", illustrates the blessing of fulfilling this promise.

Because the Roman Catholic Church supplemented the Scriptures with unbiblical doctrine, they lost faith that the Scriptures would THOROUGHLY EQUIP God's people for all good works. It does not matter WHAT a man speaks, it does not matter HOW he speaks, it, ONLY matters WHAT A MAN BELIEVES. If there is no faith, there will be no miracles.

The early Church of Jesus Christ in the second and third centuries began to slip into being a bishop-driven organization where the Bishop of Rome was decreed to be the chief apostle and men viewed other bishops in other cities as especially gifted and wise apostles. As the Roman Catholic Church became more influenced by the heathen cultures it eventually morphed into the Unholy Roman Catholic Church, and it is no surprise that by the third and fourth centuries, miracles were rare, if present at all.

CESSATION OF THE DOCTRINES OF GRACE

Just look at the one-thousand-year period of darkness from around 300-500 A.D. to the Reformation in 1517. During this time, THE DOCTRINES OF GRACE and the SIMPLE GOSPEL OF GRACE were virtually never preached. Most Christians DID NOT believe or teach that we are saved by grace through faith in Jesus Christ ALONE. The precious doctrines of grace were compromised by adding church tradition both oral and written. Sola Scriptura was unknown to Pope, priest and parishioner alike.

This occurred because of a self-serving mismanagement of Scripture, a greedy desire for power and control, and a suspect morality that was not concerned about compromising Holy Scripture with unholy idolatry. DID GOD WITHHOLD HIS GRACE BECAUSE THE TIME OF GRACE HAD PASSED? Did people NO LONGER NEED HIS GRACE because the Word of God was finally completed or the last apostle died? Of course not! But God would no longer respond to an idolatrous people that looked to men and the culture for the answers and not EXCLUSIVELY to His Holy Word. He could not bless His people with His grace because they chose NOT TO ABIDE EXCLUSIVELY in ALL of His Word. Instead they chose to abide in the words of the Roman Catholic church.

THE AGE OF GRACE DID NOT CEASE, but men, because they WOULD NOT BELIEVE the Scriptures, FRUSTRATED THE GRACE OF GOD. It was not God who removed the grace of God that comes by faith, it was the Roman Catholic Church that led the people into a gospel of works and a false faith steeped in tradition. They taught the people to trust in the words of the Pope, the Cardinals and other leaders. Doctrine was interpreted for them by an "intellectual" elite that eventually included the authority of Greek philosophy. Unbelievable damage was done to the people of God during those times and even continues today as the Roman Catholic Church flourishes around the world. No doubt, many in the Church, because they were never taught the simple gospel message of grace, WERE NEVER EVEN BORN AGAIN.

We are still clawing our way out of these spiritually dark times and are far from being fully in the light. When we say that certain Scriptures no longer apply to God's people, WITHOUT GOD TELLING US THEY NO LONGER APPLY, we are treading in dangerous territory. Both the Cessationists of little faith and the Continuationists of hyper-faith are guilty of elevating the opinions and powers of men too highly. The men of the Reformation inherited many extra-scriptural doctrines. Along with denying the possibility that the gifts and ministries still could exist as powerfully as they did in the early Church, infant baptism continued in the Protestant Reformation.

Also, the Protestants saw that there were few, if any, miracles after the first several hundred years of Church history and many miracles that had been reported were PATENTLY FALSE. Usually these miracles were accompanied by the presence of Mary. Protestants of the Reformation chose the unbiblical doctrine of Cessationism, based upon the ACCURATE testimony that most, if not all, miracles were fraudulent. Basically, they chose to believe the opinions, the teachings, and the traditions of men who observed the corrupt Roman Catholic Church. They did not take into account the corrupt doctrine and practices of the unholy Roman Catholic Church. This attitude is similar to people looking at the terrible things that the Catholic Church did during the Spanish Inquisitions and then saying that Christianity is evil, and Jesus Christ was a fraud.

CESSATIONALISTS SAY, NO MORE PROPHECY!

The Cessationists say that because the canon of Scripture closed with the writings of the apostles and their authorized companions that "THERE'S NOTHING LEFT. The man of God needs no additional revelation from God, he has it all right here. Jesus is calling and teaching by His Spirit through a 2-3000 year-old best seller. The Spirit speaks only in and through the inspired Word."[27]

It is ABSOLUTELY TRUE that there is nothing left to add to the Scriptures. Whenever an individual or a church or a denomination adds ANY WORD OR PROPHETIC UTTERANCE to the Scriptures, you then KNOW that is the work of a CULT! The Book of Mormon is clear evidence that the Church of Latter-Day Saints is a CULT! The Scriptures are complete, and they are sufficient. ALL OF THEM are to be heeded by God's people. NONE ARE TO BE IGNORED! **We need no other writings to guide us.** However, our sovereign God, at times, will have one of His children give an individual or a church an URGENT WORD of correction, direction, warning, or promise. This word is to be judged and evaluated regarding whether it is Scriptural, timely, and appropriate for the recipient of the word. These individual words are NEVER TO BE ADDED TO THE CANON OF SCRIPTURE. It must be noted, however, just as Agabus was moved upon by the Holy Spirit to give warning and direction to God's people regarding an upcoming earthquake and just as Philip had four daughters that prophesied to God's people without adding one word to the Scriptural canon, so OTHER men and women have been moved upon by God to prophesy direction, warnings, correction, and comfort to God's people.

Are the words of these men equivalent to Scripture? **OF COURSE NOT!** Whenever they conflict with Scripture they are to be ignored. Whenever they add to the Word of God, they are to be ignored. Whenever THEY SUBTRACT FROM THE WORD OF GOD, their message is to be ignored. We must view their words, NOT through the lens of culture, church tradition, or THE OBSERVATIONS OF FOOLISH MEN, rather through the only clear lens: THE HOLY SCRIPTURES THEMSELVES. The Scriptures are most certainly sufficient, and NONE of their instructions are to be dismissed by ANY generation. We are not to dismiss the Scriptures concerning marriage, divorce, or the Biblical directives concerning the roles of Christian husbands, wives, and children because we live in a different age or culture. We are not to dismiss the Scriptures concerning the miraculous gifts and ministries because most Christians have not seen REAL GIFTS in operation; all they have encountered are false gifts.

The Scriptures STILL instruct us to seek the best gifts, especially prophecy. Prophecy, in the sense of being of being one of the best gifts is SO IMPORTANT because it provides direction, confirmation, comfort and EVEN CONVICTION to the recipient. This gift adds to the person's understanding. But, it adds NOTHING to the Scriptures.

1 Corinthians 14:1 (NASB) Pursue love, yet Desire Earnestly Spiritual Gifts, but ESPECIALLY THAT YOU MAY PROPHESY

Just as the sufficiency of Scripture is not responsible for the disappearance of the doctrines of grace, so the sufficiency of Scripture is not responsible for the disappearance of the miraculous spiritual gifts and ministries. The fact that the doctrine of salvation by grace through faith essentially ended by 300-500 A.D. is not the result of the completion of the Scriptures or the death of the last apostle. EVERY generation must heed ALL the Scriptures. When they fail to do so, that generation will lose the ability to trust that His grace is sufficient or that ALL of God's UNALTERED word is for ALL of God's people for EVERY generation!

CHAPTER 17: THE USE AND MISUSE OF THE MIRACULOUS GIFTS

Cessationist Says Gifts are Different Today
Biblical Speaking in Tongues:
    Hearing in the Hearers Own Language
    Gift of Tongues in the Public Assembly
    Self-Edification
    Being Baptized w/ the Holy Spirit
Gift of Prophecy
Gifts of Healing
Why So Few Miraculous Gifts Today
Charismatics Disregard Biblical Rules
Conclusion
The House of God

CESSATIONISTS SAY GIFTS ARE DIFFERENT TODAY

Tom Pennington, a cessationism apologist, says "If the Spirit were still gifting believers today with the miraculous gifts, they would be the same gifts that we find in the New Testament. However, the Charismatic gifts claimed today bear almost no resemblance to their New Testament counterparts." [28]

JWK: I WHOLE-HEARTEDLY AGREE that MOST charismatic gifts and ministries bear LITTLE resemblance to their New Testament counterparts.

BIBLICAL SPEAKING IN TONGUES

HEARING IN THE HEARERS OWN LANGUAGE

Tom goes on to says "Consider, for example, the gift of tongues. According to Luke in Acts 2, The New Testament gift was the capacity as manifested at Pentecost to speak in a KNOWN HUMAN LANGUAGE." [29]

Acts 2:1-6 (NASB) When the day of Pentecost had come, they were all together in one place. 2 And suddenly there came from heaven a noise like a violent rushing wind, and it filled the whole house where they were

sitting. 3 And there appeared to them tongues as of fire distributing themselves, and they rested on each one of them. 4 And they were all filled with the Holy Spirit and began TO SPEAK WITH OTHER TONGUES, as the Spirit was giving them utterance. 5 Now there were Jews living in Jerusalem, devout men from every nation under heaven. 6 and when this sound occurred, the crowd came together, and were bewildered because each one of them was hearing them speak IN HIS OWN LANGUAGE.

This manifestation of tongues is BUT ONE MANIFESTATION of the gift of tongues: on the day of Pentecost each heard the message in his own language. To limit all utterances of tongues as being the same as this reference to Acts two is TAKING THE PART FOR THE WHOLE. There are THREE other manifestations of tongues mentioned in the New Testament.

GIFT OF TONGUES IN THE PUBLIC ASSEMBLY.

1 CORINTHIANS 14:27-28 (NASB) If anyone speaks in a tongue, it should be by two or at the most three, and each in turn, and one must interpret; 28 but if there is no interpreter, he must KEEP SILENT in the church; AND LET HIM SPEAK TO HIMSELF AND TO GOD.

1 Corinthians 14 mentions very specifically that the message in tongues in the public assembly needed to be ACCOMPANIED BY AN INTERPRETER. It is obvious that all the people in the public assembly did not hear the message in tongues in their own language. Rather the message in tongues needed to be interpreted by one who had the gift of interpreting messages in tongues. If there was no such person, and the speaker in tongues was not able to interpret the message, then that message must NOT BE GIVEN IN PUBLIC. The one speaking the tongue must do so silently and either speak to himself or speak to God.

In Pentecostal circles, speaking in tongues in any form is becoming rare, and worse, when it is practiced, it is not practiced Scripturally. There is still a smattering of churches, typically small ones, that allow message in tongues to be delivered in the public assembly. In practice, some churches want the speaker in tongues to produce a written summation or an oral recitation of what he is about to speak as an interpretation. Most churches want to make sure that no negative or corrective interpretation would be spoken that might offend anyone in the congregation. Due to the popularity of community style churches, Biblical messages in tongues, which can be quite strident, are becoming obsolete.

SELF EDIFICATION

This is not the gift of tongues to be used in the assembly, nor is it the ability to speak in tongues and have people understand the message in their own language. The third use of tongues is for the individual Christian himself.

1 Corinthians 14:28 (KJ21) But if there is no interpreter, let him keep silence in the Church, AND LET HIM SPEAK TO HIMSELF AND TO GOD.

If someone in the assembly feels a strong impulse to deliver a message in tongues but there is no opportunity to do so, or there is no one to interpret the message, he must stifle the oral expression and speak to God silently under his breath in praise or prayer
.

1 Corinthians 14:4 (NASB) One who speaks in a tongue EDIFIES HIMSELF

This might be an utterance that forms in the mind during a church service. This tongue can be expressed during a time of prayer or contemplation. It might be used to gain edification regarding Scripture or in decision-making. This is a personal tongue that the speaker employs for the purpose of, "EDIFYING HIMSELF". This manifestation of tongues is not the same as was poured out on Pentecost when each heard the message in their own language nor is it the gift to be used in the general assembly. REMEMBER, Spiritual improvement or edification is pleasing to God and good for His people. It is not the act of a selfish person, rather it is the act of a person who hungers and thirsts after righteousness. ALSO, it is not merely an ecstatic outburst, but a genuine appeal to God for Spiritual self-improvement.

BEING BAPTIZED WITH THE HOLY SPIRIT

Acts 10:44-47; 11:1-3; 15-18 (NASB) While Peter was still speaking these words, the HOLY SPIRIT FELL UPON ALL THOSE who were listening to the message. 45 All the circumcised believers who came with Peter were amazed, because the gift of the Holy Spirit had been poured out on the Gentiles also. 46 FOR THEY WERE HEARING THEM SPEAKING WITH TONGUES AND EXALTING GOD. Then Peter answered, 47 "Surely no one can refuse the water for these to be baptized who have RECEIVED THE HOLY SPIRIT JUST AS WE DID, can he?" 11:1 Now the apostles and the brethren who were throughout Judea heard that the Gentiles also had received the word of God.

2 And when Peter came up to Jerusalem, those who were circumcised took issue with him, 3 saying, "You went to uncircumcised men and ate with them." 15 And *Peter said* "As I began to speak, the Holy Spirit fell upon them JUST AS HE DID UPON US at the beginning. 16 And I REMEMBERED THE WORD OF THE LORD, HOW HE USED TO SAY, .'JOHN BAPTIZED WITH WATER, BUT YOU WILL BE BAPTIZED WITH THE HOLY SPIRIT.' 17 Therefore if God gave to them THE SAME GIFT as He gave to us also AFTER BELIEVING in the Lord Jesus Christ, who was I that I could stand in God's way?" 18 When they heard this, they quieted down and glorified God, saying, "Well then, God has granted to the Gentiles also the repentance that leads to life."

In chapter10 of Acts, Peter relates the incident where the Holy Spirit fell on the Gentiles who were listening to his message and he and his circumcised brothers were amazed because "the gift of the Holy Spirit had been poured out on them also. For they were hearing them speaking with tongues and exalting God." Peter "...remembered the Word of the Lord, how He*(Jesus)* used to say, 'John baptized with water but you WILL BE baptized with the Holy Spirit.' 17 Therefore if God gave to them THE SAME GIFT as He gave to us also AFTER BELIEVING in the Lord Jesus Christ, who was I to stand in their way?" In this case, the evidence that they had been baptized in the Holy Spirit was, as Peter put it, "for they were hearing them SPEAKING WITH TONGUES AND EXALTING GOD."

Many Cessationists believe that there is no subsequent Baptism in the Holy Spirit. Some believe that we are all baptized in the Holy Spirit when we get saved. The Scriptures indicate that we are baptized in the Holy Spirit AFTER we believe in Jesus Christ (either immediately after or later).

There may be an INITIAL BAPTISM OF THE HOLY SPIRIT immediately or shortly after a person is saved but Acts 11:17 clearly states that this experience is AFTER BELIEVING. The Bible speaks of this in ACTS 11:16. The Baptism with the Holy Spirit is much more dramatic and life-changing than delivering a message in the public assembly or edifying oneself in prayer, or to gain Godly understanding. This experience both on the Day of Pentecost and after the Day of Pentecost was most certainly a supernatural experience that moved the people to spontaneously worship God and likely deepened their faith. This baptism in the Holy Spirit is what enabled Peter to preach the gospel of Jesus Christ with great boldness on the day of Pentecost and enabled Stephen to preach to men while they were stoning him. The baptism in the Holy Spirit empowered George Whitfield to preach in a way that caused men to fall on their faces and repent of their sins and give their lives wholly to the Lord Jesus Christ. John Wesley, after he was baptized with the Holy Spirit preached with a fervor and a power that caused men to fall over in his presence and cry out to God for mercy. This same baptism of the Holy Spirit empowered Arminians and Calvinists alike to boldly proclaim Jesus Christ and Him crucified both in the British Isles and the colonies of America. This mighty baptism in the Holy Spirit awakened both New Testament Christians and men and women in England and America in both Great Awakenings to fall desperately in love with our Savior and our King, Jesus Christ. This mighty immersion of heart, mind, and soul into the midst of the powerful and loving Spirit of God ignited the flames of evangelism and spread the gospel throughout the world in the eighteenth and nineteenth centuries.

GIFT OF PROPHECY

Cessationists consider the nature of the gift of prophecy among today's Charismatics and Pentecostals to be faulty.

TP "The New Testament gift and today's manifestation are two different things. Contrary to charismatic doctrine, nowhere does the New Testament distinguish the Old Testament prophets from the New Testament prophets. Instead, the New Testament equates Old Testament prophecy with New Testament prophecy. Just like the Old Testament prophets, their words were to be evaluated against previous revelation, but once it was approved, as we saw in Acts 2, their prophecies were added to the teaching of the apostles to form the foundation of the Church. So New Testament prophecy then is DIRECT, INFALLIBLE REVELATION. That is not what is called prophecy in the twenty-first century charismatic movement

" Wayne Grudem, admits that prophecy as it is practiced in the charismatic movement should not be prefaced with 'thus says the lord.' Instead, he suggests that prophecies in the charismatic church today should begin with, quote: 'I think this is what the spirit might be saying.' THAT IS NOT THE NEW TESTAMENT GIFT OF PROPHECY." [30]

JWK Gruden's remarks, which on their face, are somewhat humorous, carry a frightening degree of truth. The issue is no one should ever say, "Thus says the Lord," if he is unsure of the word he speaks. He can express that word as "This is what I'm thinking" or as Gruden puts it "This is what the Spirit MIGHT BE SAYING", BUT THAT IS NOT PROPHECY! A prophetic utterance is a word spoken by a Christian who has the gift of prophecy, given directly to him by the Lord for a specific time, place and audience. Tom Penning's observations and analysis are MOSTLY true.

Since the completion of the Scriptures, NO PROPHECY is EVER to be added to the Church's revelation. There certainly were MANY prophecies in many different congregations during the time when Paul wrote his instructions regarding the gifts of the Holy Spirit, and MOST CERTAINLY virtually none of those prophecies were ever added to Scripture. The same is true today. SCRIPTURE IS COMPLETE! NO TEACHING OR PROPHECY should EVER add or subtract from the Scriptures.

IN TODAY'S CHURCH not only is prophecy understood differently, it is also practiced carnally. Many of the so-called prophets and prophecies that are heard in Charismatic churches are at best highly suspect and at worst demonically inspired. Most of the people (NOT ALL) that speak, "messages from God" are false prophets or prophesy falsely. Just as in New Testament times, in today's Church, both Charismatic and non-charismatic, false prophets, false prophecies, false teachers and false teachings are commonplace. Throughout the New Testament Age false prophets and false teachers ministered error. Simon Magus (Acts 8:9-24), Elymas (a.k.a. Bar-Jesus Acts 13:6-12), Antichrist (1 John 2:18-19), Jezebel – not to be confused with the Jezebel of the Old Testament. (Revelation 2:20), the false prophet of the book of Revelation: 16:13, 19:20, 20:10 and the false teachers in 2 Peter 2:1 are all Bible examples.

All prophetic utterances most certainly MUST be a DIRECT INFALLIBLE REVELATION, a divinely inspired Word from the Lord. Scripture however, in 1 Corinthians 14:29, tells the others to pass judgment on the word that is delivered. In the Old Testament, the word also had to be judged. The fact that others had to judge whether the word was from God or not, does not diminish the responsibility of speaking as an Oracle of God. In fact, Scripture directs all speakers: teachers, pastors, evangelists, prophets and apostles TO SPEAK AS ORACLES OF GOD. (1 Peter 4:11). Delivering a false prophecy, teaching a false doctrine, preaching a false word most certainly deeply grieves the Spirit of God. False teachers and false prophets ALIKE will be severely dealt with by God.

Before we can re-enter the realm of Scriptural prophecy, the Church must change her ways. Today, most in the Church, no longer desire greatly to abide either in the Word of Christ (the Scriptures) or in the holiness of Christ. Many do not think it is necessary to be a disciple of Christ. Many believe in cheap grace and cheap holiness. We no longer depend COMPLETELY on the Bible and we no longer depend on the COMPLETE Bible as being relevant regarding conduct or duties. How can we expect to move and achieve the complete will of God when we ignore or discredit ANY Scripture?

Even in the INCREDIBLE days of the New Testament Church, before the end of the New Testament Church Age, men needed to judge whether the word was Scriptural, whether the word was spoken at the right time and whether the word was appropriate for the people who heard the word. Prophecy is not to be understood differently today than it was in 1 Corinthians chapter 12, however most practitioners of prophecy are not prophets and do not prophesy by the Spirit of the Lord and many Bible teachers are not teaching the true and complete Word of God. Today most "ministers of the Lord" rationalize away the Scriptures they either can't do or won't do and insist that they are no longer for today. Two glaring examples are 1) How we view divorce and remarriage and 2) How we view the supernaturally miraculous gifts of the Holy Spirit.

GIFTS OF HEALINGS

Tom Pennington says, "Consider another example, the gift of healing. In the New Testament when someone with the New Testament gift of healing used his gifts, the results were complete, immediate, permanent, undeniable, every kind of sickness, every kind of illness. The purported healings of today's faith healers are the antithesis of those Biblical miracles. They are incomplete. They are temporary, at best. And they are unverifiable. [31]

Mark 8:23-25 (KJ21) And He took the blind man by the hand and led him out of the town. And when He had spit on his eyes and put His hands upon him, He asked him if he saw anything. 24 And he looked up and said, "I see men as trees, walking." 25 After that He put His hands again upon his eyes and made him look up; and he was restored and saw every man clearly.

One of Jesus's miracles took a little time and a second treatment to become complete. This indicates that some healings are not immediate. When Jesus prayed for the blind man and his response was, "I see men as trees, walking" Jesus had to administer healing one more time. Unfortunately, with many charismatics, they use this one LONELY Scripture as an excuse to tell people why they are not healed immediately by their prayer. But, our only guide for conduct and expectation being the Holy Scriptures, shows us that there may be OCCASIONAL EXCEPTIONS to an immediate healing, but they are RARE!

Tom goes on to say, "There is a disparity between New Testament and modern-day healings as well" [32]

For the most part, TOM PENNINGTON IS TOTALLY CORRECT. I have experienced and observed incredible supernatural healings, but for every supernatural healing I have observed or heard about, I have seen literally HUNDREDS that were phony as a three shekel note. I DO understand that there is a temptation in Charismatic meetings to focus on healing headaches, fibromyalgia, lower back pain, and hurts from the past (I've seen plenty of those). That is CERTAINLY NOT the type of healing that was ministered in the New Testament.

WHY SO FEW MIRACULOUS GIFTS TODAY

The gifts and ministries of the Holy Spirit don't move today as they did in the time of the early Church because we in the 21st century Church, just as the early Roman Catholic Church, HAVE CEASED TO ABIDE IN JESUS CHRIST AND HIS WORDS HAVE CEASED TO ABIDE IN US. We have, like the Roman Catholics, "Christianized" secular practices such as psychology and science so we could be more acceptable to our culture. In the Pentecostal and evangelical movements many church leaders and their congregations have forsaken the unadulterated Word of God as their guide for their marriage relationships and even their sexual practices. If we want to see the power of God as it existed in New Testament times, we must once again ABIDE IN JESUS CHRIST AND HIS UNADULTERATED WORDS MUST ABIDE IN US. How can we expect to experience the power of the HOLY SPIRIT in ministry if we deny the necessity of living HOLY LIVES? ALSO, how can we expect God to use us in miraculous ministries, IF WE DON'T BELIEVE that it is possible for Him to do so?

Once again, we should judge Scripture by Scripture! We should not judge Scripture by Scripture plus the opinions of "learned scholars" whether they are from the distant past or whether they are modern interpreters. We tend to practice, Sola Scriptura PLUS! We quote sources that range from the traditions of men to science that contradicts Scripture. Some are even influenced by the conduct of men. We rely upon the views and opinions of men even if these views are not articulated clearly in Scripture. That goes for both the hyper-faith crowd and the little faith crowd. We must be people that travel the narrow way and practice Sola Scriptura (Only Trust the Scriptures) and Omnis Scriptura (ALL the Scriptures) AS IF THE LIFE OF THE CHURCH IN AMERICA DEPENDED UPON IT: BECAUSE IT DOES!

CHARISMATICS DISREGARD BIBLICAL RULES

1 Corinthians 14:23-40 (NASB) Therefore if the whole church assembles together and all speak in tongues, and ungifted men or unbelievers enter, will they not say that you are mad? 24 But if all prophesy, and an unbeliever or an ungifted man enters, he is CONVICTED BY ALL, he is CALLED TO ACCOUNT by all; 25 the SECRETS OF HIS HEART ARE DISCLOSED; and so he will fall on his face and worship God, declaring that God is certainly among you. 26 What is the outcome then, brethren? When you assemble, each one

has a psalm, has a teaching, has a revelation, has a tongue, has an interpretation. Let all things be done for edification. 27 If anyone speaks in a tongue, it should be by two or at the most three, and each in turn, and one must interpret; 28 but if there is no interpreter, he must keep silent in the church; and let him speak to himself and to God. 29 Let two or three prophets speak, and let the others pass judgment. 30 But if a revelation is made to another who is seated, the first one must keep silent. 31 For you can all prophesy one by one, so that all may learn, and all may be exhorted; 32 and the spirits of prophets are subject to prophets; 33 for God is not a God of confusion but of peace, as in all the churches of the saints. 34 The women are to keep silent in the churches; for they are not permitted to speak, but are to subject themselves, just as the Law also says. 35 If they desire to learn anything, let them ask their own husbands at home; for it is improper for a woman to speak in church. 36 Was it from you that the Word of God first went forth? Or has it come to you only? 37 If anyone thinks he is a prophet or spiritual, let him recognize that the things which I write to you are the Lord's commandment. 38 But if anyone does not recognize this, he is not recognized. 39 Therefore, my brethren, desire earnestly to prophesy, and do not forbid to speak in tongues. 40 But all things must be done properly and in an orderly manner.

Tom Pennington says, "Tragically most Charismatic practice today completely disregards those clear Biblical commands. The result is not the work of the Spirit, but it is a work of the flesh, clear rebellion..." [33]

Unfortunately, here, Pennington speaks the truth! While the little faith people choose to rationalize away the Scriptures regarding the miraculous gifts and ministries, the hyper-faith people choose to abuse the precious gifts and ministries of the Holy Spirit by not following the rules laid down in Scripture and worse! There is virtually no SCRIPTURAL discipline in the Churches! Most charismatic churches will give NO OPPORTUNITY to deliver a prophetic word of correction or judgment in the assembly. Also, most so-called prophets and apostles no longer abide in Jesus Christ and His Words don't abide in them. Genuine prophecy and prophets have virtually disappeared from most Pentecostal and Charismatic churches. The main utterances allowed are those that are positive and support the denomination, the Church, or the leadership of the Church. And unfortunately, they typically have the stench of rotting flesh about them.

Equally true is that there is NO DECLARATION FROM SCRIPTURE THAT SAYS THAT THESE GIFTS STOPPED after the last apostle died or after the Bible was completed. The denial of the application of key portions of Scripture by the men of little faith plus the corruption of the gifts in the Pentecostal and charismatic churches is merely evidence that the current Church is spiritually sick and in GREAT need of help. If the Church in America does not repent deeply, only judgment from God or severe punishment can be expected. However, in this section of Scripture, it states, in:

1 Corinthians 14:24 (NASB) "But if all prophesy, and an unbeliever or an ungifted man enters, he is CONVICTED BY ALL, he is called to account by all; 25 the SECRETS OF HIS HEART ARE DISCLOSED; and so he will fall on his face and WORSHIP GOD, DECLARING THAT GOD IS CERTAINLY AMONG YOU."

This is another manifestation of **God's convicting power working through one of His gifts. And if we ever needed a wave of conviction to sweep through our churches, it is now!**

CONCLUSION

It is most illogical to view God as someone who would tantalize us by instructing us to seek for and minister in the magnificent, supernaturally miraculous power of His Holy Spirit, and then, upon the completion of the Greatest and only Perfect Book that was ever written, would rescind a significant portion of the New Testament Scriptures and not explain WHY HE DID SO. We face a supernatural and supernaturally powerful enemy. These God ordained supernatural, miraculous and COMPASSIONATE abilities would assist greatly in the defeat of our powerful enemy! If we want to win the *Battle for the Church*, we must return to THE EXCLUSIVITY AND THE FULLNESS OF HIS WORD! We must embrace both SOLA SCRIPTURA and OMNIS SCRIPTURA!

THE HOUSE OF GOD

This house is not only beautiful but extremely useful. It has a comfortable family room and many bedrooms where you can relax and be refreshed. It has a great kitchen where magnificent food is prepared. It has several workrooms and offices and even has a supernatural miracle room for the purpose of restoring health and well-being not merely to the inhabitants of the house, but also to those in the neighborhood to show how wonderful, powerful and COMPASSIONATE is the One who planned the construction of this home.

This home has a special instruction manual written by The Planner. This book was compiled from the time of Moses to the time of the apostles. This manual was written so the inhabitants of the house could learn how to bring glory to The Planner, His Father and The Mighty Holy Spirit. This PERFECT book gave all the instructions necessary for the people of God to be filled with faith, become strong in the Lord, be more faithful, and fully equipped to defeat the enemy and restore the bodies, minds and hearts of whosoever would listen to their ETERNAL message.

Upon completion of this Book of Instruction, an angelic being from another kingdom came to the people who lived in the home and told them that they could use every part of the home, except the Supernatural Miracle Room. They were also to disregard the parts of The Book where it mentioned supernatural miracles. He explained to the people that the parts of this book that discussed supernatural miracle ministry, such as the ministry of miracles, prophecies and even the miraculous and compassionate ministry of healing were no longer available to the people of God and should be ignored. He said that the supernatural miracle room should be boarded up because The Planner said that after His perfect book was finished and the great and powerful original apostles died, miracles such as prophecy, tongues and healings by those with gifts of healing were no longer necessary and, in fact were FORBIDDEN by The Planner.

He said that the time of supernatural miracles had served its purpose and now these miracles were past history and had nothing to do with the present time. To avoid confusion, he said it might be necessary to remove those parts from the instruction manual. The angel said that the miracle room was no longer necessary because the original twelve apostles and their predecessors were the only ones that God ever commissioned to use this room. The people were disappointed, because the instruction book said that, "These signs shall follow THEM THAT BELIEVE (and all who lived in the house were Believers): in My Name shall they cast out devils; they shall speak with new tongues; they shall take up serpents, and if they drink any deadly thing it shall not hurt them. They shall LAY HANDS ON THE SICK AND THEY SHALL RECOVER." Nowhere in this great book did it ever say that the supernatural miracle room would be closed to God's people who lived in this house. But the angel insisted that they needed to ignore the Scriptures instructing the people to use the miraculous gifts. He assured them, however, that the rest of the book was still good. And in fact, because the rest was so good, it was no longer necessary to use the part about the miracles.

The people were sad, but they passed this message on to the rest of the people in the house. Most of the people understood that the supernatural miracle room was off-limits to the current occupants of the home. If anybody tried to get into this room, they were branded by the New Age Scribes and Pharisees as fools. After a while only a few approached its door. A little later, most forgot there ever was a supernatural miracle room for anyone except prophets and apostles from a time long, long ago.

SECTION 6: GAME CHANGER-- THE DESTRUCTION OF THE FAMILY

CHAPTER 18: FOUNDATION FOR WARFARE: LOVE AND SUBMISSION
  LOVE AND SUBMISSION
CHAPTER 19: MARRIAGE AND DIVORCE
CHAPTER 20: AN EPISTLE FROM HELL:
  DOES THE BIBLE SAY THE WIFE IS SUPERIOR?
CHAPTER 21: AN EPISTLE FROM HELL:
  DOES SCIENCE SAY THE WIFE IS SUPERIOR?
CHAPTER 22: TO BE OR NOT TO BE..A DOORMAT!
CHAPTER 23: EXTREME SOLUTIONS

Satan's failure to stop the Reformation in Germany in the 16th century was the most terrible defeat he had experienced since The Resurrection. For over 1000 years he had been the power behind the largest cult in the world, the Roman Catholic Church. He kept idolatry alive by introducing heathen doctrines and practices into the Church. He kept salvation by works alive and established rules that crippled and perverted the clergy. By the fifth century, he had virtually destroyed the power of Christianity. The Church was a mere shell of what the apostles had left and it became The Church of the Walking Dead.

The Reformation in 1517 changed all that. The new Church that protested the Roman Catholic Church embraced much more of the Scriptures. Salvation by grace through faith alone was restored and the policy of adapting some heathen practices for church use was abandoned. Consequently, the reformers experienced the power of the Holy Spirit in the two Great Awakenings that followed.

In response to the worldwide successes of the Reformation and the great awakenings, Satan had to come up with some new strategies. Instead of a wholesale takeover of the Church as he had successfully accomplished in earlier years, He was able to convince various groups that the Bible was neither sufficient nor complete. He particularly attracted people that objected to the Bible's concept of Hell. He raised up groups that added supplementary books or beliefs to the Scriptures. In some cases, these writings essentially canceled out some Scripture and replaced it with more pleasing promises. In some cults, every human being goes to heaven. Many introduced new teachings into the curriculum, often denying the deity of Jesus Christ. Others allowed for multiple wives. Eventually, many mainline Protestant churches were compromised by worldly philosophy and psychology.

The post-reformation cults and the liberal protestant churches took much away from Biblically oriented Christianity, but it was not enough. Satan needed a master plan and a strategy that would weaken the entire fabric of Christianity as he had once done with the Roman Catholic Church. He needed something MORE UNIVERSAL to bring down the Church of Jesus Christ.

Satan observed that God initially chose Abraham to "direct his children and his household after him to keep the way of the Lord by doing what is right and just so that the Lord will bring about for Abraham what He has promised him. (Genesis 18:19 NIV)." Satan recognized that if he could destroy the father's leadership in the family, he would weaken the family to such an extent that, the Lord would not be able to bless the families and consequently it would be much easier to destroy the Church of Jesus Christ. This new master strategy of Satan started in the latter part of the 18th century and by the middle of the 19th century with the emergence of the false sciences of evolution and psychology, he was ready to implement his master strategy. Charles Darwin and William James popularized this new "scientific" viewpoint. Karl Marx, Friedrich Engels, and a little later, Vladimir Lenin were the founding fathers of Communism – an Antichrist political system. "Destroy the family, you destroy the country" [34] is a quote attributed to Vladimir Lenin. Particularly useful was the new science of psychology. Male oversight of the family was considered unnecessary and often harmful. Because it produced guilt, the Bible was considered to be out of date. The challenge of male leadership in the family started to produce stress that previously did not exist between the husband and the wife. Satan continued to chip away at the Bible's view of marriage and family through the available media of the time. Freedom became an important word, particularly in psychology. Women needed to be free from male domination. Children were encouraged to stand up and resist the unfair treatment of their parents. Sexual freedom was encouraged, regardless of marital status. By the 20th Century he even enlisted sympathetic pastors and Bible teachers to be his spokesmen. He gave great power and authority to those men and women who were able to weaken the Church and assist him in his plan to destroy Christianity.

To destroy the family, he needed, first and foremost, to destroy the institution of marriage. He needed to cause the men not to love their wives like Christ loved the Church and he needed the women to stop submitting to their husbands as unto the Lord. He needed to cause them both to be unfaithful in their God-given duties and unfaithful with their bodies. Most importantly, he needed to make them uncaring about their spouse. He knew if he could destroy marriages, he could enlist the children for his cause. He knew that this strategy would be one of the most effective strategies that he had ever employed to gain control of mankind. He understood perfectly that this was not just a new denomination he was forming, but this was a new idea he would implant in the existing churches. To accomplish this, he needed willing and enlightened church leaders.

From his 19th century vantage point, he could see the tremendous successes that would occur in the next 100 years and he rejoiced at the prospect of seeing marriages fall apart, parents abandon their children, children abandon their parents and most importantly, CHILDREN ABANDON THEIR FAITH in Jesus Christ. With his intellectual understanding of Scripture, he could calculate that in the future these policies would weaken the church and thereby weaken the nation so that parents would kill their own children and children would despise their own parents.

In the 1960s, with the sexual revolution, the rise of feminism and the acceptance of birth control and abortion, women felt a freedom that they had never experienced. Men also were quite happy to see women finally liberated from their fear of socially inappropriate sexual activity and pregnancy. With the loosening of the divorce laws and the Churches more sympathetic view of unscriptural divorce, Christian women and men alike were less inclined to obey the Scriptures regarding their responsibilities of oversight, submission, and raising their children for the Lord. The Church no longer changed the culture; the culture NOW was changing the Church. All in all, Satan's attack on the Christian family has been ONE HELL OF A SUCCESS!

CHAPTER 18: FOUNDATION FOR WARFARE: LOVE AND SUBMISSION

Introduction
Biblical Oversight and Submission
Equality of Believers and Mutual Submission?
God's Plan: Submission and Love
Wives, Be Subject to Your OWN Husbands
Husbands: Be Responsible and Exercise Authority
Conclusion

INTRODUCTION

The title for this book is *Battle for the Church*. So far, not much attention has been given to the Christian warfare chapter in Ephesians Chapter 6 because we must first understand the importance of the chapter that precedes the warfare chapter. Ephesians chapter 5 is the oversight and submission chapter. Without a proper understanding and application of these concepts as Scripture defines them, no soldier can fight effectively. If the enlisted men are not submitted to the officers over them, the chance of success in the battle is greatly diminished. If the officers do not care deeply for their men and are not given authority over the enlisted men, chaos ensues.

The most important reason we have failed in our spiritual battle against Satan is because we have neglected or perverted the section that stresses oversight and submission: Ephesians chapter 5:21 to chapter 6:9. We have twisted and weakened the Scriptures in this section to fit our own desires and the culture of the 21st century. We have minimized its importance. It is no coincidence that God deals in detail in this chapter with what our conduct should be ESPECIALLY IN OUR MARRIAGES. God's people must be entirely submitted to these precious Words before we can accomplish the powerful works of warfare in chapter 6 of Ephesians. If we want to wage war against Satan and his soldiers we need to learn HOW TO LEAD and HOW TO FOLLOW, WHO TO LEAD AND WHO TO FOLLOW. The reason Satan has attacked marriage in our culture and country is because this relationship is the most fundamental and important relationship among Christians. At one time America honored the values of scriptural Christian marriage more stubbornly than any other nation.

During this period, the enemy suffered defeat after defeat and lost much precious ground in Western Europe and America. BUT he came to realize that the best way to defeat us was to destroy or pervert Christian marriages as defined by the Scriptures. This relationship is a living example of the relationship between Jesus Christ and His Church. Our enemy has been successful in ruining our marriages and thereby ruining our families. He has created movement after movement in our culture to tear down the authority of the husband and cause the wife to resist the scriptural oversight of her husband. Even most husbands now have no desire to be the head of their wives or to love their wives like Christ loves the Church. This lack of respect for God-ordained authority in the marriage is rampant both in our culture and our churches.

This lack of respect and love for our spouses and the lack of respect of children for their parents has affected other authorities in our country. Our law enforcement officers no longer can count on respect from the citizenry. The police are targeted for ambush and are mocked and maligned by angry crowds of lawless losers. Teachers must capitulate to the statutes that force them to let their students do what they want to do. If we are to win the *Battle for the Church*, we need to understand that Christian marriage is the front line of this great war and the Church must honor and respect God's plan regarding scriptural leadership and submission in the marriage relationship.

Many people are concerned that difficult times, tribulation, or judgment will come to United States of America and they are doing what they can to prepare for these events. There are televangelists selling food packages that will last for 25 years; many recommend the purchase of guns: everything from personal weapons to assault rifles. This is done to prepare people for the time in America when civil war or chaos runs rampant and our neighborhoods become lawless.

It is important to prepare for difficult times in America. We may have food shortages; we may need protection from violent criminals and even armed government police or soldiers. The government may sanction armed Antifa soldiers or Black Panthers to oversee neighborhoods. We even may lose the precious freedom that God has granted us over the last several centuries to keep order in our cities.

But ALL THESE PREPARATIONS WILL MEAN NOTHING if we have not prepared our families by the Scriptures to resist our Real Enemies with the power of the Holy Spirit. Better to have no guns and no food supplies and prepare ourselves SPIRITUALLY. Remember the Jewish Zealots who militarily opposed Rome and were wiped out. The disciples of our Lord Jesus Christ, even though most were killed, never resisted with any military force but only with the power of the Holy Spirit and the perfect Word of God. They survived to build the greatest spiritual movement that the world has ever seen. We and our loved ones may suffer and even die at the hands of Satan and his followers, but only a thorough spiritual preparation will preserve us to fight and defeat him. We must prepare both ourselves and our families with knowledge of and obedience to the Scriptures. This protection will not merely help guard our homes and our bodies but will prepare our hearts and souls to thrive and survive during difficult days that may come in our lifetime or the lifetime of our children.

If it does seem right to resist the government with military power, like our forefathers did in the 18th century against the British, we STILL need to be obedient to the Word and be empowered by the Holy Spirit.

BIBLICAL OVERSIGHT AND SUBMISSION

A smooth functioning family unit that heeds God's Word to the husband, wife, and children must be the foundation for spiritual success in any church, denomination or movement. The study of the Scriptures and the application of its principles are most important. You must STUDY DILIGENTLY the Scriptures that deal with the relationships and responsibilities of the husband, the wife, and the children. Before we look at those Scriptures, we must BELIEVE THOROUGHLY that the Bible is the SOLE OBJECTIVE SOURCE of all the truth that we need in order to serve God, experience His love. and defeat Satan in the *Battle for the Church*. The Scriptures themselves proclaim that truth. This Scripture has been repeated MANY TIMES in the *Battle for the Church*

2 Timothy 3:15–17 (NIV) ...From infancy YOU HAVE KNOWN THE HOLY SCRIPTURES, which are able to MAKE YOU WISE for salvation through faith in Christ Jesus. 16 ALL SCRIPTURE is God breathed and is useful for teaching, rebuking, correcting and TRAINING IN RIGHTEOUSNESS, 17 so that the servant of God may be THOROUGHLY EQUIPPED for EVERY good work.

WE MUST TRUST THE SCRIPTURES because they guard us against the evil men and impostors that will PERVERT HIS WORD and draw us away from its pure and perfect power. Today, Christians who are concerned about the government legitimatization of same sex marriage SHOULD BE MUCH MORE CONCERNED about the unscriptural neglect and misuse of God's Word regarding marriage, divorce, remarriage and the raising of children.

If the Church does not repent of the sin of watering down the responsibilities of men and women regarding marriage and divorce, the Church will NEVER function with the power and the purpose that God proclaimed for us. The

Lukewarm Church will just die off, and in a century or two or ten, God will raise up a people that desire to trust in and live in His entire Word. We must study and read EXACTLY what the Scriptures say regarding these topics. We may not understand and agree with all the Scriptures, but we must believe and practice them all. Obey the Word, not because you understand all the ramifications, but because you believe the Word is true and YOU LOVE TRUTH. In the world, we must understand before we can believe. In God's realm, we must believe and trust in His Word BEFORE WE CAN UNDERSTAND His Word.

EQUALITY OF BELIEVERS AND MUTUAL SUBMISSION

Ephesians 5:21 (NLT) And further, submit to ONE ANOTHER out of reverence for Christ.

The Life Application Study Bible (LASB) commentary regarding Ephesians 5:21: "Of course, both husbands and wives should submit to each other, just as both should love each other. Paul emphasized the EQUALITY OF ALL BELIEVERS IN CHRIST." [35]

Galatians 3:28 NASB There is neither Jew nor Greek, there is neither slave nor free man, there is neither male nor female; for you are all one in Christ Jesus', [36]

LASB: But he (PAUL) did not suggest overthrowing Roman society to achieve it. Instead, he counseled all believers to SUBMIT TO ONE ANOTHER by choice – wives to husbands and ALSO HUSBANDS TO WIVES; slaves to masters and ALSO MASTERS TO SLAVES; children to parents and ALSO PARENTS TO CHILDREN. This kind of mutual submission preserves order and harmony in the family, while it increases love and respect among family members.'" [37]

JWK: This interpretation of the MUTUAL SUBMISSION Scripture and THE EQUALITY OF ALL BELIEVERS Scriptures are MAJOR heresies of the New Age Church. This Christian Feminist movement has an agenda: it wants to be Christian AND fit into the politically and religiously correct 21st century culture. This is not possible. In order to justify their position, they need to go outside the Bible, or they need to interpret the Bible in such a way that certain Scriptures have lost their true meaning. They essentially are denying the fact that a man has a special place of leadership in the Christian marriage. The man is the head of the woman even as Christ is the head of the Church and the woman must submit to the man as unto the Lord. It does not say that the woman is the head of the man and the man must submit to the woman. That authority is destroyed if this doctrine is practiced. Those who practice and teach the mutual submission doctrine in this way are compromising with the culture so they can build a bigger church because they have been duped by the barrage of anti-male feminist propaganda and the supposed equality of the sexes.

Scripture does not even hint that husbands are to submit to their wives or masters to their slaves or PARENTS TO THEIR CHILDREN. The absurdity of believing that parents need to submit to their children is beyond reason or spiritual sanity. Certainly, we see that there are children in the 21st century world who DO feel free to tell their parents what to do and there are parents who are willing to submit to their children for the sake of peace. But the real need of the child is to honor his parents and submit to them. By doing so, according to the fourth commandment, they will have a long life.

BASICALLY, submitting one to another IN THE SCRIPTURES is a relationship where one type of person submits to another type. For example, children submit to their parents, slaves to their masters, wives to their husbands. In the secular realm, privates to sergeants, but sergeants do not submit to privates. Those in authority do not by the nature of the relationship submit to those under their leadership. They serve, but in their service to those under them, they would NEVER relinquish their authority as leaders. Generals never submit to privates. Jesus was a servant to His disciples, but He NEVER relinquished His headship over them or submitted to ANY of their dictates.

Galatians 3:28 (NASB) There is neither Jew nor Greek, there is neither slave nor free man, there is neither male nor female; for you are all one in Christ Jesus.

Galatians 3:27-29 (AMP) FOR ALL OF YOU WHO WERE BAPTIZED INTO CHRIST, into a spiritual union with the Christ, the Anointed, have clothed yourselves with Christ; that is, you have taken on His characteristics and values. 28 There is NOW NO DISTINCTION IN REGARD TO SALVATION, neither Jew nor Greek, there is neither slave nor free, there is neither male nor female; for YOMISCELU WHO BELIEVE ARE ALL ONE IN CHRIST JESUS. NO ONE CAN CLAIM A SPIRITUAL SUPERIORITY. 29 And IF YOU BELONG TO CHRIST; IF YOU ARE IN HIM, then you are Abraham's descendants, and spiritual heirs according to God's promise.

The Life Application Study Bible (LASB) commentary said, "Paul emphasized the equality of all believers in Christ".[38]
JWK: NOWHERE in ANY Scripture is "the equality of all believers" mentioned. Galatians 3:28 does not even mention the word equality. Paul is not abolishing

the concept of Jews, Greeks, slave, free men or males and females, nor is he making them equal.

What Scripture IS saying is that our primary identification is no longer our race, our nationality, what sex we are or if we are free men or slaves. Our PRIMARY IDENTITY IS THAT WE ARE HIS and we are all in Christ! The Scripture does refer rather to UNITY in Christ (you are all one in Christ Jesus) and all have EQUALITY OF OPPORTUNITY: Jews, Greeks, slaves, free men, men and women are all united in Christ Jesus and ALL HAVE EQUAL OPPORTUNITY to belong to the body of Christ. ALL have equal opportunity for salvation, redemption and absolute success in the Kingdom of God. ALL can be His spiritual children. On this planet, some are Greek, some are Jews, some are slaves, some are free man, some are males, and some are females. In God's economy regarding the people in His Church, some are subordinate to others and some have authority over others. THIS EQUALITY IN OVERSIGHT THAT IS TAUGHT in many congregations has damaged millions of families! But we ARE all to work together as One Body to glorify God before men and be diligent to obey the Scriptures regarding OUR OWN duties.

THE LASB COMMENTARY says, "Of course, both husbands and wives should submit to each other (5:21), just as both should love each other." [39]

JWK: Regarding loving each other, the Bible teaches the husband is to love his wife AS CHRIST LOVES THE CHURCH and the younger women are to be taught by the older women TO LOVE THEIR HUSBANDS. Scripture commands husbands and wives to love each other. But nowhere in the Bible is there a Scripture that tells the husband to submit to his wife, either directly or by implication. And there is no directive in Scripture for the wife to be the head of her husband and sacrifice herself for him.

The husband's directive to love his wife as Christ loves the Church and for him to give himself for her is CERTAINLY as difficult as the wife's commandment to submit to her husband as unto the Lord. To do so he must put aside his own selfish interests so that he can properly and lovingly care for her. This directive implies that there may be great sacrifices he must make in loving his wife in a scriptural manner.

The woman is called to submit to her husband as her head even as the Church is to submit to Christ. Both the husband and wife are called to OBEY AND SUBMIT to the Scriptures and do what God directs them to do.

GOD'S PLAN SUBMISSION AND LOVE

ACCORDING TO SCRIPTURE: In the Christian marriage the woman submits to her husband as unto the Lord and recognizes that he is her head and the man loves his wife like Christ loves the Church, sacrifices himself for her and washes her with the water of the Word. If either spouse decides that they choose to not fulfill their God-ordained duties in the marriage, the one who chooses to fulfill their God-ordained duties will be BLESSED BY GOD and the one who neglects their God-ordained duties will be CHASTENED BY THE LORD or possibly even worse. Disobedience to the Words of our Lord Jesus Christ is a serious matter.

EPHESIANS 5:22-26 (NLT) For wives, this means submit to your husbands as to the Lord. 23 For a husband is the head of his wife as Christ is the head of the Church. He is the Savior of His body, the Church. 24 As the Church submits to Christ, so you wives should submit to your husbands in everything. 25 For husbands, this means love your wives, just as Christ loved the Church. He gave up His life for her 26 to make her holy and clean, washed by the cleansing of God's Word.

THE COMMENTARY in LASB SAYS, "Why did Paul tell wives to submit and husbands to love? Perhaps Christian women, newly freed in Christ, found submission difficult; perhaps Christian men, used to the Roman custom of giving unlimited power to the head of the family, were not used to treating their wives with respect and love.
"IN PAUL'S DAY, women, children and slaves were to submit to the head of the family: slaves would submit until they were freed, male children until they grew up, and women and girls their whole lives." [40]

Hebrews 13:8 (NASB) *states that* **Jesus Christ** *(and the Holy Scriptures which reflect His heart, soul and mind)* **is THE SAME YESTERDAY AND TODAY AND FOREVER.**

JWK What happened in Paul's day is not the issue. The circumstances of Paul's day have NOTHING to do with our obedience to the Word of God today. We must trust and obey ALL the Scriptures in EVERY CENTURY regardless of the culture or the circumstances.

The Bible was not written for any single time frame; rather it was written for EVERY age in history. It was not written because of the way people of the first century lived, it is a timeless book for every century and every culture. It is based on God's perfect understanding of the human condition of His creation: both men and women. The Scriptures are completely valid and completely relevant to every age. This book was written with mankind in mind, not men and women who were newly freed in Rome. It really doesn't matter why the

Bible tells us what to do. These Scriptures were written for the glory of God and for the good of man! What really matters is that we do it, AS UNTO HIM. What really matters is that we believe it is for us to obey the Scriptures with faith and love. Our obedience is never dependent upon our spouse's conduct. We, FOR CHRIST'S SAKE, must trust Him and obey His Scriptures.

THE LASB COMMENTARY says "How should a man love his wife? (1) HE should be willing to sacrifice everything for her, (2) make her well-being of primary importance, and (3) care for her as he cares for his own body. NO WIFE NEEDS TO FEAR SUBMITTING TO A MAN WHO TREATS HER IN THIS WAY." [41]

JWK He MUST make great sacrifices for her; he must make her SPIRITUAL WELL-BEING OF PRIMARY IMPORTANCE; not grant all her carnal desires . Jesus didn't sacrifice everything for the church's fleshly desires. Certainly, we need to care for our wives as we care for our own bodies. But there are times when we need to deny the cry of OUR flesh or the cry of HER flesh.

These duties are no less difficult than for the wife's duties to submit to her husband as unto the Lord, to quietly receive instruction with entire submissiveness and to love their husbands even when it is difficult to do so. The issue is NOT a wife, fearing or not fearing to submit to a man who is willing to sacrifice everything for her. The issue is SUBMITTING AS THE BIBLE DIRECTS HER TO SUBMIT SO SHE CAN PLEASE THE LORD JESUS CHRIST by her loving and sometimes sacrificial obedience. This is equally true for the husband. Please note: the commentary does not mention that, "no husband needs to fear loving a wife like Christ loves the Church if she graciously submits to him as unto the Lord." It isn't a question of a husband loving his wife like Christ loves the Church being easier if she submits to Him. He Is to obey the Scriptures so he can PLEASE THE LORD JESUS CHRIST and count himself worthy of the grace that God has poured out on him.

WIVES, BE SUBJECT TO YOUR OWN HUSBANDS

Wives are NEVER directed to be subject to their pastors, Christian counselors nor ANY OTHER MAN in the same way that they submit to their husband. The Christian counseling movement has done much to undermine the authority of the husband. In many Charismatic and Evangelical Churches, the pastor or counseling elder has usurped the authority of the husband. Most of these churches are much closer to the Roman Catholic model than they are to the Protestant Reformation model. While the Bible in 1 Corinthians 11:3 says, "But I would have you know that the head of every man is Christ, and the head of the woman is the man, and the head of Christ is God." The pastor is not the head of the man: Christ is the head of the man. In the Roman Catholic Church, the confessing priest has much more authority than the husband with the wife, because it is with her priest in the confessional booth that the wife shares her most personal problems. In the charismatic and evangelical churches, the husband is looked upon as not really equipped to deal with the deepest problems of his wife. As in the Roman Catholic Church, the charismatic and evangelical churches have "special" ministers, such as Bible school trained pastors, elders or paid counselors to deal with the wife's problems, especially her problems with her husband.

Ideally the husband should be taught by the pastor or his father on how to be the proper spiritual leader of his wife. Unfortunately, most charismatic and evangelical churches are afraid to teach the man that he is the head of his wife even as Christ is the head of the Church. They are afraid of teaching the man that he is the primary authority that must guide his wife into true spiritual blessing. Some leaders understand that they would lose much power in the Church if they gave that power, authority, and RESPONSIBILITY back to the husband where it scripturally belongs. Some leaders have been taught that men in general are unequipped and cannot be trusted to lead their wives because of their inherent insensitivity, lack of ability to communicate and childish nature. Many pastors, elders, and even counselors reinforce this poor image of men through their sermons, teachings and psychological counseling.

They imply that the woman would do much better if she talked with a professional who has had proper training and the necessary experience that would help her to become happier in her marriage. This of course is a usurpation of her husband's authority and an establishment of their own authority in her life. This is one of the reasons that we see so much adultery and romantic entanglements develop between pastors or leaders with female members of the congregation. The sympathetic wisdom of the pastor or elder is very attractive to an upset woman. Likewise, the trusting appreciation of a hurting woman is attractive to a pastor, elder or counselor. Scripturally illegal relationships between an elder and a counselee can begin in the counseling room.

This is one reason why the Bible counsels the older women to minister to the younger women. However, it is imperative that the older women love their husbands and are scripturally submitted to them. The practice of pastors running off with secretaries, piano players or other members of the congregation has become prominent in the 20th and 21st century church in America. This was uncommon in the Reformation churches of the 16th and 17th centuries and the Revival churches of the 18th and 19th centuries.

Unfortunately, most Christian women today are not taught to love their husbands and their children by the older Christian women. Usually they are taught how to navigate carefully in the marriage using manipulation to create a happy relationship. A prominent woman radio psychologist recently wrote a book entitled "The Proper Care and Feeding of Husbands". The title itself suggests strongly that the author and her audience viewed men in the same light as either pets or small children. In the Church, there are both Christian women and Christian men who voice this same attitude towards men. I DO understand that the title was a joke: but it was a bad joke. Situation comedies make their living by making men look like fools. What is worse, many pastors and teachers make fun of men from the pulpit. Few pastors or teachers joke about the weaknesses of wives. God is not pleased when church leaders make fun of either husbands OR wives.

HUSBANDS: BE RESPONSIBLE AND EXERCISE AUTHORITY

In churches in America, families must function with authority and responsibility. There must be leaders and there must be those who submit. The head of this army is not the husband: the head of this army is Jesus Christ.

The husband is submitted to Jesus Christ. And the wife is submitted to the husband as unto Jesus Christ. The husband has the responsibility to love his wife like Christ loves the Church and lead his wife with sacrificial love, never compromising the Scriptures. The wife has the responsibility to love and submit to her husband as unto the Lord. ONLY THEN can they raise children who will be submitted to their parents and submitted to the Lord Jesus Christ. The parents have the responsibility of leading and loving their children according to the dictates of Scripture. The children have the responsibility of obeying and honoring their parents and trusting that God will give them the best life possible if they do so.

Jesus Christ must be the foundation of the family. And the godly family is the foundation for every aspect of the Church and its power in the community, the culture, the nation and the world. When this happens, if both husband and wife fight hard to trust God and raise their children according to His precepts, then Satan will be defeated and the Church will be restored, and the culture and the nation will be restored and experience the greatest glory in its long history.

Unfortunately, many spiritually lazy Christian men would rather be properly cared for and fed than assume their God-given responsibility to properly care for and protect their wives. They are perfectly satisfied to relinquish leadership in order to obtain carnal comforts. They are even taught by some Christian men's groups that the wife's approval of their conduct is the primary validation of their spiritual progress.

God has given the husband spiritual authority to lead his wife and his family. A major portion of that authority is the responsibility to understand, trust in and teach spiritual principles to his wife and children. He must be Biblically prepared to answer any questions she has about spiritual matters, either by personal Bible study or elder counsel.

1 Corinthians 14:35 (NLT) If they *(wives)* have any questions, they should ASK THEIR HUSBANDS AT HOME, for it is improper for women to speak in church meetings.

The husband's responsibility according to the New Testament is to know the Scriptures well enough to answer her questions. He should learn to study the Scriptures, using a concordance (Strong's is excellent) a Bible Commentary (Matthew Henry is great) so he can find the answer to her questions. If he still does not know, then he should ask an elder or the pastor to teach him what the answer is. Then he can go to his wife and teach her. This enables him to maintain the spiritual authority in his household. This is not a choice! This is a commandment of our Lord Jesus Christ. To avoid doing this is to disobey God. It is false humility and is a selfish act.

Many men are willing to be an equal partner in the marriage relationship because the phony interpretation of mutual submission is what they are taught by their Christian leaders. Marriage in the Scriptures is not an equal partnership. Headship of the man and submission to him by the woman is not partnership. There is only one head in the marriage relationship and that is a man. If we look at nature, we see that a two-headed animal is a FREAK. Many Christian marriages are FREAKISH. If Scripture taught mutual submission, Jesus Christ would never have gone to the cross because His Bride the Church would never allow Him to do so.

Neither is the husband to abdicate his responsibility to be the head of the woman. On Judgment Day, this will not go well for the men who stand before the Lord and say that they relinquished the headship that God commanded them to exercise because he and his wife got along just fine without him being her head as Scripture dictates. Or he will use the excuse that the Word regarding marriage was only meant for Christians living in first century Ephesus.

Some men are willing to assume God's directive to love their wives as Christ loves the Church; however, they're not willing to be the head of the wife for fear that they would be considered chauvinistic or his wife would make him miserable if he did so. For men to please God, they must function with both responsibility AND authority. Anyone who assumes responsibility without authority functions in the same way as a slave or a child. Even though many pastors make fun of men from the pulpit, Christian men are NOT children nor are they slaves. Christian men in the marriage relationship are commanded to have both responsibility and must be allowed to exercise that authority. The authority that the husband has is not given to him by his wife. It Is commanded of him by his Lord, Jesus Christ! He does not earn this authority; He is commanded to have this authority and function in it. He must exercise that authority even if his wife won't submit to him as unto the Lord. Peace and unity are never to come about by breaking God's Word.

Some men have absolutely no desire to love their wives as Christ loves the Church. Usually this is from sheer unadulterated selfishness. They would much rather work hard, make money, and contribute little spiritual direction to their wives or children. They look upon the married years essentially as an extension of their adolescence. The contributions they make to the family are basically financial and for this, after working hard they want to relax and enjoy themselves. They leave the raising of the children to the wife and expect little in return. They allow the wife to run the family and manage their lives because that leaves them more time to do what they want. This attitude is most unchristian. They are always puzzled why their children rebel and their wife is so loveless. These so-called Christian men have no desire to study the Word so they can rule their households well. They are not interested in discipling their wife and their children and see them progress as spiritual beings. They are not concerned about what Scripture says. As Christian men, they will suffer because the Lord must discipline and chasten them so they will repent and obey His Word, especially regarding their God-given marriage and family duties.

Some women are willing to sacrifice being loved like Christ loves the Church just so they can be the head of the household, the family, and their husbands. They believe that because they are women and understand men better than men understand women, they will do a much better job in ruling the household and their husbands. Perhaps that's the way it was in their own household: their single or divorced mother was in charge and they never were under male leadership at home. These women, like their lukewarm husbands, will also need to stand before God and be evaluated regarding their obedience to the Word. They too will suffer the chastening hand of the Lord.

CONCLUSION

Even though the Church in America may not change this century regarding Scripture's policies regarding oversight and submission, that does not need to stop any of us from returning to the Spirit and the Word of Scripture regarding these vital subjects. In twenty-first century Christianity, there are no issues more important to born again Christians than trusting and obeying these Scriptures. By simply trusting in and obeying these life-giving directives in the New Testament, we can ensure a safe haven for our families in an increasingly dangerous culture.

CHAPTER 19: MARRIAGE AND DIVORCE

Love and Reverence
Why Christians Have Difficult Marriages
Consequences of a Scripturally Inappropriate Marriage
Miscellaneous Instructions to Wives
Miscellaneous Instructions to Husbands and Fathers
Miscellaneous Instructions for Both Husbands and Wives
Divorce Is Not the Unforgivable Sin,
   But that is NEVER the Point!
Consequences of Divorce in Our Society and in the Church
What Does God Want Us to Do?
Blessings of a Scriptural Family

LOVE AND REVERENCE

    Ephesians 5:22-33 (KJ21) WIVES SUBMIT YOURSELVES UNTO YOUR OWN HUSBANDS, AS UNTO THE LORD; 23 for the husband is the head of the wife, even as Christ is the head of the Church, and He is the savior of the body. 24 therefore as the Church is subject unto Christ, so let the wives be to their own husbands in everything.
    25 Husbands, love your wives even as Christ also loved the Church and gave Himself for it, 26 that He might sanctify and cleanse it with the washing of water by the Word, 27 that He might present it to Himself a glorious Church, not having spot or wrinkle or any such thing, but that it should be holy and without blemish.
    28 SO OUGHT MEN TO LOVE THEIR WIVES AS THEIR OWN BODIES. He that loveth his wife loveth himself. 29 for no man ever yet hated his own flesh, but nourisheth and cherisheth it, EVEN AS THE LORD THE CHURCH. 30 For we are members of His body, of His flesh, and of His bones. 31 "For this cause shall a man leave his father and mother, and shall be joined unto his wife, and they two shall be one flesh.

32 This is a great mystery, but I speak concerning Christ and the Church. 33 Nevertheless, let every one of you in particular so LOVE HIS WIFE EVEN AS HIMSELF, and THE WIFE SEE THAT SHE REVERENCE HER HUSBAND.

This section of Scripture sums up Paul's teaching on the marriage relationship in Ephesians. Loving your wife as you love yourself is a specific reference to a general directive previously spoken in Scripture. Jesus told His followers to love others as they loved themselves. The fact it is specifically mentioned here seems to indicate that the husband must keep this Scripture in mind as he leads and loves his wife. The relationship of marriage may cause him to forget this principle, so the Holy Spirit reminds him of his duty to treat her as he would like to be treated and to love her even as he loves his own body. The woman on the other hand is told to reverence her husband because that is something that she may forget during the marriage.

Noah Webster in his American Dictionary of the English Language published in 1828 defines REVERENCE:
"Noun: Fear mingled with respect and esteem.
The fear acceptable to GOD is a filial fear, a reverence filled with awe, PROCEEDING FROM A JUST ESTEEM OF HIS PERFECTION, which produces in us an inclination to His service and an unwillingness to offend Him.
We feel reverence for a parent and for an upright magistrate.
2. REVERENCE. Verb. To regard with reverence; to regard with fear mingled with respect and affection. We REVERENCE SUPERIORS for their age, their authority and their virtues. We ought to REVERENCE PARENTS AND UPRIGHT JUDGES AND MAGISTRATES. We ought to reverence the Supreme Bearing, His Word and His ordinances. Scripture: Matthew 21:37 They will reverence My Son. Ephesians 5:33; Let the wife see that she REVERENCE her husband."

Over the years, the meaning for the Greek word PHOBETAI in Ephesians 5:33, translated here as REVERENCE, has changed from fear to reverence to respect. In Ephesians 5:33, the word phobetai best translates as reverence. The husband is to be reverenced. Not feared in the sense that we use the word today but must be more than merely respected. Pastors are to be respected but not reverenced.

The reverence that a wife is to have for her husband that God orders in Scripture is comparable in its nature to the sacrificial love that the husband is to have for his wife. The husband is called to have A DIVINE love for his wife, "as Christ loves (agapate) the Church)". So, the wife is to have reverence for her husband. Obedience to these two commandments from God can ONLY BE ACCOMPLISHED if a person is BORN AGAIN and a NEW CREATURE IN CHRIST!

Translating the word phobetai as RESPECT today is indicative of how we have changed the language of Scripture to fit our own culture. Since the early part of the 20th century, we have seen a significant change of the wife's attitude toward her husband in our culture and a lack of responsibility on the part of the husband to sacrificially love His wife like Christ loves the Church.

It must be noted that a husband's sacrificial love for his wife is not conditional upon her submitting to him. Neither is a woman's submission to her husband conditional upon him loving her like Christ loves the Church. The submission that a wife gives to her husband and the love that a husband gives to his wife is UNCONDITIONAL! The reason that both husband and wife obey the Scriptures is BECAUSE OF THEIR FEAR, REVERENCE AND LOVE FOR GOD!

If either spouse disobeys God's command for them, they should fear the consequences that will come upon them. The Lord chastens whom He loves. But, as in every case, when either spouse repents and obeys the Scripture, there will be great blessing in that life. We must never give up the battle between the Spirit and the worldly attitudes and temptations of our culture that test our flesh. These directives from Scripture are the foundations for a spiritually successful marriage and a spiritually successful family. When we ignore or resist the clear directive of God, our marriages will suffer, and our children will even suffer more. The fact that the Church ignores or rationalizes these clear directives of Scripture is the reason why Christians in the 21st century are so prone to divorce and so easily tempted to abandon the marriage for a more satisfying, if not unscriptural relationship.

In America, the divorce rate of born-again Christians in 2008 was TEN times higher (32%) than the divorce rate of ALL married couples (3%) from 1867 to 1879. In 2011 the divorce rate among Christians (32%) was just a little lower than married people who claim no faith in God.[42]

WHY CHRISTIANS HAVE DIFFICULT MARRIAGES

It is easier to love your wife as Christ loves the Church or submit to your husband as unto the Lord if they are perfect, near-perfect, very good, or even just good. But God is in control of all things. He knows what is best for you. If your best opportunity to be spiritually successful is with a near perfect spouse, that is what He will give you. The same is true for a borderline okay spouse or even a really rotten spouse. This solely depends upon your need and His wisdom. Often our need is dictated by what kind of person we are. If we were desperate for a spouse because we were lonely before we got married and were just looking for the first person that we felt would help relieve that loneliness and or help us scripturally experience sexual satisfaction, then we might have entered into a relationship that was not the best idea for our life. If we entered into any relationship without making sure the other person was a Christian; if we were merely looking for a good looking or rich or religiously successful spouse; if we were more concerned about our needs than our spouse's needs; then we were entering into a relationship that God would necessarily have to teach us lessons. Even if we loved the spouse passionately and they loved us with equal ardor, it is not enough. "All you need is love" is not true. All you need is God's absolute validation of the relationship based upon, NOT YOUR FEELINGS, but His Word in the Scriptures.

To the degree that we are outside His Word and His heart is the degree that we will need to suffer and learn from our mistakes. God will not let His true children experience true happiness in a shallow or self-seeking relationship. The very one that you chose may be used by Him to refine you and bring you to a state where you will have repented of your shallow self-seeking ways.

CONSEQUENCES OF A SCRIPTURALLY INAPPROPRIATE MARRIAGE

2 Corinthians 6: 14 (NIV) Do not be yoked together with unbelievers. For WHAT DO RIGHTEOUSNESS AND WICKEDNESS have in common? Or what fellowship can light have with darkness?
2 Corinthians 6:15 (NLT) What harmony can there be between Christ and the devil? HOW CAN A BELIEVER BE A PARTNER WITH AN UNBELIEVER?

We must be equally yoked: we must not marry unsaved people or so-called Christians who do not love Jesus Christ. However, if you bail out of that unscriptural marriage with an unscriptural divorce, no matter how unequally yoked you were, or how unhappy you were, IF YOU ARE HIS, you will be severely chastened by God's firm but loving hand.

If you are weak, selfish or are not even a true follower of Jesus Christ, you will resist, you will rebel and do everything in your power to either control or abandon the relationship. You will always look at the faults of the other and NEVER recognize your own shallow carnal heart. If you are His, He will discipline and chasten you until you get it right. You will have to stick with a difficult spouse and love and serve them as God's Word instructs you.

Are there extenuating circumstances that are not found in Scripture that can be a good reason for divorce? Each situation may present a different answer from God and His Word. Separation is a scriptural choice. However, if you separate from your spouse, remarriage to another is not a choice, except in situations where sexual sin has been committed by the offending spouse or the unbelieving spouse insisted on leaving.

1 Corinthians 7:15 (NLT) But if the husband or wife who isn't a believer INSISTS ON LEAVING, let them go. In such cases the believing husband or wife is NO LONGER BOUND TO THE OTHER, for God has called you to live in peace.

We can be certain that if we have used an unscriptural excuse to God to gain freedom from our spouse, we will be dealt with severely by Him. Perhaps the severity of our punishment will not become obvious to us until we stand before Him on the day of judgment.

MISCELLANEOUS INSTRUCTIONS TO WIVES

1Timothy 2:15 (NASB) But women will be preserved through the bearing of children if they continue in faith and love and sanctity with self-restraint.

1 Timothy 2: 15 shows us that a wife and mother is to be preserved by the BEARING of children and raising them with love and faith that comes from being born again and obeying the Word of God. She is to live a life of holiness with self-restraint and, and if possible, avoid any occupation that would hinder her from raising her children for the Lord. The Christian mother has been blessed with one of the most important MINISTRIES in Scripture: to help her husband disciple, love and faithfully prepare children to serve the Lord. This duty requires much time and sacrifice.

Motherhood for the most part is a full-time job and is a most important ministry. The dilution of this high calling of God by seeking unscriptural ministries or lucrative job opportunities has caused terrible damage to Christian families over the last century. Self-esteem doctrines have taught us that we deserve certain material blessings and must "make sacrifices" for them. At times, a woman needs to work for a godly purpose; however, at other times the great sacrifice that the couple is making IS THEIR CHILDREN. For the sake of being a good wife and mother, a couple can decide that they will live with less material advantages so they will be best prepared to raise their children for the Lord.

This does not preclude the necessity of earning a living, if necessary: because of the death, illness or the disobedience of her husband or for any other legitimate financial need of the family. Preferably, she would work in her home but working outside the home may be her only choice. Sometimes, a wife may work in order to send her children to a Scripturally Christian school.

T 2:3–5 (NASB) Older women likewise are to be reverent in their behavior, not malicious gossips nor enslaved to much wine, teaching what is good 4 so that they may encourage the younger women to love their husbands, to love their children, 5 to be sensible, pure, workers at home, kind, being subject to their own husbands so that the Word of God will not be dishonored.

EVERY CHURCH should have the more mature women who are submitted to their husbands and love them teach these things to the younger women. Not only is this Scriptural but it would be beneficial, particularly to the younger women of our generation who have not been taught by their parents or their culture to love and be submitted to their spouse.

MISCELLANEOUS INSTRUCTIONS TO HUSBANDS AND FATHERS

Colossians 3:19 NASB Husbands, love your wives and DO NOT BE EMBITTERED AGAINST THEM.

Other translations instead of using the word embitter, use the phrase. "Don't hold hard feelings" against them. Embitter is the strongest translation word. Embittered means holding bitterness. Bitterness is the fruit of unforgiveness. Unforgiveness is DANGEROUS AND PUNISHABLE BY GOD.

Matthew 6:15 (NIV) but if you DO NOT FORGIVE others their sins, YOUR FATHER WILL NOT FORGIVE YOUR SINS.

Holding hard feelings is the result of being embittered. Becoming embittered against our wives is a sin against both them and God. We must NEVER become embittered with anyone, but particularly with our WIVES. Men who don't forgive their wives will not experience the abiding forgiveness of God.

Colossians 3:21 (NASB) Fathers, do not exasperate *(provoke)* your children, so that they will not lose heart *(become discouraged)*.

You can provoke your child by teasing them. This could provoke them and cause them to lose heart. Don't expect your child to do more than he is able.

Every child is not a good student in school. Every child should learn to be DILIGENT, but God never grades you on your INTELLIGENCE. Help them all you can but don't exasperate them by continually pointing out their failures.

Ephesians 6:4 (NASB) Fathers, DO NOT PROVOKE YOUR CHILDREN to anger, but bring them up in the DISCIPLINE AND INSTRUCTION OF THE LORD.

This appeal is directed at fathers. Fathers are more likely to provoke their children to anger than are mothers. Consequently, as dads we must be CAREFUL to discipline our children when they have gone against God's Word. When they are disrespectful, cruel, selfish, or knowingly commit sins, they must be disciplined or punished. Chronic carelessness is an offense that may need to be disciplined. But because a child breaks an inexpensive or even a valuable object accidentally, this is not an offense that grieves God's heart and needn't be disciplined or punished. These are judgment calls: if a child has been warned previously about an item and is still chronically careless, then he should receive correction. In dealing with children, we must first and foremost be loving and PATIENT. It helps to remember what it was like to be 5 years old, 12 years old or even 16 years old.

1 Kings 1:6 (NLT) Now his father, King David, HAD NEVER DISCIPLINED HIM *(Adonijah)* AT ANY TIME, even by asking, "Why are you doing that?"

The Scriptures condemn David for NOT CORRECTING HIS SON and clearly illustrates the terrible judgment both he and his sons experienced. Adonijah, attempted to become heir to King David was killed at Solomon's order. Two other sons were punished by death also. Amnon raped his half-sister and was killed by his brother, Absalom. Absalom, tried to take over David's throne and, in the process, humiliated his father by sleeping publicly with his concubines. He was killed by Joab, David's military leader. David's judgment for selfishly overlooking proper discipline of these sons was to watch them die.

MISCELLANEOUS INSTRUCTIONS FOR BOTH HUSBANDS AND WIVES

1 Corinthians 7:3-5 (NLT) The husband should fulfill his wife's sexual needs, and the wife should fulfill her husband's needs.4 The wife gives authority over her body to her husband, and the husband gives authority over his body to his wife. 5 DO NOT DEPRIVE EACH OTHER OF SEXUAL RELATIONS, UNLESS YOU BOTH agree to refrain from sexual intimacy for a limited time so you can give yourselves more completely to prayer. Afterward, you should

come together again so that SATAN WON'T BE ABLE TO TEMPT YOU because of your lack of self-control.

This is most important. Reasonableness is not thrown out the window. Doing unto others as you would have them do unto you is not thrown out the window. Doing what you are physically able to do, within reason and NEVER against what you believe is sin, is reasonable. It is important that both husband and wife do what they can to satisfy their spouse. The issue is not whether you love sex; the issue is you must love your spouse enough to do what you can to satisfy them sexually. You don't want to let Satan tempt your spouse to commit sexual sin. If either spouse is tempted to view pornography because the other spouse withheld reasonable sex from their mate, BOTH have sinned.

1 Corinthians 7:10-16 (AMPC) But to the married believers I give instructions—not I, but the Lord—that the wife is not to separate from her husband, 11 but even if SHE DOES LEAVE HIM, let her REMAIN SINGLE or else be reconciled to her husband and that the husband should not leave his wife. 12 To the rest I declare—I, not the Lord, since Jesus did not discuss this, that if any believing brother has a wife who does not believe in Christ, and she consents to live with him, he must not leave her. 13 And if any believing woman has an unbelieving husband, and he consents to live with her, she must not leave him. 14 For the unbelieving husband is sanctified, that is, he receives the blessings granted through his Christian wife, and the unbelieving wife is sanctified through her believing husband. Otherwise your children would be unclean, but as it is, they are holy. 15 But if the unbelieving partner leaves, let them leave. In such cases the remaining brother or sister is not spiritually or morally bound. But God has called us to peace. 16 For how do you know, wife, whether you will save your husband by leading him to Christ? Or how do you know, husband, whether you will save your wife by leading her to Christ?

If the Christian spouse leaves for a Godly reason, such as the other spouse is a REAL danger to a family member, then that spouse is not free to marry again. That spouse must remain single or come back to the other spouse. But if any unsaved spouse wants to leave, then the Christian spouse must let them go. In these cases they are not bound to the unbelieving spouse either morally or spiritually and they are free to marry. Neither the husband nor the wife is to leave their unsaved spouse, except for sexual sin. The reason for them staying is because the Christian spouse brings holiness to the marriage and the children will remain holy. If a Christian spouse leaves their unsaved spouse, then the children would not be holy. Perhaps this means that children have a special spiritual advantage if they are with a Christian parent.

1 Corinthians 7:39 (NIV) A woman is bound to her husband as long as he lives. But if her husband dies, she is free to marry anyone she wishes, but HE MUST BELONG TO THE LORD.

A believer is bound to their spouse as long as they live. But if the spouse dies, the believer is free to marry, but THEY MUST MARRY A CHRISTIAN.

Matthew 25:21 (NLT) "The master was full of praise. 'Well done, MY GOOD AND FAITHFUL SERVANT. You have been faithful in handling this small amount, so now I will give you many more responsibilities.

Praise your child when it is appropriate. If your child does something well, either in terms of effort or diligent accomplishment, then of course it would be a good thing to praise him. Academic success is good, but pride is not worthy of praise, but must be corrected. Most parents think their children are brilliant. A slow learning DILIGENT child is a great blessing to God. A brilliant student who gets great grades, but is not diligent, does not please God. The same principle also replies to athletic skills. Some children are naturally good athletes. Others are not. Never berate a child who does not do well in sports or academics. If a child is disrespectful to his coach, teacher, or parent that is another matter.

DIVORCE IS NOT THE UNFORGIVABLE SIN, BUT THAT'S *NEVER* THE POINT!

No single issue has hurt the Church more than the epidemic of divorce. Yet we discuss and teach on the legitimacy of a literal seven-day creation or the rapture much more than we teach what God says IN THE SCRIPTURES about divorce. Or worse, we unscripturally rationalize divorce so that the divorced people in our congregations will feel comfortable. We use such phrases as, "Remember, divorce is not the unforgivable sin" This catchphrase which does not represent the spirit of God's Word has opened the floodgates for thousands of Christian men and women to feel better about divorcing their spouse.

There are legitimate, scriptural reasons for dissolving a marriage, but the phrase, "Divorce is not the unforgivable sin" seems to be so true and so rational but is JUST NOT THE POINT. The following are some unscriptural excuses for divorce: "I just stopped loving him or her", "We just grew apart", "My spouse was so controlling", "My spouse was verbally abusive and scared me," "I finally met my true soulmate: a spouse I can minister with!" And, "I need my freedom so I can be me!" If children are involved, oftentimes the initiator of the divorce will say, "We divorced for the sake of the children." This usually is just not true. If one spouse were beating the children unmercifully or abusing them sexually then, OF COURSE separation or divorce for the sake of the children would be appropriate. But usually CHILDREN ARE HURT DEEPLY by divorce.

Many unscriptural divorces and subsequent remarriages, even among clergy, fall apart and then there is another divorce. Even if the remarriage lasted until death did them part, it was still WRONG BEFORE GOD. The Scriptures are clear: unscriptural divorce and remarriage is forbidden by God. It is a sin, and certainly can be forgiven, but that should never be a reason or a pretext for ANY unscriptural divorce or remarriage. Child molestation is certainly a sin that can be forgiven by God, but that is not a reason to imply that the molestation of a child is not as serious as some people think. Thank God, in the Body of Christ we have not yet reached the depravity of saying, "Child molestation is not the unforgivable sin!" If you are a Christian, knowingly and casually sinning, you must be aware that sin invites the chastening hand of God into your life. Worse, if your confession and repentance is not deep and from the heart, you may well prove that you are not His.

Matthew 5:31-32 (NKJV) Furthermore it has been said, "Whoever divorces his wife, let him give her a certificate of divorce." 32 But I *Jesus* SAY to you that whoever divorces his wife for ANY REASON EXCEPT SEXUAL IMMORALITY causes her to commit adultery; and whoever marries a woman who is divorced COMMITS ADULTERY.

Matthew 19:8-9 (NKJV) He said to them, "Moses, because of the hardness of your hearts, permitted you to divorce your wives, but from the beginning it was not so. 9 And I say to you, whoever divorces his wife, EXCEPT FOR SEXUAL IMMORALITY, and marries another, commits adultery; and whoever MARRIES HER WHO IS DIVORCED COMMITS ADULTERY.

CONSEQUENCES OF DIVORCE IN OUR SOCIETY AND IN THE CHURCH

DIVORCE CAUSES PAIN TO CHILDREN

Besides the obvious consequences of the pain that divorce can cause the divorcing parents, there is also GREAT pain that the children experience. My wife's mother left her husband for another man and it shattered her childhood. Some children come to believe that it was their fault that their parents divorced and carry that unsubstantiated guilt. In some families, the spouse who is raising the children or shares custody, constantly blames the other spouse as being responsible for the pain that their family is experiencing. This often implants bitterness in the child's heart toward the other parent and alienates the child.

DIVORCE OFTEN BEGETS MORE DIVORCE

If your parents were divorced, it is easier for a grown child to get divorced. Likely, your divorced parent told you they divorced because their spouse was VERY unfair, cruel or just plain bad. If you become dissatisfied with your spouse, it is MUCH EASIER to follow in your parent's footsteps.

DIVORCE CAN DESTROY THE AUTHORITY OF THE HUSBAND

According to the National Center for Health Statistics…in the United States about 80 percent of the divorces are initiated by women. In 75% of divorces, the children are raised in a home where there is one female parent and either no male parent or there are a number of temporary male father figures in the home (boyfriends and/or consecutive husbands). [43]

Because there are so many divorces in our culture, many men have never had the consistent presence of one father who functioned as the head of the family. Even in religious households, often the wife was the ultimate authority to the children. Also, it is not uncommon for several husbands or boyfriends to pass through the lives of the children with no steady male figure. Because MOM was the primary authority in the family, when her sons became husbands, they were quite comfortable being submitted to their wives and having her hold the reins of authority as the head of the household.

In the Church, we have altered our doctrines concerning divorce to accommodate the changes in our culture. The UNSPOKEN thought of many church leaders is that to teach a straightforward scriptural doctrinal presentation of Christian marriage and divorce would offend a large portion of the congregation. This is true! MANY WOULD LEAVE and find a church that "understood their situation".

DIVORCE, in both our culture and in the Church of Jesus Christ, threatens to remove the husband or neutralize him as the head of the wife and leader of his household. Many husbands are NOW more afraid of offending their wives and losing their families by her divorce than they are of offending God. These men are afraid that if they go with the teaching of Scripture, they may well lose their wives and probably their children. The State and even many churches typically are not sympathetic to any husband who exercises the God-ordained authority and responsibility as set forth by the Holy Scriptures. Even evangelical and charismatic churches temper the man's desire to lead his family by Biblical standards. Many would suggest a more moderate approach and suggest to him egalitarian principles NOT FOUND IN SCRIPTURE.

WHAT DOES GOD WANT US TO DO?

The battle to establish a strong scripturally sound Christian family and not cave into the ungodly cultural pressures that have redefined marriage is THE FIERCEST BATTLE that the Body of Christ will wage. In order to gain victory over our strong and well-organized enemy, we must fight HARDER THAN HELL! Had Satan failed to destroy or weaken the Christian family as defined by the Scriptures, he would not now have taken over the educational system, the media, the courts, the culture and much of the Church. If we would not have seen the terrible divorce rate, EVEN IN THE CHURCH, we would not have experienced the pain of seeing our children abandon their Christian values when they have left our homes.

We must quit sacrificing our marriages and our children to our need for personal happiness. We must realize that the political battle and the culture battle will never be won until we win the spiritual battle and the spiritual battle will never be won until we have Christian families that will obey the Scriptures regarding marriage and raising a family! Then and only then will the Church begin to be powerful enough to destroy Satan's kingdom and build a Church that would please God, turn America upside down and take back our culture, our educational system, our court system, AND OUR CHILDREN. Only then can we begin to win the *Battle for the Church*.

We need to make decisions that ensure our children's place in heaven. Be careful that the choices made are for the glory of God and the spiritual wellbeing of your children. Giving your child materialistic advantages that you did not have when you were their age, often is not pleasing to God. Having more time to love and disciple your children and teach them the ways of the Lord is infinitely superior.

THE BLESSINGS OF A SCRIPTURAL FAMILY

Proverbs 22:11 NASB Train up a child in the way he should go, Even when he is old HE WILL NOT DEPART FROM IT.

In order to teach children properly and disciple them according to the way of the Lord, parents must be good examples to their children. Remember that your children are your disciples.

Luke 6:40 (NABRE), "No disciple is superior to the teacher; but when fully trained, EVERY DISCIPLE WILL BE LIKE HIS TEACHER."

If both mother and father obey God and His Word concerning their duties as husband, wife and parents, the children will be much more likely to obey their own duties before the Lord. And the greatest joy parents can experience is to see their children follow the Lord and love Him with a joyful heart when they are mature.

1 Timothy 1:5 NASB But the GOAL OF OUR INSTRUCTION is love from a pure heart and a GOOD CONSCIENCE and a sincere faith.

Christians who trust in and obey the Lord Jesus Christ and His Word regarding marriage are assured of having a clean conscience and a sincere faith.

Deuteronomy 12:28 NLT Be careful to obey all my Commands, so that all will go well with YOU AND YOUR CHILDREN after you, because you will be doing what is good and pleasing to the LORD...

When we are careful to obey God's commandments, especially the ones that involve our wives, husbands, and children, we are assured by Scripture that things will ultimately go well for our entire family, including our children. What's even more important, we can be assured that we are pleasing our Lord.

CHAPTER 20: AN EPISTLE FROM HELL. DOES THE BIBLE SAY THE WIFE IS SUPERIOR TO THE HUSBAND?

The Battle: the Evil Rulers of Hell Against Christ's Church
Loving Him Well **by Gary Thomas: A Critique**
Double Standard: Dishonest Scales
Gary's Scriptural Validation of the Superiority of Women

THE BATTLE: THE EVIL RULERS OF HELL AGAINST CHRIST AND HIS CHURCH

Ephesians 6:12 NLT For we are **NOT FIGHTING AGAINST FLESH-AND-BLOOD ENEMIES**, but **AGAINST EVIL RULERS AND AUTHORITIES OF THE UNSEEN WORLD, AGAINST MIGHTY POWERS IN THIS DARK WORLD.**

There is a Luciferian spark that kindles ALL bad doctrine. SATAN is ALWAYS behind any shift away from the clear message of Scripture. Whether it was his famous challenge to Eve, "Hath God said?" or Charles Darwin's On the Origin of the Species and the theory of evolution, Satan was the original author. These words always originate with him. After they are received by the secular world, they are then brought to the attention of the leaders of God's people and then they are willingly received by some pastors, teachers and special speakers.

These cunningly scripted lies are spoken first by the deceiver and gladly parroted by men and women who have little knowledge of what the Bible says. They enlighten and ignite the corrupt desires of the easily deceived men and women of the Church. These words are not the mere utterances of men of science or misguided philosophers; these are the words that come directly from the throne of Satan in his habitat in HELL. Gary's book expertly sums up the current religiously correct psychological and scientific views of the short comings of men and the superiority of women. Because of these NEW TRUTHS, is subtly suggested it that the Scriptures regarding marriage, divorce, and family must be viewed differently.

In the 19th century Karl Marx wrote The Communist Manifesto which depicted workers as victims of rich Capitalists and Charles Darwin wrote On the Origin of the Species, a book that spoke of a creative process which excluded the need for a Creator. In the 19th and 20th centuries, Satan used William James, Sigmund Freud, Carl Jung, and Carl Rogers to popularize the new so-called science of psychology. ALL of these men were atheists or agnostics. Their teachings, especially Carl Rogers's, was eventually mixed with suspect Bible teaching to form Christian psychology in the 20th century. Many modern churches firmly accept this mixture of the sacred and the secular as being balanced teaching. Rights, privileges, victimhood, and other popular politically correct doctrines are emphasized in this movement. The Christian Psychology movement has led to easier, more frequent divorce and a loss of order and respect in the home. Wives and grown children have found it convenient to embrace their victimhood and even husbands are finally starting to believe that they are really quite Ill-equipped to be the head of the wife.

Gary Thomas and other Christian psychologists have unwillingly spoken for the enemy and helped Satan strengthen his grip on America and the Church. As always, Satan's main goal has not merely been to corrupt the culture; his ultimate goal has been to cripple and destroy the power of the Church. His demonic spirits roam the earth looking for those who would receive and PASS ON his twisted and unscriptural message. This message originally comes from the throne room of Hell itself. That's why this chapter is called, AN EPISTLE FROM HELL.

Please read the entire chapter, before you evaluate it.

LOVING HIM WELL BY GARY THOMAS: A CRITIQUE

This book is just one typical example of the suspect doctrine that is being taught in churches in the evangelical and charismatic movement in America. Many similar books exist. This book is NOT written by a fringe member of the establishment church. Both its author and the book itself are endorsed by Focus on the Family, founded by Dr. James Dobson. *Loving Him Well*, previously published as *Sacred Influence*, is written by Gary Thomas, a man highly esteemed by most Evangelicals and Charismatics. The subtitle is "PRACTICAL ADVICE ON INFLUENCING YOUR HUSBAND." He has written at least seventeen other books that have been Christian best-sellers. I could not find ANY negative criticism of this man. He is a counseling hero to MANY church goers in America. Gary is not considered radical in any way by mainstream Evangelicals.

PLEASE NOTE: Whenever a passage from *Loving Him Well* is quoted, there will be no introductory words, but the letters GT, to signify the words of the author, Gary Thomas. If there are quotes from another person, this will usually be noted.

His wife Lisa says in the introduction: "Gary wrote this book partly in response to the many emails and questions received from women who had heard him speak or who had read his other books. He heard their frustration, pain, and sometimes anger at husbands who just DIDN'T seem TO BE GETTING IT."[44]

This is a major theme of the book: it is the wife's duty to teach, influence, cajole, and at times even threaten her husband so he "gets it". The title itself is a double entendre. It means loving him in a good way and loving him back to health and making him well. This is the central issue of the book: the wife must be the physician that heals her sick, innately inferior, and damaged husband back to good health. With her God-given superior feminine perspective, she can lead her husband to a successful marriage. The wife just needs to have the courage to do so.

The book gives few challenges to wives regarding their own conduct, it concentrates on two things: reminding women of their victimhood at the hands of clueless husbands and assuring them of their husbands physiological, I and spiritual inferiority. The author describes men as defective, clueless, prone to anger and often loveless.

The following are quotes from Gary's book with comments from the author of the *Battle for the Church*. Gary's comments will be preceded by GT. The author of the *Battle for the Church* comments will typically be preceded by JWK.

GT: "I'll be upfront with you: you can't change a man. But you can influence him or move him – A FAR SUBTLER ART. And that's what we're going to discuss in this book." [45]

JWK: Because men are emotionally and spiritually inferior to women, listening to his wife is his last best hope on how to become pleasing to God and in the process make their lives and their marriage much more enjoyable.

The purpose of this chapter and the next chapter is to critique *Loving Him Well*. This book contains many psychological and neurological truths from the secular realm that are at best culturally adjusted and at worst downright lies. It must be noted that the teachings of this book reflect the majority opinion of the modern evangelical movement. Some of Gary's teachings interpret Scripture in a way that agrees with the culture warriors in our country. Other teachings reflect science studied from the secular/feminist viewpoint. When Scripture is referred to, the interpretation is usually through the lens of Christian feminism. As you read this book and the remarks of Gary, it will be up to you to decide whether this critique is correct or not. Please look at ALL OF THE SCRIPTURES that are listed, both ones that he uses and ones that I refer to. One of the principles of my analysis of his book is that our behavior in a marriage must be directed and judged ONLY by Scripture and not from secular science or psychology. The Holy Scriptures trump any and every psychological analysis and scientific discovery. As was stated earlier, the controlling truth or basic premise that is written in the *Battle for the Church* is, "As the Christian family goes, so goes the Church; as the Church goes, so goes the nation." As of late, neither the family, Church, nor the nation have been going very well. The criterion for any successful Christian family is scrupulous obedience, from the heart, to God's Scriptures

DOUBLE STANDARD: DISHONEST SCALES

PROVERBS 11:1 (NLT) The LORD DETESTS the use of dishonest scales. But he delights in accurate weights.

JWK: Many years ago, a dishonest merchant would use one set of weights when he purchased potatoes and another set of weights when he sold them. Or he would use one set of weights for selling to his friends, and another set of weights for people he did not care for. This is using a double standard. The Lord DETESTS a double standard or DISHONEST weights

In American politics today, the media is supposed to be impartial. In reporting a political or cultural event, the facts should be reported without prejudice. The media should report the successes of both parties and the failures of both parties. But when this media reports 95% of the successes of one party and 5% of the successes of the other party, this is impartiality and is unfair. When the media reports 5% of the moral failures of one party and 95% of the moral failures of the other party, this too is unfair. If they report every bad rumor as truth for ONLY one party, this is not just. When they judge the acts or words using one standard for one party and another standard for the other party, this too is unfair. This is the use of dishonest scales, and Proverbs says that THE LORD DETESTS THE USE OF DISHONEST SCALES.

CNN and the left-wing media obviously favor of the DEMOCRAT party, which now has embraced Marxism. They LITERALLY HATE Christians, Conservatives and Capitalism. Consequently, they use dishonest scales

The author of the book we are critiquing has a similar approach when dealing with men and women. The deeds of men are weighed with one standard and the deeds of women are weighed with another by either ignoring them, distorting them, or justifying them. This, too, is using a double standard; this is using DISHONEST SCALES. Remember, "THE LORD DETESTS THE USE OF DISHONEST SCALES."

Loving Him Well is the perfect example of this strategy. In *Loving Him Well*, when teaching wives about their responsibilities in a relationship with her husband, Gary Thomas seldom goes into detail about her duties and often ignores them. When the subject of a husband's responsibilities is mentioned, he goes into great detail about his responsibilities and about his failures. Like the shills for the Democrat party in our country, he MINIMIZES HER RESPONSIBILITIES and concentrates on her RIGHTS and her VICTIMHOOD. "He (Gary) heard their frustration, pain, and sometimes anger at husbands who just DIDN'T SEEM TO BE GETTING IT."[46] This approach is certainly satisfactory to the women in our culture, but it is just the opposite of Scripture, which concentrate on Jesus Christ's wonderful gift to us and our reasonable but sacrificial duties and responsibilities to Him RATHER THAN focusing on OUR VICTIMHOOD at the hands of our fellow human beings.

GT: "God sees and hears everything taking place in your life and relationships. He knows the MANY WIVES WHO SUFFER in loveless marriages. he knows how men sometimes look down on women and act condescendingly towards their wives. He knows that men can provide great strength, nurture, comfort, and security but also that they can be FRUSTRATING, TERRIFYING, DEMANDING and SELFISH. He sees the women who feel trapped in difficult marriages, as well as those who enjoy relatively good marriages with men who still occasionally act foolish, thoughtless, or distant...SOME HUSBANDS WILL RESIST CHANGE NO MATTER HOW ...BRILLIANTLY their wives confront them." [47]

JWK: Certainly, that is true, but he doesn't mention the obvious truth that there are many husbands who suffer in loveless marriages. He doesn't mention that he knows how women sometimes look down on men and act condescendingly towards their husbands and can be frustrating, demanding and selfish and at times even very scary. He doesn't take note that some wives will resist change no matter HOW BRILLIANTLY their husbands confront them. BOTH HUSBANDS AND WIVES can be guilty of these sins that harm a marriage. But the author uses two different standards. He judges men severely and does not judge women at all regarding the same sins.

GT: What if your husband NEVER GETS IT? Marriage as designed by God would result in a husband loving you like Christ loves the Church... However, too many marriages are turned upside down where wives are asked to become godlike figures to their husbands, trying to rescue their husbands from ruin and destruction.... Developing new skills and PRACTICING THEM ON YOUR SPOUSE may not change your spouse but it will certainly change you and you are so important to God and loved by God. [48]

JWK: Please note, the author once again uses the term, "YOUR HUSBAND NEVER GETS IT." He teaches that it is the wife's duty for her to "develop new skills and PRACTICE them on her husband." Gary seems to be careful to avoid the phrase "teach her husband" because Scripture says, "I suffer a woman not to teach nor usurp the authority of her husband." He uses the phrase "influence her husband." At the very least, this helps her develop new skills when she practices them on her husband. I wonder what Christian women would think, if the teacher suggested to a man that he should develop new skills and PRACTICE THEM ON HIS WIFE? Of course he would be condemned as a male chauvinist and chastised by the church.

Once again , we see the double standard. Speaking to the wife, Gary suggests that it is important for the husband to love his wife like Christ loves the Church. HOWEVER, he does not suggest that the woman's duty is to submit to her husband as unto the Lord. In fact, throughout the book, he seldom mentions the wife's scriptural duties regarding her husband. Also, the phrase, YOUR HUSBAND DOESN'T GET IT is repeated often in different forms.

GT: "The challenge of marriage is that when you're married to a defective man (and ALL MEN ARE DEFECTIVE in some way), it's not limited to learning how to handle something once or twice; it's about learning to live with that defect perhaps for the rest of your life. That calls for perseverance."[49]

JWK: OF COURSE, all men are defective in some way; but all women are ALSO defective in some way too! ALL PEOPLE are defective in some way. To point out ONLY men as being universally defective in some way, but to neglect mentioning the universal defectiveness of women is using a double standard.

GT: "I have never heard of a situation where marriage made a man less angry. You should assume you are seeing at most about 75% of your future husband's temper while dating him; it's virtually guaranteed that more temper will erupt after the wedding. If the man you are dating already seems too angry for your taste, he will be much too angry after the honeymoon." [50]

JWK: This is true of any and every sin that the man OR WOMAN will manifest before marriage. If he or she is angry, if he or she is somewhat flirty, if he or she is a nag before the marriage, he or she will likely BE WORSE after marriage. This is true of ALL human beings. We tend to suppress the negative aspects of our personality while we are courting. We typically are on our best behavior. For the author to draw attention to the increase in the man's anger or any other sin AFTER marriage and not take note that the same thing will happen for the female involved in the marriage, is using DISHONEST SCALES.

GT: "Anger attracts no one; A GUY throwing a temper tantrum can look downright silly to an observer." [51]

JWK: A GAL throwing a temper tantrum looks equally silly. Once again, the author judges men exclusively. He ignores women who throw temper tantrums. AND women do throw temper tantrums!

GT: "By nature, MEN CAN BE SELF-CENTERED… This cuts to the heart of the issue, because AN ANGRY MAN often acts as though he is the only one who matters. An angry man tries to assert control, seizing the situation by force and trying to USE HIS anger to intimidate or scare the other person into doing what he wants." [52]

JWK: Both men and women, BY NATURE are extremely self-centered and can use force, anger, threats, or tears to control the situation and get the other spouse to do what they want.

GT: "Jesus said what He said about divorce to protect women, not to imprison them… Our focus must be on urging men to love their wives like Christ loves the church, not on telling women to put up with husbands who mistreat their wives like Satan mistreats us." [53]

JWK: Jesus said what He said about divorce to protect women AND men AND children. Sometimes women need to put up with husbands who mistreat them. Sometimes men need to put up with wives who mistreat them. He made divorce extremely difficult for both husband and wife. The limits on divorce were established to keep the family together except in cases of sexual sin, desertion, or life-threatening situations. Children typically suffer MOST because of divorce. When Christians marry, they should be fully aware, according to Scripture, how hard it is to get out of the marriage. They should think long and hard and make sure this is the spouse that they are willing to share their lives and, if needs be, make great sacrifices for. They need to trust Jesus Christ in difficult circumstances. Please see the next chapter "To Be or Not to Be a Doormat!"

GT: An author that Gary quotes says, "Enough is enough. we must put THE FEAR OF GOD in the hearts of THESE TERRIBLE HUSBANDS…" [54]

JWK: We must put the fear of God into ALL of God's people. For the most part we have lost the fear of God in the Body of Christ. THE FEAR OF GOD is only invoked by Gary Thomas and his friend to protect wives from husbands. Often, This is just one of MANY examples where women are victimized by men. Unfortunately, many in the Establishment Church view women as victims. One pastor in a church when teaching on the terrible sin of pornography, said that the women who exploited their bodies for money were doing so because men wanted that kind of illicit pleasure. He said that men were the ROOT CAUSE of pornography. Men who desire illicit sexual experience and the women who profit from and are willing to provide that illicit sexual experience are BOTH GUILTY BEFORE GOD.

GARY'S SCRIPTURAL VALIDATION OF THE SUPERIORITY OF WOMEN

GT: Historically, neurologically, socially & EVEN BIBLICALLY, one can make the case that women tend to be MORE INVESTED in their marriage and in their relationships than are men...Back in Genesis 3, after the fall, God tells Eve, "Your desire will be for your husband" (verse 16 NIV). The word desire has been rendered as something so strong it is "bordering on disease". It comes from a root word connoting a violent craving for something. [55]

JWK: The 1599 Geneva Bible translates the Scripture as, "Thy desire shall BE SUBJECT to thine husband, and he shall rule over thee." The 2015 New Living Translation translates the same passage as "you will desire to CONTROL YOUR HUSBAND, but he will rule over you."

Verses 14-19 of Genesis 3 are written as Hebrew poetry. Both the NLT and the GNV translate this section correctly. The GNV version of the Bible translates a more literal Hebrew rendering of verse 16 while the NLT draws a reasonable conclusion from the context. Nowhere in the Bible does it state or even imply that women are more invested in their marriages AND MOST CERTAINLY NOT FROM THIS VERSE. In verses 16-19, both Adam and Eve are cursed by God to suffer greatly. The ground will be cursed, and Adam will need to struggle to scratch out a living. Childbirth for Eve will henceforth be painful, and she is no longer to control her husband. He will rule over her.

Statistics indicate otherwise regarding women being more invested in marriage. approximately 80% of divorces are initiated by women [56], but THAT MAKES NO DIFFERENCE!. At other times in Church history men-initiated divorce more than women. The Bible is the sole, TOTALLY dependable source of truth.

This is a major flaw of *Loving Him Well*. The author seems to care little for what the Bible says. Instead of quoting directly, he makes vague references that cannot be corroborated by Scripture. The following quote is a good example: Remember, an earlier quote by Gary on page 88, which says that If you look at the line of creation, FEMALES ARE THE CULMINATION...and ONLY THEN does God rest.

You can see why many women love this teacher. This Biblically flawed analysis of Scripture is a further indication that Bible truth is never this man's agenda and especially not his area of expertise. His basic truth model is that women are superior to men and must lend their talents to influence their hapless husbands to become better spouses. Furthermore, he ignores Scriptures that indicate the weakness of women.

1 Peter 3:7 (NIV) Husbands... be considerate as you live with your wives and treat them with respect AS THE WEAKER PARTNER and as heirs with you of the gracious gift of life...

1 Timothy 2:12-14 (NIV) I DO NOT PERMIT A WOMAN TO TEACH OR TO ASSUME AUTHORITY OVER A MAN; she must be quiet. 13 For ADAM WAS FORMED FIRST, and then Eve. 14 And ADAM WAS NOT THE ONE DECEIVED: it was the WOMAN WHO WAS DECEIVED and became a sinner.

GT: "One time a Pharisee was having dinner with Jesus when a prostitute came in and washed our Lord's feet with her tears, drying them with her hair (Luke 7:36-50). This act appalled the Pharisee, but JESUS SAID, IN ESSENCE, 'YOU JUST DON'T GET IT! She understands who I am, while you, even with all your learning, remain blinded to my place and glory.' In addition to the clueless Pharisees, the MALE disciples of Jesus also occasionally REVEALED SLOW THINKING. One time, A WOMAN poured costly perfume all over Jesus' head (Mark 14:3-9.) And some of the disciple said to themselves, 'what a waste!' while Jesus thought, FINALLY HERE'S SOMEONE (A WOMAN) WHO REALLY GETS WHO I AM." [57]

JWK: Jesus uses this event to teach Simon a lesson about forgiveness. He doesn't focus on her sin or Simon's sin; instead he focuses on the magnitude of her love because HE FORGAVE HER MANY SINS. Because Simon could only see a small amount of his sins, he could not love Jesus much because, in Simon's mind, there was little for Jesus to forgive. Jesus does not denigrate Simon; instead, He teaches Simon a valuable lesson and then he exalts the woman.

This Scripture is supposed to validate the author's contention that women get it and men don't get it. Jesus instructed His disciples not to trouble the woman and He certainly exalts her, but there's no implication that Jesus was belittling the disciples. But Jesus was complementing the woman. He certainly wasn't thinking of Himself. He corrected the disciples because they were supposing that the money could have been better spent. He corrected them. He pointed out that there would always be the poor, but her wonderful act of love and worship would be known to the whole world. He teaches His disciples a lesson. He does not denigrate them. He exalts the woman who did this wonderful thing. "Finally here's someone who really gets who I am." was the furthest thing from His mind. Gary is playing to his audience when he denigrates and makes fun of men at their expense. However, this is very popular with many 21st century women churchgoers.

GT; The author encourages wives to note that "the "Bible refers to you as a Queen. Genesis 1 tells us that God blessed both the man and the woman and told them to rule (verse 28)." [58]

Genesis 1:28 (NIV) God blessed them and said to them, "Be fruitful and increase… fill the earth and subdue it. RULE OVER the fish in the sea and the birds in the sky and over every living creature that moves on the ground."

GT: As you seek to live out your calling as A QUEEN in your home [59]

JWK: We are taught in our culture that little girls are Princesses and Gary is telling us that wives are Queens. Our culture NEVER says that boys are Princes and this book makes no mention that husbands are Kings. Women are elevated and men are ignored or denigrated. Once again, dishonest scales.

GT: "Many women accuse their husbands of being uncaring or unloving when, in fact, they may just BE CLUELESS… The reality may be that THEY JUST MAY BE CLUELESS… Sadly, far too many wives assume the husband doesn't care or worse, that he's trying to make their lives more burdensome, when the reality may be that he JUST DOESN'T HAVE A CLUE. [60]

JWK: He implies that MEN ARE CLUELESS throughout the book. Women are NEVER described as clueless. Unfortunately, even in the Body of Christ, some men are clueless, AND so are some women.

GT: In describing the creation of woman: "Genesis pictures a man created with an ACUTE VULNERABILITY. He is clearly not self-sufficient; he needs SOMEONE TO COME ALONGSIDE HIM, to live this life with him." [61]

JWK: I would suggest that, after the Fall man had the need for companionship and the need for a helper. God made him a GREAT companion and helper – his wife. "ACUTE VULNERABILITY" implies a desperate need to be protected. The woman was not created to be man's protector. God is to be man's protector. Part of loving your wife like Christ loves the Church is for the husband to be the protector of his wife. Because the Bible recognizes that she is the weaker vessel, she is more vulnerable than the husband and he is expected to protect her from physical, psychological and especially spiritual harm. In doing so, he honors her as the weaker vessel (1 Peter 3:7). THE AUTHOR ONCE AGAIN TURNS THE MARRIAGE RELATIONSHIP UPSIDE DOWN. Being a helper DOES NOT include protecting his non-existent 'acute vulnerability'.

CHAPTER 21: AN EPISTLE FROM HELL: DOES "SCIENCE" SAYS, THAT THE WIFE IS SUPERIOR?

Introduction
Scientific Proof: Women Are Neurologically Superior to Men?
Astonished that Jesus had Feminine Strengths
Hierarchical Relationships Versus Egalitarian Relationships
Bad Behavior: Male and Female Violence
It's A Lie They Want to Believe
Warning from Scripture
Conclusion

INTRODUCTION

This chapter is based on Gary's use of modern science including psychology and neurology in determining why a husband is emotionally and behaviorally inferior to his wife. Virtually all the information that he has gathered illustrate this clearly. In particular, the science that he uses, tells us that a woman's brain and nervous system are vastly superior to that of a man.

MODERN "SCIENTIFIC" PROOF: WOMEN ARE NUEROLOGICALLY SUPERIOR TO MEN?

GT: You need to know that MEN TEND TO BE HYPER-SENSITIVE TO CRITICISM and judgment...this is because "The dorsal pre-mammillary nucleus (located in the hypo-thalamus) ... 'contains the circuitry for a male's instinctive one-ups-man-ship, territorial defense, fear, and aggression. It's LARGER IN MALES than in females.'" [62]

JWK: This suggests that because of the way that God created him, he can't help but be more fearful, aggressive, more inclined to practice one-ups-manship and that he is MORE SENSITIVE TO CRITICISM than women. In these areas, he is physiologically and REALLY spiritually inferior to women. Inordinate fear, hyper-aggressive behavior and ESPECIALLY not being able to receive criticism well, are ALL sinful; so is one-ups-man-ship, which is just plain PRIDE.

In the chapter entitled "Understanding the Male" in *Loving Him Well*, the author points to many current scientific discoveries regarding the male and female brain.

GT: "Male brains usually have less serotonin than female brains. Since serotonin calms people down, men are more likely to act EXPLOSIVELY and compulsively. SURPRISED? PROBABLY NOT." [63]

JWK: His somewhat snide remark is directed at women who already have a reduced respect for their husbands. Once again, the author is preaching to the choir of culturally confused church going women, who in their mind, are justifiably concerned about the failures of men in general and are strongly entrenched in their victimhood at the hands of their husbands. He confirms their highest hopes by proving that men are much more unstable than women. They are created to be naturally inclined to compulsive behavior and get upset and EXPLODE more quickly than women.

GT: " Why is your husband LESS LIKELY TO TUNE IN TO EMOTIONAL PAIN? His brain doesn't work the same way a female brain does..." [64] "It is a biological FACT that emotional conversation can feel very stressful for a man and actually increases ANGER, particularly if that conversation gets pushed on him." [65]

JWK: This most certainly is a biological fact to the radical feminists in our country. To the culturally created, victim-oriented church-going women of our country it is also a fact. Because they embrace their victimhood as a kind of badge of honor, they see all kinds of negative activity in men and only perceive themselves as victims and never perpetrators of actions that might be instigated by a hyper-sensitive nature. Both men and women typically react with anger when emotional conversation is pushed on them. Scripture does not single out men as being more angry or stressed out than women. Rather it directs both men and women alike to neither be angry nor incite anger.

Proverbs 15:1 (KJV) A soft answer turns away wrath: but GRIEVOUS WORDS STIR UP ANGER.

Ephesians 4:31 (KJV) Let all bitterness, and wrath, and anger, and clamor, and evil speaking, be put away from you, with all malice.

GT: "If you can learn to live with and appreciate YOUR CONFUSING MALE BRAIN HUSBAND through his 20s, 30s, and 40s, there's a surprising payoff in his late 50s and beyond.... Your husband is gradually growing into a person who will likely be more in tune with your emotions, more capable of making sound judgments, and more relational overall." [66]

JWK: I am concerned that Gary used the term CONFUSING MALE BRAIN HUSBAND in a denigrating, sarcastic manner. However, his conclusion about the surprisingly great payoff that wives would experience in the latter years of their marriage was a ray of light. Eventually, these hapless, over sensitive, angry young and middle-aged men WHO JUST DON'T GET IT will change. Small solace for most women who must wait DECADES for the butterfly to come out of his cocoon.

GT: "You don't get angry at a CHILD IN A WHEELCHAIR WHO CAN'T JUMP over a 3-foot pole. Will you look at your husband's emotional/relational challenges within reason as partly a consequence of NEUROLOGICAL INABILITY?" [67]

JWK: This statement ranks as one of the all-time most condescending statements that I have ever read. It is true, that in generations past many so-called funny comedians and probably even some funny pastors made insulting, condescending jokes about women. That was wrong then and this is wrong now. It's somewhat like watching the old racially insulting movies made by white Hollywood in the 1930s. They pictured most black people as lazy, stupid, and immoral, and vastly inferior to white people.

ALL the aforementioned quotes suggest that God created men to be INFERIOR psychologically, sociologically, and EVEN SPIRITUALLY to their wives. Gary is referring to a science that is not unlike the supposedly scientific discoveries made by "brilliant" German scientists in the 1930s regarding the moral and intellectual inferiority of Jews.

Gary counsels women to be sympathetic with these slow witted, tired, poorly created and emotionally DISABLED creatures. The so-called science that has discovered the innate neurological, physiological, and spiritual inferiority of men is useful to validate the politically correct social engineering that is going on in our country. Most of the social engineering has to do with perverting or destroying the Word of God. The social engineers want to redefine sexuality, marriage, the raising of children and the relationship of a husband and wife apart from Scripture. Most social engineers push the agenda of the gross inferiority of men. These God-hating PC worshipping Progressives despise Christian men being in charge of ANYONE. They believe that WOMEN would make much better Presidents, senators, Supreme Court justices, corporate heads and, if the straitlaced and old-fashioned religion of Christianity would allow it, they would make much better leaders in the Church and family. In their world ANY decent clear-thinking husband should at the very least relinquish his right to lead his wife. Unfortunately, this social engineering, like so many other unscriptural worldly notions, has invaded and will continue to invade the Church in America.

ASTONISHED THAT JESUS HAD FEMININE STRENGTHS

GT: "HOW ASTONISHING IT IS that Jesus while still so young (barely 30) when he started his public ministry, demonstrated the perfect balance of typical male and FEMIMINE strengths, courage and gentleness, forceful action and empathy, leadership and humility.[68]

JWK: The author is actually ASTONISHED THAT Jesus Christ could manifest gentleness, empathy and humility. These qualities are NOT FEMININE qualities, but HUMAN qualities. They particularly belong to men and women alike who have been BORN AGAIN and have become NEW CREATURES IN CHRIST with tender hearts of flesh and not stone. The author apparently has been immersed in way too much Oprah, Dr. Phil, Gloria Steinem, and "Christian" psychology. Obviously, this man needs more Jesus Christ, Paul the Apostle, Peter, and the pure and perfect BIBLE. It would do him well. Along with being the Creator of all things, Jesus is the PERFCT MAN and the quintessential human being.

GT: Read books that directly deal directly with humility. Pride is an ever-present foe, so make HUMILITY an ever-present friend to marriage [69]

JWK:. I would suggest that she read MORE of what the Bible says about humility. Gary or others of his ilk would be tempted to reinterpret the Scriptures in a way that would reinforce the feminist viewpoint. The following Scriptures ON HUMILITY are from the Classic Edition of the Amplified Bible.

Philippians 2:3, (AMPC) Do nothing from factional motives through contentiousness, strife, selfishness, or for unworthy ends or prompted by conceit *and* empty arrogance. Instead, in the true spirit of humility (lowliness of mind) let each regard the others as better than *and* superior to himself, thinking more highly of one another than you do of yourselves.

Ephesians 4:2, (AMPC) Living as becomes you with complete lowliness of mind, humility, and meekness, unselfishness, gentleness, mildness, with patience, bearing with one another *and* making allowances because you love one another.

Colossians 3:12 (AMPC) Clothe yourselves therefore, as God's own chosen ones (His own picked representatives), who are purified *and* holy and well-beloved by God Himself, by putting on behavior marked by tenderhearted pity *and* mercy, kind feeling, a lowly opinion of yourselves, gentle ways, and patience which is tireless and long-suffering, and has the power to endure whatever comes, with good temper.

Just as a man should concentrate on the Scriptures that teach HIS RESPONSIBILITIES as a man, a woman should read the Scriptures regarding HER

RESPONSIBILITIES as a woman. The real issue is not the phony politically correct science and psychology that many of these men and women have devised. The issue is WHO does God tell us we are, and WHAT does God tell us to do.

HIERARCHICAL RELATIONSHIPS VERSUS EGALITARIAN RELATIONSHIPS

GT quotes Ephesians 5:21 "SUBMIT TO ONE ANOTHER out of reverence for Christ." He goes on to say, "The egalitarian view sees no such thing as gender roles in marriage. Thus, every couple should make their own decisions about who does what best and then divide up the responsibilities on the basis of their individual strengths and weaknesses. In this view, marriage is primarily a collaboration that stresses MUTUAL SUBMISSION." [70]

"JUST ABOUT EVERYTHING taught in this book *(Loving Him Well)* would work IN...THE EGALITARIAN... VIEW OF MARRIAGE."[71]

JWK: Egalitarian means that everyone has equal authority in relationships. For example, if the military were egalitarian, then a private would have as much right to give an order to a sergeant as the sergeant has to give an order to a private. If the private were smarter and more learned than the sergeant, then, in his area of superior knowledge, he would decide what the unit should do. Hierarchical means that some give orders, such as sergeants, and some take orders from the sergeant such as privates. Privates must obey and submit to the orders of the sergeant. We accept hierarchy in virtually every relationship situation in our culture EXCEPT marriage! We recognize that employees should do what the boss tells them, and children should obey their parents. But in the Church, many have an EGALITARIAN view of marriage! This interpretation says that husbands are not really the head of the wife and wives do not need to submit to husbands: they both are equal in authority and must both submit to each other.

BAD BEHAVIOR: MALE AND FEMALE VIOLENCE

GT:"Men are biologically LESS IN TUNE WITH THE CONSEQUENCES OF BAD BEHAVIOR. The anterior cingulate cortex, which is the fear of punishment area of the brain, is smaller in men than in women. Furthermore, testosterone decreases worries about punishment. The prefrontal cortex... focuses on good judgment and works as an inhibiting system to put the brakes on impulses and is larger in women and matures faster in females than in males...biologically, a case can be made that IT ACTUALLY IS EASIER FOR WOMEN TO 'BEHAVE.'" [72]

JWK: This ability of women to behave better than men is not mentioned in Scripture, and if you would look at real life, you must conclude that the statement is not true. Fallen human beings and saints alike ALL exhibit bad behavior.

GT: "Male violence creates havoc in homes across the world. You can hardly pick up a newspaper without reading at least one account of the DESTRUCTIVENESS OF MALE anger and VIOLENCE in VIRTUALLY ALL THE ASPECTS OF SOCIETY." [73]

JWK: Male violence is a tremendous problem. From 1933 to 1945 in the Nazi genocide and mass murder, soldiers under Adolf Hitler killed 20,946,000 men women and children.[74] Since World War II, In ALL THE WARS IN ALL THE WORLD including both combatants and noncombatants, 42,000,000 men, women and children died because of wars being fought all over the planet.[74]

But female violence also exists and has produced death far exceeding the destructive wars fought almost exclusively by men over the last 75 years, the paltry 42 million people killed was far exceeded in less than fifty years in America alone by the willful "mass murder of over fifty million unborn children. During 2010–2014, an estimated 56 million induced abortions occurred EACH YEAR worldwide. This number represents an increase from 50 million ANNUALLY during 1990–1994."[75] That is over 200 MILLION murders in only 4 years! These tragic homicides, in many cases, were perpetrated by selfish and violent women because they wanted their freedom and did not want to not be shackled down at home by an unwanted child.

REGARDLESS of the culturally charged scientific discoveries about the woman's ability to behave better than men. THESE WOMEN WILL GO DOWN as the most prolific mass murderers in history. FEMALE VIOLENCE, in the last 50 years, IS FAR WORSE THAN MALE VIOLENCE.

IT'S A LIE THEY WANT TO BELIEVE

2 THESSALONIANS 2:10-11 (KJV) ...THEY RECEIVED NOT THE LOVE OF THE TRUTH, that they might be saved. 11 and for this cause, GOD SHALL SEND THEM STRONG DELUSION, that they should BELIEVE A LIE

There are some in the Church that DON'T love the truth and look for teachings that would help them avoid truth. BUT in order for them to be successfully convinced of the innate superiority of women, they MUST IGNORE the Holocaust of ABORTION perpetrated BY WOMEN because it goes against their core beliefs. Gary's teaching is the PERFECT SOLUTION because it IGNORES the RESPONSIBILITY that WOMEN bear in this terrible crime. In order to convince people in the Church that women make much better leaders than do men, HE MUST IGNORE THIS HORRIFIC SIN. Because Christianity holds this sin in such high contempt, Gary cannot acknowledge this sin as being violence by women.

How can this author and so many evangelical Christians believe the lie that men are more violent than women? Because IT'S A LIE THEY WANT TO BELIEVE. They don't want to believe the truth because THE TRUTH would interfere with their agenda. So, they concoct a lie that similarly inclined people COULD accept as "truth". The fake news media tells lie after lie about Conservative Presidents, congressmen, Supreme Court nominees, and Christians. They get away with it because many in this country WANT TO BELIEVE THAT LIE. In the Church, people are hungering for lies that will make them rich, help them feel good about themselves and many women want to cast off the shackles of "male domination" by their husbands They want to be fed lies that denigrate men and exalt women. They are ESPECIALLY concerned about the Scriptures that take away a woman's right to do whatever she thinks best.

WARNING FROM SCRIPTURE

2 Timothy 3:1-2,5-7,14-15 (AMPC) But understand this, that IN THE LAST DAYS WILL COME PERILOUS TIMES of great stress and trouble that are hard to deal with and hard to bear.2 For people will be lovers of self and utterly self-centered, LOVERS OF MONEY and aroused by an inordinate, GREEDY DESIRE FOR WEALTH, 5 For ALTHOUGH THEY HOLD A FORM OF PIETY AND TRUE RELIGION, THEY DENY AND REJECT AND ARE STRANGERS TO THE POWER OF IT. Their conduct belies the genuineness of their profession. Avoid all such people. TURN AWAY FROM THEM! 6 For among them are THOSE WHO WORM THEIR WAY INTO HOMES AND CAPTIVATE SILLY AND WEAK-NATURED AND SPIRITUALLY DWARFED WOMEN, loaded down with the burden of their sins AND EASILY SWAYED AND LED AWAY by various evil desires and seductive impulses. 7 These weak women will LISTEN TO ANYBODY WHO WILL TEACH THEM; they are forever INQUIRING and getting information but are NEVER ABLE TO ARRIVE AT a recognition and knowledge of THE TRUTH.14 But as for you, CONTINUE TO HOLD TO THE THINGS THAT YOU HAVE LEARNED and of which you are convinced, knowing from whom you learned them,15 And how from your childhood you have had a knowledge of and been acquainted with THE SACRED WRITINGS...

There are teachers today who lead spiritually dwarfed women FAR AWAY from the Word of God. These GULLIBLE WOMEN will listen to teachers who oppose the truth of God's perfect Word and will do ANYTHING to relieve themselves of their God-given responsibility to obey the Scriptures. Men too are deceived and convinced to disobey Scriptures. . IT IS A FAKE TEACHING that BOTH men and women want to believe.

2 Timothy 4:3 (AMPC) For the time is coming when people will not tolerate or endure sound and wholesome instruction, but, having ears itching for something PLEASING AND GRATIFYING, they will gather to themselves ONE TEACHER AFTER ANOTHER TO A CONSIDERABLE NUMBER, chosen to satisfy their own liking and to foster the errors they hold.

CONCLUSION

The men and women that reject the tempting teaching of the world that has caused millions of churchgoers to embrace their victimhood need to turn to the Scriptures that demand sacrifice and suffering from both men and women alike. As they do so, they will experience great joy. Only submission to the COMPLETE, UNADUTERATED WORD OF GOD will bring us the joy of the Lord!

Please read the WHOLE NEXT CHAPTER, "To Be or not to Be a DOORMAT!"

CHAPTER 22: TO BE OR NOT TO BE …. A DOORMAT!

Introduction
Instructions to Husbands and Wives
Instructions to Slaves
You Must Follow in the Footsteps of Jesus Christ
The Key Issue Regarding Being a Doormat
Instructions to Husbands: IN THE SAME WAY
Instructions to Wives: IN THE SAME WAY
Conditions for a Blessed Christian Marriage

INTRODUCTION

Gary Thomas characteristically says, "MEN CAN BE VERY CRUEL with their cutting comments…Your husband's angry response will tempt you to become even more of a DOORMAT. This "MARTYR" method of marriage shortchanges both husband and wife." [76]

The Life Application Study Bible in its commentary on Ephesians 5:21-26: regarding submission says, "Submitting to another person is an often-misunderstood concept. It does not mean BECOMING A DOORMAT." [77]

JWK: This Scripture and this concept are CERTAINLY misunderstood and abused in the 21st century Establishment Churches. Whenever I have heard speakers or commentators, teach on this Scripture regarding marriage, after reading that the wife is to be subject to their husbands as to the Lord, they are always careful to say, "But remember this! You wives are NEVER to let your husband make A DOORMAT of you." He also warns the husbands, regarding his wife's submission. He says," How terrible it is that a husband would make A DOORMAT of his wife." DOORMAT is a Christian codeword for the oppressive way that Christian men treat their wives. Some men and women may even believe that the word DOORMAT is in Scripture. It certainly is true that there are mean or cruel men that are married to Christian women who have taken advantage of the submission of their wives. However, it is equally true that there are mean or cruel women married to Christian men that have taken advantage of their husbands responsibility to love their wives like Christ loves the Church and are called to give themselves up for their wives and serve their needs as Christ served the needs of the Church.

The modern commentaries and most evangelical teachers NEVER exhort the wife to NOT take advantage of her husband's love and make him a DOORMAT for her own desires. To address wives in this manner would fly in the face of political correctness and would greatly abuse the religious correctness which dominates the 21st century Church. Being a doormat is a very unpleasant experience. It is humiliating and uncomfortable to be taken advantage by someone else. BUT it can happen to anybody. It happens to both women and men. IT EVEN HAPPENED TO JESUS!

INSTRUCTIONS TO HUSBANDS AND WIVES

Ephesians 5:22-26 (NIV) WIVES SUBMIT YOURSELVES TO YOUR OWN HUSBANDS as you do to the Lord. 23 For the husband is the head of the wife as Christ is the head of the Church, His body, of which He is the Savior. 24 Now as the Church submits to Christ, so also wives should submit to their husbands in everything. 25 HUSBANDS LOVE YOUR WIVES just AS CHRIST LOVED THE CHURCH and GAVE HIMSELF UP FOR HER 26 to make her holy, cleansing her by the washing with water through the Word.

GT: "In her role as an inspirational speaker, Jo has met many women whose husbands have COWED them into an unhealthy DOORMAT mode. Sadly, sometimes this posture gets couched in religious language and represents a complete misreading of Biblical submission." (Jo is Jo Franz an inspirational speaker and acquaintance of Gary Thomas). [78]

JWK: It is clear from Scripture that men should not, "cow" their wives or anyone else into submission. Neither should either parent "cow" their children into an unhealthy doormat mode. Nor should a wife "cow" her husband into an unhealthy doormat mode so she can get what she wants.

However, the Scriptures in 1 Peter 2:18–3:9 discuss how the victims of inappropriate oversight and even inappropriate submission are to respond. First Peter discusses the issue of BEING A DOORMAT for someone else's desire. The slave with a physically abusive and cruel master, the wife with the domineering cruel husband and the husband with a rebellious, cruel wife.

This section on Scriptural submission to God's Word in first Peter, can be VERY PAINFUL! Should one spouse be a doormat for the other?

INSTRUCTIONS TO SLAVES

1 Peter 2:18-20 (NLT) You who are slaves MUST SUBMIT to your masters with ALL RESPECT. Do what they tell you—not only if they are kind and reasonable, but EVEN IF THEY ARE CRUEL. 19 For GOD IS PLEASED when, conscious of His will, you PATIENTLY ENDURE UNJUST TREATMENT. 20 Of course, you get no credit for being patient if you are beaten for doing wrong. But IF YOU SUFFER FOR DOING GOOD and endure it patiently, GOD IS PLEASED WITH YOU.

JWK: The pattern for proper behavior for God's people is established in these verses. Slaves are to submit to cruel masters and if they do so and suffer unjust treatment for doing good, THEY PLEASE GOD! But if they suffer for doing wrong, they get no credit or approval from God.

YOU MUST FOLLOW IN THE STEPS OF JESUS CHRIST

1 Peter 2:21-23 (NLT) For God called you to do good, even if it means SUFFERING, just as Christ suffered for you. He is your example, and YOU MUST FOLLOW IN HIS STEPS 22 He never sinned, nor ever deceived anyone. 23 He did not retaliate when he was insulted, nor threaten revenge when he suffered. he left his case in the hands of God, who ALWAYS JUDGES FAIRLY.

1 Peter 2:21 makes it clear, Since Christ suffered for us, WE MUST FOLLOW IN HIS STEPS. The suffering that Christ suffered for us FAR SURPASSED "BEING A DOORMAT". We must leave our painful experiences with our spouse to the Lord and trust that God is a fair judge and will work things out according to His justice and His mercy. He will be pleased with our obedient and submitted behavior. If we do not submit to His Word but exalt ourselves above His Word, we grieve His Holy Spirit.

He is our perfect model of submission. He became much more than a doormat. Most certainly, the Scribes, the Pharisees, the Romans and most of Israel walked all over Him. But they did much more than merely wipe their feet on Him. They humiliated Him, they crushed Him, they beat him so badly that He was not recognizable as a man. Oftentimes, both husbands and wives according to first Peter, are called to endure treatment that is cruel and is tantamount to being a doormat. But we are called to FOLLOW IN HIS STEPS.

The remarks in first Peter indicate that slaves, husbands, wives, and even our Lord and Savior Jesus Christ sometimes must suffer and be treated cruelly. Whether you are a wife who needs to submit to a cruel husband or a man who needs to love a cruel wife, if you seek Him diligently, he WILL change you, your circumstance and your marriage. One of the best prayers that a person in a difficult marriage can pray is "God give me a heart of divine love and honor for my spouse. Give me the strength and the will to take up my cross daily, deny myself, and follow You and Your Word for Your sake and Your pleasure". When we sacrificially obey Him, that gives Him great pleasure and we do find favor with God! When we SIN and disobey the Scriptures regarding our spousal responsibilities, and are harshly treated, He receives no pleasure and we find no favor from God.

THE KEY ISSUE REGARDING BEING A DOORMAT

1 Peter 2:23 (NLT) HE LEFT HIS CASE IN THE HANDS OF GOD, WHO ALWAYS JUDGES FAIRLY.

Like Jesus Christ, we must trust God because when we leave our case in the hands of God, HE ALWAYS JUDGES FAIRLY. We must trust, even if it means painful sacrifice, HE ALWAYS JUDGES FAIRLY. We know that the greatest blessings for us and the greatest joy for God are when we obey His Word, ESPECIALLY when it hurts!
For both the husband and wife, this painful sacrifice of suffering at the hands of a disobedient spouse may be the only way you can bring peace and ultimately joy to your marriage. The key is trusting that God will work things out to your benefit when you walk in sacrificial obedience. If you want peace and the joy of the Lord in your marriage, YOU MUST suffer for His Namesake, even from your spouse. BUT THE BLESSINGS OF PLEASING OUR LORD ARE INCALCULABLE!

INSTRUCTIONS TO HUSBANDS: IN THE SAME WAY

1 PETER 3:7 (NASB) You husbands IN THE SAME WAY live with your wives in an understanding way, AS WITH A WEAKER VESSEL, SINCE SHE IS A WOMAN; and SHOW HER HONOR as a fellow heir of the grace of life, so that your prayers will not be hindered.

IN THE SAME WAY as slaves submitted to cruel or harsh masters, and Jesus suffered for us, we must follow in His footsteps. HUSBANDS are to submit to God's Word and continue to love their wives as Christ loved the Church. Even if they won't submit to them, are rebellious or even if they are cruel. At times, a husband may be a doormat to his wife's unreasonable, cruel or harsh behavior! At times, his wife may walk all over him. At times, his wife may verbally or even physically abuse him in private or in public. OF COURSE, if the life or physical well-being of the husband or his children are threatened, he has the option of separation.

At times, she may turn their own children against him for her advantage. At times, she may make him look bad to her friends. In private counseling sessions with the pastor or an elder or a "spiritual" friend, she may openly reject his headship yet willingly submit to the pastor, an elder, a friend or a so-called Christian counselor in an inappropriate way. She may even accuse him falsely. This damages her husband's headship and is demeaning to him, but HE MUST CONTINUE TO LOVE HIS WIFE AS CHRIST LOVES THE CHURCH! "He must live with her in an understanding way, as with someone weaker, since she is a woman." He is commanded by the Scripture to SHOW HER HONOR as a fellow heir of the grace of life! Even if your wife treats you harshly, you must respect her and love her as Christ loves the Church. You must submit to the Scriptures and put up with her as a servant would put up with a cruel master.

INSTRUCTIONS TO WIVES: IN THE SAME WAY

1 Peter 3:1-2 (NASB) IN THE SAME WAY, you wives, be submissive to your own husbands so that even if any of them are disobedient to the Word, they may be won without a word by the behavior of their wives, 2 as they observe your chaste and respectful behavior.

IN THE SAME WAY AS SLAVES SUBMITTED TO THEIR MASTER wives are to submit to their CRUEL or HARSH husbands. "Disobedient to the Word" means just what it says: it is NOT merely an unsaved husband, but a husband who is DISOBEDIENT TO THE WORD OF GOD! "Won without a word" means won over to obedience to God's Word WITHOUT SPEAKING A WORD OF CORRECTION OR REBUKE. Even if you believe that the Scripture only refers to an unsaved husband (and many commentators do), how much more should the wife submit to a fellow believer than to an unbeliever? In our politically correct country and some religiously correct churches, harsh words are grounds for a woman to divorce her husband. HOWEVER, Scripture makes it clear: this is the way the wife wins over her husband so that he becomes obedient to the Word of God, because he observes the "chaste and respectful behavior" of his wife. J.B. Phillips says " pure and reverent behavior"

At times, a wife may be a doormat to her husband's cruel or harsh behavior! At times, her husband may walk all over her. At times, the husband may verbally or even physically abuse her in private or in public. OF COURSE, in cases of physical abuse that threatens the health or life of either the wife or her children, the wife has the option of separating from her husband.

At times, her husband may turn their own children against her for his advantage. At times, he may make her look bad to her friends. Sometimes during corporate prayer times at church, he may uncover her sin for all to see. In private counseling sessions with the pastor or an elder or a "spiritual" friend he may accuse her falsely or uncover her sin and shame her. She is STILL to submit to him in the same way that a servant submits to his cruel or harsh master and Jesus suffered for His Church..

Many Christian women would balk and deny the validity of this teaching and follow the teaching of the Lukewarm Church and the poor commentaries they have fostered. THIS IS BEYOND BEING A DOORMAT! In the eyes of many 21st century women, submitting to a husband who is cruel or harsh is worse than being a fool! But Scripture offers justice from God to the one who sacrificially obeys.

1 PETER 3:3-6 (NASB) Your adornment must not be merely external such as braiding the hair, and wearing gold jewelry, or putting on dresses; 4 but let it be the hidden person of the heart with THE IMPERISHABLE QUALITY of A GENTLE AND QUIET SPIRIT, which is PRECIOUS IN THE SIGHT OF GOD. 5 For in this way in former times the holy women also, who hoped in God, used to adorn themselves, being SUBMISSIVE TO THEIR OWN HUSBANDS; 6 just as SARAH OBEYED Abraham, calling him lord, and you have become her children if you do what is right WITHOUT BEING FRIGHTENED BY ANY FEAR.

The Scripture speaks of Sarah as being the mother of submitted women. Likely, it was because her disobedient and cowardly husband Abraham was willing to allow his wife to marry two different men at two different times to save his own life. He was afraid he would be killed if the rulers knew that Sarah was his wife. Each ruler took her for his own because they thought she was Abraham's sister (she was Abraham's half-sister: Genesis 12 and 20). This despicable act of Abraham greatly compromised his wife. Apparently, Sarah in her obedience to cowardly Abraham was not frightened by any fear. She is God's example to the Church of a submitted wife who trusted that God would work all things out for her good AND THEN SHE WATCHED HIM DO IT! This adornment is not merely superficial; this adornment MUST come from her heart. The adornment is "the imperishable quality of A GENTLE AND QUIET SPIRIT."

It certainly is easier for a husband to love his wife like Christ loves the Church if his wife submits to him as unto the Lord. It is also easier for a wife to submit to her husband if he loves her like Christ loves the Church. But even if your spouse treats you cruelly, you must follow the INSTRUCTIONS OF OUR LORD. Wives must submit to cruel husbands and husbands must love cruel wives. He must love her like Christ loves the Church even if she constantly threatens him or attacks him cruelly. Likewise, the wife is to submit to her husband even if he threatens her or attacks her cruelly.

If we can endure cruel or harsh treatment as the Lord endured cruel or harsh treatment, we can HOPE FOR eventually an atmosphere of harmony, sympathy, brotherly love, kindheartedness and humility of spirit in our relationship with our spouse. At times, our spouse will be a doormat; at other times, you will be a doormat. But the reward for trusting in and obeying God's Word is PEACE, SPIRITUAL PROSPERITY and the joy of making God smile in approval and love for you.

CONDITIONS FOR A BLESSED CHRISTIAN MARRIAGE

1 Peter 3:8-9 (NLT) Finally, all of you should be of one mind. SYMPATHIZE WITH EACH OTHER. Love each other as brothers and sisters. Be tenderhearted and keep a humble attitude. 9 Don't repay evil for evil. DON'T RETALIATE with insults when people insult you. Instead, pay them back with a blessing. That is what God has called you to do, and He will grant you HIS blessing.

These verses refer to slaves, Masters, husbands, and wives. In this context it is particularly important for married couples to obey these Scriptures. Versus 8 and 9 imply that at times both men and women will have differing viewpoints, be unsympathetic, unloving, hardhearted or proud. ESPECIALLY, we must repress the almost overwhelming desire to return evil for evil and strike back verbally when we are attacked verbally by our spouse. Instead of retaliating in like manner, we are to pay them back WITH BLESSING! Sometimes, WE NEED TO BECOME DOORMATS for Christ's sake.

If both husband and wife can endure the pain, cruelty and harsh treatment of their spouse and obey God's Word, He will grant them a blessing. Even if ONLY ONE SPOUSE responds with sacrificial obedience to His Word, that spouse will receive a blessing. For one thing, you can experience the joy of knowing that, as the obedient spouse, you bless the heart of God.

In a Christian marriage, as in all other Christian pursuits, very few unconditional rights are given to us. Most blessings are contingent upon obedience. If we want mercy, we must be merciful. If we want to follow Jesus, we must take up our cross daily. IF we walk on the narrow road, we will experience life everlasting. God does not give us a bill of rights as our Constitution does. He gives us a Book of Responsibilities and Privileges. If we want eternal life, we MUST BELIEVE in the Lord Jesus Christ. If we want a happy marriage, we must fulfill the responsibilities that God gives us as wives and husbands. According to first Peter, we don't even have the right to respond in kind: we cannot return an insult with another insult. In fact, we have the responsibility to be kind to a cruel spouse. If we suffer because we have been disobedient to God's Word regarding the treatment of our spouse, no blessing comes to us because we have sinned.

Romans 8:28 (NASB). And we KNOW that God Causes ALL THINGS to work together for good to those who love God, to those that are called according to His purpose.

REMEMBER, these Scriptures are only for Born Again Christians who have New hearts and are New creatures in Christ. However, if you don't really believe this and are not really called by Him and don't really love Him enough to obey Him, you are in great trouble. If you are a stubborn child of God who would rather risk receiving 1,000 stripes from the hand of Him who loves you, rather than obey Him, He most certainly will chasten you.

You may resist, you may rebel and do everything in your power to either control or abandon the relationship. You may always look at the faults of the other and NEVER recognize your own carnal heart. If you are His, you will be disciplined and chastened until you get it right, even if it means, when your mate treats you badly. To please Him, the husband must love his wife like Christ loves the Church, and the wife must submit to her husband as unto the Lord. For His sake, you will stay with a difficult spouse and love and serve them as God tells you to do in His Word.

CHAPTER 23: EXTREME SOLUTIONS

Hitler's Final Solution: Eliminate the Jewish People
Margaret Sanger's Final Solution:
   No Masters, Gods, or Unwanted Children
Satan's Final Solution: Destroy the Family.
   and-the Church Will Fall
EXTRMELY Offensive Scripture
   To WOMEN in the Establishment Church
It's an Old Strategy with a New Twist
EXTREMELY Loathsome Teaching
Why God Made Marriage and Divorce EXTREMELY Difficult.
Extreme Consequences of Divorce
The Most Extreme Solution in History

HITLER'S FINAL SOLUTION: ELIMINATE THE JEWISH PEOPLE

The Final Solution for the Jews in Europe began in Nazi Germany and other European nations in the 1930s. It culminated with the death of over 6 million Jews and the crippling of a religion and a culture like nothing the world had ever seen. Before these mass murders could take place, the propaganda machine of the Nazi party had to convince Germany and the rest of the world just how evil the Jews were. "Brilliant" Nazi scientists declared that Jews were physically and morally inferior to the other races, with a natural proclivity towards evil and a lack of love for anyone who is not Jewish. They were referred to as pigs and rats. They were considered dangerous to the culture and the nation. They were even portrayed as intellectually inferior. Eventually, they were stripped of any position of power or authority and were systematically removed from the educational system. Very few nations and individuals fought for their rights. It was only near the end of World War II that people discovered how effective The Final Solution had been. When the concentration camps were liberated by the Allied powers, they discovered the horrific life these people had endured before they were exterminated. Over 6 million Jews had been murdered. At that time, Hitler's Final Solution was one of the most successful acts of mass murder in history.

MARGARET SANGER'S FINAL SOLUTION:NO MASTERS, NO GODS, AND NO UNWANTED CHILDREN

In the 20th century, before the Nazis came to power, another FINAL SOLUTION began. Margaret Sanger's attack on the Biblical teachings regarding God, marriage and unwanted children. In America she became a hero to millions of young women in the feminist movement. She published a newspaper called The Rebel Woman. On the front page of every issue the masthead read NO MASTERS, NO GODS!

Her endgame was twofold: destroy the authority of the husband over his wife and by doing so give women the right to do whatever their hearts desired, particularly in regard to their unwanted children. This allowed women to end both unwanted male oversight and prevent or destroy the lives of unwanted children. Ms. Sanger believed in eugenics (the science of producing better human beings). She strongly believed that birth control, particularly practiced by less intelligent, less affluent and less able individuals, would strengthen the human race. In 1921 she founded the American Birth Control League which later became The Planned Parenthood Federation of America and organized clinics in Harlem. In her later years, while she was president of the International Planned Parenthood Federation, she and her organization advocated for the decriminalization of abortion laws. In 1973, the federal government made abortion legal in the United States and abortion clinics became common in every large city in America.

While Hitler's Final Solution was temporarily successful, Margaret Sanger and those who shared her viewpoint are still accomplishing much for their true leader Lucifer, Satan, the god of this world. As was mentioned in Chapter 21, in the last 50 years, in America alone, over 50 million unborn children have been systematically slaughtered by women willing to have their children murdered by the new American Storm Troopers: the abortion doctors. These selfish and benumbed women acted in the same capacity as a Mafia Don would act when he would call a professional killer to eradicate an enemy.

Sanger's war against Biblical doctrine concerning the role of the wife has been almost completely victorious in our culture. In many churches, practically speaking, the husband's headship of the woman has been virtually destroyed. The wife is no longer expected to submit to her husband as unto the Lord. If Margaret Sanger were not writhing in hell, she would be applauding the world AND THE CHURCH for embracing so many of her views.

SATAN'S FINAL SOLUTION: DESTROY THE FAMILY AND THE CHURCH WILL FALL

Satan clearly understood that God's order of authority in marriages and families was important in establishing the Lord's Kingdom. As was spoken earlier in this book, he observed that God initially chose Abraham to "direct his children and his household after him to keep the way the Lord by doing what is right and just so that the Lord would bring about for Abraham what He has promised him."

Genesis 18:19 (NASB) For I have chosen him, so that HE MAY COMMAND HIS CHILDREN AND HIS HOUSEHOLD after him to KEEP THE WAY OF THE LORD by doing righteousness and justice, so that the LORD may bring upon Abraham what He has spoken about him.

Satan recognized that if he could destroy the father's leadership in the family, he would weaken the family to such an extent that, the Lord would not be able to bless the families and consequently it would be much easier to destroy the Church of Jesus Christ and even the United States of America would eventually fall to the enemies of God. Satan understood that faith in and obedience to the Word of God, especially His Word on marriage, is the cornerstone of a strong Christian church. His best strategy was to go after the leader of the home.

In the New Testament, God's purposes for His people were even more detailed and more specific. If Satan could get the leader of the Christian household to voluntarily relinquish his responsibility and authority over his wife and family or if he could get the wife and family to ignore or disrespect that authority, he KNEW he could destroy the Christian family and subsequently CRIPPLE THE CHURCH virtually beyond repair.

As in the garden of Eden where Satan was able to cause the First Family to be banished from the garden of Eden by deceiving the woman, so today, he has used deceptive teachers in the Church who have been blinded to the truth of Scripture to deceive the wife and cause her to ignore or dilute her husband's authority as her head. Lies, innuendos, half-truths and clever editing of the Bible have accomplished much for the god of this world. Even as millions of unborn children have been systematically slaughtered, so millions of families have been weakened and painfully destroyed by unscriptural marriage practices and divorces. Consequently, millions of children have suffered both emotionally and spiritually.

To their discredit, many false teachers, counselors, and pastors know that if they can get the wife to stray away from the authority of her husband, they can have much more influence in her life. The more they can convince the wife that she is an innocent victim of an abusive, clueless husband, the more they can feed her the poisonous fruit of rebellion against God's Word regarding her marital duties. Even if she does not leave her husband, Satan can teach her to use her newfound knowledge to control her husband and get him to go along with her plans for the children and their marriage. Of course, to Satan, DIVORCE IS FAR PREFERABLE.

This divorce strategy has caused great rejoicing in the halls of hell. As was mentioned in Chapter 19, The divorce rate in the Church is 10 TIMES HIGHER in all America than it was 150 years ago. With over 30% of "Christian" marriages ending in divorce, we have almost caught up with the non-Christian divorce rate. Approximately 80% of all divorces are initiated by the wife and 75% of children whose parents are divorced live with their mothers.

Female headship in the home is thus being perpetuated in both the world and the Church. The children look to the mother for leadership because that is the way they grew up. Many only have seen a woman as the head of the household. All this makes it much easier for Satan to convince grown children who get married that female headship is the norm.

This is why Satan initiated his FINAL SOLUTION. If you can destroy God's order of authority, then the Church will be destroyed or greatly weakened, and God's people and the nation will be much easier to conquer. Satan's Final Solution and master plan to weaken the Church has been extraordinarily successful. The Church is no longer able to stop the Paganization of our nation, our culture, our educational system, and our courts. If the Church does not repent, the Church itself will be judged by God Himself. As in times past, Satan has SUCCESSFULLY influenced men and women to alter the letter and intent of the Holy Scriptures.

EXTREMELY OFFENSIVE SCRIPTURE
TO WOMEN IN THE ESTABLISHMENT CHURCH

1 Timothy 2:11-15 (NIV) A woman should learn IN QUIETNESS AND FULL SUBMISSION. 12 "I DO NOT PERMIT a woman to teach or to assume authority over a man; 13 for Adam was formed first, then Eve. 14 and Adam was not the one deceived; it was the woman who was deceived and became a sinner." 15 but women will be saved through childbearing if they continue in faith, love and holiness with propriety.

To the modern culturally over-sensitive church, this section of Scripture, 1 Timothy 2: 11-15 CANNOT BE TAUGHT as it stands. It offends every molecule of our media dominated minds. We are taught by television situation comedies and commercials that women are not merely equal with men, but they are superior to men in most ways. In the Church, these Scriptures are the very reason that we must dismiss the Scriptures as being our exclusive source of wisdom. To the lukewarm Establishment Church, these Scriptures JUST GO TOO FAR! Women need to Learn in QUIETNESS AND FULL SUBMISSION? The response typically is, " REDICULOUS! That is NOT WHAT IT MEANS! Women are forbidden to have authority over men in the Church AND their husbands? The New Age Church with its egalitarian view of women and men CANNOT ACCEPT the truth of these Scriptures. Most New Age leaders contradict these Scriptures and give women authority over clueless men both in the home and the Church. Because Eve was created AFTER Adam signifies to Gary Thomas and others that the woman is "the CULMINATION of ALL CREATION" (Please see page 91.). Therefore, to the minds of many Bible teachers, 1 Timothy 2: 11-15 CANNOT POSSIBLY invalidate a woman to teach or have authority over ANY man.

Many churches today have women pastors, elders, and teachers of men. Many of the fabulously wealthy TV teachers and evangelists that teach both men and women are women. Women evangelists commonly hold meetings for the purpose of teaching both men and women.

Verse 15 is especially outdated. The implication is, except a woman is called to a life of singleness to serve the Lord, that she should expect to be married and bear children and continue a life of faith, love and holiness with dignity. The notion that a Christian woman should expect to live a life where she is married and bearing children as her paramount ministry for the Lord is virtually absent in the Lukewarm Churches today. IT MUST BE NOTED that, like most other sections of Scripture, these teachings are not addressing the world, but rather ONLY Christian believers. These Scriptures refer to born again Christian women who are NEW CREATURES IN CHRIST.

IT'S AN OLD STRATEGY WITH A NEW TWIST

In the second and third centuries Satan began to add, subtract and redefine the Word of God. The Catholic Church added the traditions and stories about the early Saints to buttress their own interpretation of Scripture. In the Bible, a heathen goddess is referred to both as the Queen of Heaven; in the Roman Catholic Church, Mary became the Queen of Heaven AND the mother of God. She was more beloved and respected by the Roman Catholics than Jesus Christ

Himself. In the 19th century, the Church of the Latter-Day Saints decided to add the Book of Mormon to their canon of scriptures. In the 20th century, the secular psychology of Carl Rogers and others was eventually mixed with suspect Bible teaching to form the new science of Christian Psychology. Rights, privileges, and victimhood are emphasized in this movement. The Christian Psychology movement especially has done great harm to the Scriptures regarding the roles of husbands and wives.

EXTREMELY LOATHSOME TEACHING

This section includes quotes from *Loving Him Well*. Much of the doctrine of this book is covered and critiqued in chapter 20 and 21. These practices are taught throughout the movement. The quotations referred to in *Battle for the Church*, are typical of the teachings in Establishment Churches.

1 Peter 1:7 (NIV) THESE TRIALS have come so that the proven genuineness of your faith of greater worth than gold, which perishes even though refined by fire may result in praise, glory and honor when Jesus Christ is revealed.

GT: Commenting on these verses, Gary Thomas says, "These verses, 1 Peter 1:7 ... SHOULDN'T BE MISUSED TO KEEP WOMEN TRAPPED IN A PERSECUTING MARRIAGE." [79]

JWK: This is an EXTREMELY FEARFUL response to a Scripture that was designed to help Christians understand that the trials they go through were for the glory of God and produced fruit that would last forever. To switch the focus from this to the problem of women being persecuted by men is illogical and is an attempt to make a point that the Scripture is in not making. 1 Peter 2:18-3:7, illustrates the suffering and pain in relationships that both men and women may have to endure to please the Father. For further information, read or re-read chapter 22 of this book: To Be or Not to Be... A Doormat.

Dr Melody Rhode who is a friend and mentor of Gary Thomas, the author of *Loving Him Well* discusses two men: Mark and Jim. The following situations are described in chapter 3, pages 49 through 63 of *Loving Him Well*.

"MARK admits to CONTROLLING behavior. JIM has 100 reasons for his chronic unemployment for more than a decade... At the heart of their problem is a condition that is called 'FUNCTIONAL FIXEDNESS' which can be defined in the form of a question: 'What if your HUSBAND isn't motivated by your pain? WHAT IF HE'S ONLY MOTIVATED BY HIS?...

"'FUNCTIONAL FIXEDNESS' can be used to describe a MAN who will never be motivated by his wife's pain but IS ONLY MOTIVATED BY HIS PAIN. For change to occur, he has to feel HIS OWN DISCOMFORT... So, FUNCTIONAL FIXEDNESS IS A MOTIVATIONAL AND SPIRITUAL DISORDER COMMON AMONG MEN, but also is present in many women... It shows a lack of empathy and spiritual maturity. HE NEEDS A COMPELLING REASON to change and it needs to be more compelling than your unhappiness or private misery with the situation... You must be willing to CREATE AN ENVIRONMENT IN WHICH THE STATUS QUO BECOMES MORE PAINFUL THAN POSITIVE CHANGE." [80]

"One woman begged her husband (JIM) for more than a decade to get more serious about pursuing a job. He always had a fresh excuse about why he couldn't. She finally had enough and FILED FOR DIVORCE, and in his desperation to get her to change her mind, her husband landed a job within 30 days. Is that a coincidence or is it just evidence that HE WASN'T motivated by her frustration, he was MOTIVATED only BY THE PAIN HE WOULD FEEL over losing his wife." [81]

JWK: Nowhere in Scripture does it say that a wife may divorce or threaten her husband with divorce if he is lazy or incompetent. Nowhere in Scripture does it say that a lazy incompetent wife can be divorced or threatened with divorce by her husband. Imagine if a husband filed for divorce from his lazy, incompetent wife who suffered from "functional fixedness". Imagine the response of the Church! This man would be considered cruel and unreasonable. Of course, THE AUTHOR IS ONLY SPEAKING TO WOMEN. I doubt that Gary or his mentor would give the same instruction to men. Likely, they would tell the man to search his own heart and see if he had done anything to cause his wife to not function well in her wifely duties.

The author is suggesting that a woman can use divorce to get what is necessary for her sense of well-being. She can use divorce to get her husband working and providing adequately for the family. The author has gone beyond Scripture when she did not object to her client filing for divorce to correct her husband. Such an action is totally against Scripture. God values MARRIAGE AND THE FAMILY much more than this. Divorce is not a scriptural solution to change conduct of a lazy or incompetent spouse.

GT: "Another wife had been complaining for more than a decade about a CONTROLLING husband (Mark)... She kept trying to tell him she couldn't breathe, but he didn't pay much attention until she met with a lawyer to FILE FOR DIVORCE and rented an apartment." [82]

JWK: First of all, CONTROLLING is used in TWO ways. To describe someone who forces you to do things their way; this can be DANGEROUS or very annoying. Secondly, to a person that does not like to be told what to do, they will define people who tell them what to do as being controlling. People who want to get out of a relationship often WEAPONIZE the term controlling.

..... Again, imagine a husband complaining that for more than 10 years he had a controlling, nagging wife and he kept trying to tell her that he couldn't breathe, but she didn't pay much attention until he met with his lawyer TO FILE FOR DIVORCE and rented an apartment. The Church would not tolerate the husband doing such a cruel thing. But in this book, it is considered a REASONABLE ACTION FOR THE WIFE TO THREATEN HER HUSBAND or even commit the sin of unscriptural divorce to get her husband shaped up. Perhaps the wife's mentality was, "If I can't get my way, it's the highway!"

GT: I've seen God work in so many miraculous ways when A WOMAN BECOMES STRONG." The author sums it up with this remark: "As your brother in Christ, I'm encouraging you to be BOLD, COURAGEOUS, AND STRONG." [83]

JWK: By filing for divorce to get your husband to be less controlling or to incentivize him to work harder for his wife and family is not a sign of spiritual strength, but of SPIRITUAL WEAKNESS. Would a man be considered bold, courageous, and strong if he divorced his wife so she would shape up and become more helpful, hard-working, or less controlling? OF COURSE NOT! However, the author's praise of these women sounds like the way the feminist democrats and the media characterized Professor Christine Blasey Ford. She accused Brett Cavanaugh of sexually attacking her 30 years ago. They praised her for BEING STRONG, but in the end, it became evident that she was not entirely truthful. The problem is that now we are told that we must ALWAYS BELIEVE THE VICTIMIZED WOMAN (except. OF COURSE, if she is accusing a democrat).

In the 18th and early 19th centuries, women understood that their basic Christian duties were to be a good wife, a good mother, submit to their husband as unto the Lord and be a helpmate. They understood that the Bible did not tell her to be a teacher and molder of her husband. Men were expected to be strong hard-working leaders that provided for their families, protected them, loved their wives and children in a sacrificial way and washed their wives with the water of the Word. During this period, the divorce rate was much lower, the incidence of school shootings was way down, the children had much more respect for their father, mother, teachers, and the law. Most importantly, the probability of a child retaining his faith even after he entered young adulthood was much higher. True faith was sustainable because the Church was more Scriptural. The country and the culture were much more Christlike because the Church had embraced and experienced the Reformation and two Great Awakenings, and MOST IMPORTANTLY taught the clear meaning of Scripture regarding marriage and divorce.

WHY GOD MADE MARRIAGE AND DIVORCE EXTREMELY DIFFICULT.

MATTHEW 19:8-11 (NASB) He *said to them, " Because of your hardness of heart Moses permitted you to divorce your wives; but from the beginning it has not been this way. 9 And I say to you, whoever divorces his wife, except for immorality, and marries another woman commits adultery.10 The disciples said to Him, "If the relationship of the man with his wife is like this, IT IS BETTER NOT TO MARRY." 11 But He said to them, "Not all men can accept this statement, but only those to whom it has been given.

Even the apostles of Jesus understood that marriage was an extremely difficult relationship and they also understood that the ability to divorce your wife had been changed to such a degree that they said, perhaps it is better not to marry. One reason He made marriage and divorce so difficult is that HE WANTS TO BE SURE THAT CHRISTIANS MARRY WISELY and remain committed to their spouses. He wants them to COUNT THE COST, which can be much self-sacrifice, but the rewards are that a successful Christian marriage will produce MORE disciples for Jesus and will also cause God to be pleased. It is important to choose a person who loves Jesus AND HIS WORD more than they love you. Christians should get married because they believe that they will be better able to glorify God by being married then by being single. But remember when you marry, God DID explain His program to you. The scripturally legitimate ways out of marriage are few: basically, your spouse's sexual sin or death.

To succeed spiritually and glorify God in your marriage, the ONLY way to do so is to embrace ALL of God's word and use it EXCLUSIVELY as a guideline for your conduct as a couple. No true Christian should ever be swayed by ANY so-called scientific discovery that twists or countermands the Scriptures. Over the last 100 years, as the Church has slipped further away from the Word and our culture and has become aggressively anti-authority, we have rejected the authority of the Bible, the husband, the parents oversight of their children and even the law of the land. If we choose to either come against, compromise, or ignore the Scriptures concerning our marriage, we will fail God. These are extreme statements in our moderation-mad churches. Because people of the broad way church can't find enough real evidence in the Scripture to counter God's demands regarding divorce, marriage, and remarriage, they make subtle appeals to secular "science", psychology, and history.

No Bible believing Christian should ever embrace these practices. Those that teach these principles are either fools or frauds and, in some cases, will be cast into the false teachers' section of Hell.

EXTREME CONSEQUENCES OF DIVORCE

When a child has been raised in a divorced family where the mother has been the family head (often helped by the government), the child grows up with little respect for men and in some cases great faith in the government which helps provide the food and money.

In cultures, communities, or congregations where there is a majority of children without fathers, we see a much greater disrespect for authority in general than we do in cultures, communities, or congregations where there is an active and committed father who is the head of the wife. In the last 50 years, we have become a country where MANY children have NO consistent FATHER either by the father's choice, the mother's choice, or their choice. We have seen students from grade school to college universities actively and sometimes violently reject authority on their campuses. In our largest cities, we see MANY communities that hate the police and anyone who has the authority to enforce the law. We are even witnessing the murder of law enforcement people in our country. This is due in part to the fact that we have abandoned the Scriptures regarding the authority and the responsibilities of ALL family members. We are on the fast track to becoming a LAWLESS nation. Revolution or civil war may be the result because EVEN THE CHURCHES have little respect for God's perfect law.

THE MOST EXTREME SOLUTION IN HISTORY

Even though God has made EXTREMELY difficult demands on both men and women, He Himself has made EXTREMELY PAINFUL SACRIFICES for us! He has gone to EXTREME measures to redeem mankind. He sent his Only Begotten and Uncreated Son from the Perfect Love of timeless eternity to live among a sin-filled and cruel race of rebels who were righteously condemned to death. He then tells this Perfect Son who was filled with love for His Father that He must die on the cross for our sins and that He must be forsaken by His Father and BE SEPARATED FROM HIM. This act of sacrificial love both on the part of the Father and the Son accomplished more than the redemption of mankind. When the Son of God rose from the dead, He also empowered those that would trust in Him to have the power and the will to obey whatever God asked them to do. He caused these believers to be born again and become new creatures in Christ with new hearts and new desires. He also gave them supernatural power over sin. What is equally important, God gave His people a flawless handbook that shows us the way clearly and shows us how to appropriate His love and that power. Everything He has done for us and everything He demands of us is because of His great love and IS FOR OUR GREATEST GOOD AND HIS GREAT GLORY. This indeed is THE MOST EXTREME SOLUTION IN HISTORY!

SECTION 7: LAST WORDS

CHAPTER 24: THE RULE OF LAWLESSNESS
CHAPTER 25: THE GREAT SHAKING, THE SECOND STORM, AND PEARL HARBOR: THE GREATEST AWAKENING

The title of Chapter 24, "The Rule of Lawlessness" reflects the current attitude of both the country and the establishment churches in America. Many in the church, disregard the LAW OF GOD, and the HARD DEMANDS of Scripture. Consequently some Christians no longer believe that the First Amendment must be enforced equally for ALL people. Many believe that because of white male privilege and systemic racism, certain groups need not obey. In the secular realm, the equal application of the rule of law is virtually NEVER considered. The First Amendment is only for people who support the politically correct interpretation of social justice.

Chapter 25 uses three images to describe the present and future state of the Church of Jesus Christ in America. The Great Shaking describes the sovereign work of God in separating the lukewarm establishment church members from Christians whose hearts are wholly after God. It also depicts what the Church looks like today, and what the church will look like after the Great Shaking. The Second Storm describes God's attempt to awaken His people to the reality of the battle that they must fight and the response of the people to God's attempt to rouse His people from their deep sleep. Pearl Harbor highlights how people must choose between what they want and what God demands. Some will sacrifice all of their desires so they can obtain the great prize; others will sacrifice their souls to a great temptation.

CHAPTER 24: THE RULE OF LAWLESSNESS

Introduction
A Day that May Live in Infamy
Kristallnacht: Nazi Law and Order in Germany
Kristallnacht in America?
The Response of God's People
Does the Church Bear Any Responsibility for the Chaos?
The Focus
What Can We Expect?
What Must We Do?
   We Must Repent of Our Wickedness
   We Must Grieve and Lament for the Sins of the Church
Daniel's Prayer for God's People

INTRODUCTION

When I began writing this book in 2018, I supposed that we would have possibly a decade or more to get ready for the wave of great difficulties, punishments or the ultimate judgment that would come upon the church in America. However, the events in the last months have possibly shortened that timetable. At the very least God once again is trying to rouse us out of our deep slumber. Hopefully, some will WAKE UP! The shutting down of our economy seemed possibly appropriate at first, but as it lengthens, it seems ill-conceived and somewhat contrived. Threatening to arrest church goers and imprisoning small business owners for violating social distancing policies was severe. Many Democrat state governors and city mayors particularly seemed to be anxious to shut down the economy and control their people.

A DAY THAT MAY LIVE IN INFAMY

On May 25, everything escalated. Floyd George, a black man was killed by a white policeman who placed his knee on Floyd's neck and would not get off. Floyd died and the policeman was charged with murder. Shortly after that, cities all over the nation reacted with demonstrations that turned violent;

property was destroyed, businesses looted, and more lives were lost. Black Lives Matter was at the forefront of the protests and the Democrats and their allies, the media and entertainment industry rallied to their defense. Many Establishment Evangelicals and Charismatic leaders supported this cry for "Social Justice." They seemed at that time to ignore the looting, destruction of property and the murders committed by the lawless demonstrators.

The same mayors and governors who came down hard on those who defied social distancing in their churches and businesses, did nothing to stop the Black Lives Matter mob from defying the social distancing policy. In fact they gave in to virtually all of their demands. They encouraged the protesters and treated the looters and destroyers of property with great mercy! The Seattle, Washington mayor even let them occupy and supervise a portion of their city (without social distancing). Democrat mayors and governors called for the police to not arrest looters, except if they were violent. This was the height of hypocricy. The RULE OF LAWLESSNESS was practiced in many cities and the crime rate has accelerated exponentially. Politically, it has been a great move for the democrats: they have greatly increased their chances of winning the Presidential election in November.

As the support of the fascist, extreme, left wing group Black Lives Matter party grew, it became an unforgivable social crime to disagree with their views. Media people were fired from their jobs for suggesting that the demonstrators went too far. Church leaders, sports commentators, NFL football players, coaches, and even the commissioner of the NFL joined in supporting this radical cause. Some were fired and some were beaten for showing support for conservatives. Young people, old people, rich people, and poor people began to understand that any criticism of the Black Lives Matter movement would be punished severely. All over the world people demonstrated and voiced their support for this movement. What is happening in the United States of America is the closest thing to the French revolution that we have ever experienced.

There has been an organized effort to change our culture and our political system. If Capitalism does not fall, it will certainly be readjusted. Many are bowing down to this monstrous movement. Christian NFL players, especially white players, have publicly repented and profusely apologized for not supporting Colin Kaepernick when he and others knelt before the playing of the national anthem in defiance of America and in support of Black Lives Matter. SO FAR, I have heard no Christian football players stand up for the rule of law, either the law of our Constitution or the Law of God written in His Holy Scriptures. MOST have capitulated to the cries of the crowd. The RULE OF LAWLESSNESS now rules our streets. in DEFIANCE to THE LAW OF GOD!

As in Nazi Germany, Communist Russia, Cuba, and China, people are apologizing and repenting of their crimes against political correctness, or as it used to be called, the Party Line. Many Christians choose to identify with the social justice movement more than they focus on resisting the LAST DAYS LAWLESSNESS that is clearly seen today. They apparently are willing to sacrifice THE SCRIPTURES to please man. They now support the group that hates policemen, hates America, barely tolerates white men and if these Christians don't know it now, they will soon find out, this group also hates Christians and the Bible. The radicals believe that Christianity is the religion that the white man has used, and is still using, to enslave black people and women.

A terrible storm and a great shaking are upon us NOW! The progressively weakening walls of God's church are an attractive target for the increasingly confident Left. God's people are ASLEEP. They are satisfied that they are rich and in need of nothing. The Establishment Church sees no flaws in their message, their methods, or their men. They don't believe that God needs to shake the church in America out of her deep sleep. They believe the Church is fully awake! Many are totally confident that God will bail us out of this minor setback, and we will get through this, just like we got through 9-11. Make no mistake! THIS IS NO 9-11! This is the current gang of left-wing fascist Democrats taking full advantage of a crisis. They have parlayed a pandemic into an attack on law and order with looting and murder. When the Left in this country takes full control of America, it may be only a short time until they blow down the walls that protect Gods people and THEN they will destroy Capitalism and use THEIR MILITARY to uphold THEIR LAW and THEIR ORDER. The leader of Black Lives Matter just announced that the statues of Jesus Christ and His mother must also be destroyed.

KRISTALLNACHT: NAZI LAW AND ORDER IN GERMANY

"Kristallnacht, (German: 'Crystal Night'), also called the Night of Broken Glass initially occurred on the nights of November 9th and 10th, 1938, when German Nazis attacked Jewish persons and property. The name Kristallnacht refers ironically to the litter of broken glass left in the streets. The violence continued during the day of November 10, and in some places acts of violence continued for several more days. On the evening of November 9, 1938, carefully orchestrated anti-Jewish violence 'erupted' throughout the Reich.

"The pretext for these acts of terrorism was the shooting in Paris on November 7 of the German diplomat Ernst vom Rath by a Polish-Jewish Student, Herschel Grynszpan. News of Rath's death on November 9 reached Adolph Hitler in Munich, Germany. There, Minister of Propaganda Joseph

Goebbels, after conferring with Hitler, harangued a gathering of old storm troopers, urging violent reprisals staged to appear as 'SPONTANEOUS DEMONSTRATIONS.'

"Just before midnight on November 9, Gestapo chief Heinrich Müller sent a telegram to all police units informing them that 'in shortest order, the police were to ARREST THE VICTIMS'. Fire companies stood by synagogues in flames with explicit instructions to let the buildings burn. They were to intervene only if a fire threatened adjacent 'Aryan' properties. It was given an oddly poetic name: Kristallnacht—meaning 'crystal night' or 'night of broken glass.' This name symbolized the final shattering of Jewish existence in Germany. After Kristallnacht, the Nazi regime made Jewish survival in Germany impossible. The Nazi government barred Jews from schools on November 15 and authorized local authorities to impose curfews in late November." [84]

KRISTALLNACHT IN AMERICA?

NOT YET, but we have seen a preview. Our Left-Wing Nazis, such as Antifa, Black Lives Matter, the Black Panthers, and the Democrat Party, are less selective in their mayhem. They rioted and looted the stores of the rich and the poor alike without regard to religion or race. Many did so because of their hate. Others did so because they were thieves by nature. Others did it because it was FUN! Still others did it because they understood that it was IMPORTANT TO MAKE A POLITICAL STATEMENT about their strength and their willingness to do whatever it takes to overthrow Capitalism and America. ALL did it to test the will of Conservatives and Christians alike. JUST HOW FAR COULD THEY GO? Their willingness to do whatever it takes was praised by the likes of Nancy Pelosi, Mitt Romney, CNN, many entertainers, many athletes, and many church leaders, and their followers, both black and white. The complicit media and the left-wing mob cry out for more love, more money, and more power. This takeover of a culture and a country may be accomplished as easily as the Nazis took over Germany. Make no mistake! When the fascist Democrats take over the house the Senate and the Presidency, there will once again be a rule of law! But the rule of law will not be the Constitution of the United States or the Law of God. It will be the laws of political correctness, enforced with a double standard. It will be similar to the laws that were established in Nazi Germany when Hitler took control. It will be similar to the laws that were established by Fidel Castro when he conquered Cuba. Make no mistake if Gentle Joe Biden wins. he will do just what he is told. He fully understands the penalty for disobedience to The Party. He will deliver the policies of those who put him in power, OR DIE TRYING!.

THE RESPONSE OF GOD'S PEOPLE

While social distancing likely has helped stem the pandemic, the selective enforcement of the policy is WRONG. Allowing mobs of demonstrators, both peaceful and violent, to congregate as they will WITHOUT ANY GOVERMENTAL ENFORCEMENT and then closing churches and places of business is an egregious use of the double standard. We have gone from social distancing to social justice not recognizing that both programs are examples of SOCIAL ENGINEERING. These programs have sent the country into the greatest economic downfall in America since the Great Depression.

The Chinese virus, the protests, riots, looting, the destruction, and takeover of property by left-wing Fascists has exposed the soft underbelly of Conservatives and Christians alike. Many churches have been afraid to petition for reopening churches and instead have embraced the charge that America is guilty of systemic or institutional racism. Some Charismatic and Evangelical churches are AFRAID to acknowledge the LAWLESSNESS of the mobs and either ignore or justify the destruction of property, the looting, and the murder of the police and civilians alike. They are afraid to see the double standard because they are afraid of offending people in the world. and possibly afraid of the attacks they may experience. Our deepest fears and our real desires will be exposed in these times that test men's souls.

It has become EASY and even popular to create upheaval. This has turned out to be a dry run for the fascist democrats to gauge the public's resistance to government control and INSTITUTIONAL LAWLESSNESS. NO ONE except radical leftists are resisting control. Not unlike the Nazis and Communists, the Democrat Party and their mindless media actually ENCOURAGE the chaos. Like their philosophical fathers, they are a protected species.

DOES THE CHURCH BEAR ANY RESPONSIBILITY FOR THE CHAOS?

Absolutely! WHENEVER the Christian church of ANY nation falls away from the Scriptures; whenever the church is more interested in pleasing men than it is in pleasing God; whenever the church WILL NOT OBEY the DEMANDING Scriptures, especially regarding marriage, divorce, and God's limitations on our sexual activity, then that church will lose its power to change the culture, the country, and the courts. In fact, the church in America has already lost its influence to bring people to Jesus Christ because of the cheap grace Gospel they preach. Their message is NOWHERE NEAR the gospel preaching of John the Baptist, Jesus, or Peter. Consequently few REAL converts are made.

America has become corrupt, NOT MERELY because of inept or dishonest politicians; not merely because of the mean-spirited media; not merely because of Hollywood or the ACLU; and not merely because OF ANY force in the world. The country will have fallen because THE CHURCH HAS LOST ITS SAVOR. The church no longer has the power to convert the culture and the country. It no longer battles the enemy trusting COMPLETELY AND EXCLUSIVELY in the Holy Scriptures. The culture and the state of the nation are THE FRUIT of the church. The church will always leaven the nation for good or for evil. In the 18th and 19th centuries, a much larger percent of our people were truly converted because the Scriptural Gospel was preached, and many were born- again with NEW hearts!

THE FOCUS

IT IS SO IMPORTANT that we NOT focus on the political process. We do so because that is much easier to focus on the politics of the world than it is to repent of the REAL sins of the church. We CHRISTIANS IN THE CHURCH are the ONLY ones that can fight and defeat Satan. The secular world is spiritually powerless, and most are blind to the existence of this devious enemy and, ALL who are not born again, are BLIND to the plan, purposes, and power of God.

WHAT CAN WE EXPECT?

Matthew 5:13 (NASB) "You are the salt of the earth; but if the salt has become tasteless, how can it be made salty again? It is no longer good for anything, except to be thrown out and TRAMPLED underfoot BY MEN.

When the church decided to be seeker friendly; when pastors decided that they could be rich and in need of nothing and still lead God's people into the promised land, THEN the church became powerless to see REAL conversions and stop the collapse of our culture and our country. Even if only ONE percent of Americans were born again and had the power of the Holy Spirit to live a holy life, that would mean that over three million people would powerfully preach the REAL GOSPEL and SURELY revival would break out in America. The alternative is not pleasant.

If God's leaders and God's people will not turn from their wicked ways, not only is the church doomed, but the nation is doomed also. A Repentant and Awakened Church is America's only hope. Only God can make America great again and He always uses His people to do so. Unfortunately, the Church is no longer the salt of the earth. The lukewarm church has trampled the Scriptures underfoot; the country has trampled the Constitution underfoot. WITHOUT REPENTANCE, eventually both Church and country will be trampled underfoot by power hungry and bloodthirsty men. We see these men and women, as we look at our country, standing at our left, licking their lips anxiously waiting forward to the time for them to be unleashed.

WHAT MUST WE DO?

WE MUST CONSIDER THAT "THERE BUT FOR THE GRACE OF GOD, GO I"

John Bradford, a preacher in the sixteenth century is said to have uttered "There but for the grace of God, goes John Bradford", he said this as he witnessed criminals being led to the scaffold. We have seen no member of ANTIFA, Black Lives Matter, or the Democrat Party go to the scaffold, but we KNOW, if they don't repent, that they will be destroyed in Hell. We also know, that if it were not for the grace of God that opened our eyes to our sinful condition and granted us faith in Jesus Christ, we would suffer the same fate that they will suffer. This is much more serious and infinitely more painful than being hanged. John Bradford understood God's grace even extended beyond this life. When he was about to be burned at the stake in 1555 he suggested to a fellow victim that, "We shall have a merry supper with the Lord this night!"

We MUST be thankful that the grace of God opened our eyes to our sinfulness and enabled us to believe in Him and if we are called to die for Him, "We shall have a merry supper with the Lord that night."[85A]

WE MUST REPENT OF OUR WICKEDNESS

2 Chronicles 7:13-14 (NIV) WHEN I SHUT UP THE HEAVENS so that there is no rain, or command locusts TO DEVOUR THE LAND or SEND A PLAGUE among my people, 14 if My people, who are called by My name, will humble themselves and pray and seek My face and turn from THEIR WICKED WAYS, THEN I will hear from heaven, and I will forgive their sin and will heal their land.

We must repent of the sins of the church and OUR OWN SINS; seek His face; humble ourselves; THEN WE PRAY! We are the ones that need to repent both personally and corporately so that the Church can have strength and be the leaven of righteousness that can change this country for Jesus Christ. The lukewarm Christian church will continue to pray; they will call for more prayer chains; they will prostate themselves and ask God to intervene. But until the

Church turns from their lukewarm, man-pleasing doctrines, HE WILL NOT HEAL THEIR LAND! In this overconfident, high self-esteem church, VERY FEW will EVER acknowledge their sins of ignoring God's laws. The INCREDIBLY profitable ministers who entertain shallow church goers have TOO MUCH TO LOSE! These shepherds have willingly led their people astray and away from the precious Scriptures so they could be RICH and successful. They have sacrificed the sheep in their own churches for their own well-being and their own pleasure. AND THEIR PEOPLE LOVE IT SO!

WE MUST GRIEVE AND LAMENT FOR THE SINS OF THE CHURCH

2 Kings 22:18-20 (NABRE) "But go to the king of Judah, JOSIAH, who sent you to seek the Lord and tell him: 'This is what the Lord, the God of Israel, says concerning the message you have just heard: 19 YOU WERE SORRY AND HUMBLED YOURSELF BEFORE THE LORD when you heard what I said against this city and its people ... You tore your clothing in despair and WEPT BEFORE ME IN REPENTANCE... 20 So I WILL NOT SEND THE PROMISED DISASTER UNTIL AFTER YOU HAVE DIED and been buried in peace."

When the BOOK OF THE LAW was read to King Josiah, he was SORRY AND HUMBLED HIMSELF BEFORE THE LORD when he heard what God said against the city and its people. He tore his clothing in despair and wept before God in repentance. The prophetess Huldah told him that JERUSALEM WOULD NOT BE SPARED the judgment of God, but that Josiah, would be spared because he cried out to God in repentance for his people.

EZEKIEL 9:1-6,9-10 (NABRE) Then He, the Lord, cried aloud for me to hear: Come, you executioners of the city! 2 And there were six men coming from the direction of the upper gate which faces north, each with a weapon of destruction in his hand. 4 ...Pass through the city, through the midst of Jerusalem, and MARK AN X on the foreheads of THOSE WHO GRIEVE AND LAMENT over all the abominations practiced within it. 5 To the others he said in my hearing: Pass through the city after him and strike! Do not let your eyes spare; DO NOT TAKE PITY. 6 Old and young, male and female, women and children—WIPE THEM OUT! But DO NOT TOUCH ANYONE MARKED WITH THE X. Begin at My Sanctuary. So, they began with the elders who were in front of the temple : 9 the guilt of the house of Israel and the house of Judah is too great to measure; the land is filled with bloodshed, the city with LAWLESSNESS. 10 My eye, however, will NOT SPARE, NOR SHALL I TAKE PITY, but I WILL BRING THEIR CONDUCT DOWN UPON THEIR HEADS.

In Ezekiel chapter 9, we see that the people who grieved and lamented over all the abominations practiced in Jerusalem WERE THE ONLY ONES that were spared the terrible judgment that was inflicted upon the city.

For us and our families, these are keys to avoid the punishment and the judgment that seems almost certain to come to the church in America in the future. We Must grieve FROM OUR HEARTS for our own sins and the sins done in the Church. How can we NOT GRIEVE AND LAMENT that Charles Spurgeon's prophecy has come true! "The time has come when the shepherds are not feeding the sheep, but THE CLOWNS ARE ENTERTAINING THE GOATS!"

DANIEL'S PRAYER FOR GOD'S PEOPLE

Someday, God's people in America may pray this prayer.

Daniel 9:4-5 10-14 (NLT) "O Lord, you are a great and awesome God! You always fulfill your covenant AND KEEP YOUR PROMISES OF UNFAILING LOVE to those who love you and obey your commands. 5 BUT WE HAVE SINNED AND DONE WRONG. We have rebelled against you and SCORNED YOUR COMMANDS AND REGULATIONS. 10 WE HAVE NOT OBEYED THE LORD OUR GOD. 11 All Israel (*THE CHURCH IN AMERICA*) has disobeyed your instruction and turned away, refusing to listen to your voice. "So now the solemn curses and judgments written in the Law of Moses, the servant of God, have been poured down on us because of our sin. 12 You have kept your word and done to us and our rulers exactly as you warned. Never has there been such a disaster ...13 Every curse written against us in the Law of Moses has come true. Yet we have refused to seek mercy from the Lord our God BY TURNING FROM OUR SINS AND RECOGNIZING HIS TRUTH. 14 Therefore, the Lord has brought upon us the disaster He prepared. The Lord OUR GOD WAS RIGHT to do all of these things, for WE DID NOT OBEY HIM.

THE BEGINNING OF SORROWS

If the Church of Jesus Christ does not repent QUICKLY then we will probably find that the events of the last three months are merely the beginning of sorrows for God's people and the American people. Never have we seen such an across the board unity against the principles of God and common sense. The entertainment industry, professional sports, the media, the educational institutions, and even politicians of both parties have become part of a movement that is out to destroy the very foundations of our country and the existence of a Scriptural Church. Of late, Satan has won greater victories than ever before in America.

This is a spiritual battle. The battle for America will only be won if God's people **BATTLE FOR THE CHURCH**. We must respond quickly and immediately. WE MUST cast aside the compromise and cowardice that we have displayed for so long. It's time for the Church to WAKE UP, GET UP, PUT ON THE REAL ARMOR OF GOD and fight like we never have before. This is America's only hope. This may well be **AMERICA'S LAST STAND!!**

CHAPTER 25: THE GREAT SHAKING, THE SECOND STORM, AND PEARL HARBOR: THE GREATEST AWAKENING!

The Great Shaking: Fall and the Rise of the Church in America
Second Storm Warning
Apostasy
Pearl Harbor: The Church Wakes Up
The Pearl of Great Price OR the Accommodating Woman
Pearl of Great Price Costs Everything You Are and All You Own
The Resurrection of the Body and The Greatest Awakening!

THE GREAT SHAKING:
THE FALL AND THE RISE OF THE CHURCH IN AMERICA

Years ago, the Lord showed me what He is to do in His Church. He showed me how He will RE-FORM His Church. He showed me a medieval-style cylindrical structure made of stones. This as God's church as it stood in the 1980s. It looked like a huge, stone, grain silo. This cylindrical structure reached ten stories high into the sky and could be seen clearly at a great distance. The Lord identified this as the current, people pleasing, establishment church that existed at that time in America. He showed me a terrible earthquake and shaking. Not only did the ground shake but the Lord laid His own hands on this ten-story building and shook it mightily. The church shook from bottom to top until all of the stones tumbled down and there remained only one large pile of stones. Then the Lord sorted through the stones and started to separate them. He threw most of them into a pile that was eventually disposed of. Then He began to build with the remaining stones. By the time He was through, I could see a stone church with the same cylindrical shape but only one story in height. The one-story church was much shorter and less conspicuous than the original, but it looked more solid and was much wider than it was tall. It was built to be unshakable by any earthquake and looked more like a fortress than a church. This new structure is God's SCRIPTURAL CHURCH built upon the foundation of His unaltered Word by the power of His Holy Spirit. This structure is God's Church that is after His own heart that He reformed for HIS use, using the good stones of the old Establishment Church.

The TRUE unity of His people will be accomplished by a great shaking, a division of the stones and a consequent REFORMATION. The true Church will be only a small percentage of the old church, but it will be unconquerable and unable to be compromised. This is the Church, built on the unshakable foundation of having a heart like David, wholly after God for Himself alone, a heart that is correctable and will do all of His will.

SECOND STORM WARNING

The Second Storm Warning seems clearer today than it was years ago when the Lord first revealed it to me. This is often true regarding messages from God. Often the words or images are not understood until the events start to take place or during the time that these events actually occur. It is a grievous error to interpret something that the Lord does not interpret for you. Unfortunately, this practice is commonplace among people who attempt to speak for the Lord. Sometimes you need to wait until events reveal the true interpretation of what is seen. At that time, as I related this word to a group of churches at a denominational prayer meeting, there were parts of the message that I did not understand, so I just spoke what I saw. Since then, as events have unfolded, I can better understand what the images represent.

In June of 1986 on a Friday morning, I was praying that God would move in a denominational prayer meeting with several Churches that night. The Lord showed me a storm that He would send to His Church. Later that night at the meeting, the anointing of the Lord came upon me in a compelling way and I spoke forth what I had seen earlier. I saw an army camp with thousands of tents pitched. It was night and most of the soldiers were asleep in their tents.

There were men and women soldiers, fully armed with guns, grenades, rocket launchers, and automatic weapons and were prepared to do battle. BUT they were sleeping very soundly and dreaming pleasant dreams. They dreamed of good times at the beach, beautiful homes, and fine luxury cars. They dreamed of getting money and spending money. They even dreamed of bigger and more successful ministries.

In the far distance, I could hear thunder rolling and see lightening flashing. A storm was brewing off to what was the east or right in my vision and the storm was being blown toward the camp of the Lord slowly but steadily and became progressively brighter and louder. Then with loud crashes of thunder and bright flashes of lightening the storm broke with full force over the camp of God. With each thunderclap and flash of lightning, the soldiers were stirred. However, VERY FEW of the soldiers woke up. The vast majority just kept on sleeping with satisfied smiles on their faces. I saw some stir and almost wake up, but they just changed position and went back to their sweet dreams. A few others woke up, grabbed their weapons, and went to stand on the walls that surrounded the camp and look out on the horizon to see if anyone was coming. The walls surrounding the camp were not fully intact and had many places where the enemy had previously broken through. These places had never been repaired, but on top of the walls there were places to stand and watch for the enemy. I saw that this was the beginning of the second storm that God would bring to God's Church but that the crashes of thunder and flashes of lightening would only wake a few of the fully equipped but peacefully slumbering soldiers. They were too busy dreaming about their comfortable churches, the success of their ministries and their material blessings. Because of this they would not wake up.

After the thunder and lightning passed over the camp of God, I saw many Civil War cannons. These cannons came from the left as I viewed this scene. The cannons were slowly but steadily rolling up to close range of the walled camp. Many were only yards from the walls. The soldiers who had awakened earlier and were standing on the broken walls shouted a loud warning to the ones who were asleep, but few stirred and even fewer got up to see what was happening. Then the cannons rolled even closer and cut loose a terrible barrage that brought down the wall that faced them. The cannons were then aimed at the people who were beginning to wake up. So devastating was their attack that most of the waking soldiers had time only to stand up and cry, "O My God," and then were quickly cut down. Most of the people were then completely awakened by the horrifying sound of the attack but were not ready. A few woke up and had time to grab a weapon and take aim at the enemy, but most of the people inside the sparsely guarded, weak, and broken-walled camp were either killed instantly or terribly injured. It was a scene of total devastation and few survived the attack.

As I finished delivering this word to the Church, the Southern California sky lit up with what was the most awesome spectacle of thunder and lightning that I had ever witnessed. It was so unusual in our area that it made front page headlines the next morning.

An interesting thing about this particular word, was that it was the SECOND storm that I had seen. Earlier, in February of that year, the morning of a revival meeting with several churches in the area, I saw a rainstorm of thunder and lightning that descended upon the Church in America. In the vision, thunderclaps announced that the storm was coming. Then the rain poured down and the lightning bolts crackled from the clouds. My first reaction to what I saw was that God was sending rain that would soften the earth for planting and provide water for the crops. I echoed my thoughts as I spoke to the Lord about this. He corrected me and said the rain was not for planting and irrigating the ground; rather the rain was for cleansing and washing away the sin of His people. There were men and women standing on top of the rain-soaked hills and the lightning bolts struck them. The bright lightening was for the people on the hill who represented leadership in the Church. The lightning flashes were to expose their unrepentant sin and the bolts that struck them were for the purpose of empowering them if they would repent. If they would not repent, then the lightening would do nothing more than cause them great pain. As the storm continued, I noticed that there were people who would run to the hills so they could experience the painful but powerful strikes of lightning. Others ran as far away as they could from the lightening because they wanted to hide their sin and had no desire to repent.

When I received this message, I asked the Lord to confirm the word I would deliver that night with actual thunder and lightning. He did not, but several weeks after the delivery of the First Storm warning, we began to see prominent ministries exposed over the next few years. Jimmy Baker was exposed with the revelation of the P.T.L. scandal. Months later, the sins of Jimmy Swaggart were made public. As was mentioned before, shortly after this message in our own denomination within a year, our divisional superintendent and our district supervisor were dismissed because of adulterous relationships.

This Second Storm prophecy WAS confirmed that same night it was delivered by a tremendous electrical storm. I felt that God confirmed this second storm vision and not the first, because the first storm happened very shortly after He told us about it. This Second Storm, however, was likely not to happen for a long time.

I don't know when the terrible attack from the left will occur, but the events that have occurred over the last thirty-four years have given great indication that things are much closer today than they were years ago. We certainly were jostled out of our sleep temporarily with the thunderclaps on September 11, 2001. These attacks and the murders of thousands of Americans were orchestrated and accomplished by men of the Middle East. The current Chinese Coronavirus pandemic and the possibly politically engineered economic collapse hopefully will wake up more of God's people to the vicious attack that will someday come. Even as I go through this manuscript today, July 11, 2020, an organization founded by Communists, Black Lives Matter, has gained the sympathy of most news outlets, the entertainment industry, the sports world, the democrats, some republicans and even many charismatics and some evangelicals.

The civil war cannons that lined up against the walls that protected the people of God were always a mystery to me. At one time, I suspected that these

Civil War cannons might indicate a literal civil war that our country would experience. I knew that they were an important part of the vision. One of the reasons was that in 1987, when our family was on a trip back east, we visited the battlefields of Gettysburg. While looking over the once blood-soaked battlefield, I felt a strong sense of God's presence and a great grief come on me that brought me to tears. This feeling stayed with me for some time and it made me think of the vision of the civil war cannons lining up against the walls that protected God's people. I wondered if it meant that someday we might have another civil war in our country, but I dismissed it at that time as being extremely unlikely. I thought perhaps it might even refer to in-fighting in the Church but thought that unlikely. At that time, I did not consider that the attack that came from the LEFT of my vision had any political implications.

The Storm that awakens some of God's people WILL precede the terrible attack from the left. These events have already begun to happen. With each terror attack and each progressively radical takeover of our culture and our country, we have heard the thunderclaps of God's warning and have been roused from our sleep for a few minutes but then we in the Church, roll over and fall asleep again dreaming our dreams of a comfortable Church life and the blessings of prosperity.

As I write on June 30, 2020, of course we have witnessed another thunderstorm, seemingly more vicious than the others. As I mentioned in the previous chapter, the murder of Floyd George on May 25 by an over aggressive policeman triggered riots, demonstrations, looting's and even murders that have caused RINO Republicans and Christians alike to draw much closer to Black Lives Matter. This organization was founded by Marxists [85A] whose goal is to overthrow capitalism. The entertainment industry and the media have aligned themselves with that organization also. As was mentioned in chapter 24, we are closer to the French Revolution than we have ever been before. But I'm concerned that most establishment Christians will at best, only notice the sins of the Left and never recognize that what is happening is merely the bad fruit that arises when a lukewarm church adapts Scripture to the culture. By doing so, this church loses the power of the Word to affect the country.

APOSTASY

2 Thessalonians 2:3 (AMP) Let no one in any way deceive or entrap you, for that day will not come unless THE APOSTASY comes first, that is, the great rebellion, the abandonment of the faith by professed Christians.

APOSTASY, Greek: a defection, to depart. An abandonment of what one has professed, a total desertion or departure from one's faith or religion. American Dictionary of the English Language 1828 Noah Webster.

Out and out apostasy is occurring in the Church of Jesus Christ today. In the last several years, two popular singers who at one time were closely associated with Christianity, denied Jesus Christ publicly. In the summer of 2019, we saw a worship leader in Australia and a pastor in America completely and totally deny Jesus Christ and Biblical Christianity. All four of these people have made it clear that they are departing Christianity and the claims of the Bible. These men and women clearly are those who commit APOSTASTY.

1 John 2:19 (NASB) They went out from us, but they were not really of us; for if they had been of us, they would have remained with us; but they went out, so that IT WOULD BE SHOWN THAT THEY ALL ARE NOT OF US.

The Geneva Bible of 1599 footnote: 1 John 2:19 "He showeth that these things fall out to the profit of the Church, THAT HYPOCRITES MAY BE PLAINLY KNOWN."

The Bible indicates that apostasy serves the Church in A POSITIVE WAY. A corrupt culture can be a great temptation to hypocrites. Hypocrites typically desire to have the best of both worlds. They want to experience the carnal pleasures of the worldly culture, but they also want to appear holy as the Bible defines holiness. When they decide to forsake the holiness of Christianity and join the culture that not only enjoys the unholy, but praises those who practice pleasures that God defines in His word as UNHOLY, they are much more comfortable. Our current culture takes JOY in creating turncoats that initially criticize ungodly conduct, but eventually see the dark light and join those who hate holiness. A turncoat "Christian" is a GREAT PRIZE to Satan. However, God does have a positive purpose in allowing turncoat Christians to become apostate. His purpose is to EXPOSE THE HYPOCRITES FOR WHAT THEY REALLY ARE, thereby producing a more HOLY CHURCH. These hypocrites, especially those in leadership positions, do great harm to the people of God because in order to justify their hypocrisy they must twist the Scriptures to fit their own carnal desires.

PEARL HARBOR: THE CHURCH WAKES UP

In December of 1984, about a week after I purchased a 1940 Cadillac sedan, I was driving around thinking about times gone by, particularly before and during World War II. Suddenly I felt that I heard the Lord say to me, very softly,

"It's 1940 and Pearl Harbor is coming to the Church." I thought about betrayal, warfare, death and awakening. I prayed to the Lord and He began to reveal more about Pearl Harbor. He reminded me of a scene from the film Tora, Tora, Tora in which one of the Japanese military leaders remarked, after their attack on Pearl Harbor, "I fear all we have done is to awaken a Sleeping Giant and fill him with a TERRIBLE RESOLVE." I wondered what it would take for the Church to finally wake up to her true spiritual condition and the awesome power that God has for her. I thought about what it took for America to wake up in 1941 to the realities of World War II. It took the destruction and decimation of airplanes and ships and the deaths of 3000 soldiers; it took suffering and anger in our country like we had not seen since the Civil War. But we did wake up. I thought about December 8, 1941 when we declared war against the Axis powers. Before that time, we were sending arms, supplies and money to our allies, but we were not sending men to fight Hitler and Tojo. We watched China, the Pacific Islands, France and much of Europe fall to Germany, Italy, and Japan, but we were not personally affected, so we did not enter the battles. It took a catastrophic event to wake us up.

    I prayed about and meditated on what I had heard until May of 1985, when I heard from God during a baptismal service in our church. The person to be baptized was an older lady who was quite concerned and even a little frightened, about being fully immersed. For fifty years, her mother had prodded her to be baptized, but she resisted baptism partly because she feared the water and partly because of her disobedience and rebellion against God. Right before I was going to enter the water with her, a message in tongues came forth from my wife. The Lord gave me the interpretation by means of the following: the word describes a future time of great hardship and great blessing for the Body of Christ.

    I saw a deep harbor with blue-green water that was clear and calm. There was a Person in the water. This Person was not swimming or standing, but just floating in a semi-upright position. He was motionless, like a sailing ship listing on a windless sea. Many Japanese Zero aircraft came in from the east and proceeded to dive bomb and strafe the listless Body; the Body began to slowly sink. There was no discernible response to the strafing and bombing that this body endured; this body just sank and as He went down, I could see that there were many little people clinging to this Body.

    As this Body sank deeper into the water, many of these small people jumped off just before they were about to sink in the water. There were thousands of people jumping off and swimming away from the slow but steadily sinking Body. Some of these people jumped onto beds, which the Lord made clear to me were beds of adultery and fornication and floated away off to the left.

Others jumped onto whiskey bottles and paddled away; still others jumped on books, and others swam off on their own strength. All of the people were floating, swimming, or paddling in the same direction. I looked over in that direction, which was to my left, and I saw an extremely beautiful, gigantic woman, with skin and clothing of a deep reddish-purple hue standing solidly on the harbor floor. She stretched out her arms toward the sinking Body and got the attention of many as she very sweetly and seductively called out, "Come unto me all ye that are weary and heavy laden, and I WILL GIVE YOU WHAT YOU WANT!"

THE PEARL OF GREAT PRICE OR THE ACCOMODATING WOMAN

The people who were jumping off were in a panic, like rats leaving a sinking ship. Some scurried to higher ground on the Body, going from the shoulders to the ears and finally jumping off the top of the head right before it went under. It was clear that, at first, THEY DID NOT WANT TO LEAVE THIS BODY, but it was equally clear that they were not going down under the water with it either. Some of the little people hung on as it sank, but after a few seconds of holding their breath, THEY GAVE UP, swam for the top, gulped a mouthful of air, and swam off towards the woman.

The Body now was completely under the water, sinking steadily toward the bottom. The apparently lifeless Body sank deeper and deeper into the clear blue-green water. As it sank, I could see at the bottom of the harbor a beautiful, large, perfect pearl with no flaws and obviously of great value. It was supernaturally large and lustrous, pure, and round. As I watched, I could see the Body change shape from that of a single being, with little people desperately hanging on it, to many little individual people swimming deep enough to get to this beautiful Pearl. As they went deeper, many chose to quit and swim to the surface for air and then go over to the beautiful woman. All who quit diving down to the pearl eventually swam over to the beautiful woman.

Today we see THE GREAT DIVISION beginning. In the future, Pearl Harbor will speed up and greatly increase the number of apostasies. Many in the lukewarm, entertainment starved churches where MANY hypocrites dwell, will be exposed to and fall away to the woman in the harbor who will give them exactly what they want. The Satanic culture will certainly have a victory, but SO WILL GOD. When the full impact of Pearl Harbor hits the Church, FEW hypocrites will remain and there will be great opportunity to preach the Word, the whole Word and nothing but the Word. This church will be much smaller and much less conspicuous, but much, much more powerful.

Matthew 13:45-46 (AMPC) Again the kingdom of heaven is like a man who is a dealer in search of fine *and* precious pearls,[46] Who, on finding a single PEARL OF GREAT PRICE, went and SOLD ALL HE HAD and bought it

THE PEARL OF GREAT PRICE COSTS EVERYTHING YOU ARE AND ALL YOU OWN

Finally, a number of these small people swam to the Pearl and touched it and embraced it. But to do this, those who dove down reached a point when they realized that their own natural ability to hold their breath and dive deeper would not be enough. Those who dove down and desired to touch the Pearl all came to understand that they would have to expend all of their natural strength before they could touch and embrace this Pearl of Great Price. This didn't keep them from diving down though, because the closer they got to the Pearl, the more of His beauty they saw.

THE RESSURECTION OF THE BODY AND THE GREATEST AWAKENING!

I saw many touch and embrace the Pearl and then immediately shoot straight up. As each of these little people shot up from the floor of the Harbor, each had the Pearl. As this group of individuals rose higher and higher, they all became One Body again. By the time all these Pearl laden people reached the surface they burst forth from the waters as One Body, the Body of Christ. These people were manifestly His own possession and they in turn possessed the Pearl of Great Price, Jesus Christ Himself.

As the Lord was showing me this beautiful picture, He spoke to me and said, "Even as Jesus came out of the waters of His baptism with a powerful anointing of the Holy Spirit, so My Body will come out of Pearl Harbor with a new and powerful anointing of My Holy Spirit, and a new and deadly ability to fight the enemy and defeat him." He said that there would come upon the Church of Jesus Christ a Pearl Harbor experience like our country experienced on December 7th and 8th in 1941.

He said that when the Body of Christ begins to sink under the water because of a devastating attack of the enemy that will surely come, MANY will choose to desert our Lord Jesus Christ because they do not esteem the Pearl of Great Price (Jesus Himself) worth the price, which is death to their own selfish desires. They will not make the selfless effort of love to dive deeply enough to embrace Him because they do not love Him more than their own lives. Many will choose not to identify with what they assume to be a defeated individual or group. They look upon themselves as winners and will not identify with a Jesus that is apparently being defeated. They will choose to identify with the beautiful woman of the harbor who gives them what they want. As the vision showed, many leapt off the sinking Body because the woman of the harbor promised them great blessings and success. Because of this they went to her. Many others did not feel that it was necessary to pay such a high price to apprehend Jesus, and they felt that the beautiful woman would give them the Jesus they wanted on their own terms.

As the Body of Christ came out of the waters of baptism, the Lord said that His Body was now fully alive and would fight the enemy with purpose and real supernatural power. From then on, His Body would use REAL weaponry of the Spirit. He spoke so clearly to me about the weapons. He said, "Even as the United States entered the Second World War using conventional weapons to fight the enemy, and ended the war with the atomic bomb, a weapon beyond their comprehension; so, My people will begin this Spiritual war with conventional group weapons in the Spirit, but by the end of this war, they will be using nuclear bombs of the Spirit". The Lord made it clear that those who were sacrificing EVERYTHING for Him, would come out of the water equipped with a God-given anointing to REALLY heal the sick, work miracles, and deliver those in demonic bondage. He also made it clear that before the warfare ends, we will be moving in a dimension of spiritual warfare that is unimaginable to us at this time. We will do greater works than Jesus did, and we will see the demon hordes routed as never before.

After this message in tongues and interpretation was given, my attention turned back to the woman who was to be baptized. Then the Lord said that the Pearl Harbor experience for His Church would be like this woman's baptism. I closely watched this baptism to see what the Lord meant. The woman was very nervous and quite afraid of going under the water. I assured her that she would be all right. After several moments of prayer and a short teaching on what baptism represented, she was plunged underneath the water. She came out of the water with her hands lifted up, praising God. I had not told anyone what the Lord told me about this woman's baptism, because I did not know exactly what was going to happen. When she recovered her composure, she began to testify about what had just happened to her. She said that she was extremely fearful at first, but that when she got under the water a Beautiful Peace swept through her, and all her fear was gone. This beautiful peace became joy as she came out of the water and she praised God for His great comfort, love, and mercy.

I believe that God was showing us that we need not fear what He will put us through. His purpose is to bring us peace, joy, cleansing, and above all, power to fight the *Battle for the Church* and win the war and Glorify Him! He was also showing us that His Church will go through a baptism. It is a baptism of the Body of Christ. It is a death and a resurrection. We must trust Him to bring us out of the deep sleep that we now live in and into the glorious resurrection power of His Son. We must understand that a harbor is a place of SAFETY and REFUGE. The Pearl of Great Price is located in the only harbor that will provide refuge and safety, and ALL who believe in Him will be more than willing to dive into that harbor and pay the price of dying to their own desires.

Pearl Harbor is the death and resurrection of the Body of Christ, being prepared to do His work in His way, with His heart. It is the final separation of people who have a whole heart after God, being purified and separated from people who build the kingdom to please the people. It is the final AWAKENING blast of the trumpet of God to rouse His people for battle. It is the judgment that begins with the house of the Lord. It is the refining fire that separates the gold from the dross. It will be preceded by the Lord dealing with His true people to both survive and desire this final preparation for battle. It is the promise of unmatched power and purity: power over sin, power over the enemy, power to live a virtuous and holy life, and power to glorify our Heavenly Father through Jesus Christ by the power of the Holy Spirit. Even now, God is dealing with those in the Church even as God dealt with David. Whenever David would start to fall asleep to God's purity and purpose, the Lord would abruptly DEAL with David to AWAKEN Him. God did not waste this kind of effort on Saul because Saul CHOSE to be asleep to God and His desires.

Pearl Harbor is a warning of betrayal and disaster. The Church in the past has gone through many Pearl Harbors. Jesus was betrayed and killed and rose again. English Puritans that came to America experienced Pearl Harbor in the early 17th century and survived because they would not obey the religious laws that the Church of England tried to force upon them. They fled England and eventually sailed to the New World, where they laid the spiritual foundation for what eventually became one of the Greatest Awakenings in the history of the world. John Bunyan wrote Pilgrim's Progress at the bottom of the harbor as he was betrayed by the Church of England and thrown in jail for preaching in a way that did not conform to this Church's liturgy. Had he given in and done that which they asked, he could have been a free man. But for conscience sake he chose not to do so. Because of this uncompromising obedience to the Scriptures and to God Himself, he was able to rise to the highest place in the history of Christian literature. Today he still blesses us with the fruit of that resurrection power.

To those who are not awake and prepared, Pearl Harbor will come suddenly and tragically, as a thief in the night, and they will be swept away to Great Deception. They will be content to casually swim over to the woman in the harbor who promises to give them what they want. This woman represents a religious system that will say what the people want to hear. She will be all things to all people. To the cruel, she will help them be cruel. To the greedy, she will help them be greedy and satisfy their desires., to those that want control, she will teach them how to have loveless dominion. To those who want grace with no responsibility, she will give them LAWLESS GRACE. To those who LOVE THE LIE, she will make them rulers in her vast kingdom. To those who JUST WANT TO FEEL GOOD, NO MATTER WHAT, she will, for a season, give them the desires of their hearts. All she wants in return is THEIR ETERNAL SOULS.

Pearl Harbor will be an expected ordeal, a call to arms, and a prelude to Great Victory. The initial stages will be the harbinger of the greatest move of God in History: the greatest Revival and the greatest manifestation of real - based uncompromising and costly Christianity that the world has ever known. Bible.

ENDNOTES

Introductory Material
1. Thanks to Escape Radio Show circa late 1940s (similar style to THEIR introduction)

SECTION 1: THE DUTIES AND POWER OF THE CHURCH

2. Worldometer. coronavirusworldometers.info/

CHAPTER 2: HISTORY LESSONS
3. https://study.com/academy/lesson/the-dark-ages-definition-history-timeline.html
4. Wikipedia "Opium of the People": from Marx's work A Contribution to the Critique of Hegel's Philosophy of Right,
5. Rules for Radicals;. Acknowledgement by Saul Alinsky

SECTION 2: CAN JUDGMENT BE VERY FAR OFF?

CHAPTER 3: SHRINE PROSTITUTES IN THE TEMPLE OF GOD
6. Pornography & Media Addiction (PMA) The New Epidemic in the Church
7. CITY VISION UNIVERSITY https://library.cityvision.edu/pornography-and-media-addiction-new-epidemic
8. Today's Christian Woman fall 2003
9. 9/21/07 – https://www.TechMission.org/ PMA
10. Pornography and Media Addiction: The New Epidemic.

CHAPTER 4: CORRUPTION IN AMERICA & THE CHURCH
11. The divorce rate in our country has more than quintupled in the last 100 years
12. Steve Mencher June 19,2013: report from the Council on Foreign Relations AARP
    (tps://www.aarp.org) Boomers once led
13. James Dobson: Hide or Seek, p 10
14. Ruth Graham: These Last Days News - June 1, 2015

CHAPTER 5: EVIDENCE THAT DEMANDS A VERDICT
15. Dr James Dobson: What Wives Wish Their Husbands Knew About Women
16. Charles Edward White: "What Wesley Practiced & Preached About Money"

Christianity Today: CT Pastors WISDOM AND TOOLS FOR YOUR CALLING.
CHAPTER 7: JOSIAH REVIVAL
17. *LOVING HIM WELL* BY GARY THOMAS: p 27

SECTION 3: PREPARING FOR DIFFICULT DAYS

CHAPTER 8: TEACHING GOD'S PERFECT WORD
18. Wikipedia Under "Living Constitution" P 295
19. What Russia Intends: Peoples, Plans, Policy of Soviet Russia. Bruce Hopper London: Cape 1931 P 83

CHAPTER 11: GRIEVE AND LAMENT FOR THE SINS OF THE CHURCH
20. OPEN OUR EYES, LORD
https://openoureyeslord.com/2010/12/28/is-sin-missing-the-mark/

SECTION 4: ENEMIES LIST

CHAPTER: 12: KNOWING THE ENEMY
21. www.Scienceline.org/2008/12/ask-rettner-sea-level-rise-al-gore-an-inconvenient-truth
22. https://www.seattlepi.com/ae/movies/article/Hollywood-takes-liberties-with-true-stories-but-1195421.php
23. https://nypost.com/author/johnny-oleksinski/ SEE Falling Upwards: How We Took to the Air by Richard Holmes
23A. History of Bible Translating
http://www.historyworld.net/wrldhis/PlainTextHistories.asp?historyid

SECTION 5: HAS GOD RESCINDED THE SUPERNATURAL GIFTS?

CHAPTER 15: IS SUPERNATURAL MINISTRY FOR TODAY'S CHURCH?
24. Tom Pennington, "A Case for Cessationism" (Tom Pennington) @https://www.gty.org/library/sermons-library/TM13-7/a-case-for-cessationism-tom-pennington

CHAPTER 16: CESSATIONIST VIEW OF THE ROLE OF MIRACLES
25. B. B. Warfield quoted by Tom Pennington in "A Case for Cessationism" @ https://www.gty.org/library/sermons-library/TM13-7/a-case-for-cessationism-tom-pennington p202
26A. "A Case for Cessationism" (Tom Pennington) @ Ibid.,

26B. How to Pray the Rosary, United States Conference of Catholic Bishops @https://www.usccb.org/prayer-and-worship/prayers-and-devotions/rosaries/how-to-pray-the-rosary

27. B. B. Warfield quoted by Tom Pennington in "A Case for Cessationism" @ https://www.gty.org/library/sermons-library/TM13-7/a-case-for-cessationism-tom-pennington p 204

CHAPTER 17: THE USE AND MISUSE OF THE MIRACULOUS GIFTS
28. Ibid.,
29. Ibid.,
30. Ibid.,
31. Ibid.,
32. Ibid.,
33. Ibid,

SECTION 6: GAME CHANGER - THE DESTRUCTION OF THE FAMILY

34. p.220 @https//libertytree.ca/quotes/Vladimir.Lenin.Quote 4180

CHAPTER 18: FOUNDATION FOR WARFARE
35. (LASB) p 2008 under Ephesians 5:22-28(commentary section)
36. Ibid., under Ephesians 5:22-24
37. Ibid., under Ephesians 5:22-24
38. bid., under Ephesians 5:22-28
39. Ibid., under Ephesians 5:22-28
40. Ibid., under Ephesians 5:22-24
41. Ibid., under Ephesians 5:25-30

CHAPTER 19: MARRIAGE and DIVORCE
42. http://www.barna.com/research/new-marriage-and-divorce-statistics released/; p100
https://divorce.lovetoknow.com/Historical_Divorce_Rate_Statistics
43. Briggs & Allen: American Law & Economics Review. published 2000 AND https://www.divorcesource.com/blog/why-women-file-80-percent-of-divorces/ p91

CHAPTER 20: AN EPISTLE FROM HELL:
   DOES SCRIPTURE SAY WIFE IS SUPERIOR?
44. Ibid., *LOVING HIM WELL* BY GARY THOMAS: p 11
45. Ibid., p 15

46 Ibid., p 11
47. Ibid., p 16
48 Ibid., p 14
49. Ibid., p 43
50. Ibid., p 142
51. Ibid., p 153
52. Ibid , p 159
53.Ibid., p 166
54.Ibid., p 167
55.Ibid., p 23
56. p 256 Briggs & Allen: American Law & Economics Review. pub 2000.
57. Ibid., p 28
58.ibid., p 37
59. Ibid., p 92-93
60. Ibid., p 86-87
61. Ibid., p 112

CHAPTER 21: AN EPISTLE FROM HELL:
   SCIENCE SAYS," WOMEN ARE SUPERIOR"
62. LOVING HIM WELL BY GARY THOMAS: p 82
63. Ibid., p 121
64. Ibid., p 122
65. Ibid., p 155
66. Ibid., p 135-136
67. Ibid., p 125
68. Ibid., p 137
69. Ibid., p 160
70. Ibid., p 108
71. Ibid., p 109
72. Ibid., p 266
73. Ibid., p 163
74. Military casualties of war, P.5/10
75. Reported annual abortions Guttmacher:1973-2018-
https://christianliferesourses.com/2018/04/15/u-s-abortion

 CHAPTER 22: TO BE OR NOT TO BE …. A DOORMAT!
76. *LOVING HIM WELL* BY GARY THOMAS: p 146
77. P 270.LIFE APPLICATION BIBLE   p 2008 under Ephesians 5:21-26
78. LOVING HIM WELL BY GARY THOMAS: p 148

CHAPTER 23: EXTREME SOLUTIONS
79. Ibid.,
80. Ibid., p 49-51
81. Ibid., p52
82. Ibid, p 52
83. Ibid, p 54-55

SECTION 7: LAST WORDS
CHAPTER 24: The Rule of Lawlessness
84. Michael Berenbaum under Kristallnacht
@https://www.britannica.com/event/Kristallnacht
85A. What's the Origin of the phrase 'There but for the grace of God, go I' ?
https://www.phrases.uk/meanings/ther...
CHAPTER 25:THE GREAT SHAKING,THE SECOND STORM,PEARL HARBOR: AND THE GREATEST AWAKENING,
85B. https://nypost.com/2020/07/01/the-agenda-of-black-lives-matter-is-far-different-from-the-slogan/

BIBLIOGRAPHY

A W Tozer
Arnold Dallimore
Athanasius
Bible Gateway
Bible Hub
C S Lewis
Charles Spurgeon
Chuck Smith
David Wilkerson
Dr J Rodman Williams
Dr William Brandt
Gary Thomas: *Loving Him Well*
George Whitefield
Iain Murray
John Chrysostom
Jonathan Edwards
LIFE Application Study Bible (LASB)
Martin Luther
Martyn Lloyd Jones
Mathew Henry
Noah Webster:1828 Webster's American Dictionary
Phillip Schaff: History of the Christian Church
Saul Alinsky: Rules for Radicals
Tom Pennington
Wikipedia
William Tyndale

ABOUT THE AUTHOR

Over the years, I have seen great changes in the Church and the Culture. Since I started writing this book 3 years ago, DRAMATIC changes have occurred, especially this year. The Scriptures are my ONLY standard for Evaluating these changes.

If you want to reach me by email my email address is:

jimkehrli@yahoo.com

www.ingramcontent.com/pod-product-compliance
Lightning Source LLC
Chambersburg PA
CBHW061631040426
42446CB00010B/1362